DATE DUE			
Mar 16 '67			
Mar 10 '69			
Mar 31 '69			
Nov 24 '71			
Jan 10 '73			
Apr 13 '79			
Apr 25 '80			
Oct 6 80			
GAYLORD			PRINTED IN U.S.A.

THE UNDERDEVELOPED AREAS WITHIN THE COMMON MARKET

THE UNDERDEVELOPED AREAS WITHIN THE COMMON MARKET

BY SERGIO BARZANTI

PRINCETON, NEW JERSEY
PRINCETON UNIVERSITY PRESS
1965

CONTENTS

CONTENTS

CONTENTS

CONTENTS

THE UNDERDEVELOPED
AREAS WITHIN
THE COMMON MARKET

"It is indispensable to underline the interdependence of the European movement and of the regional economies, for it poses a problem upon which may depend, after all, the final success of the European idea. The alternative is the following: either the European institutions will be able to set up the appropriate machinery to promote a balanced development of the different European sectors, and in this case Europe will triumph; or else the Common Market will aggravate regional imbalances and then there will come about, sooner or later, and after the convulsions suffered by any living organism in a state of disequilibrium, the ultimate death of Europe."

> Jacques Chaban-Delmas, President of the French National Assembly

"The great gaps between the living standards and the economic level of development of the European regions will not automatically be counterbalanced in the framework of a liberal economic policy and thanks to a competition free from all distortion. The diversities of historical origin account for the fact that the different regions are not in the same stage of development to start with, so that the realization of the Common Market could, above all, bring about a strengthening of the existing gaps."

> Commission of the European Economic Community

INTRODUCTION

The world is rapidly moving towards a general rearrangement of its political configuration and an evolution in its organization. We of the West often find ourselves facing problems we do not fully understand, and in which we perhaps do not wish to become involved. But, whether we like it or not, there are powerful forces reshaping the world and one of these is the drive toward "regionalism." The outstanding example in modern times of this associative trend among adjacent countries is that of European integration, known as the "Common Market." This successful phenomenon has caught the imagination of the world, and has given rise to deep feelings of hope and fear on both sides of the Iron Curtain.[1] It is, however, undeniable

[1] Examples of this reaction—(a) The late President Kennedy, in his famous speech delivered at Philadelphia on July 4, 1962, asking for a Declaration of Interdependence: "But I will say here and now on this day of independence that the United States will be ready for a Declaration of Interdependence—that we will be prepared to discuss with a United Europe the ways and means of forming a concrete Atlantic Partnership—a mutually beneficial partnership between the new union now emerging in Europe and the old American union founded here 175 years ago." Quoted in *The Atlantic Community*, Winter 1963–64, p. 477. (b) The position of Moscow until very recently can be summarized by these excerpts from the Soviet paper, *Krasnaya Zvezda*, June 6, 1963, which in an article entitled "The Ideological Foundation of NATO" says that (underlying the movement for the integration of Western Europe) "is the reactionary ideology of Europeanism, a kind of cosmopolitanism, behind the smoke screen of which steps are being taken . . . to knock together a large association representing state monopoly capital . . . which has found its fullest embodiment in the European Common Market . . . an alliance of monopolies against the interests of the working people." Now, it seems that a thorough reappraisal has been decided upon by the Kremlin: "The Soviet Union, which in the past has denounced the European Common Market as an expression of 'monopoly capitalism' is believed to be getting ready to adjust its relations with the six-nation economic organization . . . . the Russians in the not-distant future will accredit a mission to the Brussels headquarters of the economic community, as capitalist industrial countries already have." *New York Times*, May 6, 1964.

1

that a state of disarray has prevailed in the European Community since General de Gaulle's famous press conference barring the admission of Great Britain was held on January 14, 1963. Paul-Henri Spaak wrote: "this day . . . is fated to go down in history as the 'black Monday' of both European policy and Atlantic policy. What occurred that day was something more significant than the mere dooming of negotiations between Great Britain and the European Community. It was, in plain fact, an attack on the Atlantic Alliance and the European Community. . . ."[2]

Events like this tend to concentrate public attention on the purely political aspects of European integration. From the strictly economic viewpoint, however, several questions remain to be solved, and some of them threaten the consolidation of European unity perhaps as much as the disruptive political forces that have been so spectacularly in evidence lately.

Among the most serious problems is that of regional imbalance due to the underdevelopment of some areas of the Community. This imbalance, within the framework of a complicated construction like that of European unification, has serious repercussions on economic stability, which, in turn, entail consequences in other, disparate fields.[3]

There are a number of "minor" underdeveloped regions in the Community, ranging from Schleswig-Holstein, part of Bavaria and Lower Saxony in Germany, to Borinage in Belgium, Friuli in Venetia, Northern Italy, and others. However, while these areas present problems which need not be insurmountable, there are at present a few major areas

[2] Article entitled "Hold Fast" in *Foreign Affairs*, July 1963.

[3] "One of the most important tasks for the Economic Community, and one of the touchstones of its success, will be not only to integrate the economies with each other, but to integrate the regions by means of a more rapid development of those which, within the limits of the national economies, have remained underprivileged." Communauté Européenne du Charbon et Acier (CECA)—Haute Autorité, *Septième Rapport Général sur l'Activité de la Communauté* (Paris: Service des Publications des Communautés Européennes, 1959), p. 55.

of underdevelopment in the Europe of the Six which constitute the real "hard core" of this phenomenon in the Community. These can be broadly identified as the "Mezzogiorno d'Italia" (comprising continental Southern Italy, plus the islands of Sicily and Sardinia), and South-West France, together with other scattered regions of France (Corsica, Brittany, and the Alpine region). The reasons for underdevelopment in these regions are, however, different and cannot always be considered in the same general context.

One recent development—the new category of European associate state—will greatly enhance the importance of the problem of regional inequalities and the necessity for finding a solution. The Treaties of Association between the European Economic Community and Greece (November 1962) and Turkey (September 1963), and the application for associate membership by Spain, suggest that additional countries with large underdeveloped regions may eventually become part of the Common Market.[4]

Although Greece and Turkey, and certain other European nations which might be admitted to the EEC in some form of associate status in the future, will present additional problems of underdevelopment to the Community, the present analysis will not concern these areas since the methods to be used within the context of the Treaty of Rome are quite different from the special provisions envisaged by the Treaties of Association with Greece and Turkey.

If the problem of underdevelopment in the European Economic Community is to be faced with any possibility of success, the place to start is Southern Italy, where destitution and backwardness are far more pronounced than in any other area in the Community.[5] A balanced, long-range

[4] In the case of Spain, there are, at least for the time being, political obstacles to the admission of that nation even to associate membership. See article "Spain outside the Door", *Time*, April 3, 1964.

[5] "Italy has the distinction—and the challenge—of combining one of the most advanced industrial economies in western Europe with

program will have to be planned and patiently carried through before lasting favorable results can be achieved. A similar project will obviously have to be undertaken in the underdeveloped regions of France and of the rest of the Community,[6] but there the problem is less urgent and less difficult to solve.

Meanwhile, although the much hoped for "European Federal Government" is, for the time being, only an idea, though a fascinating one, the task of regional development is entrusted to the national governments, and therefore, among other disadvantages, the plans lack any coordination and their effectiveness is diminished and retarded.[7] Thus, for a better understanding of the problem, it is advisable to examine thoroughly the plans and the activities of the national governments directly concerned with regional development. Only the work of the Italian and French Governments falls within the scope of this book, because the two major groups of underdeveloped territories within the Community are located in these two countries.

First, however, it is advisable to give a brief explanation of what is meant by underdeveloped regions in the context of this work.

When we speak of underdeveloped areas, our thoughts turn automatically to the poor countries of Asia, Africa, and

---

some of the poorest and most backward areas." *The Economist*, March 28, 1964.

[6] "The regional policy should be one which aims at organizing the Community space in such a way as to balance the progress of the different socio-economic regions of which this space is formed, whilst maintaining their necessary diversity." Communauté Economique Européenne, *Exposé sur l'Evolution de la Situation Sociale dans la Communauté en 1960*. (Paris, Service d'Information des Communautés Européennes, 1961), intro.

[7] In this connection, *Le Monde* (Sélection Hebdomadaire) of June 7, 1962, states: "So a great breach is constantly open on one side of our planning, which threatens to reopen the question of the very essence of all our organizational efforts. There is only one way to fill it: the adoption by other countries of our own methods and the creation of a European economic policy, at least to coordinate investments."

Latin America. It seldom occurs to us that similar conditions exist in our Western world. There are, however, areas in certain Western countries where development is slow and backward in relation to the rest of the country. Even in the United States pockets of underdevelopment—and sometimes rather large pockets—can be found. Of course, this does not mean that these regions are underdeveloped in an absolute sense: they are simply underdeveloped vis-à-vis the rest of the country. In comparison with even the most progressive areas of, say, Guinea or Haiti, they certainly would not be considered underdeveloped. The depressed areas of what is now the European Economic Community are depressed in respect to other areas of the Community in general and to their national state in particular.

In Western Europe it is especially, but not exclusively, the regions bordering the Mediterranean Sea that are largely affected by regional underdevelopment. The backward areas are so large that the economy of the country to which they belong is slowed down and weakened by their existence. This is particularly noticeable in Italy, where the difference between North and South is enormous. A traveler who leaves Rome, southbound, soon finds himself in a different world; even when he reaches Naples, the largest city to the South, the contrast with Milan, Florence, or Rome will strike him immediately. It is clear that Naples is the center of a poor region, quite different in character from the Northern part of Italy.

The national governments of France and Italy have for a number of years been trying to attack and solve the problems of underdevelopment within their own countries. These attempts gained momentum after the end of World War II, and the first concrete plans aimed at tackling the problem were undertaken in the early 1950's: the Ten-Year Plan (Piano Vanoni) and the Cassa per il Mezzogiorno (Development Fund for the South) for Italy, and various all-embracing regional projects for France. These plans are all the more laudable since the national economies of the two countries were still very insecure at that time due to the war; Europe was living from day to day, supported by the most spectacular and successful operation launched by the United States during the whole postwar period—the massive European Recovery Program, better known as the Marshall Plan.[8] We shall not go into the details of this; what must be pointed out here is that, in spite of good intentions and the generally efficient implementation of the Marshall Plan on the part of all concerned, the results in the poorest regions were somewhat disappointing. The problems were alleviated, but certainly not eradicated. On the basis of past experience it seems that, in spite of great efforts, they will not be solved by national governments; it is indeed certain that "the reinforcement of European solidarity is the indispensable condition for finding a satisfactory answer to the problems of underdevelopment."[9]

The underdeveloped areas of the Community may be divided into three categories, each showing one or more of the characteristics common to regional underdevelopment in an industrialized Western country.

(a) The first category is made up of the underdeveloped areas *par excellence:* the Southern part of the Italian peninsula and the two largest Mediterranean islands, Sicily and Sardinia. The general condition of these regions, due to a number of factors which will be examined further on in this work, is extremely backward, not only in relation to the

[8] "The basic idea of the Plan was the fostering of European self-help through economic cooperation between all countries accepting American assistance. This cooperation, supplementing the domestic policies and efforts of each nation concerned, would eventually make Europe more economically self-supporting and thus reduce her requirements for outside assistance." Paul Alpert, *Twentieth Century Economic History of Europe* (New York: Schuman, 1951), p. 379.

[9] Communauté Européenne, *Où en est le Marché Commun?* ("Les Cahiers de Communauté Européenne," No. 6; Paris: Service d'Information des Communautés Européennes, 1961.)

other countries of the Community but also in relation to the rest of Italy. "The South is still remote from most of the things that strike the northern European as new. It is still part of another world, as if the Spanish heritage lingered on at one end of the peninsula while the other has almost jumped the Alps into northern Europe. . . ."[10] The people live in ignorance, with medieval concepts of honor, of relations between employer and employee, and between the sexes; some of them have a propensity to take justice into their own hands and to consider its regular administration something that must, if possible, be avoided and which has, in any case, been imposed by a government which has always been considered in many respects "foreign" to the region.

(b) The second category comprises those areas with naturally poor soil or harsh climate, or those which are too mountainous, or of an essentially rocky and barren nature, such as the Massif Central, the region of the Pyrénées, and the Alpine region in France. Also, because of human action or natural causes, these regions are largely outside the main currents of traffic, and this is another factor in their retarded development.

(c) The third category consists of zones which may have prospered in the past by carrying on certain activities such as coal mining, or textile-making. Now, however, they are forced to curtail production sharply due to a decrease in demand for these items, and structural unemployment results. We find such areas mainly in Southern and Central France.

If a laissez-faire type of economy were applied in the Common Market area, the probable outcome would be that the underdeveloped regions would lose further ground compared to the advanced areas of the Community. Industry and wealth would be polarized around certain zones, and agriculture would also be confined to specific

[10] *The Economist*, March 28, 1964.

fertile areas (the remaining agricultural products would be imported from abroad, in exchange for industrial products). Today's underdeveloped regions would grow in size and their economy would gradually deteriorate to form practically deserted areas (South-West France, which has already been undergoing this process though on a smaller scale, has been called "le désert français").[11] As we have stated, the national governments have been trying for some time to solve the problem by means which are certainly unorthodox from the viewpoint of Ricardo or Adam Smith.

Apart from strictly economic provisions, a basic "psychological" revolution is also needed. It will be no easy task to change the present mentality of the French and Italian small farmer or "petit entrepreneur" whose horizons are narrow indeed and whose way of cultivating and of carrying on their enterprises responds to very limited, local needs. They regard this simply as a means of making a living (generally a rather meager one), and have no personal ambition or real desire for aggrandizement—indispensable factors in spurring them toward the major effort required if positive results are to be achieved or at least aimed at. The small farms or the small shops owned by these people have belonged to their family for generations; they accept it as natural that they will follow in their elders' footsteps and that what has been good enough for their parents and for them will also be good enough for their children. This

[11] "Even if it could be reckoned that the progress registered in the center will eventually reverberate towards the extremities, past experience ought not to leave too many illusions on the inevitability of this process, and it actually incites the thought that *it will be necessary to aid, and even to stimulate it, by all the means compatible with the rules regulating the functioning of the Common Market.*" (emphasis supplied) CEE, *Exposé 1960*, intro. And *Communauté Européenne* (the monthly bulletin published jointly by the Executives of the European Communities), No. 7, July 1963, thus summarizes the question: "In sum, if regional economy is entirely abandoned to the free play of economic forces, it is to be feared that the disparities between the regions of Europe will increase, as the highly developed regions attract more and more of the economic potential."

phenomenon, of course, is by no means confined to the underdeveloped areas of France and Italy. It is also widespread, though in smaller measure, in the more developed regions of the two countries, as well as in other countries. The point to be emphasized is that, in view of the surrounding poverty and lack of outlets and resources in the underdeveloped regions, the owner of even a tiny patch of land or a small stationery shop in some village in Calabria, for instance, thinks himself fortunate compared to the propertyless and destitute "braccianti" (farm workers) or "disoccupati" (unemployed) around him. He is more interested in conserving what he already owns than in launching into new ventures.

The most urgent task ahead is to instill in the younger generation, especially by means of long, patient effort in the schools, a feeling of being "European," demonstrating to them that their future is linked with that of Europe, and not confined to the old, traditional boundaries.[12] They must realize that all Europe is their hunting ground and that life can offer them ample opportunity and practically unlimited

[12] In an article entitled "L'Europe des Etudiants," Louis Armand states: "It is only by mixing the youth (of the various countries) that a real European spirit will be created, that the new unity of what will be the Europe of tomorrow will be forged." La Nef (Cahier No. 10): *Quelle est cette Europe?* ed. J. Monnet, P. Uri, R. Mayer, E. Faure, *et al.* (Paris: Juillard, April-June 1962), p. 21. And Giulio Pastore, Minister for Southern Development in Italy, writes, "The economy of a territory is strengthened and becomes lively when, besides the physical infrastructure, it may rely upon a social and human milieu substantially ready to face the tasks of development. . . . The centuries-old depression has begot a society which, through the power of limited groups and an ill-conceived function by the ruling circles, particularly in the past, has been relegated to the margins, making out of them a conglomeration of subordinates and protesters, rather than citizens. The traditional position which entrusted the equilibrium of the social situation to the spontaneous capacities of individual initiative and abilities, and to the rejuvenating forces linked to the succeeding of the generations, is today clearly inadequate, above all in the underdeveloped regions." Centro Studi della Cassa per il Mezzogiorno, *La Politica di Sviluppo nel Mezzogiorno* ("Quaderno 39," Rome, December 1960), p. 27.

possibilities. In this, the example set by the United States will be a fertile ground for ideas. It will be a long process, however, and it does not seem that much can be accomplished with the older generation. But for the youth of today the reasoning may be far different when they come to be producers themselves; they will have been "conditioned" by their education to the vision of a large territory providing a great market with all its ensuing possibilities.[13] Also, of course, the conditions under which they operate will be far different; for instance, all the paperwork which is now necessary to get goods through customs barriers, to obtain export permits from the respective Commerce Ministries, to get foreign exchange, etc., will be eliminated, under the provisions of the Common Market. A Sicilian handicraftsman will be able to load his wares on a mule's back, walk down from his little village perched on a mountain top to the nearest railway station, and ship his products to Hamburg without any formality as he now ships them to Rome or to Florence.

The increased purchasing power brought about by general prosperity is another factor not to be overlooked. When, as is already happening, particularly in France and Italy, great numbers of people can turn, because of improved economic conditions, from the purchase of essentials to nonessentials (as has been the case in the United States for a considerable time now), new, unexpected outlets open up

[13] "This accommodation of the mind and the imagination of man to the concept of supranational government in Europe has continued in more recent years through the discussion generated by the treaties for Euratom and the Common Market. Now that these treaties have been ratified, federation ceases to be an academic concept both as respects the daily life of some 160 million Europeans and as respects their ideas of state and government." Arnold J. Zurcher, *The Struggle to Unite Europe* (New York: New York University Press, 1958), p. 166. See also François Fontaine, "La Jeunesse est-elle européenne?" *Quelle est cette Europe?* p. 122: "The observations made by us are confirmed by systematic polls. More than half the young people between twenty and twenty-five think that the great questions of our age cannot be solved in the national framework."

for all kinds of produce hitherto considered a luxury; in Europe, these include the handicrafts, wines, fruit, etc. of the underdeveloped regions.

Now, let us examine the causes of underdevelopment: as previously stated, some are natural, like poverty of the soil, dry or extreme climate, mountainous terrain, etc.; others are due to the actions of man through the centuries. For instance, it is man's fault if certain regions of France have been almost entirely cut off from the communications system of the nation, which is all centered around the capital; it is man's fault that the system of "latifundia" developed in Italy, increasingly pauperizing once fertile regions, or if care has not been taken to avoid the creation of problems deriving from soil erosion or from deforestation. And, even if initially spurred by natural causes, i.e. the location of deposits of coal and iron ores, it is man who has brought about the concentration of industry in certain areas. It is now increasingly difficult to undo what has been done over many, many years; even if other sources of energy (oil now and, later, atomic power) are in part replacing coal and will do so even more in the future, the concentration of factors of production is already a fact. A policy of decentralization is obviously necessary, for it is true that "free trade can modify the economic structure (of a nation) and build up a new, integrated structure; but, left to itself and unregulated, nobody can guarantee that this new structure will be in line with the exigencies of harmonious expansion or of balanced development."[14] Actually, the regional development of these depressed areas of the Community will also be an outlet for capital which is rapidly accumulating in the treasuries of some Member States and which, if left unused, will bring about serious problems. Here again, as private capital follows certain laws, the task of the Executive of the Common Market will be to encourage investment in the underdeveloped regions, with capital moving freely from

[14] *Mondo Economico*, No. 28, July 15, 1961.

11

nation to nation, no longer hindered by bureaucratic barriers. This objective is now being pursued by the national governments.

As for incentives to private industrial investments (in Southern Italy) the list is impressive. Such incentives include income tax exemptions; duty exemption on imports of construction materials and machinery; reduction in transportation rates and in sales taxes on power consumption and purchases of machinery and materials; grants of land; grants of part of the costs of buildings, road and railroad links, water main and sewage connections; low-interest, long-term capital loans; assistance in plant design, market studies and in training labor.[15]

Furthermore, the law can prescribe that a certain percentage of the total investments of public concerns must be put to use in the underdeveloped areas, as is now the case in Italy.

An important objective will be to create the rational bases which are absolutely necessary before a general uplifting of the depressed regions can be brought about. Coordination of these will result in important savings of time, effort, and money.[16] For instance, there is little sense in building two big electricity-producing plants in Sardinia and Corsica at the same time, supplying a quantity of energy in excess of

[15] *Italy—An Economic Profile, 1962*. Study prepared by the Commercial Office of the Italian Embassy, Washington, D.C., June 1963. Similar provisions have been applied to the underdeveloped regions of France by the French Government.

[16] "There are too many examples of imbalances within the national economic areas where competition is free to expect the progressive integration of these within a Community which should determine, by the fact of its existence, a more harmonious evolution. . . . It appears, in fact, that it is not possible to entirely abandon to the natural course of things the task of directing the social development of the Community in the ways of harmony and of final convergence such as the Treaty foresees, and that, without threatening free competition— the indispensable leaven of common progress—a better coordinated effort should be proposed to the Member States, so as to attain these objectives more surely and, in any case, more rapidly." *Exposé 1960,* intro.

the local needs of either of the two islands, when it would be much cheaper to build only one and install a system of cables and controls whereby the newly obtained electric power could be used on both sides of the seven-mile strait of St. Boniface which separates the two islands. By the same token, it is illogical to subsidize a mine in, say, Sicily, when the same product can be obtained at much lower cost, including transportation, from a mine in the Massif Central. Conversely, coordinated planning would mean, for instance, that certain vegetables and other agricultural produce, which are very cheap throughout the Mezzogiorno and the South of France, would not also be grown in other parts of the Community under the protection of the national State. In many cases, state financing would be necessary; for example, to enable the farmer to use modern methods of production, to irrigate his land, build roads, etc. But this temporary assistance would be discontinued once the situation was corrected.

In France, a decentralization of industry has been attempted and the establishment of new factories encouraged in the regions of Central and South-West France and Brittany where they would perform a very important function as the nuclei of new industrial zones. In Italy, the objectives of both the Ten-Year Plan of Development and the Cassa per il Mezzogiorno have been only partially attained, and it is clear that at the present pace the problem of Southern Italy will not be solved for a long time to come.

In the framework of limited economic expansion, it is difficult to conceive of a concrete policy of regional development.[17] Perhaps the underlying reasons for underdevelopment must be identified with lack of coordination on the

---

[17] *Réalités*, No. 161, June 1959, in an article on the underdeveloped areas of Europe, has this to say: "The best way to eliminate these structural weaknesses is not so much to solve them one by one but to push the *European ensemble* [emphasis supplied] into a massive and constant expansion."

national level, and with the application of obsolete methods to the means of production in the regions concerned.

The purpose of the present work can now be clearly established. It is assumed that the construction of the new Europe will proceed and that, perhaps after a transition period in which something similar to "l'Europe des Patries" (or "des Etats") in a confederal form is created, a more solid organization will unite the hitherto sovereign states composing the Community.[18] And, most important from our viewpoint, "In reality, the Europe taking shape under our eyes is assuming the physiognomy of a Europe of the regions, and, eventually, the Europe of tomorrow will be less a Europe of the nations, built by history, than a Europe of the economic regions. It is not Europe of the States, it is not even Europe of the nations, but it is already a little the European fatherland."[19] Temporary setbacks will be overcome. In fact, history teaches us that confederal institutions are generally only a necessary stage towards a tighter, federal construction. Otherwise, when a confederation has served its purpose, or is under a certain amount of strain, it will cease to exist. The contrary is true when the former sovereign states relinquish part of their sovereignty to a federal, or "supra-national" authority, and when the relations between this and the component states are care-

---

[18] M. Spaak concludes the previously quoted article in *Foreign Affairs:* "Within the European Community, we must continue the work auspiciously begun. If possible, we must skip some stages of tariff abolition, advance toward a common policy in trade, transport and social affairs, tackle the great monetary problem, work out an agricultural policy, and, by avoiding autarchy and protectionism, demonstrate that the European Community is an open organization. These ideas are still held today by the overwhelming majority of European statesmen. They are shared by the overwhelming majority of European peoples. Let us not, then, be dismayed. . . . The dissident element constituted by current French policy may be a cause of delay, but it cannot prevent the ultimate success of the great undertakings to which Europe and the United States have set their hands."

[19] P. B. Couste, Président de la Fédération des Jeunes Chefs d'Entreprise d'Europe, in *Communauté Européenne*, No. 12, December, 1962.

fully regulated by constitutional law, which is accepted as the "law of the land," thus covering all the territory of the federal state. Therefore, a law issued by the Central Authority in Strasbourg, or Brussels, or wherever the capital of Europe is located, will be equally valid in Italy and in the Netherlands, in France and in Germany, etc., even if it apparently favors the interests of one Member State over another. Those whose interests are allegedly endangered would have recourse to all the constitutional means provided in order to have the law repealed or modified. However, they could not simply refuse to abide by it.[20] Once that point has been reached, *les jeux sont faits*—and, even if the speed is uneven and the direction unsure, the end is nothing but political unification.[21]

Two ideas should be emphasized: the two basic concepts of space and time as applied to the Community. Certainly, if the Community, which is now limited to six Member States, is eventually to include all, or even most, of the nations that have applied, or will apply, for full or associate membership, modifications of the present treaties are unavoidable. But, even so, they must not reach the point of transforming the structure into a conglomeration of

[20] It is otherwise very probable that ". . . In time of stress, because of inflationary pressures or a serious recession, a national government might well apply defensive measures without too much regard for the policy of its neighbor states in the Community." Zurcher, *op. cit.*, p. 160.

[21] "If our European institutions are at present limited to economic affairs, they represent however the beginning of the United States of Europe. It is now necessary to make them more democratic, to gradually extend the European method to new domains and finally to prepare the creation of a European political authority under democratic control." Jean Monnet. "The Federal Government and the Italian Government are favorable to a new development of the existing European communities. In their opinion, the European Economic Community should be completed as rapidly as possible by the creation of political forms of cooperation." Chancellor Ludwig Erhard of Germany and President Antonio Segni of Italy, in a joint communique, following the visit of the former to Rome, in February 1964. Both quotations from *Communauté Européenne*, No. 3, March 1964.

15

sovereign states which can form little more than a free-trade association. In that case, the dream of European Union will be shattered, at least for a long time, and Europe will have proved constitutionally incapable of ever attaining the place in the world that it should rightfully hold.[22] It is undeniable that such danger exists, but it is also certain that many forces, deriving from both the purest ideals and the most prosaic vested interests, combine to counter it.

As far as time is concerned, we are now living in a period of history when profound changes take place around us with almost incredible frequency. In the last few years, satellites have been launched, men have repeatedly orbited the earth, and intercontinental television has become a fact. What is more, this process of acceleration seems to intensify. Plans are made, and huge amounts of money are allocated, to put a man on the moon by 1970; other seemingly fantastic achievements are certainly in store for mankind. Therefore, when we talk of "Federal Government of Europe," "Central Government," or "European Authority," we believe that there is an excellent chance that such a body will actually exist at a time that cannot, perhaps, be fully evaluated now.[23] It must not be forgotten, after all, that it took a long

[22] This danger has been clearly seen by Gen. de Gaulle. In his very controversial press conference of January 14, 1963, he said, among other things: "We have to agree that the entry of Great Britain and then of other states would completely change the complex of arrangements concerning ententes, compensations, and other regulations that have already been established among the Six, because all these states, like Great Britain, have some very important peculiarities. Then, the construction of a completely different Common Market should be envisaged. But that which would be built by eleven and then by thirteen and maybe eighteen, would no doubt look different from that which has been built by the Six. . . . It is easy to foresee that the cohesion of all its members, who would be very numerous and very different, would not stand up for long. . . ." *Le Monde* (Sélection Hebdomadaire), January 16, 1963.

[23] Even the government of the Member State which allegedly is further away than the others from this concept—France—no doubt agrees that it will become reality in the future. The *New York Times* of May 27, 1963, states that, according to some of "France's leading

time for Germany to travel the distance from the Zollverein (1834) to the proclamation of the Empire (1871). And in that case there was a cultural homogeneity much greater than that existing between the Western European states. However, the tempo of historical transformation and development is accelerating and therefore it seems that these considerations will also apply in this case.

Now, finally, let us again turn to the problem of regional underdevelopment in the Community, a major question that may hamper, twist, retard, or even endanger the actual realization of European unity.

As we see it, the national governments will only be able to *improve* the absolute, and perhaps even the relative, position of the French and Italian depressed regions, but will not be able to *solve* the problem. Only a European Government, clearly endowed with supra-national powers, will have the necessary strength and potentialities to achieve this goal.[24] But, in order to do this, two conditions are necessary: (a) a policy of laissez faire is incompatible with any program of development of the depressed regions; therefore deep, extensive, continuous, and vigilant intervention by the

---

diplomats . . . an exclusively European force cannot be established until there is a European political authority or government capable of deciding how and when to use such weapons. That day, the French say, is at least a decade away, despite progress toward European economic union."

[24] The pronounced intervention of the European Authority in economic matters is indispensable if a well-balanced development between the various regions and branches of the economy is to be attained. *Le Monde* (Sélection Hebdomadaire), June 7, 1962, thus states: "That intervention of the Community is necessary: procedures must be elaborated that permit its enactment, safeguarding in the meantime the interests of those to whom such measures should be applied. By virtue of the principle that a production is justified by its social usefulness, and not only by the individual profit that can be made out of it, the government should be able to impose certain curbs or to create such conditions that certain types of production, by their own nature the most profitable, cease to be so if they are damaging the Community, and, conversely, may attract private initiative, when most desirable from a social viewpoint."

European Government is necessary; (b) this intervention cannot be limited to a series of uncoordinated, spasmodic efforts which will necessarily result in a variety of local or sectoral improvements, modifying some facets of the problem, but not solving it: a comprehensive program on a European scale must be devised and applied by a European Authority. Actually, this program should not only concern certain regions, or sectors of the economy of the Community, but *the economy of the Community as a whole*.[25] It should be drawn up closely following the guiding principles of the French plan; this contention will be analyzed later in the present work.

To sum up, therefore, the writer believes that the solution to the problem of regional underdevelopment in the Community can be found in a European framework and in a partially regulated economy.

If the policy outlined above is put into effect, then regional underdevelopment will become only one of the problems in the general picture of economic expansion, directed by the Federal Government of the United States of Europe, with the participation of both private and public capital and enterprise.[26] A policy of continuous and regular expansion, and of full employment not depending exclusively on the

[25] From a conference held by Prof. Georges Vedel, of the Faculté de Droit et des Sciences Economiques, University of Paris, on occasion of the Congress of European Students, organized in Toulouse in October 1961 by the Fondation Européenne de la Culture: "Economic integration is of such a nature as to accentuate certain imbalances and to increase the underdevelopment of certain regions, unless it be guided by a political will. It is necessary to practise an orientation of development, a 'lay-out' of the European territory. This 'lay-out' of the territory must follow economic criteria. But it also entails political criteria: Europe cannot be concentrated in certain prosperous industrial sectors, surrounded by an underdeveloped *no-man's land*" [in English in original]. Reprinted in *Communauté Européenne*, No. 11, Nov. 1961.

[26] "An effective combination of public and private initiative, with adequate proportions and institutions, is an axiom which is no longer discussed theoretically, at least by those who are really competent and responsible." Giulio Pastore, *Per lo Sviluppo della Sardegna* (Quaderno No. 29. Rome: Centro Studi della Cassa per il Mezzogiorno, 1958), p. 13.

fluctuations of the market and on the capricious laws of supply and demand, will be the best guarantee for fostering the steady development of the impoverished regions of Europe.

There is of course the opposite thesis, proposed by a different school of thought, whereby strictly economic criteria should prevail over other considerations. The followers of this thesis believe that the plans for the development of Southern Italy, as well as for the South-West and other regions of France, are proving partly unworkable and are, in effect, a burden on the general economy of the two nations—expansion is slowed down, sometimes considerably, due to this massive, expensive aid, and results are not easily discernible. Attempts to industrialize these regions are *uneconomic*, therefore they should be abandoned and surplus labor from the underdeveloped regions should move to Northern Italy, to the Paris region, and to North-East France, where manpower is in demand, and where it would certainly be cheaper and easier to use these human resources in a more rational way.

This line of reasoning may have some merit, as far as the present is concerned, but has two main faults: if the migration to the industrialized parts of the countries involved continues, the underdeveloped regions of today will stay that way *ad infinitum;* actually the gap that divides the two groups of regions would rapidly get wider and wider, and we should have a deterioration of the present situation. Italy and France would be roughly divided into two sections: a progressive, industrialized, modern, active, and wealthy half, and a dormant, backward half, almost deprived of industry—practically another world, although theoretically indistinguishable on the map from the rest of the nation. Indeed, this is unfortunately the situation obtaining in these two nations. The propositions set forth in this book are aimed at improving this situation, possibly to modify it radically, and finally to correct it.

We must keep in mind not only the immediate future, but

the role that these regions will be called upon to play in the larger unit of the Common Market, of which they should be vital components, not deadweights braking the progress of the rest of the Community.

Secondly, as we shall see repeatedly throughout the book, "another factor which sometimes aggravates the shortage of skilled manpower is the lack of mobility of the workers. For example, there is the case of skilled moulders in France who preferred to be specialized workers in other branches of industry and to receive lower wages rather than change their residence with a view to obtaining employment in their specialized field, even with housing provided."[27] These people are human beings, with sentimental attachments to their own habitat, and they refuse to be moved about by virtue of some abstract economic law. The governments have to take this into consideration and act accordingly; a similar problem affects the depressed areas of Kentucky, West Virginia, and Pennsylvania in the United States. In fact, it will be very interesting to compare the ways in which these problems will be tackled by the United States, Italian, and French Governments. Up to this time, indications are that the Johnson Administration's philosophy on the subject does not differ too much from that of the two European countries.

If regional equilibrium can finally be secured in the Common Market, this will spell the end of the present state which finds unemployed labor, land, and other resources in some parts of the Community, and a shortage of the same factors in other places.

This work will start with an analysis of the reasons for the formation of the underdeveloped areas in France and Italy, particularly from an historical viewpoint. The

[27] United Nations—Economic and Social Council, Economic Commission for Europe, *Report on Manpower Problems in Europe in 1963.* Transmitted by the International Labour Office (Document E/ECE/ 508, Geneva, February 27, 1964).

analysis will be complemented by descriptions of the present state of the regions examined, covering some of the most important aspects of human activity. The treatment given to the Italian and to the French regions will be uneven for several reasons; first of all because, as already stated, the magnitude of the problem in the South of Italy is much greater than that of the backward areas in France. Secondly, certain issues are peculiar to one area but practically irrelevant to the other, for instance, crime in Southern Italy or underpopulation in South-West France. Also—and this is significant because it concerns the whole study—while Southern Italy and the Islands can be considered as a unit and therefore statistics and other data can often be found which apply to them as an integral whole within the statistics and data of the nation, this is not true of France, partially because of the scattered character of her underdeveloped regions. Furthermore in Italy a geographical region generally corresponds to an administrative region but in France the regional subdivisions retained only historical value following the Revolution—the Metropolitan territory now being divided into ninety *départements* whose borders very often do not correspond with the historical limits of preexisting regions. Sometimes national statistics, covering the whole of France, have been given, but obviously these have only an indicative value.

These factors are also reflected in the method of dealing with the subjects covered. In Chapter I which is descriptive, Southern Italy has been treated as a unit, whereas the various depressed regions of France have been examined separately. Some underdeveloped but less important French regions, such as Roussillon, Béarn, Limousin, etc. have not been treated specifically, although it is to be understood that they follow the course of the large neighboring regions of Languedoc, Aquitaine, Massif Central, and so forth.

This is followed by as thorough an examination as possible of the action taken by the national governments of

Italy and France to overcome the problem of regional underdevelopment in the territories of the two nations, within the framework of European integration.

The free movement of workers, goods, capital, and services within the Community and its potential and actual consequences on the underdeveloped areas forms the subject of a separate chapter. This chapter also includes an examination of the two financial institutions created by the Common Market Treaty, the European Investment Bank and the European Social Fund, which have particular relevance for the underdeveloped areas.

A detailed analysis is then made of a problem which is one of the most difficult to solve in the Community (as evidenced by the long-drawn-out meetings of the Executive of the EEC in December 1961–January 1962, December 1963 and 1964)— agriculture. Its relevance to the underdeveloped regions will naturally be given paramount consideration. The solution consists in creating a market on a European scale, regulated by the proper European agencies.

The other main aspects of regional underdevelopment— transportation, industry, and power—and their solution in the larger European Community are dealt with in such a way, it is hoped, as to convey a clear picture of these facets of the general problem and the prospects of solving them.

An activity which is becoming especially important now, with the steady rise in living standards within the Community and the consequent increased motorization and general affluence of the West Europeans, is that of tourism. Many zones of the Italian South, three large Mediterranean islands—Sicily, Sardinia, and Corsica—and some of the depressed regions of continental France are ideally suited, potentially at least, to a mass exploitation of this activity. We shall examine this and try to evaluate the impact of the lowering of barriers within the Europe of the Six on the tourist activities of the underdeveloped regions examined in this study.

The last chapter consists of an analysis of the two most widely known examples in history of the integration of industrialized with mainly agricultural (and under-developed) regions, with little or no governmental inter-vention: the unification of North and South Italy and the reunification of the North and South in the United States following the Civil War. Lessons have been drawn from these events that apply to the present problems of European integration. This is followed by a discussion of the role of the prospective European government.

A summary of the problems and possible solutions in the Mezzogiorno and the French underdeveloped areas follows, concluding with a final appraisal.

The hope is that this study of the general problem of European unification and the detailed examination of one of its most negative facets may contribute toward a lasting solution and aid in counteracting the potentially disruptive forces presented. European unification is a fascinating subject.[28] It cannot be denied that the obstacles to be over-come are many and difficult; however, in the present world situation, we are becoming accustomed to living with difficulties and insecurity.[29] While the "solutions" to world problems are often clumsy and inconclusive, the fact that *something* is being done in a given area, and in this case in Western Europe, gives rise to hope. Perhaps the example thus set will bring constructive results to other areas and people. Central American, South American, African, and Asian nations have all tried, though with little success, to

[28] As Walter Hallstein puts it: "We are not integrating economies, we are integrating policies. We are not just sharing our furniture, we are jointly building a new and bigger house." *United Europe: Challenge and Opportunity* (Cambridge, Mass.: Harvard University Press, 1962), p. 66.

[29] "Each generation, no doubt, thinks of itself as destined to remake the world. Mine knows however that it will not remake it. But its task is perhaps greater. It is that of impeding the unmaking of it." Albert Camus, speech of acceptance of the Nobel Prize, Stockholm, 1957.

form their own common markets, and the Soviet bloc has also appropriated the idea. The enormous repercussions that the Common Market is having in the United States,[30] is also a sign of the importance it has assumed. A solution to the problem of regional underdevelopment in Europe will contribute to increasing the momentum for continental unity, the favorable consequences of which, not only for Europe, but for the West as a whole, are too clear to need explanation.[31]

A number of sources, mainly, but not exclusively, French, Italian, British, American, and "European" (that is, publications of some of the official and unofficial European organizations), all of which are fully described in the bibliography, have been used. The writer translated into English all the quotations from French, Italian, Spanish, and Latin.

Grateful acknowledgment is made to the following

[30] These extend to military, political, economic considerations, etc. President Johnson stated: "Progress toward an integrated European Community will help (the Alliance's capacity to influence events in the world at large constructively) and thus to strengthen the Atlantic Community. A more cohesive and powerful Europe within a developing Atlantic Community is needed to undertake the large tasks which lie ahead. The essentially national and loosely coordinated efforts of the past no longer suffice." President Johnson (then Vice-President), address on the occasion of the 10th Anniversary of SHAPE, April 6, 1961. Reprinted in *The Atlantic Community*, Winter 1963–64, p. 483.

[31] "And as Europe moves towards unity, its role and responsibility, here as elsewhere, would and must increase accordingly." President Kennedy, Frankfurt address, June 25, 1963 (full text in *New York Times* of the following day). The future key position of Europe is also foreseen by the Secretary-General of the United Nations, U Thant, who stated that "In the seventies, if there are seventies, the world will witness four big powers—the United States of America, Europe, Russia, and China." *New York Times*, June 29, 1963. And the urgency of this enterprise is underlined by General de Gaulle who, in one of his rare press conferences, said: ". . . in particular the direct contacts which are being established again between the Anglo-Saxons and the Soviets, and which risk influencing her own destiny, should convince Europe that now is the time to be herself or otherwise she risks never being so." *Le Monde* (Sélection Hebdomadaire), July 31, 1963.

24

organizations for supplying much of the information and material used in this study.

La Section Culturelle de l'Ambassade de France—New York.

The French State Tourist Office—New York.

L'Ufficio Informazioni annesso al Consolato Generale Italiano—New York.

The Office of the Commercial Counselor at the Italian Consulate-General—New York.

The Italian State Tourist Office—New York.

L'Office Statistique des Communautés Européennes—Luxembourg.

Le Service d'Information de la Haute Autorité—Luxembourg.

Le Service d'Information de l'OECD—Paris.

Le Service d'Information des Communautés Européennes —Paris.

Le Sécrétariat de la Commission de la Communauté Economique Européenne—Brussels.

Le Service des Publications des Communautés Européennes—Paris, Brussels, Luxembourg.

The Administration of the Cassa per il Mezzogiorno—Rome.

Various Services of the United Nations Secretariat—New York.

I wish to acknowledge the valuable advice furnished at various stages of the manuscript by Dr. Arnold J. Zurcher, Dr. Ludwik Krzyzanowski, Dr. Thomas Hovet, Dr. Feliks Gross, and Col. Roman Michalowski, all of New York University. Particularly close to me, during and after the drafting of the study, was Dr. Paul Alpert, also of New York University. The manuscript was thoroughly read and analyzed by Professor Douglas Dowd of Cornell University, whose advice and critical appraisal has had a decisive effect on the final version. My wife Jean, though laboring under exceptionally heavy family responsibilities, found the time, the strength, and the will to type, research, advise, criticize; without her assistance and encouragement, this study probably would never have materialized. She deserves all my gratitude.

CHAPTER I

Regional Underdevelopment in the South of Italy, Central and South-West France

DISPARITY OF DEVELOPMENT BETWEEN NORTH AND SOUTH OF ITALY

GEOGRAPHIC FEATURES

The area encompassed by the term "Mezzogiorno," (the Land of the Midday Sun) comprises the five mainland compartments or regions of Abruzzi-Molise, Campania, Basilicata, Apulia, and Calabria,[1] and the islands of Sicily and Sardinia, with a total surface area of 47,400 square miles and a population of more than eighteen million. The terrain, dominated by the Apennine chain of mountains, is extremely rugged, though some areas have great scenic beauty. Due to its geographical position, with the sea surrounding it on three sides, the area has mild winters and very hot summers.

The poor nature of the soil and the climatic characteristics have deeply influenced the structure of the Southern Italian economy. Only about 15 per cent of the land is flat and suitable for cultivation, while 50 per cent is hilly and the remainder mountainous.[2] The mountains, however, are not

[1] Each compartment contains several provinces, which are again divided into 1,750 communes.

[2] See SVIMEZ (Associazione per lo Sviluppo del Mezzogiorno), *Notizie sull' Economia del Mezzogiorno*, (Rome, 1956), p. 30. Hereinafter cited as *Notizie*. It is interesting to note the comparison between mountainous, hilly, and plain land in the two parts of Italy:

	North	*South*
Mountainous	3,511,000 hectares	2,631,500 hectares
Hilly	2,078,900 hectares	6,177,300 hectares
Plain	3,538,200 hectares	1,663,400 hectares

sufficiently high to ensure year-round snow, thus most of the rivers have only a short life and are dry for a good portion of the year. There is only one rainy season—during the winter months—when the plains become waterlogged and the rivers flood. The rest of the year is a period of drought, with obviously serious consequences for the agricultural economy. In addition to poor soil, which is lacking in mineral reserves, there is a tremendous problem of soil erosion: the hill slopes are composed primarily of clays which are liable to landslips during the winter months. Average rainfall during the years 1942–51 was only 900 mm., and in the plains was as low as 450–550 mm.[3] This paucity of rain has produced a serious irrigation problem, and it is because of this that the funds provided for the development of Southern Italy have been, and will continue to be, dedicated largely to irrigation and land reclamation projects. A report prepared by SVIMEZ (Association for the Development of the Mezzogiorno) for the International Bank for Reconstruction and Development stated:

> The problem of water supply, no less than the land reclamation program, is one of the key problems of Southern Italy which is still far from being solved; the task is to improve an indispensable service, the insufficiency of which stands seriously in the way of any attempt at promoting the economic and social development of large areas in Southern Italy.[4]

THE ORIGINS OF THE "QUESTIONE MERIDIONALE"

Ancient History

In ancient times, the regions now constituting the Mezzogiorno of Italy underwent alternate periods of

---

It must be remembered that the South covers only about 40 per cent of the surface of the whole of Italy.

[3] C. Maranelli, *Considerazioni geografiche sulla Questione Meridionale* (Bari: Laterza, 1956), p. 25.

[4] P. Saraceno, *Economic Effects of an Investment Program in Southern Italy* (Rome, SVIMEZ, 1951), p. 7. (Published in English.) A report

prosperity and depression. This assumes some significance since it indicates that agriculture has at times flourished in spite of unfavorable natural conditions; and the Greeks, the Romans, and the Arabs certainly did not have at their disposal today's technological methods. The present under-developed regions of the Mezzogiorno achieved a large degree of fertility and prosperity under all these con-querors. The Magna Grecia, which comprised most of continental Southern Italy and Sicily, attained an un-paralleled affluence and development. The Romans, who succeeded the Greeks in the domination of Southern Italy, came to consider parts of it, especially Sicily and Campania, as "the granary of Rome." However, in Cicero's times, the exploitative character of Verre's administration rapidly ruined the hitherto prosperous Trinacria. The great orator describes this calamitous event thus: "Large numbers of peasants fled, renouncing the lands inherited from their fathers. Sicily had the aspect of a country over which a con-tinuous and cruel war has been fought. The plains and hills, which I had once seen so prosperous and verdant, had fallen into waste and abandon."[5] Furthermore, the con-quest by Rome of the then-fertile lands of North Africa made the Eternal City turn to them for cereals since they could be produced there cheaper and in much greater quantities. Sicily and parts of Southern Italy thus lost the preferential treatment they had received until then.

Meanwhile, as a beginning to the imbalance that has perpetuated itself throughout the centuries until our day, new methods of cultivation, improvements of various kinds, rotation of crops, etc., progressively lifted the general agri-

---

prepared as part of the documentation submitted to the International Bank with a view to obtaining a loan to be utilized for the financing of an investment program in Southern Italy.

[5] "Diffugerant enim permulti, nec solum arationes sed etiam sedes suas patrias . . . reliquerant. Sicilia mihi visa est ut eae terrae solent in quibus bellum acerbum diuturnumque versatum est. Quos ego campos antea collesque nitidissimos viridissimosque vidissem, hos ita vastatos nunc ac desertos videbam." Cicero, *In Verrem*, iii. 18. 46, 47.

French Underdeveloped Regions

cultural level of Northern Italy. Furthermore, the scourge of malaria, probably brought from the Orient, hit Southern Italy in the 4th century A.D. and spread rapidly, favored by climatic conditions. Very little could be done in those days to counteract this illness, and the desolation it brought was certainly not a negligible factor among the causes that

30

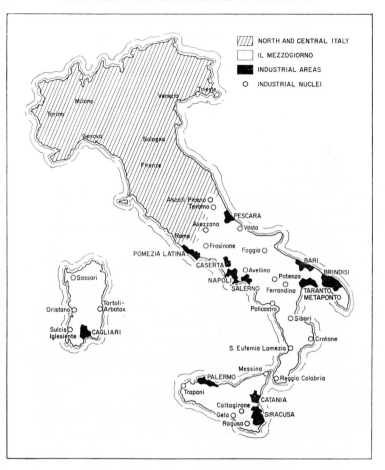

Industrial Expansion in the South of Italy

contributed to the underdevelopment of the area. When the
Roman Empire broke up and dissolved, the Northern parts
of the country were successively invaded by waves of
barbarians who, along with destruction, also brought new
life and vitality to these lands. Such invasions, however,
took place on a much smaller scale in Southern Italy;

31

furthermore, the invading barbarians did not generally settle there, but returned to the North or went on to Africa after exhausting the local possibilities for plunder and destruction. Eventually, the North gradually settled down under the domination of the invaders (principally the Longobards, followed by the Franks) who, despite all their shortcomings, were not lacking in the qualities of dynamism and enterprise. Southern Italy, however, became a part of the Byzantine Empire, the main characteristics of which were immobility and intensive and indiscriminate exploitation.

So for centuries the destinies of Northern and Southern Italy became completely separate, and this partition is probably at the root of present economic and sociological conditions that distinctly mark the division of the Italian nation into two parts, one utterly different from the other.

The Middle and Modern Ages

In the 8th century, the Arabs invaded Sicily and parts of Sardinia and Calabria. Under Arab rule, which was enlightened and as little motivated by exploitation as a foreign domination can be, Sicily and the other small areas occupied by the Moslems underwent a quick recovery; at the end of their stay (11th century), they left behind a vastly improved organization, particularly in agriculture.

In 1040 the Normans came to Southern Italy and settled. Their administration was very efficient and honest. The Normans did introduce, however, the system of feudalism which, particularly in Southern Italy, was to have such disastrous consequences, both because of the extension of latifundia (which we shall examine in detail in Chapter IV) and because of the sharp division of the population into two classes—the landowners and the people who worked the land for them. Even today the structure of Southern Italy basically follows these lines, and this is one of the primary causes of the backwardness of the region.

Then new invasions, neither of which brought any benefit to the Mezzogiorno, followed one another in quick succession: those of the Angevins and the Aragonians. Southern Italy rapidly reverted to the state of destitution and devastation of pre-Arab times.

Thus the feudal system continued to condemn the country to immobility while no moneyed bourgeoisie arose as in the more and more prosperous Maritime Republics and Free Communes of the North. Two events dealt the final blow to the Mezzogiorno: the shifting of maritime traffic from the Mediterranean to the Atlantic, consequent to the discovery of America, and the Spanish occupation and domination of Southern Italy, which lasted for centuries and was an outstanding example of maladministration and exploitation.[6]

Cut off from the new sources of riches, already suffering from centuries of foreign domination, with unfavorable climatic conditions, poor soil, and a very tight and oppressive feudal system, Southern Italy entered a period of stagnation and resignation which, to all intents and purposes and in spite of many attacks on it, continues to this day and presents a very difficult problem to solve.[7]

New ills were from time to time added to the old: in Napoleonic times, the necessity of supplying the French armies with wood, together with that of finding new land needed to grow cereals, mainly for the same purpose, brought about massive deforestation. This entailed the most disastrous consequences for Southern Italy in view of the irregular and torrential character of its rivers which now swept away the land along their banks. This soil erosion

[6] "All that was left by the feudal lords to the government of the resources of Southern Italy went in the direction of Spain." Carlo Scarfoglio, *Il Mezzogiorno e l'Unità d'Italia* (Florence: Parenti, 1953), p. 95.

[7] "The relation between North and South is part of the knot that ties together all the Italian problems, which essentially are problems of integration between continental and Mediterranean regions of the country." Francesco Compagna, *Mezzogiorno d'Europa* (Rome: Editoriale Opere Nuove, March 1958), p. 51.

process made gigantic inroads in a relatively short time. Finally, mainly for political reasons aimed at keeping the country separated from the new currents of liberal thought then prevailing in Europe, the Bourbons, after their restoration, erected a real curtain around their kingdom, a curtain that embraced all intellectual as well as commercial activities.[8]

Unification with the North

We shall analyze in detail later in this study the consequences of unification with the North in the years following 1860 and continuing until present times. It is enough to say here that from an economic viewpoint the way in which unification was carried out was completely irrational. In effect, the Piedmontese government gave free rein to the interplay of economic forces which, according to their reasoning, should by themselves have taken care of the situation in a relatively short time and abolished the gap between the relatively wealthy and industrialized North and the poor, disorganized South, essentially dedicated to agricultural activities. Today, after a century, the South is still suffering the consequences of this policy, and, indeed, it seems to some that this situation will be everlasting.[9] In a few years it became apparent, even to the more reluctant

[8] "It is worthwhile to remember that in the last years of the reign of Ferdinand II even the foreign representations of the Kingdom of the Two Sicilies abroad were headed only by Chargés d'Affaires; similarly, the Ministries at home were headed not by Ministers but by Directors. All this was to avoid the power and prestige deriving from the title of Ambassador and Minister." Ruggero Moscati, *Il Mezzogiorno d'Italia nel Risorgimento* (Messina: d'Anna, 1953), p. 40.

[9] ". . . the gap, the abyss, that separates Italy into two will never be filled." Corrado Barbagallo, *La Questione Meridionale* (Milan: Garzanti, 1948), p. 38. Also: "The most typical and most serious case of unbalanced regional development is that of Italy. Industrialization has affected the North almost exclusively. The South suffers not only from the lower agricultural revenue, but furthermore is less productive than the North. This does not mean that there is not also an agricultural overpopulation around the industrialized regions in the North, but this can be gradually reabsorbed. To the contrary, agricultural overpopulation is found throughout the South. The disequilibrium

minds, that unification had cost the South dearly and that the hoped-for results would never materialize. Thus originated the so-called "Questione Meridionale" (Southern Question) which has been plaguing Italy ever since, bringing tremendous negative consequences to the economic life of the nation, and certainly proving deleterious to its position and prestige in the world.

HISTORY OF GOVERNMENTAL INTERVENTION IN
SOUTHERN ITALY

In the first forty years following Italian unification practically nothing of any consequence was done to alleviate, in any lasting way, the problem of Southern Italy. This was due to many reasons, but chiefly to the intrinsic economic weakness of the young nation which was striving to achieve a position on the international scene not really compatible with her potentialities. In any case, whatever the reasons, the problem gradually became more serious and massive emigration deprived the country of millions of its citizens. Politically the South was in a continuous state of unrest due to the extreme degree of destitution; banditry was widespread and law and order were nebulous concepts, especially in certain parts of the area.

The first politician to make concrete proposals aiming at industrialization of certain parts of Southern Italy, principally Naples, was Luzzatti; he was followed by Salandra, who pointed out to Parliament the need for an aqueduct in Apulia and various urgent projects which could stimulate trade in the South. Finally, Zanardelli, the Prime Minister, promised to act upon these recommendations. Better still, he

can be translated into a series of comparative figures:

Region	Territory	% Income	Rate of Gross Investment	Demographic Growth
Centre-North	59	79	74	35
Mezzogiorno	41	21	26	65
Italy:	100	100	100	100"

Source: CECA, *Septième Rapport Général.*

went personally to perhaps the poorest region of the Mezzogiorno, Basilicata, to acquire first-hand knowledge of the problem. This was a momentous occasion, because Italian prime ministers before him had generally been too busy to go further south than the suburbs of Rome. Deeply impressed by what he saw, he elaborated on his return a comprehensive program: roadworks, water supply, reforestation, works to regulate torrents and river courses, taxation changes, etc. He also initiated a fight against illiteracy. But it took a long time to embody these provisions into law, and a much longer time—in some cases from twenty to thirty years—to bring them to reality.

Even when something was done, however, it brought no real solution to the problem. Two special laws were promulgated: in 1904 in favor of Basilicata, and in 1906 for the industrialization of Naples. More were subsequently approved for Calabria, Sicily, and Sardinia. All of them were poorly implemented, and some actually only enlarged the bureaucracy, creating a good deal more expense and confusion. Furthermore, they were not all-embracing schemes of regional development, but concerned single, uncoordinated projects, with consequent waste and added inefficiency.

One of the most outspoken critics of this state of affairs was Sonnino; when he finally became Prime Minister in 1906 he soon prepared a grandiose project for Southern Italy. This would have been the first really "organic" attempt to solve the problem, should his Cabinet have been in power long enough. Unfortunately for the Mezzogiorno, its lifespan was very short and the laws did not get beyond the drafting stage. His successors abandoned the project—the budget had, after all, to be balanced. Parliament instead decided to promote an inquiry, which was carried out in 1907 and, in high-flown language, expressed in fifteen volumes what everybody knew about conditions in the South.[10]

[10] The following is an excerpt from the Conclusions of the *Report of the Parliamentary Commission of Enquiry* (Rome: Istituto Poligrafico dello

Thus things dragged on with very little change for several years. Then came the war against Turkey (1911–1912); in the "patriotic" frenzy the South was forgotten. Meanwhile, the clouds on the European horizon were becoming increasingly black. Mussolini and d'Annunzio were inciting the crowds to "sacred duties," "expansion," etc. Who had any time or energy left to think of the Mezzogiorno in its misery? Then came World War I, followed by the reconstruction of the devastated areas (all in the North) and the whole economy. This was followed by the rise of Fascism, which had entirely different plans for Italy, none of which included the South.[11] Fascism aimed at bringing "civilization" to Africa (at least this was the official propaganda line) and in the process it forgot "Italy's own Africa."[12] Next came the Spanish Civil War, and finally World War II, which prevented even a minimum attempt at solving the Questione Meridionale. From 1943 until the end of the war, the Mezzogiorno was occupied by Allied troops while the North, or most of it, remained under German occupation, a fact which contributed further to accentuating the division between the two parts of the country. At the war's end, this

---

Stato, 1907): "The lands of the Mezzogiorno, with the exception of a few fertile areas in Calabria, Apulia and Sicily are mostly arid and unproductive. . . . Main obstacles to progress in agriculture are the destruction of woods, malaria, latifundia, lack of water. . . . The people in general live a life of dire poverty . . . illiteracy is widespread . . . the astonishingly high emigration represents a hard necessity . . . the future of the Mezzogiorno depends not only on the diffusion of culture and on the existence of large communications media, but above all on reforestation."

[11] "Fascism cancelled the Questione Meridionale from the Italian political lexicon. . . . Thus, denying the existence of the problem, they were not faced with it, so that, in the final analysis, its seriousness was enhanced: this seriousness appeared in its entirety after the war." Compagna, *op. cit.*, p. 7.

[12] In an article entitled "Milan", appearing in *Holiday*, August 1961, it was stated: "Recently, when Averell Harriman came to Italy to ask the Italians to take their proper share in investing money in underdeveloped countries, the Milanese businessmen replied, unanimously, that Italy had its own Africa: it began a hundred kilometers south of Rome."

time the South, on whose soil most of the fighting had taken place, was even more devastated than the North, which was also ravaged by the continuous air raids.

This, then was the situation which the Italian Government inherited in 1945. We shall see in a later chapter how it proposes to solve it.

VARIOUS INTERPRETATIONS OF THE CAUSES OF THE "QUESTIONE MERIDIONALE"

It is interesting, for a better understanding of the reasons which brought about the "Questione Meridionale," to give a few examples of the interpretation of the problem as expounded by some of Italy's outstanding scholars (almost all "Meridionali" themselves) who specialized in the subject.

Francesco Niceforo and Cesare Lombroso elaborated theories related to a pretended "racial inferiority" of the people of Southern Italy.[13] They mainly set out to find a justification for the backwardness of most of their people in comparison with the inhabitants of the North.

Benedetto Croce and Giustino Fortunato stressed the poverty of the soil and the climate as the main reason for the underdevelopment of the area. In the words of Fortunato:

Southern Italy, contrary to what some still believe, is worth very little, for conditions of climate, soil, and geographic structure are utterly unfavorable to its development; the two halves of Italy were painfully put together during the domain of pagan Rome, but are inhabited by two different peoples who happen to speak the same language; since then, in the whole economy of the Meridione, there has lain the tragedy, made graver

[13] See Niceforo's two works on this subject: *L'Italia Barbara Contemporanea* (Palermo: Sandron, 1898), and *Italiani del Nord e del Sud* (Turin: Bocca, 1901).

by human ignorance, of a people compelled to isolation in a country essentially poor.[14]

Arturo Labriola applied his Marxist interpretation of history to the evils of Southern Italy, and saw the reasons for the stagnation of the Mezzogiorno in the absence of a class struggle, and in the twisting of the dialectic process conducive to progress.

Gaetano Salvemini thought that, as the ills of Southern Italy derived mainly from the despotism and mismanagement of the upper classes, the granting of universal suffrage would bring about new management, more representative of the masses of the people, which would eliminate the former evils. He also supported the federalist thesis, on which subject many other outstanding "Meridionalisti" shared his ideas.

According to de Viti de Marco, the "Questione" derived mainly from a mistaken distribution of taxation, and was essentially connected with freedom of trade and customs tariffs. He was also strongly in favor of decentralization.

Francesco Nitti in his turn examined the problem mainly from the financial view, and pointed out that the impoverishment which had fallen upon the South was due to the excessive taxes paid, mainly to the benefit of the industrial North. This was due to a miscalculation of the potentialities of the South, not taking into consideration the poverty and the decadence of agriculture.

These are only some of the main theories advanced; many others have been elaborated, and all emphasize different aspects of the problem.

PRESENT SITUATION

General and Social Aspects

A brief description of the general situation in Southern Italy, particularly the state of destitution common to great

[14] G. Fortunato, *Il Mezzogiorno e lo Stato Italiano* (Florence: Vallecchi, 1926), 1, p. 10.

parts of it, is advisable. Nothing could be easier, in view of the abundance of material, than to embark upon a colorful description of poverty in the Mezzogiorno; we have tried, however, to sketch a general view of the situation.

We have also endeavored to avoid succumbing to the strong temptation to overemphasize or to philosophize on the miserable conditions found in what is today the extreme south of the European Economic Community and will perhaps tomorrow be part of an even larger community.[15] Figures, however, are furnished liberally, and their harsh impact may be more effective than a colorful description. In addition to sections dedicated to the problems of unemployment, migration, demography, and education, it has also been thought proper to present a synopsis on delinquency in the South. In fact, until this centuries-old plague has been conquered by a profound attack *on its causes*, the problem of Southern Italy will not have been solved. In this task the help of the Community can be of great value, especially if its Member States agree to participate in the industrialization of the area and consequently contribute to its economic rebirth. Signs of this participation are already visible.[16]

---

[15] ". . . These problems must be seen in the framework of the most modern exigencies deriving from integration between Western Europe and Southern Europe. The Mezzogiorno d'Italia can and must be considered the 'pilot zone' of this integration, inasmuch as it is the only region of Southern Europe that is included in the Common Market. . . ." Compagna, *op. cit.*, p. 84.

[16] See for instance the following statement made by Ludwig Erhard when he was West German Minister of Economic Affairs: "The efforts of Italy to eliminate the Southern problem pursue a genuinely European objective. . . . The Federal Government offers German enterprises all possible support for them to cooperate in the economic development of the Mezzogiorno. . . . DM. 50 million have been allocated to finance enterprises that operate in Southern Italy. In recent months greater participation and cooperation by German firms in important economic development projects is being seen in Italy. I would foresee that Italo-German cooperation may extend, in ever-growing measure, from the sector of research and exploitation of the

REASONS FOR UNDERDEVELOPMENT

(a) *Poverty*. It may be said that the wartime fighting in the Italian Mezzogiorno had a beneficial effect, in a certain way, on the local population: for the first time, most of them realized that life did not necessarily have to be the kind they lived. Observing the Allied soldiers—the abundance of everything from food, good clothes and money to the high degree of motorization, as well as listening to the tales of the many U.S. soldiers of Italian descent who could speak the local dialects—they developed a yearning to improve their miserable lot. This yearning no doubt contributed to urging the Government to take measures which for several years now have been working effectively, even though somewhat unevenly and perhaps too slowly, to improve conditions. Certainly the problems to be faced are formidable, but credit must be given to the Italian Government for attempting to find a solution and not evading its responsibility.

To open this description of the state of poverty in Southern Italy, let us quote Professor Saraceno of the Cassa per il Mezzogiorno (Southern Italy Development Fund):

It is estimated that the per capita income in the South is at present slightly over 50 per cent of the national average and 40 per cent of that of the Northern regions. Incidentally, it may also be of interest to note that it is 22 per cent of per capita income in the United States. But what is even more serious than the disparity between income levels in the North and the South is the fact that the mechanics of the country's economic growth have been such, at least until a few years ago, as to widen rather than reduce the existing gap.[17]

---

sources of power to all sectors of industry and agriculture." Quoted in Compagna, *ibid.*, p. 59.

[17] Pasquale Saraceno: *The Economic Development of the Mezzogiorno* (Milano: Giuffrè, 1955), p. 4. A report presented by SVIMEZ to the Conference on Underdeveloped Areas sponsored by the Centro Nazionale di Prevenzione e Difesa Sociale di Milano, 10–15 October, 1954. Published in English.

He confirms this assertion with a table, reproduced here as Table 1.

TABLE 1
PER CAPITA INCOME
(1928 = 100)

Year	Northern Italy	Southern Italy	Whole Italy	Ratio N.-S.
1928	100	100	100	1
1938	104	98	102	0.94
1948	95	75	89	0.79
1953	135	106	126	0.78

In 1951, the Chamber of Deputies of the Italian Parliament decided to set up two commissions of inquiry to make exhaustive investigations into the extent of destitution and unemployment throughout the country. A summary in English of their report is to be found in the *International Labour Review* of January 1955, published by the International Labour Organisation, Geneva. Table 2 shows the distribution of poor families on a geographic basis, and it will be noted that by far the greater number are in the South and the Islands.[18]

From these figures it may be seen that, whereas in the North 15 families out of 1,000 are classified as having a very low standard of living, the proportion rises to 248 per 1,000 in the Islands and 283 per 1,000 in continental Southern

[18] The definition of "low" and "very low" living standards given in the table is arrived at by certain very complex calculations which take into account the consumption of meat, sugar, wine, and other basic foods, living accommodation, and so forth, resulting in a figure indicative of the average for a family unit. Although this method is open to criticism, it yielded results that, if examined in the light of other factors, fit in reasonably well with the purposes of the inquiry. "These data would appear to justify the distinction drawn between low and very low living standards. There is room for argument as to whether the dividing line between the two groups should have been higher or lower. This, however, does not alter the fact that a large number of families belong to the lowest category—their living standard is far below any acceptable average." Lodovico Montini, "The Parliamentary Inquiry into Destitution in Italy," *International Labour Review*, LXXI, No. 1 (Geneva: ILO, January 1955), p. 8.

Italy. The report also points out that the maximum destitution is found in Basilicata with 332 and Calabria with 377
per 1,000. The much higher percentage of poor families in

TABLE 2
GEOGRAPHIC DISTRIBUTION OF POOR FAMILIES[19]

Region	Very low living standard		Low living standard	
	Number	*%*	*Number*	*%*
North	89,000	1.5	225,000	4.3
Center	118,000	5.9	195,000	9.7
South	802,000	28.3	624,000	21.9
Islands	358,000	24.8	301,000	20.6
Total	1,367,000	11.8	1,345,000	11.6

the South is indicative of the great difference in standards of
living between North and South. This is still true today.[20]

The Commission also inquired into the dietary habits of
poor families; the most disquieting data by far are those
referring to families in the South. The quality and quantity
of food falls in direct proportion to the increase in the size
of the family, until it reaches a daily minimum of 2,195
calories per person for families of nine persons or more. The
diet of poor families in the South scarcely reaches an average
of 2,270 calories daily, which includes a negligible amount
of protein (only 8 grams); meat consumption is only 8.6
kilograms per annum. These six million poor, with their
limited family budgets and inadequate diets, are the product
of all the factors that cause poverty: lack of work, skill, and

[19] *Loc. cit.*

[20] "The arid South, despite all the Italian Government and U.S.
aid money poured in, is still primarily a land of hunger and hopelessness. In startling contrast gleams the prosperity of North Italy, which
has replaced the U.S. as the near and visible promised land in the
dreams of impoverished Sicilians and Calabrians. 'California begins
at Milan' runs the current folklore of South Italy and each day
hundreds of sourtherners board northbound trains to seek the living
wage they cannot find home." *Time*, Jan. 12, 1962.

education, poor salaries, poor health conditions, inadequate social welfare facilities, etc.

A separate inquiry on poverty was conducted by the Istituto Centrale di Statistica in 1953, and this is summarized in the February 1954 issue of *Informazioni SVIMEZ*. It found that about one-half of all families in the South were living in poverty, reaching a peak in Calabria, where agricultural families were destitute in the proportion of 73.2 per cent. Of Southern families, 15.5 per cent were living under the poorest housing conditions, 56.9 per cent had totally inadequate diets, and 10.6 per cent the most ragged clothing.

Conditions prevailing in the cities of the South are no better than in the countryside; we shall select the two largest and most indicative among them, Naples and Palermo. As far as Naples is concerned, the Parliamentary Inquiry revealed the following:

Even the most casual observer in Naples cannot fail to be struck by the number of listless, healthy-looking young men to be seen loafing about the city's streets and squares. According to reliable estimates, some 80,000 persons in the city do not know when they get up in the morning what they will eat that day or whether they will eat at all.

The pressure of population has become excessive because of the lack of opportunity for emigration. Out of 1,100,000 inhabitants, only 28 per cent are employed, most of them in small businesses. The employment service has 110,000 names on its books, and these only account for a part of the unemployed population. . . .

Although Naples needs a minimum of 4,000 schoolrooms, it has only 2,000 at present, 900 of them in makeshift premises. Many of the public services, such as water and sewerage, are inefficient, unhygienic and primitive. Symptomatic of the position are the large number of bankruptcies, the number of protested bills, the infant mortality rate, and the low income per head, which is less than 80 per cent of the national average. But the worst problem is housing—19,000 homeless people are living in huts and caves. At the "Albergo dei Poveri" families are housed in huge, badly ventilated halls. In the former Votta schools the situation is no better, and huts have had to be built in the courtyards. The hospitals are inadequate, with 6.1 beds per 1,000 inhabitants as compared with 9.84 for Northern Italy. The dispensaries are too few in number and specialist medical care is almost non-existent.[21]

In the case of Palermo, the French magazine *Réalités* published the following article on the work of Danilo Dolci, the young ex-architect from the North who is devoting his life to improving the lot of the people of Sicily by using somewhat unorthodox methods and, in so doing, running counter to the Italian Government and the Church:

First there is Palermo: of its 550,000 inhabitants, 200,000 are living in poverty and 70,000 are unemployed. Just a few yards behind comfortable homes begins a city of ruined shacks where tens of thousands of men, women and children huddle in unimaginable sanitary conditions. Between the prison, the cathedral and the marble court-house there lies Cortile Cascino, its alleys paved with filth, its windows covered with torn sheets, its vermin, cellars, thieves, beggars and rats (a little girl once died there, her head gnawed by them).

If you walk into one of these gloomy holes . . . then you will begin to realize what poverty can be . . . in a cellar measuring five feet by eight and almost completely occupied by a four-poster bed, a pregnant woman explains that seven people sleep here; the three adults along the width of the bed and the four children along its

[21] Montini, op. cit., p. 12.

length: "When it's warm, we throw sawdust on the floor and lie down on it."

"In this alley," a schoolteacher told me, "only six out of eighty children go to school." Nearly all of them suffer from chronic bronchitis and various skin ailments caused by vitamin insufficiency. Beginning at the age of six months, a baby lives on olives, bread and spaghetti. The average inhabitant eats five pounds of meat a year. At Palermo, you see cases which you can hardly believe exist in Europe: families living in beach cabins; an old man scrapes the heels of pipes and chews them to remind himself of the taste of tobacco; a father who, in his abjection and suffering, has forgotten whether he has lost two or three children. When a loaf of bread costs 120 lire (20 cents) and when a man has an income of 400 lire (65 cents) a day and has to support five children, his choice is rather simple: steal or die. Dolci took a poll of 500 of the "disoccupati" who play cards near the railway crossing. He found they had worked an average of ninety-eight days in the year.[22]

Unfortunately, the task of giving some kind of financial help to these destitute people falls chiefly on administrations which are themselves poor and can give little or no relief where it is most needed.

(b) *Education.* The backward position of the South is if anything even more evident in the field of schools and instruction. One of the most serious aspects of the economic depression in this area is found in the lack of skilled labor

[22] Interview with Danilo Dolci, *Réalités*, No. 131, October 1961. As far as the countryside is concerned, Dolci has taken a typical village, Trappeto, and translated this frightening misery into figures: "Six hundred poor families live in 700 rooms. They share these rooms with 5,000 animals. 600 mothers have lost 1,014 children, 633 of them before they were one year old. 100 women who were questioned said that they had been pregnant 827 times. They had lost 213 children. During the same survey, a doctor discovered in these 600 families 545 cases of malaria, 241 cases of typhus and 293 cases of trachoma."

and the existence of vast numbers of people with no general or technical knowledge whatsoever; many of them will never benefit from the advantages brought to Italian labor by the European Economic Community.

One of the causes for the persistence of illiteracy in Italy has certainly been the slow development of national unity, and the uncertainties deriving from it. The result is the practical isolation of entire regions and social strata; this was especially true during the last decades of the nineteenth century when economic and social conditions in the South were very low indeed. And, of course, as in practically all regions and nations of the world, the disappearance of illiteracy is directly linked to rising living standards and to industrialization; it is certain that the relative improvement which has been making itself felt in Southern Italy since the formation of the European Community will have a decisive effect on finally eliminating this plague.[23]

According to a survey made in 1950, for every one hundred inhabitants over six years old, in the South twenty-four were illiterate, compared to five in the North.[24] At the time of marriage, about 0.5 per cent of those in the North were still illiterate, as against 8.2 per cent in the South. It is also to be noted that in the South a high percentage of children leave school before finishing the primary grades—only about one-third complete the first five grades. The situation in secondary education is even more serious; there are insufficient school installations and services, and people are too poor to send their children to higher schools.

In spite of these many handicaps, however, the final objectives of the schools in Southern Italy are: (a) to provide education for the mass of the people, with all the ensuing benefits; (b) to encourage the formation of an intelligentsia

[23] "A culture only develops on a powerful material basis." René Courtin, *Le Marché Commun* (Paris: Editions de l'Epargne, 1958).

[24] SVIMEZ, *Statistiche sul Mezzogiorno d'Italia, 1861–1950* (Rome: 1954), *passim*.

mainly dedicated to the solution of problems pertinent to the Mezzogiorno, and not, as has been the case so many times in the recent past, a group of brilliant but unorganized representatives of its culture.

Soon after the war, when it became apparent that the Southern Italian problem had to be eliminated once and for all and that one of the most important weapons to help in the fight would be the eradication of illiteracy, the State assigned one billion lire out of its meager budget to the Scuola Popolare, which had the task of fighting all forms of illiteracy and semi-illiteracy among adults. The Scuola operates almost exclusively in Southern Italy. It purports not only to give sound bases in literacy to its students, but also to imbue them with a spiritual, moral, and cultural education which can contribute to really fitting them for modern life. In slightly more than a decade of full activity, the results of the Scuola Popolare are very encouraging:

Courses for illiterate adults: 44,346 with 821,732 students;
Courses for semi-illiterate adults: 64,087 with 1,226,199 students;
Orientation courses: 37,083 with 701,666 students;
Special courses: 7,918 with 158,850 students;
Refresher courses (for people who once knew how to read and write, but who had subsequently forgotten or were about to forget): 25,126 with 615,424 students;
and many more.[25]

[25] Presidency of the Council of Ministers: *Documenti di Vita Italiana* (Rome: Istituto Poligrafico dello Stato), No. 93, August 1959. Hereinafter cited as *DVI*. One of the most effective organizations in the struggle for the eradication of illiteracy in Italy is the Unione Nazionale per la Lotta contro l'Analfabetismo, which aims at wiping this plague from the Mezzogiorno. Incidentally, the Association is also well-known in the United States and has benefitted from the material and moral support of, among others, the Ford Foundation and the American Friends Service Committee. The activity of the UNLA takes place through provincial centers—64 in Italy as a whole, all but 2 situated in the South. There are 35 in Calabria, 4 in Campania, 12 in Sardinia, 2 in Sicily, 8 in Basilicata, 1 in Abruzzo. The Centers give

The sums appropriated to Scuole Popolari have gradually been increased in the yearly budget of the State: thus from the billion lire of the year 1947–48, they rose to 2 billion in 1952–53 and for the year 1961–62, to 3 billion 341 million lire.[26]

(*c*) *Demographic factors.* Since unification, the population of Southern Italy has risen from 9.8 million to more than 18 million. The ratio of inactive to active persons has more than doubled in the South since 1871 and whereas in 1871 each active person had to support 0.67 inactive persons, in 1951 he had to support 1.74 inactive persons. The greatest demographic changes have, however, taken place since the end of World War I. The birth rate in the South decreased from 33.7 per 1,000 in 1920–22 to 27.3 in 1949, whereas in the North it declined from 28.6 to 17.5 in this period. The death rate in the North, however, decreased only from 16.7 to 10.7 per 1,000, whereas in the South there was a phenomenal drop of almost one-half, from 19.6 to 10.9. The natural increase in the South in 1951 was almost 75 per cent of the population increase for the whole country.[27]

In the years 1951–60, the natural increase in the population of Southern Italy was more than double that which took place in the Center-North, 2,611,000 against 1,252,000; in the context of the total population of Italy, the increase in the Mezzogiorno has contributed about 65 per cent of the total natural increase. This demonstrates the major demographic weight of the southern regions, which are characterized by a much higher birthrate than that of the regions of the Center-North; however, in the years considered there has been a reduction in such rate, as in 1951

---

both elementary and more advanced education to adults, and the number of those assisted approximates 22,000.

[26] It is encouraging also to see that a recently approved Ten-Year Plan allocates an amount of 40 billion lire in the next six years to the fight against illiteracy. *DVI*, Nos. 108–09.

[27] Data from SVIMEZ, *Popolazione e Forze di Lavoro* (Istituto Centrale di Statistica, Rome, 1954).

this was 24.6 per thousand in the South, and 14.8 per thousand in the Center-North, while in 1959–60 it was respectively 22 and 15 per thousand people.

The higher birthrate in the South can be attributed to the ignorance of the population and the influence of the Catholic Church, and any deliberate policy of birth control would be unacceptable to the majority of Meridionali on religious grounds. However, it may be expected that, with an improved level of living and the enlightenment of the population, the birthrate may decline as it has in the rest of Italy in recent years.

In considering the demographic situation in the South, it is important to note the density and the pattern of distribution of the population.

The average population density in the South is 148 inhabitants per square kilometer, as compared with 171 in the North, but it is notable that this density varies considerably with the area concerned. Four regions—Campania, northeast Abruzzi, Apulia, and south and west Calabria—have high densities, then there is a zone of slightly lower density across the peninsula between Naples and Foggia, with areas of very low density in the Apennines. Strangely enough, in the hilly zones of the South, population density is greater than in those of the North, whereas in the North the plains are more populated. This is due to the fact that the flat lands of the South suffer from bad climatic conditions, and there is a considerable incidence of malaria. Also, as a result of the many invasions of the South in years gone by, people tended to congregate in the higher areas for safety, and settlements gradually grew up. It is interesting to note that Southern Italy contains the area with the maximum density for the country (332 persons per square kilometer) in Campania, and also the lowest (56 per square kilometer) in Sardinia.[28]

The population is mostly concentrated in big com-

[28] SVIMEZ, *Notizie*, p. 3.

munities of a mainly agricultural character, with only a few dwellings scattered between the big centers. Very large urban areas are rare. This is the characteristic settlement pattern, but, with the improvement of economic conditions in general, and communications in particular, the elimination of malaria, land reform, etc., it appears to be destined for a profound change.

(*d*) *Emigration*. One of the main safety valves for the growing population in the South during the last decades of the nineteenth century and in the first years of this century was emigration, either towards the industrial North of Italy and the rest of Europe, or else abroad, mainly to the Americas. Overseas emigration amounted to about 200,000 per year from 1901–1913, but after World War I sank to 46,000 in the twenties, and 10,500 in the thirties. The decrease was partly due to the antimigration policy of the Fascist Government, and also to the immigration barriers erected by many countries between the wars, particularly by the United States. By 1952, through the efforts of the Italian Government, overseas emigration reached 138,000, of whom 71,000 were from the South.[29]

It is clear that the emigration restrictions of the last three decades have undoubtedly been a strong factor in the deteriorating population situation and, though emigration in itself is not a solution to the problem of the Mezzogiorno, it is certainly an important factor.[30] Now, however, the formation of the Common Market is throwing an entirely different light on this problem. Thus we find:

A quota of the excess Southern population will emigrate to the North . . . and another quota will emigrate within Europe to the countries that have in recent years

[29] INEA (Istituto Nazionale di Economia Agraria), *Annuario della Agricoltura Italiana, 1952–53* (Rome: Istituto Poligrafico dello Stato, 1954), p. 461.

[30] "Even in 1960, 55,326 persons emigrated by sea and air from the Mezzogiorno, while only 18,504 emigrants originated from the North." *Prospettive Meridionali*, No. 1, January 1962.

51

attained full employment and that, in spite of the progress towards automation, will in the next few years represent a sizable labor market. They will have no other reserves to tap except that of the Mezzogiorno d'Italia, which is now the Mezzogiorno d'Europa. . . . Then, numerous problems, old and new alike, will arise: industrial zones, city planning, building, community services, communications, power costs, etc. And, foremost, that of qualifying men for industrialization and for emigration.[31]

(e) *Unemployment and Underemployment.* The overpopulation and geographic characteristics of the Mezzogiorno, along with lack of capital investment and, until 1950, of Government planning, have served to create a serious and tragic problem of unemployment and underemployment, which, only now, particularly since the coming into being of the Common Market, is being relieved.

No statistics on the present state of unemployment may be entirely relied upon, partly because it is difficult to distinguish unemployment from underemployment; furthermore, as the question of unemployment is one of the trump cards in any political struggle, naturally the Government tends to minimize the figure, whereas the Opposition tends to exploit it to the full.[32]

[31] Compagna, *op. cit.*, p. 82.

[32] According to the *Yearbook of Labour Statistics, 1963* (International Labour Office, Geneva, 1964) unemployment in Italy at present, in its chronic manifestations, is limited to certain areas of the South. The number of unemployed decreased 17 per cent from 1962 to 1963 and in October 1963 actually reached a minimum of 2 per cent of the available labor force, that is 413,000. One of the means of reaching this objective has been the enactment of a law for the prolongation of the period of obligatory schooling, so that several thousand youngsters have been taken out of the labor market and sent back to school. (*passim*)

"In Italy, the most acute employment problem is still that of regional imbalances, but the number of unmet applications is steadily decreasing. . . ." Economic and Social Council of the United Nations, Economic Commission for Europe, *Report on Manpower Problems in Europe in 1963, op. cit.*

The exact picture of the labor situation in Southern Italy is difficult to assess because of the great mass of underemployed workers, of "born" unemployed, who have never held a regular job and whose existence is ignored in the statistics: young people who, even though looking hard for a job, have never found one, and old people who theoretically have a pension that will support them but who in reality must keep working, even spasmodically, and for a pittance, in order not to starve. Of these categories, the greatest by far is that of the so-called under-employed, the majority of whom are in the South.

According to the criteria followed by the Istituto Nazionale di Statistica in the sectors of industry, transport, communications, and services, there are two categories of underemployed workers: those who work less than fifteen hours (compared to an average of forty-five per week in these activities for the ordinary worker) and those who work between fifteen and twenty-four hours. The others are considered fully employed (it is clear that this criterion of evaluation is arbitrary, to say the least).

In the agricultural sector, however, (where, it must not be forgotten, the proportion in Southern Italy is about 52 per cent of the whole), the figures for the composition of the working population are as follows.

During the period 1861–1951, the percentage of agricultural workers in the North has diminished from 57 per cent to about 37 per cent, whereas the percentage of industrial workers has increased from 26 per cent to more than 40 per cent. The percentage of people engaged in tertiary activities and services rose from 17 per cent to 23 per cent. Conversely, in the South the percentage of agricultural workers underwent only minor changes in this period, the figure being 57 per cent in 1861 and 52 per cent in 1951. The percentage of industrial workers not only has not increased, but has actually diminished by exactly 2 per cent, from 30.4 per cent to 28.3; people engaged in tertiary

53

activities now form a percentage of 19.4, while at the time of unification the figure was 12.4 per cent.

TABLE 3
COMPOSITION OF ACTIVE POPULATION IN 1861, 1936, AND 1952[33]
(Percentages)

	1861			1936			1952		
	N.	M.	I.	N.	M.	I.	N.	M.	I.
Agricultural sector	57.3	57.2	57.2	44.0	56.9	48.1	36.6	52.3	41.6
Industry, transport and communications	25.8	30.4	27.6	36.8	27.6	33.9	40.2	28.3	36.4
Tertiary activities	16.9	12.4	15.2	19.2	15.5	18.0	23.2	19.4	22.0
Total	100	100	100	100	100	100	100	100	100

N: North; M: Mezzogiorno; I: Italy

We have more precise data, computed by INEA (Istituto Nazionale di Economia Agraria) in 1952 from the census of 1951.[34] According to this, against a theoretical level of full employment for an agricultural worker of 271 days, there was an effective average of 195 in the North and 153 in the South, a level dangerously near to being only half that considered the yearly average for full employment.

The situation has improved a great deal in the years since these figures were published. At the beginning of the nineteen sixties, the Commission of the European Economic Community summarized it thus:

It is under the impulse of certain migrations towards the industrial regions, no doubt, or abroad, that unemploy-

[33] SVIMEZ, *Notizie*, p. 16. Preceding data also taken from same source, *passim*.

[34] INEA, "Indagine sulla stagionalitá e sul grado di impiego dei Lavoratori in Agricultura" appended to *Atti della Commissione Parlamentare d'Inchiesta sulla Disoccupazione* (Rome: Istituto Poligrafico dello Stato, 1953), *I*, 2.

ment has receded, in a relatively substantial manner, in regions like Venetia, Romagna, or Abruzzi. Conversely, the situation has improved only very slightly in this matter in the South of the peninsula, where in Sicily it seems to be even somewhat more serious. The problem of unemployment continues therefore to exist in all its gravity in the South of Italy, in spite of emigration and of the systematic effort of the public powers to assure a better equilibrium in regional development. The Government now aims to find a definite solution to this problem by the enactment of regional development plans based on *state intervention larger than that hitherto employed.* [emphasis supplied] The elaboration of the first of these plans—the Plan for the Economic Rebirth of Sardinia—was completed in 1960, and it envisages a much heavier financial assistance than that foreseen by the Cassa per il Mezzogiorno.[35]

TABLE 4
CRIMES REPORTED TO POLICE IN THE PERIOD 1957—1959

	1957	*1958*	*1959*	*%1958*	*%1959*
				(base 1957 = 100)	
North	124,928	122,719	134,991	98.2	108.0
Center	67,098	64,402	62,662	96.0	93.4
South	108,178	107,202	110,834	99.1	102.5
Islands	52,390	52,244	53,048	99.7	101.3
North	192,026	187,121	197,654	97.4	102.9
South	160,568	159,446	163,882	99.3	102.1
Total Italy	352,594	346,567	361,536	98.3	102.5

(*f*) *Delinquency.* The Istituto Centrale di Statistica published in September 1960 an interesting study relative to the geographic distribution of delinquency in Italy.[36] The data are presented in Table 4 since they are relevant to our study;

[35] CEE, *Exposé*, 1960, p. 42. Further discussion of this problem will be found in Chapter III, of this study.
[36] All data on delinquency are taken from *DVI*, Nos. 108–09.

data referring to the North of Italy have also been added in order to allow comparison. In some cases, the study divides Italy into four parts, instead of two, as normally practiced, but then it also gives the total figure for the North (North plus Center) and for the South (Mezzogiorno plus Islands).

In the North (excluding the Center), with 44 per cent of the total population, the percentage of crimes is 36.1; conversely, in the South, the opposite is true: with 37.7 per cent of the population, it has 45.6 per cent of the crimes.

The highest crime rate is the unenviable possession of Sardinia, 1,033 for every 100,000 people, followed by Calabria and Lazio 960, and Apulia 933. The figure for Sicily is 790. It must be pointed out, however, that these figures are only approximate examples of the crime rate, especially for the South, since a high percentage of crimes committed there never reach the ears of the police.

Political Aspects

The present political situation in Southern Italy has been shaped by many of the same conditions that have contributed to the underdevelopment of the area and to the formation of the personality of the Southern Italian: the division of Italy into two parts by an imaginary line that runs across the country south of Rome, the lack of general education, the degree of poverty, and the legacy of the past. The division was accentuated after World War II, for the North had been under Nazi domination and reasserted itself in a long and bloody partisan struggle, especially in the great industrial cities of Milan, Turin, and Genoa. The poverty of the South was aggravated by destruction from the heavy fighting that took place there, and it was too obsessed with its own problems to give much attention to what was happening in the North.

The influence of the Catholic Church, traditionally conservative, has always been much stronger in the South and, strangely enough, the Mezzogiorno had a deep affection for the Piedmontese monarchy, stemming from the lack of political education and, again, from the past, which was but a succession of foreign kings and emperors from diverse families and various origins. Nothing in this heritage, therefore, was conducive to arousing republican feelings. The North, however, with the tradition of the Maritime Republics, a much higher standard of life and education, and twenty years of collaboration by the monarchy with Fascism, was definitely antimonarchist. After the War, therefore, we find a North, leftist and republican, facing a South, rightist and monarchist. As the elections of 1946 and 1948 showed, these differences were not as great as had been thought, and many people voted unpredictably. In the referendum of 1946, however, the majority voted for the abolition of the monarchy.

These sympathies for the monarchy in the South were to some extent a negative expression of discontent with the Central Government, it being a Southern tradition to blame the Government, rightly or wrongly, for their miseries—for overtaxation and all types of exploitation. In Sicily, these feelings are so strong that a separatist movement was set up soon after the War and the Movimento Indipendenza Siciliana (Sicilian Independence Movement) was formed, with the declared objective of seceding from Italy and forming a separate Sicilian state. We also saw at this time a resurgence of banditry in the island, led by the famous Giuliano gang.[37] After some bloody fighting, the Central Government succeeded in suppressing these movements, but it was realized that, in order to placate these exceptionally strong Sicilian feelings, a certain amount of self-administration would be necessary for the island, within the framework of the Italian Republic.[38]

[37] A detailed and fascinating account of this period is given in the *New Yorker* magazine, February 15, 1964, in an article entitled "The Honored Society."

[38] By constitutional law of February 26, 1948, Sicily is today one of the five regions of Italy to which a degree of autonomy in internal

In Sardinia regional autonomy was also granted by the Central Government.

In continental Southern Italy expressions of discontent are diminishing as the standards of living and education continue to rise slowly but appreciably. The benefits of action taken by the national Government are making themselves felt and the young people are at last beginning to have some hope for the future.[39] This is a period of formation and transition which will decide the political shape of Southern Italy in years to come.

REASONS FOR REGIONAL UNDERDEVELOPMENT IN FRANCE

The problem of underdevelopment in France has peculiar features which sharply distinguish it from the problem of the Mezzogiorno. First of all, it must be pointed out that it is not a problem of the same magnitude because France as a whole offers many more outlets to her people so that they do not need to remain confined in the areas which present few possibilities. It is enough for them to move to another part of the country, where they will probably not find it difficult to obtain a new and better situation than their previous one. Also, for the most part, the land is generally not naturally hostile, either in the soil itself or in climatic conditions, water resources, etc. As a matter of fact, in many

---

matters has been granted. Actually, Sicily is, together with Sardinia, the region of Italy most different from the others. Certainly the fact that they are both islands and have been constantly at the crossroads of civilization, invaded by successive conquerors throughout the ages, weighs heavily on the character of their inhabitants. So, also, do the barrenness of the land and the extremely hot, dry climate.

[39] "No matter whether we take into consideration the average income, the family income, or the personal salary, Italy still shows a considerable lag compared to other countries, evidently linked in large part to the heavy influence on the national average of the overpopulated regions of the South. But progress over the last few years permits the conclusion that this general lag has ceased to grow bigger, and that now it is only a question of narrowing the gap between the revenues of the Northern regions and those of the less-developed areas." CEE, *Exposé 1960*, intro.

cases the land is potentially good, but it happens to be underpopulated and underindustrialized, or, to use a contemporary expression, "underdeveloped," mainly because of a phenomenon peculiar to France, i.e. the centralization of practically all activities—industrial, intellectual, bureaucratic, and so forth—in and around Paris, to the detriment of all the other regions, and specifically those that we are about to describe.[40] The island of Corsica has its own particular reasons for underdevelopment.

The French Government had several times before World War II taken action—although with not very encouraging results—aimed at breaking the system that threatens to suffocate all French activity (ironically, harmful to Paris itself, creating many problems of overgrowth) and which slows down levels of production and of living that would otherwise benefit the whole nation.

Some explanation is needed to elucidate the reasons for this phenomenon which has assumed more and more serious proportions; since the end of World War II, the French Government has had to take steps to counteract it with a series of measures which will be considered later.

Alexis de Tocqueville, describing the conditions existing at the time of the French Revolution, says: "At the time of the Fronde, Paris was only the largest city of France. In 1789, it is already the whole of France."[41] A cursory survey

[40] "The economic and industrial anemia which affects the Atlantic side of France is essentially due to a dangerous under-equipment and to its peripheral situation. This tends to accentuate its isolation within the Common Market. (However) . . . the reasons for its inferiority are not beyond repair. . . . Actually, the 'drying up' of the economy of the South-West is only relative. This large area which, from Nantes to Montpellier, includes about forty *départements*, has extremely important potential riches in store. Its two metropolises, Bordeaux and Toulouse, constitute powerful poles of economic development and cultural attraction; they are important enough to capture part of the current that at present leads the majority—and the most active part—of the available population towards the capital." Jacques Chaban-Delmas, "De Bordeaux à l'Europe," in *Quelle est cette Europe? Op. cit.*

[41] Alexis de Tocqueville, *L'Ancien Régime et la Révolution* (Paris: Lévy, 1856), 2nd edn., p. 139.

of French history shows us that almost everything of any importance that has happened in France in the last two or three hundred years has taken place in Paris. Regimes have been made and unmade, republics have alternated with kingdoms and empires, all because of decisions taken in Paris, often provoked directly by the people rising in arms against the government of the time. And the rest of the nation, with some notable but hapless exceptions, followed.

The reasons for this overconcentration go back in time, but it assumes great proportions with Louis XIV, the Sun King, who made Paris part of his personal "rayonnement." The events of the French Revolution, too, contributed much to enhancing the importance of Paris relative to the rest of France. Lastly, Napoleon conceived the idea of transforming Paris into an immense city, a city of several million inhabitants, "something fabulous, colossal, unknown up till now."[42] So the centralization continued and, even after the fall of Napoleon, it increased throughout the Restoration, the July Monarchy, the Second Republic, the Second Empire, the Third, Fourth, and even the Fifth Republic. The question is not one primarily of physical and demographic growth: in this Paris is not alone and other big cities of the world have advanced with the same rapidity. The administrative system is so centralized in Paris that the Ministries of the capital decide practically everything that shall take place throughout France—even the details. The *longa manus* of Paris is everywhere.[43]

[42] *Mémorial*, as quoted in J. F. Gravier, *Paris et le Désert Français* (Paris: Flammarion, 1958), p. 11.

[43] Gravier goes on to say that "In fact, the central administrations—often, thanks to the weakness of their Ministries, in real feudal tradition—correspond directly with their outside services, completely ignoring the authority of the local Prefect. We then see a truly vertical compartmentalization of the State, divided into several fiefs, each of which is ruled by a powerful 'corps' extremely jealous of its responsibilities: Inspection des Finances, Mines, Ponts et Chaussées, Génie Rural, etc. If it happens that the engineers of the Génie Rural and of the Ponts be at odds about the draining of a swamp in Languedoc,

Administrative centralization, however, is only one aspect of the general centralization of all French life around Paris. Let us take the railways, for instance. It was in the 1830's that the Government then in power, that of Louis-Philippe d'Orléans, decided to accept a proposition to build a "star-shaped railway network, centered on the capital." The scheme was gradually enacted and around the middle of the nineteenth century we see that a dozen lines were already radiating outward from Paris. The North was not linked directly to the East, nor Lyon to the West, nor even Toulouse to the Pyrénées. And, furthermore, the communications serving Paris were much more rapid and had the best rolling stock available. As time is so important in business, all communications between the provinces and Paris are thus heavily favored. The traditional business patterns existing before the advent of the railway have been disrupted; regional and local commerce is directed toward Paris, and becomes increasingly dependent on the capital, ready to prosper or to suffer according to its fortunes. And, apart from the many attractions of the city itself, since Paris is also the center of bureaucracy, industry, credit, etc., we see an accelerated movement of business concerns and people alike toward the capital, at the expense of the rest of France. Those regions which, either because of natural causes or geographic location, were left out of the famous "star" rail network slowly decline and wither away, losing their industry and more and more of their population, which has to be replaced, at least partially, by foreign immigration.

---

the question is brought to Paris to be discussed by two Inspectors-General; if they do not reach agreement, all the complaints in the world by the Prefect will not prevent the swamp from staying the way it is for as many years as necessary, until Divine Providence takes a hand and incites the enemies to smoke the peace pipe. Generally speaking, the French administrative system is characterized by a powerlessness to decide any important business on the spot; not only this, but also many questions of a very local character are preferred to Paris." *Ibid.*, p. 12.

One-half of France is practically excluded from the modern economy and makes no appearance in the contemporary market either as producer or consumer. France, peasant France, has no organized provincial markets at all. Her agricultural market is the Paris Halles, the picturesque, hopelessly overcrowded and overflowing "belly of Paris," bursting at all its seams, which has become the belly of the whole country. . . . The empty and impoverished life of most French villages and provincial towns, whose monuments bear witness to a former vitality, is the result of this centralism. Not only was the road and rail map of France laid out like a spider's web radiating from Paris, but everything that used the web—men, goods and energy—was caught up in it. All France was laid waste and her vital energy sucked into Paris.

There is scarcely a big concern that does not feel compelled to maintain its head office at great expense in Paris, the place of prestige, of useful contacts and combinations, and at the same time the only place where it is possible to minimize the fearful but inevitable bureaucratic entanglements by direct contact with the Ministries. Even the agricultural economy of this peasant country is directed towards Paris, or alternatively, where no contact with the "Paris network" has been established, has become ossified into a closed, archaic, village economy.[44]

Paris monopolizes not only the business life of France, but also the intellectual. Apart from the various theatrical and artistic activities which are mainly confined to the capital, university life is also heavily centered there. Over 40 per cent of all university students in metropolitan France are graduated from Paris, and all the prestige "Grandes Écoles," École Normale Supérieure, École Polytéchnique,

[44] Herbert Luethy, *France Against Herself* (New York: Meridian Books, 1957), pp. 20–21.

etc., are located in Paris.[45] Here again, this intellectual concentration, leading to the desire of many students to remain in Paris after termination of their studies, is deleterious to the equilibrium of the provinces, parts of which are thus transformed into an intellectual, as well as a material, "desert."

Of course, the industrial revolution also contributed to strengthening this super-concentration in the Paris region, reaching its zenith when the two giants of the French automobile industry, Renault and Citroën, established their factories in Paris.

If there is to be a solution to the disproportionate growth of Paris compared to the rest of France, it must be a solution worked out as part of an organic plan, for, as we have seen so many times in the past, single decrees or projects which are not related to others achieve very little. Sometimes they actually have results contrary to those expected. If a solution is to be found on the European rather than on the national level, then certain realities must be squarely faced.

To begin with, a look at a map of France shows that the regions of the so-called "désert français" will, perhaps even more in the ensemble of the European Economic Community than in the national state, be cut off from the main lines of communication along the Member States. New roads and railways will be built, but they are certain to be located far from the South-West region of France.[46] The

[45] However, efforts are being made now to promote the decentralization of at least some of these "Ecoles." The IVth Plan foresees a four-year transfer program (1962–65) and, among others, the following institutions are to be moved from Paris to the underdeveloped regions: the Public Health School to Rennes; the Aeronautical School to Toulouse; the Marine Engineering School to Brest; and the Marine Fishing Institute to Nantes. *France and Economic Planning*, Ambassade de France, Service de Presse et d'Information, New York, 1963, p. 34.

[46] In this connection, J. Chaban-Delmas writes: "The remedies applied (by the national government) are not up to the magnitude of the problems confronting the region. What is essential and urgent is to disengage the South-West, to put it in direct relation with the dynamic regions of Europe. A massive and efficacious intervention of

same also applies, for geographic reasons, to Brittany and probably to Savoy, in view of its very rugged character unsuitable for regular channels of communication.

BRIEF HISTORY AND PRESENT SITUATION OF THE UNDERDEVELOPED REGIONS OF FRANCE

After an examination of the appalling conditions in the South of Italy, an analysis of the present situation of the underdeveloped regions of France shows by contrast a much lesser degree of hopelessness and destitution. As a matter of fact, conditions are quite different in many respects. The only French underdeveloped region whose aspects approximate those of the Italian South, particularly those of the neighboring island of Sardinia and, to some extent, Sicily, is Corsica. This island will be dealt with separately. Furthermore, while it is not difficult to consider all the Italian underdeveloped regions together under the heading "Mezzogiorno," "Meridione," or simply "the South," a grouping of the French underdeveloped regions is much more difficult, for they present widely differing characteristics that render categorization almost impossible. The most realistic arrangement, we believe, is to distinguish them as follows: (a) Central France or Region of the Massif Central (Limousin, Auvergne, and parts of Quercy, Périgord, etc.); (b) South-West France (Languedoc, Roussillon, Pyrénées, Aquitaine); (c) Brittany; (d) Corsica; and (e) the Alpine region (Savoy). In contrast to the method followed for Southern Italy, each underdeveloped region will be treated separately.

---

private investment is not to be expected unless the State solves this extremely important problem, which is the preliminary condition for a renovation of the economic structure. To remedy the peripheral situation of the South-West, it is paramount to establish, in the first order of priority, good, diversified and rapid communication lines which will facilitate human and commercial relations with the other French regions and with the whole area of the Common Market." *Op.cit.*, p. 13.

The Massif Central

The region of the Massif Central is not an area with its own historical characteristics; rather, its unity is mainly based on geographic considerations, and it is from this aspect that it will be described. The area usually given this name covers about 27,000 square miles, most of them at an altitude of at least 1,800 feet above sea level. For our purpose, we may consider eleven *départements* lying entirely within the area: Ardèche, Lozère, Aveyron, Nièvre, plus Auvergne (Allier, Puy-de-Dôme, Cantal, Haute-Loire), and Limousin (Creuse, Corrèze, Haute-Vienne). However, the area also includes parts of Bourbonnais, Forez, the Bas-Languedoc (Cévennes, Espinouse), Guyenne (Mons de Lacaune), Quercy, and Périgord. In this area there are about three million inhabitants, representing roughly half the national average per square mile.

In the *départements* just mentioned, all lying within the Massif Central area, there has been an over-all decrease of 26 per cent in the population during the years 1886 to 1954. The depopulation process reached its maximum in the Ardèche and Creuse (35 per cent) and in Lozère (40 per cent). Out of the twenty-five *départements* of continental France that have lost more than 10 per cent of their population in the years between 1936 and 1954, fifteen are contained, partly or in their entirety, in the Massif Central region. This, then, forms the last great area of demographic depression, in full contrast to the demographic progress of most of the nation. Actually, if we examine some areas smaller in size than a *département*, say the cantons of Neuvic-d'Ussel and Maymac in the Haute-Corrèze, and those of Valgorge and Pont-de-Montvert in the Cévennes, they have lost about 35 per cent of their population in the years 1936 to 1954. A very high rate of emigration over immigration is also found in the *départements* of Aveyron, Cantal, Corrèze, Creuse, and Haute-Loire. The rate is always higher than

65

6 per cent, with a maximum in Lozère, where it reaches 12 per cent.[47]

Some of those concerned with these problems seem to assume a fatalistic attitude and accept the fact that, under new economic exigencies and conditions, the Massif Central region is becoming a "pole of repulsion." This is a very superficial judgement in view of the variety of local situations and the findings of experts regarding possible economic activities in the region. An economic and demographic rebirth of the whole area of the Massif Central is possible, and should be channeled in three parallel efforts basic to the development of these regions: (1) the quantitative and qualitative improvement of agricultural production and of industries connected with the agricultural products of the region (canning, etc.), the forestry products (wood and woodpulp), and light industry in general; (2) the introduction of heavy industrialization and the improvement of mining; (3) the systematic development of tourism in the region.

We shall see in following chapters how these provisions can be made operative.

Languedoc

This is the "area where the *langue d'oc* is spoken" ("*oc*" meaning "yes") in contrast to the other regions of France where the *langue d'oïl* (modern "oui") is spoken. Up till the tenth century its history is not very different from that of most French provinces: first a number of Gallic tribes, then a long Roman domination, then the barbarian invasions (Visigoths, Suebi, and Vandals), until the Franks conquered it in the eighth century. The Dukes of Toulouse became prominent in the region in the eleventh century and by the end of the twelfth century their supremacy was recognized throughout the region, encompassing some of the richest cities in one of the most cultured parts of France.

[47] All data from Gravier, *op. cit.*, and *The Statesman's Yearbook, 1963* (New York: St. Martin's Press), *passim*.

Actually, the country had no natural geographic unity. Stretching over the Cévennes into the valleys of the upper Loire on the North and into those of the Upper Garonne on the West, it extended to the Pyrénées on the South and the rolling hills along the Rhône on the east. Its unity, therefore, was entirely a political creation, but nonetheless real, for it was the great state of the Midi, the representative of its culture and, in some measure, the guardian of its peculiar civilization.

Unfortunately, religious persecutions brought about by a local heretic sect (the Albigensis) brought destruction on the region for a long period of time, and much of the country was burned and ravaged. Finally, in 1229, part of the region came under the direct rule of the King of France, and the rest followed in 1271.

After a few decades of consolidation, Languedoc increasingly came to be regarded as a source of revenue by the Kings of France, who dispatched Governors to it with the precise duty of raising money for the King's always-needy Treasury. They acquitted themselves so well in their task that in a relatively short time the once prosperous region was turned into a needy, poor one. Louis d'Anjou and the Duc de Berry, both brothers of the King of France, were outstanding in this work of pillage (fourteenth century). A great peasant revolt finally broke out in 1382–83 but this was suppressed in a sea of blood. As a collective punishment, taxes were further increased and the situation became chaotic. Many peasants refused to cultivate their land under these conditions, and fled to the "maquis" to become outlaws.

After several ups and downs, the country revived somewhat, but the scars left by the religious persecutions and the exploitative taxation system remained. Protestantism was still a powerful force; civil wars, mainly over religious causes, again ravaged the country until the Edict of Nantes, which allowed a certain religious liberty, was granted in 1598. Civilian strife, however, continued for a few more decades, until finally the King of France managed to eradicate Protestantism as a political force. In 1685 the Edict of Nantes was revoked and new rebellions broke out. Most notable was that of the Camisards (they used tactics strikingly similar to what we now call "guerrilla warfare"). They ravaged the country for about fifteen years beginning in 1702. After this, Languedoc became more or less completely integrated with France.

Languedoc was for many centuries a very active region in many economic endeavors. Its geographic position was then advantageous, situated as it was between Italy, Spain, and the Garonne Valley and it therefore functioned as the crossroads for traffic between these regions.

At the end of the Middle Ages, the currents of traffic slowly started to shift, diminishing the role hitherto played by Languedoc. This process, however, gathered momentum after the discovery of America, and the entire Mediterranean area was deeply affected by this. The new currents of traffic decisively contributed to separating the South of France from the regions of the north and east.

A great change occurred at the beginning of the nineteenth century, when the industrial revolution brought great promise of development to the region, which was rich in coal. For a few years, industries were actually established, particularly around the coal areas of Decazeville and Alès. But these industrial activities, instead of continuing their expansion, progressively slowed down until they reached the present decline and stagnation.

This apparently strange phenomenon was due to a series of factors, geographic as well as economic. In fact, the industry of Languedoc soon found itself in a disadvantageous position in respect to that of the north and east, due to its peripheral placement and to the fact that an aggregation of factors of production increasingly began to take place around those regions.

Furthermore, most of the coal mined in Languedoc was

68

not of a very high quality, making it unsuitable to support a steel industry of vast dimensions.

Another important cause of underdevelopment is the fact that this region lacks any important industrial or administrative center; consequently capital tends to be invested elsewhere.

Particularly during the nineteenth and twentieth centuries, the most important activity was wine growing. Actually, this trade became so important that the whole economy of Languedoc tended to become based on it. Capital, therefore, when employed in the region, tended to shy away from industrial investments and to concentrate on the more profitable wine-growing activities.[48] However, an increase in the quantity of production, combined with fierce competition from the other wine-growing regions of France and from Algeria, suddenly plunged the region into a crisis of overproduction from which it has suffered ever since.

While at peak times the flourishing vineyards favored the establishment in Languedoc of certain ancillary industries (chemical fertilizers, distilleries, etc.), its decline also spelt a regression of these industrial activities, some of which became marginal and some disappearing altogether. Capital, old and new, tended to flee towards the prosperous regions. Most regional banks have gone bankrupt since the turn of this century, thereby depriving Languedoc of a very

[48] "Just before the revolution there were for instance in Hérault and in Gard 40,000 workers in the wool industry. At Montpellier, five large factories with several hundred workers each, were engaged in the manufacture of cotton handkerchiefs. In 1785, Chaptal et Bérard founded at Montpellier the very first chemical factory in France, which employed seven hundred workers in 1850 when it shut down, in spite of the many orders waiting to be filled. . . . The collapse of these industrial activities, of which only vestiges remain today, took place in the middle of the 19th century, at a time when considerable profits deriving from agriculture led to the transformation of an upper class with industrial origins into a rural bourgeoisie." *Revue de l'Economie Méridionale*, No. 38, April–June 1962.

important element in its over-all development. Thus wine-growing, either directly because it drew off investments from local industrial activities, or indirectly, through its domination of numerous industrial sectors, has not only impeded the industrial development of the region, but in its decline has dragged the whole area in its wake.

The region is about 13,400 square miles in area, with a population of some 2,400,000.

Aquitaine

Aquitaine has a surface of less than 29,000 square miles, with a population of 3,500,000. The population density in the region is always low, particularly in the *départements* of Ariège, Gers, Landes, and Lot. No industry whatsoever exists in seven out of the eleven *départements* of which the region is composed. This is a summary of conditions in Aquitaine, and from this it can be inferred that the problem of the region is essentially one of underpopulation. We shall see what is being done, and what should be done, to face this situation in succeeding chapters. First of all, let us give a brief historical sketch of the region.

This region was named Aquitaine (Aquitania) by the Romans who occupied it after the name of the original inhabitants of Iberian origin, the Aquitani. Administratively, it was one of the five divisions of Gallia, and in the third century it was subdivided into three districts: Aquitania prima, secunda, and tertia. It was conquered by the Visigoths in the fifth century. Then Clovis, King of the Franks, defeated Alaric II, Visigoth King, near Poitiers in 507 A.D. and annexed the province. After the Franks' conquest, Aquitaine became a region united by rather tenuous links to the French crown, until Peppin the Short reasserted them in 768. The region was given by Charlemagne to his son, Louis, as a vassal kingdom in 781, but after a century of semi-autonomy it again became a possession of the French king in 877. By the eleventh century it had become a very important duchy, strategically located to control France south of the Loire. In 1152, Eleanor of Aquitaine married Henry II of England and the region became an English possession, following from then on the fortunes of the other English domains in France.

In the tenth century, the province's name was corrupted and it came to be called Guienne, which was also the name of a specific region, corresponding roughly to the Roman Aquitania Secunda. After a century of wars and devastation, it reverted to the French crown at the end of the Hundred Years War (1453). Guienne eventually formed a government, which included Gascony, with its capital in Bordeaux, and this lasted until the end of the French monarchy.

Partially isolated, Aquitaine is the most underdeveloped large region of France. While this was not very noticeable until the middle of the nineteenth century, it then became more and more evident, due to the rapid advance of most other regions and its own uneven progress.

South-West France has not always been a poor region. On the contrary it prospered while the great commercial currents passed through it, up to the sixteenth century. But even later, in spite of momentary setbacks, the region managed to secure for its inhabitants a reasonably acceptable standard of living, certainly not lower than that of the rest of France. Several artisan activities, light industries, etc. gave the area a sufficiently diversified economy, not based exclusively on agriculture. The real series of blows to the region, from which it never recovered, came in the middle of the nineteenth century, when the process of centralization around Paris assumed such proportions that this whole area was practically severed from the momentous developments taking place in the more advanced parts of France. The structure of the railways, which left it almost completely isolated from the main lines of communication with the commercially most important parts of France, and the almost complete lack of suitable supplies of coal (then the only known form of industrial energy) rapidly contributed to push it further into the background. Two serious crises befell Aquitaine at that time: a commercial crisis, particularly over the imports of wheat, and the catastrophic spread of a vine-disease (phylloxera) which destroyed most of the vineyards that constituted one of the major riches of the region. With the exception of Charentes, where there was some changeover towards an economy based on cattle-raising and dairy products, the local inhabitants took these successive blows passively, and accepted the increasingly advanced state of impoverishment of the region. Their passive reaction also led to demographic and self-imposed economic limitations which produced not stagnation but actual regression. For instance, in the last forty years almost all the rural cantons have experienced a continuous loss of population, averaging about 35 per cent. In 1954, the *département* of Lot had less than half the inhabitants it had in the middle of the nineteenth century.

Furthermore, the Pyrénées, in spite of the relative ease with which they could be crossed, became more and more a barrier to the normal development of traffic between the Iberian peninsula and South-West France; the reasons can be found in the isolationist policy of Spain and in the general stagnation of its economy, which lacked the dynamism to contribute the necessary vitality to an important two-way traffic between the two nations. This part of France therefore rapidly became a real "dead end," cut off at the same time from the main sources of supply, and from commerce with the rest of France and with Spain. Capital, of course, fled the region; the artisan activities, deprived of outlets, quickly declined, and so did agriculture. In the period 1851–1954, the area lost 600,000 inhabitants, that is 20 per cent of its population. Actually, some *départements* lost more: Lot, 50 per cent; Gers, 28 per cent; Ariège, 26 per cent; Tarn-et-Garonne, 23 per cent. The situation appeared almost hopeless just before World War I but after

72

the end of the war a considerable immigration from the other regions of France, and from abroad (Italy and Spain) replaced in part the original inhabitants of the region who had moved elsewhere. In 1936, the number of foreigners in the *départements* of Gers and Lot-et-Garonne was about 10 per cent. After World War II, there was some demographic revival but even so it has been calculated that the number of adults in 1965 will be more or less the same as that in 1954, and that only immigration (and in this the potential Italian immigration from the Mezzogiorno can be particularly welcome) will permit an increase in the number of inhabitants in the now sparsely populated region.

However, in the last few years a new element, with the potentiality of entirely changing the stagnant economy of the region, has come about: the discovery and exploitation of natural gas at Lacq and oil in the Parentis area. Of these, we shall write extensively when we examine the power resources in the underdeveloped regions and their relation to the European Economic Community (Chapter V).

In the period 1911–1954, the population density per square kilometer fell from 49 to 46. Actually, in about one-fifth of the region, it does not even reach 20. This contrasts with the average in France: an increase from 75 to 78. It is therefore easy to conclude that the region as a whole cannot, without radical changes in its economy, procure work for all its people, and emigration from it will continue unabated. The standard of living is only about 75 per cent that of the national average. In 1954, the proportion of workers in industry and commerce with an income lower than 300,000 francs per year, was over 65 per cent in Tarn-et-Garonne and reached 78 per cent in Gers, where the average wages were the lowest in France: 254,000 francs. (Over-all French average: 39.1). The number of cars was 22 per 1,000 inhabitants, compared to the national average of 33.

Logically, in view of the low purchasing power of the population, a very important factor has to be added to the

73

other disadvantages that plague the industrial and commercial activities of the region. The small local industries, in view of the limited margin of profit, cannot reinvest much in the modernization of their plants and therefore lose further ground in competition with products from outside the region, from places where such disadvantages do not exist. Very often, the government is tapped for direct or indirect subsidies, but such intervention will cease, at least in principle, when the Common Market operates in full, as the rules to preserve competition forbid any kind of financial support. However, in the framework of the European Economic Community, Aquitaine and the surrounding regions will benefit for a while at least from the special provisions set up for the underdeveloped regions, and it is hoped that eventually they will reach an economic level not too far behind that of the other European regions.

Brittany

Brittany has an area of approximately 13,650 square miles and it constitutes the western peninsula of France. It is divided into five *départements*, and the capital city is Rennes. The population is about 3,200,000.

Throughout its history Brittany has had a somewhat different development from that of the neighboring regions. This is in part due to its peninsular position, which fostered its autonomous growth, and partly to the character of the inhabitants, some of whom, in the so-called "Bretagne bretonnante" descend from the Celts and speak a language closely related to Welsh, although all speak French as well. Movements for autonomy arise once in a while, but they assume a character of protest against the Central Government and are of little consequence. These tendencies to autonomy seem to be a recurrent phenomenon in underdeveloped areas, as we see also in Sicily, Sardinia, etc.

The history of Brittany is that of the rest of France until the end of the Roman occupation in the fifth century A.D.,

74

which was immediately followed by waves of Celts from Britain, fugitives from the Saxons. Next the Normans tried to impose their suzerainty on Brittany, but the fierce and independent character of the inhabitants did not allow them to make much progress. Britain and France then alternately predominated in the peninsula, although the inhabitants did not want either. Finally, however, Brittany's independence was ended by the French who, in 1532, annexed it by marriage, although at the same time giving it some freedom and guarantees. From then on, the history of Brittany becomes practically indistinguishable from that of France.

The region is not underdeveloped in the general meaning of the word; only parts of it are actually poor, mainly dedicated to scraping a scanty crop from a sandy and barely productive land. However, some zones, noticeably the basin around Rennes, are very fertile and productive. For Brittany, the problem is not so much that of widespread underdevelopment as that of unequal development and of imbalance between agriculture and industry. The latter is scattered and little developed, much of it dedicated to processing and canning local agricultural products. Actually, we shall find an analysis of the ills besetting Brittany in the chapter on agriculture which, with fishing well behind, constitutes a major activity of the region. In recent years, and especially in 1961, several peasant riots have marred the calm of the region and we shall assess how the economic unification of Europe can help to solve Brittany's agricultural problem by opening up new outlets for exports and perhaps helping to solve, indirectly, the problem of rising unemployment. Indeed, the increased demand within the common tariff limits will increase the number of jobs available in other parts of France which will then be able to absorb some of the surplus labor of Brittany. This labor, however, will be of agricultural origin and therefore a great deal of retraining will be necessary.

Corsica

Corsica, the beautiful Mediterranean island, has a history very similar to that of the main islands of the western Mediterranean: Sicily, Sardinia, and the Balearics. Because of its insular position, it was, in pre-Roman times, successively in the hands of the Etruscans, Phoenicians, and Carthaginians. However, they occupied only parts of the coastline, which was sufficient to serve their trading purposes. Furthermore, the island's inhabitants were warlike and fierce. Even Rome experienced serious difficulties and conquered the island only after a century of intermittent fighting. Upon the disintegration of the Roman Empire, the island was invaded by the Vandals and then the Goths. The Byzantine Empire held it for a short time, and it was also for brief periods under the domination of the Lombards and the Franks. It was invaded by the Arabs early in the eighth century and they were not expelled from their last stronghold until the middle of the tenth century. It is interesting for our purposes to note that the southern part of the island, held more continuously and more firmly by the Saracens, was plundered by them with devastating effect, while the rest of the island, even though ravaged by warfare, was more stable and productive under a system similar to the feudal one. Pisa, Genoa, and the King of Aragon, sometimes together and sometimes separately, had the upper hand until, in 1568, Corsica was subdued by Genoa which remained in sole domination until 1729 when a series of revolts broke out in the island. Genoa was finally easily persuaded by France to sell all her rights to the island in 1768.

The period from the end of the Arab domination up until the time when the French took over was a black one for the Corsicans. There was no adequate administrative system, and in the absence of justice the people took the law into their own hands by means of the vendetta. The Genovese, who were concerned only with squeezing as many taxes as possible out of the population, neglected to defend the island so that the coast was open to the ravages of the Barbary pirates, and floods and plagues also occurred during the sixteenth century. The population tended to move further and further into the dry interior, allowing the most fertile coastal areas to become malarious swamps.

From 1768, when the French took over, the history of Corsica becomes part of the history of France—or vice versa, according to some Corsicans, overwhelmed by memories of Napoleonic times.

The same phenomenon that took place in the Italian South and in Sicily and Sardinia, and which is common to underdeveloped areas situated within industrialized states, took place in Corsica: a continuous, sizeable emigration towards the more advanced parts of the mainland, and also an invasion of the bureaucracy, army, and police.

The island is 3,367 square miles in area. The population reached its peak in 1936 (322,854). After World War II, contrary to most of the rest of France, there was a steady decrease: 267,873 in 1946, 246,995 in 1954. A slight recovery took place in the early sixties (275,563 in 1961). The *département* has the highest proportion of illiterates in France.

From the physical viewpoint, the island is rugged and partly barren, but beautiful and picturesque, with short, torrential rivers and a Mediterranean climate.

Light industry is little developed and depends generally on agriculture or fishing (canning, etc.). Heavy industry is nonexistent. Fishing and hunting are abundant. There is some mining but this is not very developed. Imports are far ahead of exports, and there are very poor communications systems, with almost no good roads or railroads. The Corsicans speak an Italian dialect and French, and are in great majority Roman Catholic. They are polite and

77

hospitable, with high standards of morality, but show little enthusiasm for economic development and a certain lack of enterprise.

The Alpine Region

The Alpine Region is composed of the *départements* of Haute-Savoie, and Savoie, plus parts of Isère, Hautes-Alpes et Basses-Alpes, and Alpes-Maritimes. It is not underdeveloped in the sense of the other regions we have already described; indeed, its condition is peculiar, as its very mountainous nature, harsh climate, and rocky soil are much more responsible for its present state than human causes. And also, its underdevelopment is very irregular; for instance, large areas in the two *départements* of Savoy are very active and affluent, due to winter sports activities. Most depressed is the southern part of this region, as far as the beginning of the Alpes-Maritimes.

Historically, much of the region can be identified, roughly to be true, with the history of the House of Savoy. Indeed, Savoy proper is a recent acquisition of France, having belonged to that country for only slightly more than a century; indeed, it was annexed in 1860, as part of an agreement between Napoleon III and Victor Emmanuel II, King of Italy, as compensation for French help to Italy during the previous year in the war against Austria. But, throughout the centuries, its history has been subjected to its geographical position, astride the borders of France, Italy, and the German Empire.

The population of the Alpine areas is very unevenly distributed, depending on the activities prevalent in the respective areas. The *départements* of Hautes-Alpes and Basses-Alpes have, in their mountainous parts, rather poor and backward economies; the situation must be corrected soon, in order to arrest the progressive depopulation of the area. The inhabitants of this region generally live in the valleys, or on their slopes, provided these are exposed to the

78

sun; big villages are the most usual form of human habitation, although scattered houses or tiny groups of houses are also found.

The main cities of Savoy are Chambéry, the capital of the region, Annecy, Aix-les-Bains, and Chamonix. In the southern part of the Alps, Briançon, a large tourist center on the upper course of the Durance, and Digne, a market city, deserve mention.

The two *départements* entirely situated in this region, Haute-Savoie and Savoie, have a total area of 4,162 square miles. The area of the whole region is about double this figure. The population of Savoy is almost 600,000; of the whole area, upwards of 800,000.

This concludes the background material on the underdeveloped areas within the Common Market, including a brief history of each area as well as a summary of the present situation. We shall now turn to an examination of the subject proper.

CHAPTER II

What Has Been Done to Redress the Situation

REGIONAL IMBALANCES IN THE EUROPEAN ECONOMIC COMMUNITY

The European Economic Community is made up of a heavily industrialized zone in the Center and North, surrounded by moderately industrialized regions, and finally an outer circle (except in the North) composed of more or less underdeveloped regions. Thus, the more economically advanced zones are congregated around an axis running from the Netherlands to Northern Italy, through the valleys of the Rhine and the Rhône. This area comprises: 30 per cent of the territory of the Community; 45 per cent of the population; and 60 per cent of its total ecomonic production. Conversely, the outlying regions represent: 70 per cent of the territory; 55 per cent of the population; but only 40 per cent of production.

To look at the Community as a whole, there is an evident opposition between a middle bloc of regions with strong economic vitality which, from the beaches of the North Sea to those of the Mediterranean, contains all the large industrial areas of the Community and a series of less dynamic peripheral regions, whose backwardness in relation to the others is *important to a greater or lesser degree but tends, as a general rule, to increase rather than to diminish.* [emphasis supplied] The first group has attained a very high, more or less uniform level of employment and productivity. The second offers, on the contrary, a gamut of situations all more or less clearly short of the optimum of employment, of which that of the South of Italy is by far the least satisfactory. And while the first group of regions offers possibilities of employment which generally tend to be greater than the local resources . . . the regions of the second group are still, in differing degrees, zones of repulsion. It is no doubt in the natural order of things that the vital forces of the Community will continue to concentrate in the zones which insure the greatest efficacy for their employment, and which are, furthermore, those where the territories of the six countries border each other. But it would be prejudicial to the long-term equilibrium of the Community that this phenomenon continue indefinitely.[1]

The disparities in per capita income between the different regions of the national states reach the proportion of 5:1 in France, 4:1 in Italy, and only 2:1 in West Germany. The underdeveloped areas present the following characteristics: unemployment, underemployment, and often irrational utilization of available labor; obsolete production techniques; a low standard of living; scarcity of local capital; and insufficiently developed agriculture. In these regions 40 per cent to 70 per cent of the active population work in outmoded agricultural enterprises. This percentage goes down to 5 per cent in the most advanced provinces of the Community.

The regional inequalities within the community are therefore very evident. They represent obstacles, brakes, and potentially disruptive elements in the way of unification. They are, in fact, an invitation to protectionism, escape clauses, preferential treatment, subsidies, and all the factors which go against a liberalization of trade; also, in the last instance, protectionism and nationalism go together.

The discovery of new sources of energy such as natural gas in Aquitaine, and the building of petro-chemical plants

[1] See CEE, *Exposé 1960*, intro.

in the South-West of France, in Sicily, and in Apulia have opened new horizons to the areas concerned. These improvements are based on the development of already existing resources, but paramount importance must also be given to encouraging man's own natural talents. The national governments, as well as the authorities of the Common Market, have already taken many active measures and they will now be examined.

GENERAL OUTLOOK OF THE FRENCH ECONOMY

Her long tradition of immobility and protectionism[2] provoked violent arguments about the wisdom of France participating in the Common Market before a complete modernization and overhaul of the French economy could be made.[3] It was asserted that the French economy had no chance against the modern, aggressive, and dynamic German industrial machine; it was feared that hordes of Italian *disoccupati* would flood into France, disrupting the local economy and noticeably lowering the standards of living. Lastly, the underdeveloped regions feared that the Common Market would mean a rapid acceleration of the process which was already turning them into deserts; for if the economic protection under which they were still able to subsist was dismantled, the inhabitants and industries in these areas would move into the more advanced regions, leaving vast empty spaces behind them. For it is indeed

. . . by far the most important fact that new enterprise tends by preference to establish itself in the regions where

[2] Protectionism in France was systematized by a law promulgated on January 11, 1892. But even in the nineteenth century free trade took place practically only in the period 1860–1877. For a detailed explanation, see *La Politique Commerciale et Douanière de la France* (Paris: Service Economique Francais, May 1958), Supplement No. 113, pp. 496–504.

[3] One of those against it was former Premier Mendès-France. "(Pierre Mendès-France) has always pointed out with force the necessity of making the French economy healthier before exposing it, with the suppression of all commercial barriers, to European competition." *Réalités*, No. 161, June 1959.

its promoters believe they will be able to find rapid satisfaction for their essential needs: near the great consumer markets, the great conglomerations of skilled labor; near the great intellectual centers; in the regions where great building possibilities are found, particularly pre-existing industrial plants; near the great communication, water and power distribution networks.

All of this, which is true in the national economies, even when they evolve without too many imbalances, *would be even truer in a European economy* [emphasis supplied], taking shape under the immediate impulse of a competition whose diverse elements would not be constantly regulated. It may therefore be believed that an intra-European division of economic activities, if effected in anarchic competition, would play in favor of the present great industrial regions, and to the detriment of regions that, for historical reasons, have until now remained on the fringe of development activities.[4]

Insofar as the fears of the French are concerned, however, there is ample factual evidence now, after a few years of operation of the Common Market, that they were unfounded. The French economy as a whole, and the underdeveloped regions no less than the others, within the limits of their possibilities, have shown spectacular qualities of adaptation and resilience.[5]

---

[4] CEE, *Rapport 1958*, p. 317.

[5] "From having virtually exhausted its exchange reserves in 1957, France entered 1962 with a reserve of almost $3 billion. In the meantime it had repaid all the debt incurred during the stabilization period, liquidated its liabilities under the European Payments Union, and participated in the IMF's grant of assistance to the United Kingdom in July 1961. The transformation of the French external accounts has been such that short-term foreign assets now more than cover even long-term liabilities. Besides accumulating reserves rapidly, since it emerged from the stabilization period late in 1959, France has attained annual rates of growth of domestic product among the highest in Western Europe." United Nations: Economic Commission for Europe: *Economic Survey of Europe in 1961*. Geneva, 1962, chap. I, p. 32.

REGIONAL POLICY

The policy of regional expansion in France has received double support, from the ever greater influence of the European Economic Community Treaty and from the Plan d'Equipement et de Modernisation that will soon be described. Indeed, in certain respects, the latter can almost be considered a function of the first; or, at least, it is strongly influenced by the present impact and by the promise of transformations brought about by the Treaty of Rome.

There is clearly noticeable, on scanning through the successive Plans, a progressive preoccupation by the planners with regional development. Indeed in the IVth Plan (1962–65), a new and perhaps revolutionary concept has prevailed, that of "tranches opératoires." "These 'operational sections' will contain not only the objectives of public investments but forecasts on the creation of new employment and of private investment. They will be completed by studies stretching beyond the limit of 1965, destined to put in evidence the technical and human factors acting in long term on the geographical distribution of populations and activities."[6] The relatively small unit of the *département* has been consolidated into larger units, regions. The concept of region thus acquires official sanction. The 90 *départements* of France have been divided into 21 regions, following criteria based on economics, history, and geography. Such regions have an average of between one and two million inhabitants. The only exception, for understandable reasons, is the Paris region of about 8 and $\frac{1}{2}$ million people. This is possibly only the first step toward a further consolidation of the 21 regions into a smaller number, 7 to 10; these regions would then be of European dimensions and constitute a stage in the regionalization of Europe.

In order to evaluate the over-all approach of the French

[6] Bernard Cazes, *La Planification en France et le IVme Plan* (Paris: Editions de l'Epargne, 1962), p. 238.

government to the problem of regional underdevelopment, it is essential to examine, at least to some extent, the French Plan which, as we have just seen, ". . . is characterized by a stronger effort . . . to articulate national and regional directives. . . . In each region the Plan must fix the order of priorities for the projects to be realized between 1962 and 1965 so as to add to the sectoral pattern of the national plans a regional dimension."[7]

A brief analysis of the French Plan is also necessary because, as we shall see later on, a plan on a European scale is possibly the solution to the regional problems of the European Economic Community and such a plan should be patterned after the principles of the French Plan. Actually, once the economic frontiers among the Six have disappeared, one is inconceivable without the other.[8]

[7] *Ibid.*, p. 237.

[8] M. Jean Boissonnat stated in *Communauté Européenne*, No. 7, July 1962: "We talk in France with satisfaction of the Fourth Plan but we have to ask ourselves if to prepare a Fifth Plan which is exclusively French makes any sense, in view of the fact that in 1967, '68 or '69, the economic life of the Member States will, under the impact of the Common Market, be well on the way to a total transformation." And Pierre Pflimlin, former Premier of France: "Economic forecasts, investment programs, risk being gravely affected by the investments realized in the other member states of the Common Market. I am persuaded that either we shall in France have to renounce really serious and efficient planning, or we shall have to envisage planning on a European scale." Reported in *Le Fédéraliste*, No. 4, December 1962 (article "Planification Européenne et Planification Nationale). *Mondo Economico*, February 2, 1963, so describes the situation: ". . . the planners' task was infinitely easier in the framework of a more or less closed market like that of the French Union between 1948 and 1958, than it is today, in a regime of borders which are either open, or at least moved to the very limits of an area which extends from the Channel of Sicily to the North Sea . . . of this the French planners are quite aware: therefore, the insistence with which they require the adoption by the other members of the Community of a system of planning similar to that existing in France. This is a logical, though incomplete, pretension. To be efficient, therefore, a European Plan presupposes a political unification, not only an economic one, of the participant states, i.e. the centralization, in the political field, of the "fundamental choices' of the Community."

Furthermore, as the Common Market is a new economic entity and for this reason particularly susceptible to many imbalances and actual or potential upsets and weaknesses, a carelessly directed or supervised period of adjustment could be deleterious to certain sectors and to economically backward regions of the Community, with consequences that could be felt for quite a long time after complete unification becomes a fact. The usual and classic example of unification a century ago between the industrialized Italian North and the agricultural South, with its sparse light industries, many of them still in the embryo stage, is an ominous lesson of what may happen in similar cases when the State does not intervene and leaves the necessary adjustments to "natural economic forces." The lesson has not been lost on the European authorities, and it appears very probable that no new "Mezzogiorno" will come about as a by-product of European integration.

The Plan

The French Plan came into effect at the end of World War II when the French economy, along with the economies of all the other European nations, was in a deplorable state.[9] As the necessary private capital for a quick reconstruction of the disrupted French economy did not exist, the State, with considerable United States aid, took upon itself the task of rebuilding it. "It cannot be said that France had to make a choice, because there was no choice for her, except between certain decadence or the road to economic rehabilitation through modernization and equipment of the

[9] "By its background, as well as by its positive contents and also its defects, this plan is fairly representative of post-war economic trends in Western Europe. The Monnet Plan goes back to the fact, acknowledged during the war and the German occupation, that the pre-war structure of France, based mainly on a balance between agriculture and industry, had been proved by events to be a source of weakness and not of strength." Alpert, *op. cit.*, p. 314.

productive apparatus and its methods."[10] Little time was allowed to elapse between the decision and the publication of a decree in the *Journal Officiel* of January 3, 1946, to the effect that "it has been decided to inaugurate a first comprehensive plan for the modernization and the economic equipment of Metropolitan France and the Overseas Territories, to develop national production and foreign exchange, to increase output, to insure full employment of labor and finally to raise the standards of living of the population by improving the conditions of the environment."

Three administrative organs were created by the decree, each concerned with different stages in the elaboration of the plan: (1) Commissions (permanent and *ad hoc*), (2) the Commissariat Général au Plan, and (3) the Conseil. *Grosso modo*, their tasks were divided thus: the first was to do the "field work" and research; the second to elaborate the data, coordinate them with the data furnished by other Commissions and finally transmit them to the Council, composed of the Ministers concerned, plus the representatives of the interested unions, management, consumers, etc. In the last analysis, the Government would make the final decisions, which were also approved by Parliament.[11]

Three such plans have been completed so far and a fourth is now being enacted. The last plan, covering the period 1958–1961, foresaw an annual increase of 4.9 per cent; the new plan foresees an annual rate of growth of 5.5 per cent.[12]

[10] France, Secrétariat Général du Gouvernement, *L'Economie Française* (Paris: La Documentation Française, 1959), p. 16.

[11] It should be pointed out here that the first Commissaire-Général au Plan was M. Jean Monnet, perhaps the foremost exponent of the movement for European integration. As he and many people in high positions in the EEC are in favor of a European plan, there are good chances that a system similar to that adopted by France can be applied by the Community; also, it so happens that the organs of the EEC are strikingly similar in function and in hierarchic position to those proposed for the development of the Plan in France. Thus its adoption by the EEC would be greatly facilitated.

[12] "Between 1961 and 1965, the annual growth of domestic product (in France) is set at 5.5 per cent, or 4.6 per cent per head of popula-

In the framework of the West European type of economic set-up, it is true that there would seem to be:

> . . . a contradiction in terms—a four-year plan for what is essentially a free enterprise economy. . . . But the performance has been good enough to cause other countries, notably Britain, to take a closer look at the French experiment, with the idea perhaps of imitating it. This can only work if everybody plays the game. If the railways or chemical industry do not invest "up to the target" the demand for machinery and steel will be "under target." But because all the major industries are associated in drawing up the plan . . . practically everybody does play the game. Thus all win.[13]

---

tion. This compares with an average during the fifties of 4.5 per cent (and 4 per cent per capita). Although the ambitiousness of the plan is recognized by the French planners, its targets are believed to be feasible (so long as the assumptions on the allocation of the increase in product to end-uses are respected) without straining resources or upsetting external equilibrium." ECE, *op.cit.*, p. 34.

[13] *New York Times*, August 21, 1961. Perhaps a few more quotations may help to give a better understanding of the meaning of the word "Plan" as it is applied to the French economy. One is by François Perroux, the well-known French economist: "In practice, the French plan is often devised and put into operation under the preponderant influence of the large enterprises and the large financial organizations." Another by M. Le Brun, from a speech made at a Trade Union Congress: "The Plan is essentially agreed upon between top representatives of capital and top representatives of the State, the first normally having more weight than the second." Both statements reported in *Le Monde* (Sélection Hebdomadaire), March 14, 1962. This newspaper, in its issue of April 24, 1963, reprints the following data, extracted from "La Planification Française" by M. Bauchet, Editions du Seuil, Paris, 1963:" . . . the composition by function or profession of the 3,137 persons who have participated in the commissions and working committees charged with preparing the Plan is:

Entrepreneurs and Management Representatives, 40.7%
Farmers, 3.4%
Peasant Unions, 1.0%
Unions of Workers and Professionals, 7.9%
Government Officials and Experts, 47.0%"

It is therefore somewhat exaggerated to fear it as ". . . a diabolical invention, carried by the juggernaut of Communism, and destined to

REDRESSING THE SITUATION

According to studies made on behalf of the Statistical Office of the Communities,[14] the average yearly per capita income of the inhabitant of the Common Market area is equivalent to $871.

> Expressed in dollars at the official exchange rate, the average income would be about $850 per capita (for the whole Community). Such evaluation, however, does not correspond to internal prices which, in the United States —particularly because of rents and services—are much higher than in Europe. In real purchasing power . . . five countries of the Community have an average per capita income very comparable to that of each other, varying between $1,000 and $1,100 per year, which however, if Italy is included, decreases to $950. . . . The present gap in the average standard of living between Italy and that of the other Member States of the Community is partly explained by still-high unemployment which is, however, tending to diminish because of the rapid expansion in Italy . . . between the North and the South of that country . . . the average of $600 per annum is composed of $800 in the North and only $360 in the South.[15]

If the base $871 = 100 is taken, the index so formed may vary from a maximum of 186 in parts of West Germany, an overindustrialized area, to only 26 for certain of the poorest provinces of Southern Italy.

---

favor the birth of a real Leviathan, eager to strangle free enterprise." *Loc.cit.*, December 5, 1962.

[14] Prepared in the form of a report presented to the plenary European Parliamentary Assembly on May 22, 1960 by the French Deputy, M. Bertrand Motte, on behalf of the Commission for a Long-Term Economic Policy, for Financial Questions, and for Investments of the EPA. Reproduced in *l'Economie*, No. 759, January 12, 1961.

[15] *CEE, Rapport 1958*, p. 18.

In France, the overpopulated Paris region has an index of 166, which is the maximum for the country, thus making the 38 for Corsica seem even worse than it is in comparison. A brief examination is necessary in order to obtain a clearer impression of the state of backwardness of the economies of the underdeveloped regions in respect to the rest of France and the European Economic Community as a whole.

Besides the Paris region which, as we have seen, reaches 166, 22 more regions of France have an index surpassing 114. The influence of the Paris region on the French economy as a whole is overwhelming:[16] it includes one-sixth of the entire French population, one-quarter of the industrial population, and one-third of the administrative and commercial services.

The regions of the Nord, Alsace-Lorraine, Alpes, and Rhône Valley vary between 118 and 137. These areas contain the main coal basins, a considerable part of the production of energy, almost all the iron ore, and an important proportion of the steel, mechanical, chemical, and textile industries. As far as agriculture is concerned, the yield is average, with the exception of the Nord, with predominance given to cattle-raising and growth of cereals.

The index 113—118 can be applied to Picardie, Champagne, and Haute Normandie. The other regions of France —all those considered in the present work—vary between 75 and 95. Far behind comes Corsica, with an index of 38, and an average per capita income of about $330 per annum. These regions are characterized by a stagnating economy which the national government is now trying to revive in order to prepare them for their new role in the Common Market. The main characteristics of these areas also include: underpopulation (except in Brittany); a "family" system of

[16] It must be emphasized here that this does not apply only to the economic field. As Luethy states: "The Paris monopoly of the market applies to things of the mind just as much as it does to cauliflowers. Paris has turned the rest of France into an intellectual desert." H. Luethy, *France against Herself* (New York: Meridian Books, 1957), p. 23.

agriculture; and obsolete methods of cultivation and marketing of products.

In conclusion, a summary of the French economic situation shows that:

(a) The Paris region is still by far the center of practically all French activities—economic, political, administrative, and industrial, as well as intellectual. The *départements* of Paris (Seine and Seine-et-Oise) account for one-fifth of the national income and, together with ten others around and to the east of them, they produce 45 per cent of the national product, occupying 38 per cent of the active population.

(b) An imaginary line stretching from Le Havre to Marseilles truly divides France in two. To the east of this line we find slightly more than a half of the national territory, including the Paris region, of course, which contains two-thirds of the population, occupies 66 per cent of the workers, and creates 72 per cent of the national product. In eight *départements* in this half of the country we find that more than 50 per cent of the active population is engaged in industrial activity (compared to the national average of 36 per cent). Also, in several *départements* of this region the average income surpasses the national average by more than 25 per cent. Agricultural production is divided about equally between the two halves, while 78 per cent of industrial production takes place in the eastern area.

On the contrary, to the western half of the line, less than 25 per cent of the active population is employed in industry, with the exception of the four *départements* of Calvados, Loire-Inférieure, Gironde, Haute-Garonne, where however the number does not attain the national average of 36 per cent. This area includes only one *département* where the average income is higher than the national average, while in many *départements* it is more than a quarter less than the average for the country.[17]

[17] The above statistics taken from Pierre Maillet, *La Structure Economique de la France* (Paris: Presses Universitaires de France, 1958), p. 75–76.

Programs of Regional Development in France

As a foreword, it must be said that a program of regional development can only be efficacious when the economic structure of a region is *permanently* modified by the changes brought about by the program. Otherwise,

> . . . the risk will remain that the regional establishment of new economic activities would have a tendency to develop as it does today, that is preferably in those regions already well-equipped with transportation facilities, power and industrial plants of all kinds. Such a risk must be avoided if we are to prevent competition from leading to a heavier industrial concentration, and to an increase in the degree of underdevelopment in the present backward regions.[18]

If permanent changes do come about, then the economy of the region undergoes a reorientation; a new backbone is built and around it many economic activites become possible and viable. The economic destiny of the region becomes tightly linked to the new framework, that is, to the provisions that are destined to improve the economic situation. For instance, the rational irrigation of a region means that the kind of crops grown hitherto may be replaced by some other, more profitable ones, and the results prove far better. Consequently, the standard of living of the farmers concerned improves, their increased purchasing power fosters a multitude of new activities in the region, and the population is not only encouraged to stay, but new immigrants may arrive from other regions of France and of the European Economic Community, especially from overpopulated Southern Italy.

The similar construction of a nucleus around which the region may be revitalized is possible also in industrial activi-

[18] CEE, *Rapport 1958*, p. 319.

ties. For instance, if a factory powered by atomic energy is installed in a region where hitherto no industrial activity of any importance had taken place because of a lack of coal in the neighborhood, other activities must necessarily spring up in great number and then, attracted by the awakening of the region, private capital, always in search of suitable places to make investments, will find it profitable. Such private capital is available not only in France but also in other member countries of the Common Market, especially Germany. It is important that the country be a member of the European Economic Community because the investment can then be better stimulated and directed by a federal European Government.

Conversely, however, this system of nuclei is not always the most advisable one, for a variety of reasons—geographical, for instance. In a mountainous region, even if a factory is opened in one valley, the impact in regard to the next valley, separated from it by a chain of high mountains with no quick communications between them, will be negligible. Therefore, in these cases, the development program cannot be based on one or two big undertakings, in the hope that they will polarize around them the new economic activities of the region. For these regions the programs must consist of a multiplicity of relatively small works, whose execution is entrusted to a variety of bodies, both in public and local administrations and private enterprises.

In this connection, it must be said that remarkable, and sometimes spontaneous, cooperation has taken place on the regional departmental level between professional organizations, local authorities, and trade unions; also the agricultural organizations have often participated in the planning of regional development. However, the old characteristic of the French administration of being completely centered in the Ministries and in the high authorities in Paris still remains. Therefore, the former agencies have slightly more of an advisory character, while the really important decisions

93

are made in Paris. However, their advice has great value and weight and is generally taken into account.

The first laws concerning regional development go back to 1951, long before the signature of the Treaty of Rome, but at a time when the European Coal and Steel Community was already in the making and it became apparent that European integration would soon, in one form or another, be a living reality. The financial provisions can be divided into three categories:

(a) In the areas presenting the characteristics of underdevelopment, a special "equipment bonus" equal to a maximum of 20 per cent of investments may be granted. This subsidy can also be allowed for scientific research, reconversion of labor, and reclassification.

(b) State-granted long-term loans, with low interest rates, may be made for the partial financing of programs of decentralization, reconversion, specialization, rationalization, and modernization.

(c) Financial aids may be given to the Societies for Regional Development.

In fiscal matters, tax relief or exemption may be allowed in certain cases:

(a) to enterprises which are carrying on rationalization, reconversion, decentralization and/or creation of new activities in the underdeveloped areas;

(b) to certain bodies (labor or professional organizations) aiming at reforming the professional structure of certain activities, particularly on a local or regional basis.

These great programs of regional development are being accomplished according to the basic principles of economic development: first of all, a certain region, well-defined from a geographic and economic viewpoint, is selected; then the program is planned in a "global" way, i.e. to embrace all the activities insofar as possible which contribute to the goal of full development. It is now realized that it is practically impossible to improve permanently the prosperity of a cer-

94

tain region in any one particular branch of the economy without bringing about a parallel development in others. The economic activities of a region must be considered as a whole, if durable results are to be achieved.[19] It is also of great importance to establish better human and social relations between the inhabitants of the area.

A body with the function of coordinating the various efforts, and endowed with supervisory powers, surveys and directs the over-all materialization of what has been planned and the progressive unity of all the different projects going on at once, so that one particular activity will not be supported at the expense of another or otherwise be so much ahead or behind the over-all development of the region as to upset the general equilibrium. A solution to these problems must be found rapidly, otherwise the "French economy in a few years risks meeting some real difficulties in harmonizing its active population and its production with the space available. This can only be satisfactorily solved by an active regional policy, an extension of that already initiated a while ago."[20]

FINANCING AND ORGANIZATION OF PLANS FOR REGIONAL DEVELOPMENT

The regional development projects have been realized with the aid of the State through certain public institutions, such as the Caisses des Dépôts, La Caisse Centrale de Coopération Économique, La Société Centrale pour l'Équipement du Territoire, etc., and mixed-economy companies such as Les Compagnies Nationales du Bas-Rhône, Languedoc, de la Corse, des Landes de Gascogne, etc.

The mixed-economy company is not at all uncommon in

[19] "In a policy of development, the necessity of an orderly and simultaneous evolution of *all the compartments* of economic life is paramount." Gabriele Pescatore, *Dieci Anni di Esperienze della Cassa per il Mezzogiorno* (Rome: Cassa per il Mezzogiorno, 1961).

[20] CEE, *Rapport 1958*, p. 282.

95

Europe and, within the Community, is found in France and Italy especially. In this type of company part of the capital is contributed by public agencies (local administrations, *départements*, etc.) and by the State as such directly, the other part by private enterprise. The company, which therefore undergoes strict scrutiny from the State, also benefits from many advantages entailed in State interest: technical aid, subsidies, and facilities of various kinds. The State exercises its function through a commission which makes sure that the program is being realized according to the plans put forward for it. A State controller scrutinizes its finances, but ample freedom of action is given to the administrators of the organization, who do not have to refer to him for authorization and so on, but can make whatever decisions they see fit. In this way, the mixed-economy company benefits both from the advantages of private enterprise so far as practical administration is concerned, and from the guarantees and help brought by the State's participation and control. State intervention is especially pronounced in the first stages, when the activities of the company do not yield any profit, or at least very little. In this stage, private capital alone would fight shy of the organization.[21] The State helps to set up the general structure necessary for better economic development, unhampered by responsibilities to shareholders and boards of directors. Once the base is established and the whole economic status of the region in question becomes viable, the State calls for the participation of private capital in this now going concern, to carry on what has been achieved and to attract normal, private investment.

The financing of all these projects and institutions is

[21] One of the distinguishing features of this type of company is that ". . . the State, or any other public Agency . . . acquires rights more important than would normally be warranted by the proportion of their participation in the capital of the company." J. E. Godchot, *Les Sociétés d'Economie Mixte et l'Aménagement du Territoire* (Nancy: Berger-Lavrault, 1958), p. 7.

secured by the Fonds de Développement Economique et Social (FDES), created and organized by decrees of June 30 and October 18, 1955, and by the Fonds National d'Aménagement du Territoire, instituted by decree of July 26, 1954, and successive decrees of July 23, 1956, and April 19, 1957.

The purpose of the first organization is to decide on the granting of financial aid and on tax relief and exemptions; the second aids local cooperatives, small collectives, etc., through grants and guarantees for the purchase of land and the financing of the infrastructure.

On December 31, 1958, exactly at the end of the "preparatory year" of the European Economic Community, a new type of body entrusted with regional development tasks was added: the Comité des Plans Régionaux, with the cooperation of the Interior, Finance, Economic Affairs, and Construction Ministries.

The main objective of the Comité des Plans Régionaux is to devise programs and to insure their reciprocal coordination on a national scale, with the Plan National de Modernisation et d'Equipement.

The Comité des Plans Régionaux is made up, among others, of the representatives of the Ministries concerned in the various development activities foreseen for the region. Also involved are the representatives of the Conseil de Direction du Fonds de Développement Economique et Social and other bodies such as the Comité National d'Orientation Economique, the Haut Conseil de l'Aménagement du Territoire, and the Comité de Décentralisation des Etablissements Publics.

The State also participates in, but does not control, the Sociétés de Développement Régional, which are of a semi-private character. They have the objective of participating with capital outlays in the financing of industrial or commercial enterprises or in granting loans to boost the development of regional enterprises.

Other agencies for regional development are:

The S.A.F.E.R. (Sociétés d'Aménagement Foncier et d'Établissement Rural). These Societies were founded following the "Loi d'Orientation Agricole" of August 3, 1960. They aim at generally improving and rationalizing the already existing agricultural structures by means of transfer of land and by several measures of land improvement. They are to some extent a counterbalance to the risk of "pulverization" and consequent economic nonviability of the land. In fact, one of their tasks is to try to reconstitute the optimum "family size" estate. There is a Central Society which controls Regional Societies and coordinates the activities of the latter on a national scale.

The Comités d'Expansion Régionale. The first of these Committees was created in 1954, but several subsequent laws and regulations concerning them have been promulgated in following years. Perhaps the most important is the decree of January 20, 1961, whereby rules were established concerning the constitution and the functions of these bodies. These Committees are essentially private bodies of a consultative character, formed by representatives of various groups and interests in the region. They are also assisted by a somewhat loose galaxy of local and departmental Committees that are not always necessarily helpful in the formulation of an economic policy embracing the whole region. The essential value of these Committees is that they represent the combined thinking of the most important interests in the region. Their jurisdiction is not exclusively confined to economic matters, and in actual practice almost anything concerning their territory may form the object of their endeavors. Their composition is such that most sectional as well as geographical interests and activities of various kinds are represented. One of the problems of these agencies is that the criteria of maximum representation and maximum efficiency often clash. Consequently about 30 persons make up each of these Committees, even if adequate representation would require perhaps ten times that number. But a large representation has been deemed impractical for several reasons and, at least for the time being, a somewhat "streamlined" structure has been preferred. The financing of the Committee is done on a double base: one is a direct subsidy by the State, which does not actually alter the private character of the Committee; the other is a combination of private contributions plus contributions coming from local and regional public agencies.

Conférence Interdépartementale des Préfets. These Conferences are a most important element in the regional context and were created by a decree of January 7, 1959. They include the Préfets of all the *départements* of the region. The scope of the Conference is essentially that of administrative coordination at a regional level; details concerning their constitution and functions were given in circular letters of June 20, 1960, January 26, 1961, and December 18, 1961. It seems that, consequent to the increased importance attributed to regional matters by the IVth Plan, these Conferences will play an ever-increasing role in the general economic context of the region.

Finally, a number of individual, private development projects has been directly subsidized by the State.

SPECIFIC PROGRAMS OF DEVELOPMENT

In 1951, a law was promulgated to create central regional bodies which could coordinate a basic program of development for the region as a whole and encompass all the activities taking place in that geographical area—somewhat similar, in fact, to the Tennessee Valley Authority project in the United States. For the time being, the law applies only to a few regions of France which can be classified as underdeveloped over most of their surface. These are:

(a) Corsica, where a company created to develop the region has already been working for some time to redeem and begin exploiting the plains of the west coast over an area

99

of fifty thousand hectares. An auxiliary company is concerned with the promotion of the tourist industry and connected activities (hotels, restoration and maintenance of monuments, etc.).

(b) The highland region of Gascogne, which will take advantage of the waters rising in the Massif de Neouvieille. On completion of this project, it is hoped that eighty to ninety thousand hectares will be irrigated with this water which up till now has been largely wasted.

(c) A program of land redemption, also in Gascogne, is scheduled to transform an area of about fifty thousand hectares into fertile soil.

(d) Various parts of South-West France, where swamps are being drained and redeemed and the land so cleared devoted to grazing. About two hundred thousand hectares should be obtained by this.[22]

More programs of this kind are envisaged for other regions: in particular we may cite those of Limagne in the Massif Central, and of Brittany, both of an agricultural character; also, the project for the Garonne valley in Gascogne. According to present plans, which however are not yet codified, at least officially, the whole of Southern France from the Italian to the Spanish border should in a few years be in a position to develop into one organic unit without any perceptible structural difference.[23]

[22] The following figures show investments made during the first few years of the great regional development projects:

Type of operation	Amount invested (billions of "old" francs)			
	1956	1957	1958	1959
Bas-Rhône, Coteaux de Gascogne, Durance-Verdon, Landes de Gascogne, Corse, Marais de l'Ouest:	1.7	5.4	8.1	11.7
In billions of francs re-evaluated at 1959 price:	2.0	6.0	8.3	11.7

Source: *Rapport Annuel du Commissariat au Plan* (Paris, 1960), p. 64.

[23] *Le Monde* (Sélection Hebdomadaire), May 8, 1963, confirms that "The Mediterranean Coast, between Camargue and the Spanish

Agricultural and industrial developments are closely interrelated, and should proceed apace as much as possible in order to create the conditions for a large productive region capable of holding its own within the Community. But as the bulk of exports will, at least in the beginning, be agricultural products, a thorough reorganization of the agricultural system will be necessary, with the elimination of crops unsuitable to the region and specialization in those for which the climate, soil, and other conditions are particularly favorable. Furthermore the peasant must become accustomed to growing crops for which there is a possibility of obtaining outlets in the vast European market. Up till now, he has always traditionally grown certain products with the knowledge that, if the crop could not be sold, the State would intervene and either buy it or otherwise subsidize the farmer. Subsidies could also be granted by a European Government, but they would be of an exceptional character, following for instance a serious drought or abnormally bad market conditions.

The first concrete application of the Law of 1951 took place two years after it had come into force, that is in 1953. A special Commission pour l'Equipement et Modernisation was created by the Commissariat-Général au Plan, charged with the irrigation and exploitation of the regions of Bas-Rhône and Languedoc. At present, it is the most advanced program of regional development in the extent of its realization, besides being the most rational and complete. It foresees the irrigation of a total of two hundred thousand hectares between the Rhône and the Pyrénées, utilizing a canal from the Rhône, together with some of the rivers near the coast.

---

border will, within five or six years, be completely revamped. . . . This project . . . has been described at length by M. Maziol, Minister of Public Works, during a trip he has just completed in Languedoc-Roussillon."

A Decree issued in 1955 created the Compagnie Nationale du Bas-Rhône et Languedoc. The specification "nationale" emphasizes the fact that the aims of this Compagnie are of nationwide importance, even though concerned with only one region. It is responsible for all the activities going on in the region—industrial, commercial, and agricultural alike; up till now, its main effort has been the rapid creation of an infrastructure, so that the production of the region can be profitably increased in a short time.[24] On the agricultural level, its tasks range from gathering data on the composition of the soil to the modernization and equipment with mechanical means of the newly redeemed lands. The company also endeavors to instruct farmers on the type of crops best suited to their land, and to find outlets for them in France, in the Common Market, and in other European and world markets.

NECESSITY OF A REORIENTATION IN THE POLICY OF REGIONAL DEVELOPMENT

After some years of experience, it is now possible to make an appraisal of the new regional development policy. Such appraisal must be considered in the context of a general plan of development for the territory, conceived not only in terms of "national territory," but of "European territory," as the consequences of the Treaty of Rome become increasingly manifest. Development of these areas will shortly be dominated by the efficacy of the communication lines that not only link the different regions of France to each other, but which link them to the other regions of Europe. The economic heart of Europe beats in the Rhineland and the Lorraine Basin. It is in these regions that the most intense activity is developing and that investments reach the maximum. Beyond the Massif Central, to the West and South, a

[24] See for details article "L'Aménagement du Bas-Rhône et du Languedoc," by René Dumont, *Agriculture en France* (Paris: La Nef, Juillard, July–September 1962).

great part of the territory of France is excluded from this dynamic nucleus.[25] It is essential that these areas be brought out of their isolation and led into the productive process being carried on in the center of Europe. At the same time, they also have something to offer: their labor, their products, especially agricultural, and the possibilities of opening to the heavy industry of the East and of Germany some needed outlets in the Mediterranean. In a few years time, the possibility of saturation of the internal European markets and of the increased productive capacity of the Community will make exports even more important than they are now.

One of the most urgent tasks of the Government is that of better coordinating the too numerous Agencies, Committees, etc. which participate in the programs, frequently duplicating efforts in certain areas while other sectors are either entirely overlooked or do not receive sufficient help.

The attitude of the local businessmen is also very important. They have to reconcile themselves to the fact that an increasing industrialization of their region will attract new enterprises from outside and that therefore they will have to accept the new situation brought about by this increased competition. Consequently, certain industries, professional activities, etc., hitherto operating almost in a position of regional monopoly, will have to quickly reconvert their activities to survive, if not to increase their prosperity. Others, the most ossified, will become marginal or disappear altogether. No regional expansion is possible without hurting a number of *situations acquises;* this is unavoidable if any regional improvement is to be brought about.

France is at present the nation with the highest rate of

[25] " . . . there is no doubt that, . . . in France, the west, the center and the south-west progress more slowly than the rest of the country. If employment statistics do not always make this fact very evident, it should appear clearly from a regional analysis of productivity." CEE, *Exposé 1960*, intro.

demographic expansion in the Europe of the Six.[26] She must prepare to furnish a large number of jobs to the young people coming into the labor market for the first time. Besides demographic growth, which itself proceeds rapidly enough, several hundreds of thousands of people have been repatriated from North Africa. According to most demographers, France will be a country of 55 million people in fifteen or twenty years.

Preparing for such a certainty, and not only keeping pace with the demographic expansion but actually increasing the standard of living at the same time, is the most important long-range task of the French nation. The chance that this objective can be achieved is now immensely improved, thanks to the great possibilities offered by the European Economic Community. France is a part—and a very important part—of a European market which is already developing economic potentialities that can eventually eliminate problems of regional development. Once again, France has demonstrated an unexpected resilience[27] and, brushing aside

[26] In the Community as a whole, the population is expected to increase as follows during the period 1962–1976:

	(millions of inhabitants)			
	1962	*1966*	*1971*	*1976*
France	47.1	48.6	50.2	52.1
Belgium	9.2	9.7	9.7	9.9
Luxembourg	0.322	0.325	0.335	0.345
Netherlands	11.8	12.1	12.7	13.3
Federal Rep. of Germany	54.8	55.9	58.2	60.5
Italy	50.1	51.2	52.5	53.9
Total Community: (approx.)	173	178	184	190

Source: *Communauté Européenne*, No. 2, February 1964.

[27] The two following quotations are illustrative of the capacity of France to bounce back from catastrophe to grandeur:

"It has always been said that France was a vessel for which the tempest served as a pilot. Our fathers have fought their wars without discipline and their negotiations have been carried out without secrecy . . . We have always been the makers and the artisans of our misfortunes . . . Perhaps these disorders should bring France to the

104

all the doubts expressed even by some of her leading economists, is not only holding her own in the Common Market, but, since its very inception, has steered a straight, bold course. The results are increasingly satisfactory.[28] After all, the Common Market is essentially a French idea, and France should take the lead in developing her own creation.

GENERAL OUTLOOK OF THE ITALIAN ECONOMY

Italy is, among the six Member States of the European Economic Community, the country where the national income is lowest, having an average index for its nineteen regions of approximately 61 according to the EEC Commission scale. The western half of Northern Italy (including Val d'Aosta, Piedmont, Lombardy, and Liguria) is by far the most developed part of the country, and here the index is around 95. Two-thirds of the heavy industry of the whole country is concentrated here; the same proportion applies to textiles and chemicals. In fact this is the great productive area of Italy. The agriculture practiced here, and in the whole Po valley, is also comparatively much more advanced than that in the other areas of the country.

The rest of the North-Center covers the regions of Trentino-Alto Adige, Friuli-Venezia Giulia, Venetia,

---

ultimate catastrophe. Have not many other states perished for less than this? However, she has proved all the fortune-tellers wrong." This text, which could have been written today, was written in 1631 by Guez de Balzac and is quoted by André Maurois, *Portrait de la France et des Français* (Paris: Hachette, 1955), p. 135.

Luethy, *op.cit.*, p. 15, states: "The recurrent French miracle has been the extraordinary invulnerability of a political organism which has suffered almost unparalleled convulsions."

[28] "The stabilization measures adopted by France at the end of 1958 have produced extremely satisfactory results. . . . This progress must be partly attributed to certain outside factors, particularly to a more rapid resumption of expansion abroad and to the fact that the starting of the Common Market favored French exports just when they were benefitting from the effects of devaluation." OEEC, *L'Europe et l'Economie Mondiale* (Paris, 1960), p. 34.

Emilia, Tuscany, Umbria, Marche, and Latium, extending to a few miles south of Rome. This area is much less, as well as more sparsely, industrialized than the northwest of the country. Pockets of poverty and backwardness are not unusual and agricultural productivity is also irregular. The index here varies between 48 and 77.

The South includes Apulia, Abruzzi, Campania, Calabria, Basilicata, Sicily, and Sardinia. This area is almost uniformly underdeveloped—industrially, agriculturally, and culturally.[29] Of the 18 million people living in the South, only 17 per cent work in industry, and the average index here ranges from 26 to 39.

RECONSTRUCTION IN THE SOUTH OF ITALY

After World War II, in the framework of European reconstruction fostered by the Marshall Plan, Italy undertook as one of its main tasks to solve the problem of the South. This problem was faced energetically and it now appears that concrete, lasting results are possible, especially through the Cassa per il Mezzogiorno. The question has become even more important now that Italy's participation in the Common Market has made a solution to the problem of the South imperative.[30]

[29] "In the Southern part of the country (Italy) . . . the territory in its entirety shows the signs of a typical underdeveloped area or, to be more exact, of an area where the mechanism of development is clearly insufficient to furnish employment to the available labor and to counterbalance its natural growth." CEE, *Rapport 1958*, p. 370.

[30] "The problem of development of the Southern regions in the post-war years has been first of all the general problem of Italian economic expansion, of the enlargement of the internal market, of employment, etc.; a problem, therefore, whose solution would condition the whole Italian economy and the future itself of the industries located in the northern part of the country. And from here, in the national framework, we find the necessity for extraordinary intervention, for pre-industrialization and industrialization of the South; and in the European framework, the necessity for a more pronounced economic integration, for liberalization of exchanges, for emigration of men and immigration of capital." Compagna, *op.cit.*, p. 43.

Ten-Year Plan for Development, 1955–1964

The problem of underdevelopment in Southern Italy differs somewhat from the traditional pattern[31] since the area concerned forms part of a modern, industrialized nation. It has been realized that it is necessary to tackle underdevelopment here on an over-all basis, always taking account of the situation in the rest of the country—in short, by integrating the Mezzogiorno into the process of expansion of already existing industry.[32] To achieve this, the Government in 1954 promulgated the Plan for Development of Income and Employment in Italy in the Ten-Year Period 1955–1964—better known as the Piano Vanoni, after its author. Besides being an attempt to face the problem on a *national* scale, this was also the first time that it had been viewed from the *international* angle, for it is based on an international policy of cooperation and was presented in January 1955 to OEEC. This policy has been constantly followed by successive Italian Governments.

The main task of the Plan was to expand the industrialization of the country so that it absorbed the young people

[31] "It is as though the Italian economy were disfigured by the existence of a permanent depression, by whose effects a country of some 47 million people offers to its industry an outlet corresponding to a much smaller number of consumers." Pasquale Saraceno, *Elementi per un Piano Economico, 1949–1952* (Rome: Centro di Studi e Piani Tecnico-Economici, 1948).

[32] In this connection, the following figures concerning the structure of the productive investments in the North and in the South are of particular interest:

	North	*South*
Sector	(*respective percentages—1957*)	
Agriculture	13	26
Industry	50	27
Transport & communications	19	23
Public Works	9	19
Miscellaneous	9	5
	100	100

Source: CEE, *Rapport 1958*, p. 371.

continuously coming into the labor market, those presently unemployed and those becoming unemployed during future years as a result of technological improvements, especially in agriculture.[33]

An increase in national income equal to 5 per cent yearly is foreseen in the Plan; it aimed particularly at increasing industrialization in the Mezzogiorno. However, despite the growth of income in the South, the gross income of this area was planned to be no more than 28 per cent of the total national income, although the population was estimated to be nearly 38 per cent of the total.[34]

An important function of the Plan was to encourage private investment in the South as a necessary stimulus for industrialization.[35] In 1954, before the Plan was enacted,

[33] ". . . the definite solution of the unemployment problem created by the insufficient development of a part of the country, essentially in the South, may now be envisaged in a relatively near future." CEE, *Exposé 1961*, p. 47.

[34] It is in any case clear that the Plan had limited objectives. "The Piano Vanoni, even foreseeing for the ten years 1955–64 a rate of development equal to 9.6 per cent for the Mezzogiorno and 5.1 per cent for the North, admits that the gap will not be closed by the end of the ten years." Cassa per il Mezzogiorno, *Bilancio 1956–57* (Rome: Istituto Poligrafico dello Stato, 1957), p. xxviii intro.

[35] "The decisive importance for Italy of intensifying the process of accumulation of capital is clear. This is in fact the preliminary condition to any solution of the problem, constituted by the necessity of rapidly improving the situation of the most backward sections of agriculture and by the necessity of consolidating the competitive capacity of the extant industrial system, while extending it to the Southern regions where practically the whole excess labor supply of the country is located. This method of facing Italian problems . . . is at the origin of the Ten-Year Plan of Development, which is the basis for the present economic policy of Italy. The new fact that results from the participation of Italy in the Common Market is that whereas the Ten-Year Plan foresaw the acceleration of the process of capital formation in a non-autarchic regime, protected nevertheless by customs tariffs, today this protection must gradually disappear. This does not imply a change in direction, only a considerable acceleration in the process as foreseen in the Plan." CEE, *Rapport 1958*, p. 411. However, "external equilibrium has been reached much earlier than was officially expected (1964 was the date foreseen in the Plan)." ECE, *op.cit.*, p. 32.

108

only 14 per cent of private investment in the country was directed to the South. It was hoped that through the program of State investment a progressively attractive field would be created to induce large-scale private investment so that the role of the State might gradually diminish. This is of the utmost importance; in fact, in 1956, OEEC reported:

> The problem of unemployment in the South can only be resolved, in the sense envisaged by the Ten-Year Plan of Development, by an increase in industrialization; this depends to a large extent on the interest which Northern industries take in the South, and so far progress in this respect has been slow. . . . In the future, it will be necessary to take more concrete steps to incite private capital to invest in the industrial enterprises of the South.[36]

Public financing has been carried on primarily through the funds allotted to the Cassa per il Mezzogiorno, either directly or through the setting up of several institutes for industrial medium-term lending, which will be described at the end of this Chapter.

The Cassa per il Mezzogiorno

The South was helped along in the last year of the War and in the immediate postwar years by intense American aid, both directly and through UNRRA (United Nations Rehabilitation and Relief Agency). However, the problem then had to be tackled by the Italian Government since certain extremist and centrifugal forces had appeared, and only quick action could have saved the situation. It was clear that, if anything of a lasting nature was to be done, there were two conditions to be met: (a) to reorganize thoroughly the backward, medieval economy of these regions, using all the power of the law, if necessary, to enforce the decisions

[36] OEEC, *Situation et Problèmes de l'Economie Italienne* (Paris, 1956), p. 15.

made; (b) to create some sort of centralized organ, on an *ad hoc* basis, to coordinate the policies to be followed to that effect, to plan these policies in detail, and to work in close contact with the Government, with the credit institutes, and with private organizations of all types. The creation of such a body was decided on, and on August 10, 1950, a Law (No. 646) was promulgated to establish it. The name of the organization was to be "Cassa per Opere Straordinarie di Pubblico Interesse nell'Italia Meridionale," a rather cumbersome title which was soon replaced in practice by the simpler "Cassa per il Mezzogiorno," (Development Fund for the South).[37]

The creation of this Fund was of basic importance for the Italian economy:

(a) It was the first over-all plan to radically face and solve the problem of the underdeveloped Mezzogiorno, overcoming, in a common draft, different and sometimes clashing competences, either administrative or territorial. Naturally, special provisions for Southern Italy as a whole, or for certain specified provinces, or cities, existed before the Cassa; however, the lack of coordination between them had reduced their effectiveness, besides creating considerable waste and bureaucratic slowness and impediments. Now, the State, the local bodies, and the private firms could develop their activity according to a definite plan, long-range in its essence, and not linked to the budgets and diverse exigencies of the various administrations. As Professor Pescatore has pointed out, "The Cassa is a new entity, on which has been conferred a new organization, peculiar to it, allowing it to operate within a more elastic and supple framework which, by reason of the diversity of the laws

[37] Called "extraordinary" because to the Cassa are entrusted those projects for which the regular machine of the State is not usually competent. They are the programs that "break through" the environmental situation, and which, after the initial impetus has been given, must be taken over by the normal administration.

which govern them, is not usually accorded to normal institutions."[38]

(b) It had the character of being, not a substitute for the various State administrations, but of integrating them as the promoter of a much larger, long-range program which could go beyond the financial limitations imposed by their budgets; the scope of the program was not the profit of certain enterprises, or the benefit of a limited number of people, but the improvement of the standard of life of all the people living in the area, and their final integration into its economic and social life, on a par with the rest of the nation.

(c) It was a model for the long-delayed reform of the Italian bureaucracy, as it demonstrated how a ". . . relatively slim, elastic Administration could operate efficiently and rapidly without too much overstaffing or unnecessary red tape."[39]

The original plan called for an average expenditure of 100 billion lire a year for a ten-year period, and was thus subdivided:

(a) land reclamation and agricultural transformation.................. 770 billion
(b) acqueducts and sewers........... 110 billion
(c) road construction and improvements......................... 90 billion
(d) works of touristic interest........ 30 billion

Total   1,000 billion lire

In January 1952 a supplementary allocation of 280 billion lire was granted to the Cassa as an additional measure

[38] Cassa per il Mezzogiorno, *Bilancio 1956–57*, p. 13.
[39] Comitato Italiano per la Ricostruzione, *Lo Sviluppo dell'Economia Italiana nel Quadro della Ricostruzione e Cooperazione Europea* [with preface by Alcide De Gasperi] (Rome: Istituto Poligrafico dello Stato, 1952), p. 85.

against unemployment (Law No. 949 of July 25, 1952). The 280 billion was appropriated in the amount of 10 billion a year for the fiscal years 1954–55 to 1959–60; furthermore, 110 billion in each of the fiscal years 1960–61 and 1961–62; consequently, the duration of the Cassa per il Mezzogiorno was prolonged for two more fiscal years. Successively, the Cassa was allowed to extend its activities also to the industrial sector, utilizing for this purpose the loans of the International Bank for Reconstruction and Development by means of the newly created regional financial institutions, which will soon be described. Also, the Cassa was authorized to issue bonds and to raise foreign loans. Finally, on July 29, 1957, Law No. 634 extended the action of the Cassa to the financial year 1964–65, making the plan a fifteen-year venture. The total funds allocated to it amount to 2,107.5 billion lire. As Minister Campilli said during the debate on September 17, 1956, before Parliament: "The new law does not constitute only a simple prolongation of the preexisting laws, but a complex of vast provisions intended to give a more decisive impetus to the development of the most backward regional economies; it constitutes the natural, necessary integration of the initial provisions."

PROGRAM

The main aim of the Cassa, at the time of its creation, was to promote fundamental land reform and projects of various kinds directly or indirectly affecting agriculture. It was also to improve the existing infrastructure and to create new bases for industry and agriculture. In fact, 77 per cent of the initial investments were intended for agriculture, 20 per cent for road improvement, aqueducts, and other basic works of various kinds. The remaining 3 per cent was to be devoted to promoting and encouraging tourism (hotel construction, restoration of monuments and other works of art).

However, it soon appeared evident that industrial development, which it was originally deemed desirable to leave to the interplay of normal economic forces should be closely

112

connected to the other three aspects of regional development. It was, in fact, perhaps the most important.

Actually, in the revised fifteen-year plan, the percentage of appropriations has been modified as follows: 55 per cent for agriculture, 30 per cent for the infrastructure, 3 per cent for tourism, and 12 per cent for industry. This time, as can be seen, industry makes its official entrance on the scene.

It must be added that there is much elasticity in the administration of the funds allocated, and that their destination can be changed according to sudden needs or new situations. The percentages are only indicative of the importance given by the Cassa to the various sectors forming the over-all picture. Also, the repartition of the Cassa's activities must take into account geographic realities; therefore, it must endeavor to carry out its work over a vast geographical area, even when economic considerations alone might indicate a contrary course.

The decisive role attributed to agriculture at the beginning of the program was due to the assumption, subsequently partially revised in the light of experience, that any further improvement in the Mezzogiorno would be practically impossible without an over-all reform in land distribution and production methods in the area. It soon became clear, however, that, without powerful intervention in the industrial field, it would not be possible to attain these objectives and to foster a reasonably balanced growth of the regions concerned. Industry was the only activity capable of creating new jobs in great numbers. It should also be noted that the intervention in favor of industry is not as limited as it appears to be in the percentage of funds appropriated. Actually, it takes place in great part in forms not immediately translatable in monetary terms, such as granting of credit through the appropriate Institutes, tax facilities and subsidies allowed by the Government at the suggestion of the Cassa, and so forth.[40] The purpose of all these actions

[40] ". . . the policy of incentives [to industry] must become a decisive factor in orientating investments in the area of the South to eventually

is to stimulate the investor to put his money in enterprises located in the South of Italy, and thereby increase the percentage of investments in that part of the country which, otherwise, would never take place. For instance," . . . between 1951 and 1959, for every 100 lire of net investment, the growth of gross product has been only 29 lire in the South compared to 46 lire in the Center-North."[41] Special institutes for the granting of short-range credits have been created within the framework of the action by the Cassa aimed at fostering aid to industry. Also, through the Cassa, arrangements have been made to obtain loans and grants through the International Bank for Reconstruction and Development and the European Investment Bank. Two of the major State enterprises, Istituto Ricostruzione Industriale and Ente Nazionale Idrocarburi, in cooperation with the Cassa per il Mezzogiorno, are investing heavily in the South.[42] Actually, this is in accordance with a law whereby they are obliged to put 40 per cent of their new investments into the Mezzogiorno. Of course, such a high percentage is only possible because they are State enterprises and their activity is not always dictated by strictly economic considerations. But, in spite of this, they are administered with wisdom and have contributed much to improving the financial and economic state of Italy in the postwar period,

---

bring about a mechanism of self-development. This goal is required also because in the next few years, with the progressive growth of the European Common Market, it will become imperative for our economy to reach high technological and competitive levels in all sectors." *Confluenze Economiche*, No. 2, March–April 1962.

[41] *Le Monde* (Sélection Hebdomadaire), October 5, 1961.

[42] "The target aimed at, which consisted of averting the tendency of Italian industrial investments to concentrate in the North, has not had any appreciable success until now . . . but, by new laws, Italian public enterprises are called upon to also participate in the industrialization of the South. However, this in no way changes the basic doctrine of the policy pursued in the South, according to which the process of industrialization will attain satisfactory results only if an important increase in individual private investments is registered." CEE, *Rapport 1958*, p. 372.

which, in highly laudatory words, *Time*[43] defines as ". . . the biggest, most sustained comback that any European nation has made from World War II ashes. Germany has had its economic miracle, and France its postwar resurgence; both are still prospering, but at a slightly slower pace."

VARIOUS FORMS OF FINANCIAL HELP

As indicated above, several different institutes have been set up to provide financing for the various schemes of development. The main ones are described here.

1. *Consorzi di Bonifica* (Agricultural Cooperatives for Land Redemption) and *Enti di Riforma Fondiaria* (Organizations for Agrarian Reform) operate together within the Cassa per il Mezzogiorno to form a new agricultural infrastructure. Their main task is that of developing and subdividing the "latifundia" and of transforming them into small and medium-size farms, following a process which includes expropriation, reassignment, and improvement of the land through technical, economic, and financial assistance, by supplying agricultural equipment, and by the setting-up of cooperatives among farmers. This reform is completed by land redemption and irrigation, and improvements in the mountain regions and agricultural areas in general.

2. The *Consorzi di Zone Industriali* (Industrial Zone Cooperatives) are helped in their work, which aims at the creation and improvement of industrial zones, by exceptional procedures of various kinds—customs, and other fiscal and financial advantages. Thus, every enterprise either directly owned by the State, or controlled by it, must by law invest 40 per cent of its total annual investments in the South. Machinery, raw materials, etc., directed to Southern Italy for aiding in the industrialization of the area benefit from special tariff reductions. This reduction is also applied to transportation by sea from the continent to Sardinia of material, machines, etc., to build new industries there. Fur-

[43] January 12, 1962.

115

thermore, for a period of ten years, the State exempts new industrial enterprises from many forms of taxation.

3. *ISVEIMER* (Institute for Economic Development of Southern Italy) and its two parallel organizations dealing with Sicily, *IRFIS* (Regional Institute for Industrial Financing), and Sardinia, *CIS* (Industrial Credit for Sardinia), have been conducting most of the financial operations in connection with the program of development for Southern Italy. Actually, ISVEIMER is not a creation of the postwar years, although it was reorganized by Law No. 298 of April 11, 1953. In fact, it goes back to 1938, when it was founded by the Bank of Naples, although its scope of operations was very limited at that time. It started to be active again in 1954–55, together with IRFIS, while CIS began to function a year later.

Financial operations undertaken by the Institute are made possible through (a) an endowment fund, whose financial support is shared thus:[44] 40 per cent by the Cassa per il Mezzogiorno, 40 per cent by the Bank of Naples, and 20 per cent by various Savings Banks, People's Banks, etc.: (b) income from banking operations effected through Mediocredito (Credit Bank for Southern Italy); (c) a special fund created under Law No. 298, of April 11, 1953; (d) the issue of bonds; (e) long-term loans from the Treasury and reemployment of income from United States surplus; (f) part of the loans from the International Bank to the Cassa per il Mezzogiorno and other funds made available by various laws.

The Institute concentrates on medium-term loans for the acquisition of plants, for the modernization or the installation of factories, etc. Loans cover from 40 per cent to 70 per cent of the total amount to be invested. In special cases, the Cassa per il Mezzogiorno may even contribute directly to

[44] All data given here are taken from *Italian Affairs, Documents and Notes*, No. 5 (Rome: Information Service, Presidency of the Council of Ministers, Sept.–Oct. 1960). Hereinafter cited as *Italian Affairs*.

the immediate needs for capital, for other uses than those described, of the new factories. Interest on loans from ISVEIMER is generally 4 per cent up to 500 million lire; 5 per cent between 500 and 1,000 million lire, and 5.5 per cent for loans of more than one billion lire. Loans are made on a graduated basis, due consideration being given to the stage reached in reorganization and to the sums already paid for work completed and machinery purchased. The maximum period is fifteen years. Five years is the average, especially for loans not exceeding 10 million lire granted to small industry.

The industries that have most benefitted from the activities of ISVEIMER are those dealing with building materials, pottery and ceramics, crystal and glass, canned food, paper, motor vehicles and machinery of various kinds, metallurgy, and textiles. The aids and encouragement offered by ISVEIMER have been extended not only to local firms, but also to those already operating in the North which were planning to open branches in the Mezzogiorno.

4. Various forms of subsidy are granted either directly by the State or by the Cassa per il Mezzogiorno. They apply in general to the creation of new industrial activities, to the setting up or improving of hotel installations (up to 50 per cent of the total cost), and to mines, prospecting, and research (20 per cent to 40 per cent). Different and even more favorable provisions are granted in the administratively autonomous regions of Sicily and Sardinia.

5. A new private institution was created in 1955—*ISAP*, Istituto per lo Sviluppo delle Attività Produttive (Institute for the Development of Productive Activities), with an initial share capital of 2 billion lire.

HOW THE CASSA WORKS

It is advisable to describe the way in which the operations of the Cassa are carried out before looking back on the first dozen years of its existence. They take place in the following

117

order: annual investment planning, project planning, project screening and approval, contract awards, and execution of work.

The first, and certainly most important, stage, is annual investment planning: directives are drafted which will channel the sum allocated for a particular fiscal year into all the projects that the Cassa will undertake that year. It coordinates the various projects, so that there can be maximum efficiency and minimum waste. Also, it must take account of the geographical distribution of projects in order to equalize activity in all areas.

The next stage is that of project planning: here the Cassa comes up against limitations in the equipment of the executive agencies and in the quality and quantity of designers. Unfortunately, this state of affairs is not the exception, and this explains the difference between the total number of works planned and the number of works actually carried out. Since the constant preoccupation of the Cassa has been improvement of project planning, sizeable sums have been appropriated for study and research.

The following stage is project screening: in this, the Cassa evaluates the projects planned and the degree to which they fit into the general picture. Of these, some are unconditionally approved, some are sent back to be revised, and some are not deemed worthy of further consideration. Most projects are approved, but it must be pointed out that the Cassa frequently cuts the estimated expenses, i.e., re-budgets them according to its own criteria.

FIRST RESULTS—AN APPRECIATION

The Cassa started its work in 1950, although in actual practice the first concrete interventions took place in 1951 after a period of orientation due to the completely new organization and personnel. "A unique criterion presided over its creation and also its enactment: to promote, in the Mezzogiorno, the development of a self-propelling [*sic,*

118

auto-propulsiva] economy."[45] In a twelve-year period it obviously is not possible to obtain decisive results and the complete structural overhaul of the economy of the South which it is desirable to achieve. However, it may be noted that, in this period, the average rate of growth both for income and for consumption has been 4.5 per cent, which is quite an achievement for the Mezzogiorno; and it must be noted too that this result is quite important in view of the fact that industry is still sparse, so that it derives mostly from public investments. We should also note, however, "the difference in proportion still existing between private investment and public investment in the two regions of Italy. In fact, following the weakness of industrial investments, which in Italy are essentially private, the total of private investments, amounting in the North to about 75 per cent of the total, can in the South be estimated at only 40 per cent."[46] As far as over-all progress is concerned, we find that the North has proceeded at about the same speed, or maybe a little faster, so that the gap between the two parts of Italy is still as wide as ever, if not wider, and the social tensions between the two halves still persist.[47]

Lastly, three important phenomena assume relevance in an appreciation of the results of twelve years of active existence of the Cassa: the infrastructure has definitely improved; agriculture is much better organized, due to land reform, insufficient as it may have been,[48] and to the improvement and redemption projects; and finally there has been the

[45] Pescatore, *op.cit.*, p. 18.

[46] CEE, *Rapport 1958*, p. 371.

[47] "The considerable economic progress realized in 1960, and the very important improvement in employment linked to this progress, have not narrowed the gap between the levels of development and employment in the North and the South of the country. The progressive reduction of this gap remains, for Italy, the fundamental objective of its structural policy." CEE, *Exposé 1960*, p. 42.

[48] ". . . it should be remembered that land reform only accounts for a negligible portion (3 per cent) of the cultivated area." *Rapport 1958*, p. 409.

birth and survival, under strictly self-supporting financing, of some sizeable industrial units. As a matter of fact, it is a deliberate policy on the part of the Administration of the Cassa, to foster the growth of "poles of industrial development" or, at least, of "nuclei of growth," to attract in the long run new capital and industries to the South.

All this, however, is far from having put the South in a condition to survive if abandoned to market forces, or even to fight with any chance of success; this is even truer in the framework of the European Economic Community.[49] Furthermore, all these problems are aggravated by the abnormal demographic growth. However, the action of the Italian Government will persist in order to alleviate, if not to solve, the problem, while waiting for a decisive and, it is hoped, final attack to be made by the European Community as a whole.

A development in this connection is the creation of a National Programming Commission whose ". . . specific task is to eliminate regional imbalances," and to accelerate and coordinate the development of Southern Italy. Its approach to the problem of development of the whole area should be modern and bold, with stress on the push towards industrialization of the Mezzogiorno in order to find employment *in loco* for the Meridionali and to raise the standard of living in Southern Italy to equal that of Northern Italy.

The financial year 1961–62, which ended on June 30, 1962, marked the conclusion of the twelfth year of existence

[49] "The South has certainly made some steps forward by itself, but these have been either by creating the infrastructure, which does not entail creating new jobs, or by setting up some industrial plants on a very local scale, and these have already been translated into a sensible improvement of the overall situation. Also, whereas a remarkable increase of employment and productivity has taken place in the industrial North–West, and notable progress has been accomplished, in these two sectors, in the North-East and Center, the South of the peninsula and the Islands have accumulated a further lag and continued to find in emigration one of the principal outlets to their difficulties." CEE, *Exposé 1960*, p. 5, intro.

of the Cassa. A balance-sheet of its activity in this period can now be made.

The number of projects approved is 217,344, for a total amount of 1.791 billion lire. Of these projects, 13,712, for an amount of 1.224 billion lire, have been used in the private sector of the economy. Contracts for public works have been awarded for an amount of 1.146 billion lire. Projects completed by the end of the first twelve years of activity represent a value of 282 billion lire.

We shall now examine briefly the results of the Cassa's activity throughout the first dozen years of its life, sector by sector.

Land Reclamation and Agricultural Transformation

As the problem of the South is essentially an agricultural one, the Cassa has been guided accordingly in its planning. An improvement in general agricultural techniques and in agricultural output is necessary if the standard of living of the population is to be raised, and impetus given to industrial and commercial activities.

Productivity in the plains depends to a considerable extent on the state of drainage and water distribution in the surrounding terrain. Also, agrarian reform, or the breaking up of large areas (with specific cultivation) into relatively small plots, must be accomplished together with a program of land transformation, i.e., cultivation methods must change and new marketing and processing facilities for agricultural produce must be created.

Not all the agricultural problems of the South have been covered by the Cassa; the State deals directly with many of them, but mutual action by the State and Cassa is coordinated and unnecessary duplications are thus, in general, avoided. The guiding criterion for division of responsibility is that the State takes care of the areas where conditions are normal, or near normal (by southern Italian standards) while the Cassa provides for zones more urgently in need of

121

assistance, or where there is greater need of capital investment on a considerable scale, or where the extreme destitution calls for vigorous and immediate measures.

The areas in which the Cassa takes action may be divided into three groups: reclamation districts, flood and erosion control districts, and zones of land reform.

Two criteria guided the formulation of the Cassa's policies in this first period, as far as agricultural production is concerned: (1) to carry out projects already decided on (before the creation of the Cassa) by the Ministry of Agriculture and inherited by the Cassa; (2) to conceive of the works always as a function of the main objective of the Cassa for the entire period of its existence, so that a *steady* increase in production and income can be achieved. To bring about this increase, prominence had to be given to irrigation, and the only feasible plan was to collect the winter waters in reservoirs in difficult geological terrain.[50] A number of problems arose in connection with this, and are still being faced. Also, soil erosion and flood control have been given special consideration, as main factors related to the whole investment program. Roadworks, electricity grids, and community centers connected with land reclamation and agricultural transformation have been given high priority. Also reforestation, both in coastal lands and in mountainous terrain has been extensively carried out, though it will obviously be some time before the results can be known.

A total of 6,643 reclamation schemes, for an amount of 581 billion lire, have been approved; 6,506 for an amount of 554 billion lire, have been commissioned; projects for 302 billion lire have been completed—all concerned with land

[50] "The completion of irrigation works represents only the first stage of the structural transformation of Southern agriculture. Upon a vigilant and continuous adaptation of these works to the real exigencies of agriculture, through the best utilization of irrigation water, depends the possibility of introducing and consolidating more productive instruments." Cassa, *Bilancio 1956–57*, p. 40.

reclamation. A very large number of projects has been approved for agricultural transformation: 201,572, amounting to more than 443 billion lire. Of these, 259 billion lire have already been spent on completed works. Furthermore, a sum of about 5 billion lire has been used for financing the construction of 212 silos.

Also deserving mention is a special effort made by the Cassa to train a number of young people to become agricultural specialists. In the first dozen years since the Cassa's creation, 21 Institutes for Professional Agricultural Specialization have been added to the few already existing. These coordinate 129 professional agricultural schools, most of them already functioning in permanent premises. Each school can accept about 100 students.

The regulation of mountain river basins is also one of the many activities of the Cassa, related to agriculture. A total of 2,084 projects has been approved, for an amount of 57 billion lire; works commissioned, 2,056 for 56 billion lire; projects already completed equal to 41 billion lire.

It is interesting to quote a few figures about the accomplishments of the Fund concerning land redemption and agricultural improvements. More than 4,300 kilometers of water-collecting canals have been dug; land in excess of 700,000 hectares has been drained or otherwise redeemed. More than 6,200 kilometers of irrigation canals have been built. Roads have been opened in former swamp areas for a total of 6,100 kilometers; 97,000 hectares have been reforested.

At the end of 1961, projects for 567,618 rural houses, storehouses, and constructions of various kinds in the countryside had been approved, as well as 3,228 small plants connected with agricultural production; 6,430 kilometers of country roads; 60,494 wells, rural aqueducts, pumping stations for irrigation, etc.; and 2,890 kilometers of electric power lines. Several thousand more projects, covering about 600,000 hectares, have been approved, and 12,783 selected

123

bulls have been distributed among Southern Italian farmers. Finally, 7,800 kilometers of aqueducts have been put into operation and 1,500 reservoirs with a capacity of more than 1,070,000 cubic meters.

Aqueducts and Sewers

The main criterion of the aqueduct program is that of providing running water for most of the inhabited centers of the South. An over-all project was planned at the beginning of the Cassa to coordinate the many projects needed, although it was assumed that the funds allocated probably would not be sufficient to realize some of them. The planners thus had a general scheme of what needed to be done, and only the most important and urgent projects were selected. The total funds allocated were 165 billion lire, whereas the entire project, if carried out, would have cost an estimated 250 billion lire. The funds actually available will, nevertheless, make possible a supply of water to an area inhabited by about thirteen million people.

For the execution of the work involved, the Cassa generally requests the help of the governmental authority, but sometimes it carries out the project itself, as it has for some of the big schemes. As far as sewers are concerned, the activities of the Cassa have been directed mainly to important urban centers, or to places of particular tourist interest.

By the end of the first twelve years, the work performed can be thus summarized: 1,741 projects approved, amounting to over 242 billion lire; projects commissioned, 1,654 amounting to 228 billion lire. Of these, projects amounting to 113 billion lire have been completed. The Cassa has also granted sums of money for building certain aqueducts and sewers, for a total amount of 5,514 billion lire.

Roads, Railroads, and Ports

One of the principal reasons for the backwardness of the Meridione was the pitiful state of its road network. Therefore, one of the most urgent problems of the Cassa was that of substantially improving the existing road system. In 1950, 52 per cent of the roads were properly surfaced in the North, while in the South the percentage was only 13.6. The Cassa tackled the problem with energy and efficiency, and the number made a spectacular jump forward to about 70 per cent in the South. The extent of roads improved was 14,600 kilometers; newly built roads exceed 2,600 kilometers.[51]

Work performed on the roads has had the highest order of priority. It is easy to see the reason for this: the entire economic progress of the Mezzogiorno is closely related to the state of its roads, and no noticeable advance could be possible without a great improvement of the system.

The Cassa first brought the roads to a minimum of six meters in width, plus embankment. The course of many roads was also improved, as well as their foundations. The road program has been very carefully planned and the factors dominating it have been strict coordination and economy. Bridge construction, insofar as roads are concerned, has been the object of particular attention, with full use being made of modern techniques.

In the first twelve years 2,334 projects, amounting to 185 billion lire, were approved; projects commissioned were 647, for a total of about 87 billion lire. Projects for an amount of about 78 billion lire are already complete.

The Cassa also participates, in its own right, in certain projects of the F.F.S.S. (Italian State Railroads) considered essential for the development of the area. The condition of the railroads being utterly inadequate in the South—much more so now in a European framework—it has been decided to push a major effort of modernization and improvement.

---

[51] "Compared to an average road density of 0.562 km. per square kilometer for the whole of Italy in 1950, the Mezzogiorno had an average of 0.354 kilometers; density in Sardinia decreased to 0.199 while in the North of Italy it attained 0.827. Furthermore, the general situation was not only characterized by the lack of roads, but also by their poor condition." Pescatore, *op.cit.*, p. 35.

125

Many lines have been electrified, some have had a second track added, and junctions, switches, etc., all have been improved. Also, a certain number of projects for the improvement of existing seaports have been accomplished, these being essential to the progress of the Mezzogiorno.

The figures for both railroad and seaport projects are the following: 213 approved, for an amount of more than 113 billion lire; 199 commissioned, for about 87 billion lire; projects for about 78 billion lire have already been completed.

Tourism

Whereas the main work of the Cassa takes place in the agricultural field, this by no means exhausts its activities. An important share is directed to the development of tourism and industrialization and to the provision of credit facilities.

The untold treasures of art, deriving from the passing of successive civilizations in the South, the Mediterranean climate, and the magnificent natural scenery, all provide a splendid background for tourist activities. These resources, however, have been only partially exploited in the past, due principally to deficiencies in communications and in accommodations. But today, with the continuous expansion of tourism, especially intra-European, it would have been illogical to overlook this source of high income. "This is a sector whose importance in the national picture in general, and in the area of Southern Italy in particular, has grown in these last years with a pace absolutely unknown in any other activity. Such tremendous development which, luckily, shows no sign of slowing down, is productive not only of beneficial social consequences, but also of substantial economic effects."[52]

The Cassa decided to tackle the problem and render accessible the main places of scenic, archaeological, or artistic beauty to the main tourist currents. It also planned to restore many of the art treasures, so that they could be

[52] Cassa, *Bilancio 1956–57*, p. 94.

appreciated in full by the visitors. These projects are closely coordinated between themselves, and also integrated with certain other projects, such as the building of roads to places of tourist importance, of hotels, restaurants, etc.

Throughout its activity, the Cassa also dealt with such different items as natural grottoes and their accessibility and exploitation for tourist purposes, and the promotion of thermal springs, especially at Ischia and Castellammare. Furthermore, the Cassa has dealt with the construction of sewers in tourist centers, and brought about considerable improvement. These measures are closely coordinated with plans for the supply of water to these towns.

In this field, 697 projects have been approved, amounting to about 47 billion lire; 647 have been commissioned, amounting to more than 43 billion lire; projects completed amount to some 23 billion lire. The whole amount at the disposal of the Cassa for help to tourist activities was originally 30 billion lire. This sum was successively increased to 40 billion by Law No. 634 of July 29, 1957, to 50,980 billion by Law No. 622 of July 24, 1959, and to 64 billion by special authority of the Council of Ministers, through a reallocation of funds.

Industrialization Credits

While the purpose of the Cassa is in the main that of aiding agriculture and other activities, in order to permanently raise the sources of income of the people of Southern Italy, aid to industry has also come to have an increasingly prominent part in the administration of the Cassa. This aid is exercised mainly in the form of industrialization credits;[53] these have been given to diverse enterprises operating in a wide variety of fields. And, whenever possible, the construction and improvement of plants to process agricultural products has been encouraged.

The Cassa's credits are granted mainly through the afore-

[53] Law No. 166 of March 22, 1952, authorized the Cassa to finance industries.

127

mentioned regional credit institutes of ISVEIMER, IRFIS and CIS. They are also effected, in part, through the disbursement of large foreign loan funds.

In the over-all framework of assistance to industry for the general development of the South, the main concern of the Cassa has been and is the financial support of the various enterprises. The field covered includes processing of agricultural produce, light and heavy industry, power stations, etc.

Following Law No. 634 of July 29, 1957, the Cassa has granted sinking fund loans for more than 118 billion lire to 1,837 small and medium industries.

Other Types of Credit

Other types of credit extend to a wide range of activities; especially important are the agricultural and the hotel credits.

The Cassa follows three systems as far as agricultural credits are concerned; an outright grant, covering 38 per cent of the amount estimated as necessary to carry on a certain project; a 3 per cent loan for the entire cost, plus a 2.5 per cent contribution to loan service; a loan on the same terms for 60 per cent of the cost, plus a straight grant, within certain limits. By June 30, 1962, agricultural subsidies of the first type had been granted to a large number of applicants.

Considerable impetus has also been given to the construction of hotels; actually the shortcomings of the hotel industry, together with the lack of communications, have been the two principal deterrents to a wide expansion of tourist traffic in most of the South. The Cassa gave considerable assistance to the construction of the Jolly chain of hotels in places "off the beaten track" and to other enterprises having similar objectives."[54]

Projects of different kinds have also been financed by the

[54] This was achieved mainly by loans, with an interest of 3 per cent yearly for a maximum of 20 years.

Cassa; for instance, 7,153 billion lire have been granted to small artisan establishments; 9,897 billion lire to the fishing industry, in response to 5,633 requests. School construction has also formed the object of contributions by the Cassa: 5,423 billion lire have already been granted. Also, 679 projects for the construction of kindergartens have been approved, for an amount of 10,824 billion lire.

ECONOMIC AND SOCIAL EFFECTS OF THE CASSA'S ACTIVITIES

Statistical data can give only a partial picture of the rebirth of the Meridione, accomplished mainly through the Cassa per il Mezzogiorno and related activities. As far as its effect on the basic problem of unemployment is concerned, this can be deduced from the following figures (valid as of May 31, 1962): 287 million workdays have resulted from projects directly connected with the Cassa. A majority of these workdays emanate from agricultural transformation—about 104 million; then follows land redemption, 64 million; roadworks, 24 million; mountain river basins, about 22 million; aqueducts, 16 million; industry, 7 million; railroads and seaports, 6 million; tourism, 3 million; silos, 648,000. Agrarian reform has produced 39.2 million workdays.

It seems that the problem is now really being faced and an attempt made to solve it with vision; the first positive results are already at hand. Moreover, it seems that the people who are directly concerned have faith in the accomplishments and over-all program of the Cassa. Of course, this does not mean that there are not shortcomings in its work, nor that the public interest is always given priority over private interests.[55] It must be remembered that the lack of sufficient numbers of skilled workers, the inadequacy of the communications network, the traditional attachment

[55] "Many observations could be made on the program and on the activities of the Cassa . . . but those on the inadequacy of its forecasts, on the mistaken ruling criteria, on the dilution and uncertainty of budgeting are the most important." Article "Cassa per il Mezzogiorno in Calabria," *Cronache Meridionali*, March 1958.

129

to old methods of land cultivation and of industrial production, the general state of backwardness, and many other related factors, are not conducive to an easy development of the program of the Cassa. However, in the light of its achievements thus far, trust must be accorded to it. It is to be hoped that, in spite of handicaps, the Cassa will carry out its task successfully. Years ago, a Meridionalista, G. Caizzi, stated: "The essential question is to know whether the Enterprise (the Cassa) will live on . . . or, if one day we shall talk of the last, expensive, deluding attempt to galvanize the Mezzogiorno with superficial special laws."[56] Now, after fourteen years of operation, it seems certain that the Cassa has brought a substantial contribution to the advancement accomplished by the South thus far.

[56] G. Caizzi, *Antologia della Questione Meridionale* (Turin: Einaudi, 1955) p. 58.

CHAPTER III

Freedom of Circulation within the Community and Financial Institutions

We shall refer the reader to the Appendices for information about the European Common Market, its history, its advantages, and a synopsis of the Treaties. Here our analysis will be confined to the problems deriving from regional underdevelopment within the Community. The sections of the Treaties of Rome and Paris concerning movement of capital, goods, services, and workers throughout the whole area are particularly relevant.

> It has become more and more evident that the great disparities existing between the levels of employment and of income inside the Community will never be eliminated, if it is just left to the play of economic forces to determine a perpetual flux of migrations to correct the situation, which effect has been proved by experience to be completely insufficient. The goal sought after, i.e. the progressive reduction of the gap between the less-favored regions, requires that a flux, in the opposite direction, of factors of production, that is of capital and skilled workers, be directed from the latter to the former, so that there develop, for local workers, more satisfactory possibilities of employment.[1]

It is clear, therefore, that the application of the principles of free circulation within the Community must be tempered by special provisions and in actual practice they must be regulated in such a way that very grave potential dangers to the less-developed regions may be avoided.

[1] CEE, *Exposé 1961*, intro.

Let us examine, therefore, this basic aspect of the Treaties' provisions insofar as the underdeveloped regions are concerned.

Principle of Free Movement of Workers

Article 48 of the Treaty states that by the end of the transition period free circulation of workers within the Community shall be assured, and continues by proclaiming that no worker shall be discriminated against on account of nationality and that he shall have the same financial and social benefits as those obtaining for local workers.[2]

However, the actual implementation of these provisions of the Treaty may be subject to several different interpretations; there are also many obstacles, apart from legal ones, to the principle of free movement, and it is not at all certain that these can all be overcome by the end of the transition period. We shall now examine the present situation and discuss some of the benefits and drawbacks to be found in a free movement of workers.

The Necessity for Movement of Workers

Decentralization of Industry

The fundamental reason for movement of workers is the old basic one of supply and demand—certain areas, heavily

[2] Even before the Common Market came into being, OEEC had realized the importance for the development of the European economy and the reconstruction of Europe which would be given by a free movement of workers within the area. Practical steps were taken to this effect. Following a recommendation of the Council on March 28, 1952, OEEC adopted in October 1953 a plan aimed at reducing the obstacles raised by the various national administrations against the movement of workers from one country to another and the granting to them of work permits. These new rules came into effect on January 1, 1954. However, it must be pointed out that they had very little effect. In its *Seventh Annual Report* (Paris, 1955), para. 110, OEEC states: "While in the majority of states employment is very high and certain sectors lack labor, above all skilled labor, the common advantages of immigration originating from the countries where unemployment and underemployment still create great difficulties, are more and more manifest. Nevertheless, movements of labor in Europe are still very limited."

industrialized, are in need of more workers; other areas with little industry and high demographic growth, have an excess labor force.[3]

The problem of overcentralization of industry and consequent imbalance in geographical distribution is an important one in the Community. As we have noted, there are great concentrations of industry in certain areas—the large zone along the Rhine, the North Italian plain, the area around Paris, Northern France, etc.

> The national economies are far from constituting an entirely homogeneous ensemble. The disparity of resources in different regions, the attraction exercised by certain centers, the cumulative effect of industrial development, which gives rise to the creation by old establishments of new units attracted by the proximity of supplies and outlets, and finally by the quality of labor, provoke important disparities in the distribution of activity and in the standard of living within the same nation.[4]

This means that in the rich, industrialized regions there is normally an intense demand for labor, and as these regions become more and more prosperous, the underdeveloped areas become proportionately and progressively poorer. The subject of imbalance and the necessity for over-all Government planning to correct it is discussed elsewhere in this study. Here, we need only stress once more that the problem must be tackled as a whole, taking into account the conditions prevailing throughout the Community. In the case of industries which have more need of labor than of special natural resources, dispersion from the "poles of

[3] "European expansion supposes that, according to the choices made, it should be possible to estimate in what measure and in what places surplus labor will appear which will have to be re-employed. *A priori*, the mind turns immediately to the underemployed agricultural workers and we are again in the midst of the problem of under-developed zones." *Réalités*, No. 161, June 1959.

[4] CEE, *Rapport 1958*, p. 51.

growth" presents no insurmountable problem. Industries may be granted special tax exemptions, credit facilities, subsidies, etc., to induce them to establish branches elsewhere.

An important role in attracting industry to the under-developed areas can also be played by the State-owned rail-roads under a policy of cheap transportation; those products which benefitted from low transport rates at the place of origin should also benefit from equally low rates in the coun-tries of transit and destination. One of the major obstacles to a dispersion of industry has hitherto been the high cost of transportation, both of raw materials and of finished goods, to the large markets, and also the high cost of power. There-fore, cheap transportation from the factory to the market should be complemented by cheap transportation of energy-producing materials (coal and oil) from the mines and refineries to the factory. Furthermore in years to come, there will be a greater use of atomic energy in the underdeveloped areas which will also help industry.

So long as the cost of the finished product is no higher than it would be if produced in the regions where they usually operate, some of the large private organizations may be persuaded to establish branches in the underdeveloped regions.[5] It will also be in their own interest to contribute to

[5] The late Pope John XXIII, in the encyclical: "Pacem in Terris" (text reprinted in *New York Times*, April 11, 1963), expressed the concept " . . . that, whenever possible, the work to be done should be taken to the workers, not vice versa. In this way, a possibility of a better future is offered to many persons without being forced to leave their own environment in order to seek residence elsewhere, which almost always entails the heartache of separation and difficult periods of adjustment and social integration." Similar ideas have also been formulated by people in positions of high responsibility in the EEC. Thus Robert Marjolin stated: "It is the industry that must go to the workers, and not the contrary." (*Le Monde*, December 10, 1961.) The advantages of possessing an unused pool of labor, which will attract new industries, rather than having to be moved to the job centers, are also extolled by *La Stampa*, December 23, 1961: "Our availability of labor, once excessive, is still such as to justify numerous new initiatives in all sectors of activity. However, the reserves are rapidly thinning out . . . the natural increase in population is now

raising the standard of living in these areas and thus indirectly increase sales of their products.

However, even if this hoped-for decentralization comes about, with subsequent increased industrialization in the underdeveloped areas, a certain excess of supply over demand for labor is likely to exist for some time to come. Conversely, the already industrialized areas, to meet the needs of the rapidly expanding Common Market, will need more and more workers.

As technological progress becomes more widespread in agriculture, this will mean that fewer workers will be employed in this sector and they will become available for the secondary and tertiary sectors. Some of them may find employment in the regional centers which are in the process of being industrialized. They will be drawn by higher wages and the attractions offered by city life and, at the same time, will still be in a familiar environment and within easy reach of their families and homes. A diminishing need for agricultural workers is one of the sure signs of economic progress, and it is hoped that continuous improvement in this direction will be possible.[6]

POSITION OF THE ITALIAN WORKER

We have discussed the reasons for underdevelopment in Italy and pointed out that the only escape thus far from the poverty and hopelessness in which these people lived was emigration. Before World War I, a massive emigration took place mainly to the New World; if this escape had not been possible, the only alternative for most people would have been a standard of living barely above the subsistence level.

limited to just covering the new needs for labor. Much foreign investment is attracted to Italy, *especially to the South, because of the abundance of available labor.*" (emphasis supplied)

[6] "The very essence of economic development is the decrease in the rate of agricultural employment in relation to total employment." (paraphrased) Benjamin Higgins, *Economic Development*, (New York: Norton, 1959), p. 2.

Aside from this permanent, overseas emigration, there was both a permanent and seasonal movement to other European countries, and, of course, internal migration within Italy —always from South to North. After World War I overseas emigration slowed almost to a trickle and consequently other safety valves had to be found. To aggravate the situation, the Fascist regime, for reasons of internal politics, not only discouraged emigration[7] but, by a deluge of propaganda, encouraged a rise in the birth rate through the inducement of a progressive scale of family allowances. With the rapidly growing population as its excuse, the Government then pursued a policy of overseas expansion justifying it by the necessity of finding room for all these people. These incentives were especially efficacious as far as the peasants of Southern Italy were concerned and some families reached the point where the "new-born" allowances from the State became a more or less permanent feature of their annual budget. The Fascist government also discouraged the movement of workers within Italy.

Different characteristics are found in the pattern of Italian emigration after World War II. Emigration assumed at this time a somewhat European character in view of the restrictions maintained by overseas areas. The destruction brought about by the war in practically all European areas made the need for reconstruction extremely urgent and produced a demand for workers, especially construction workers, with which Italy fortunately was well-supplied, particularly in the poorer regions of the South. However, economic difficulties did not allow a prompt and massive reconstruction effort; this started only after American aid was poured into Europe. The countries which actually needed certain kinds of workers were compelled to limit the numbers of immigrants they could accept. Agricultural workers were also

[7] Even so, hundreds of thousands of Italians managed to find their way abroad, not always legally. Particularly noteworthy was the agricultural emigration to South-West France.

needed, especially in France, and many of them came from Italy.

Since the formation of the Common Market, the pattern is once more changing. Improving economic conditions in the regions which used to furnish the highest percentage of emigrants, i.e., Southern Italy, and particularly Sicily, are offering some prospects to the workers, especially the young people who in the past constituted the backbone of emigration.[8] These prospects include new job openings, better social security protection, etc.[9] To these economic factors, a variety of social factors must be added. The urge to stay at home among their own people with whom they share a

[8] Even so, the percentage of decrease in unemployment is still lower in the regions of Southern Italy (Sardinia being the exception) than in those of the North. Another important factor, which greatly magnifies the difference, is shown in the fact that part of the decrease in the number of jobless in the South is simply due to their moving to the North, or abroad, especially to other Community countries. The figures give the total numbers of workers registered in the placement offices of the various areas of Italy (in parentheses the percentage of the decrease from 1960 to 1961):

	(thousands)
Piedmont, Liguria	77.2 (−14.2)
Lombardy	98.3 (−14.3)
Venetias	139.8 (−10.5)
Emilia-Romagna, Marche	204.0 (−12.5)
Tuscany-Umbria-High Latium	94.5 (− 9.8)
Abruzzi	44.9 (− 9.7)
Rome and province	35.5 (− 4.9)
Low Latium, Campania	238.1 (− 4.1)
Apulia, Basilicata, Calabria	279.8 (− 6.0)
Sicily	158.9 (− 8.5)
Sardinia	35.9 (−14.0)
Total	1,406.9 (− 9.1)

Source: CEE, *Exposé 1961*, p. 46.

[9] The Italian unions are conducting an intensive campaign of penetration and persuasion in the South among the local population. First of all, they are trying to keep the workers in their native regions and are endeavoring to increase job opportunities there. Secondly, they are attempting to infuse in the workers a sense of their own rights as workers so that if they go abroad they will be aware of the dangers of exploitation.

common language, as well as traditions and an outlook on life, is definitely stronger than the attraction of emigration, except where the latter becomes necessary due to lack of opportunities *in loco*.[10] The great cities of the North, Milan and Turin, under the impact of the Common Market are enjoying "boom" conditions and can absorb many workers from the South.[11] The Fascist law against freedom of movement within Italy was recently repealed and hence workers can now legally reside in any city. Previously, it was necessary to obtain a residence permit—available in theory to all—but it was the practice of the authorities not to give a residence permit unless the applicant had a job; however, since jobs could not be obtained without a residence permit, the result was a vicious, unending circle.[12]

---

[10] "It must be admitted that what could be called the 'preference for the place' arouses conflicts in man's choice between the way of life and the standard of life. An individual will accept being underclassed and consequently underpaid in a place in which he likes to live, rather than obtain a job to which his qualifications entitle him in a region that he thinks hostile." J. M. Jeanneney, *Forces et Faiblesses de l'Economie Française* (Paris: Colin, 1956), p. 250. And *Communauté Européenne*, No. 7, July 1963: "The pursuit of economic growth must not imply for millions of men the obligation to leave their country, to cut all social ties and to emigrate to the regions of industrial concentration to find a livelihood."

[11] However, the integration of the Southern workers with the local people is often painfully slow and difficult. "Pitiful sights occur in Turin and Milan when people from the South arrive by train to seek jobs in these boom towns. The newcomers carry all their possessions in a cardboard box, find homes only in a form of southern ghetto and face difficulty even in making themselves understood by the Northerners." *New York Times*, September 18, 1961.

[12] "The geographic mobility of workers inside their country has been facilitated by, among others, the law of February 10, 1961, which, having repealed the regulations limiting transfer to urban centers, has permitted internal migrations from one region to the other and from one city to the other, thus insuring the effective use of the right to work and of the right to choose the place of work according to the principles affirmed by the Italian Constitution, by the conventions of the I.L.O., by the treaty of Rome (free circulation of labor in the six countries of the Community) and by the European Social Charter." *Le Monde Diplomatique*, February 1964.

Now, instead of seeing great numbers of emigrants from the South lining up outside factories or anywhere else where there was a likelihood of a job, we have the quite different situation of the demand exceeding the supply, at least as far as skilled workers are concerned. To the emigrants from Sicily or Calabria the situation seems unbelievable; now, if they have a minimum of skill, their services are promptly accepted.[13] Factory agents meet the trains arriving from the South or, working through brotherhoods of Southern Italian workers resident in the North,[14] even go to their lodging places to meet them soon after their arrival and discuss the terms they can offer.

[13] An example of the scarcity of skilled workers is illustrated by the fact that, in the *New York Times* of January 10, 1962, an advertisement appeared which only a short time ago would have seemed unthinkable: a large Italian industrial group (the well-known Ente Nazionale Idrocarburi) invited "all Italian technicians and workmen resident abroad to contribute to your country's economic development. . . . Facilities will be granted for repatriation." It shows how urgent is the need for *skilled* people, even in that reservoir of labor which is Italy, and that conditions offered them must be good, if they can compare with those these workers now enjoy in the U.S. The desperate need for technicians should spur the large masses of unskilled labor now plaguing Southern Italy—particularly the young people—to take up a specialization, no matter what personal sacrifice they might have to make to achieve it. And a confirmation of this is given by *Le Monde* (Sélection Hebdomadaire) of July 31, 1963: "What illustrates even better the change which has taken place in this domain (that of unemployment in Italy) is that an Italian mechanical workshop has applied for—and obtained—authorization to import Greek workers."

[14] An interesting and characteristic trait of Southern Italians abroad, and even within Italy itself, is a sense of clannishness which keeps them together and, in the usual pattern of organized societies, helps them to find jobs throughout the period of adaptation and even afterwards. First of all, a "beach-head" is established and then those who have succeeded in settling themselves fairly quickly call their friends and relatives and generally form compact communities. This phenomenon, of course, is by no means common only to Southern Italians; however, it is interesting to note the marked difference between Southern and Northern Italians once they are abroad. Whereas the latter have much more tendency to disperse in their adopted lands and assimilate with the local population, the former generally stick together and it may take generations before they become fully assimilated in the new country.

For some of these workers who go to the North, this is just a steppingstone: after they have become more skilled and more accustomed to life in an industrialized society, they re-emigrate, most of them to West Germany, but also to France, Switzerland, Belgium, etc. The demand for skilled and semiskilled workers is now becoming so heavy that the supply will eventually dry up.[15] It is therefore important to try to tap the mass of unskilled workers in the South and in this connection the Federal Government of Germany and the Dutch Government are doing remarkable work in Southern Italy by directly financing centers for the professional training of unskilled workers.[16] Other Western European countries have also set up recruitment offices in various parts of Italy to hire labor; local employers are becoming increasingly resentful of this since they need labor themselves.[17] The economic press in Italy is aware of this

[15] This, however, is not likely to happen in the very near future. "As far as Italy is concerned, in spite of the sizeable increase in employment and the important diminution in unemployment that have characterized the last four or five years, particularly 1960, there is still a good way to go before it attains a level of employment comparable to that of the other countries and, with still overabundant reserves of labor it remains an important base for emigration. There is no doubt, however, that the evolution towards full employment is now on the march and there can be uncertainty only in the number of years it will take to attain it." CEE, *Exposé 1960*, intro.

[16] ". . . the German Government has let it be known that it is ready to contribute up to three million marks to the financing of a program of professional training of Italian workers destined to be employed in the Federal Republic—a program elaborated jointly between the German and Italian Governments under the auspices of the Executive of the Common Market. This initiative, characteristic of the European Community policy, completes the preparation of a program covering about ten thousand people, of which the first part— especially concerning the Netherlands—is already on the way to execution. Fifty per cent of the financing for this is assured by the Social Fund of the Common Market, 25 per cent by the Italian Government and 25 per cent by the recipient country." *Communauté Européenne*, No. 3, March 1961.

[17] Actually, a peculiar game has been going on for some time between foreign firms which are trying to hire Italian skilled labor, and Italian companies which want to repatriate Italian workers resident

fact, and it recurrently carries on a campaign against the principle of free movement of labor under the Treaty at the end of the transition period, saying it will not work. The once-despised Southern Italian workers who have some skills are now being fought over and sought after; those who would once work for a pittance are now becoming aware of their rights and demanding better and better working conditions.[18] Some Italian trade union leaders are vigorously campaigning for "European" salaries,[19] equal pay for equal work for men and women, for a common social security system, and for all the benefits deriving from an alignment of salaries and working conditions within the Community, based on the best prevailing ones at the time. In this, they have the letter, as well as the spirit, of the Treaty with them; in fact, Article 48, paragraph 2, states that free circulation "entails the abolition of any discrimination, based on nationality, between the workers of the Member States, as

---

abroad. For instance, according to the *New York Times* of October 19, 1963, "Italian companies are hiring Italian workers in West Germany. . . . Italy needs some of them back. . . . The return flow is mainly made up of skilled workers. It is said to be no more than a trickle, but there are reports that it has already caused some friction with German employers who count on these Italians to relieve their own tight situation. This reverse recruiting of Italian workers has been under way for only a few months, and is being done by Italian industry itself."

[18] This discussion of conditions, which to us seems so natural, is not so at all for the Southern Italians. In their own regions they were accustomed to accept whatever they could get, mostly on a short-term basis and they were pleased to take whatever the employer gave them at the end of their contract. When there are 10 or more applicants for one job, it is futile to talk of minimum wages, 40-hour work weeks, etc. The lucky one had to do all he could to keep his job and if he acquired the reputation of being a troublemaker, all possibility of finding any work in future was closed forever, unless he moved away.

[19] "As Mr. Sandri, a member of the Commission put it in the EEC's bulletin last June, the intention is that full and absolute equality of treatment will lead to the rapid replacement of the notion of the *emigrant* by that of the *European worker* . . ." *New Statesman*, December 22, 1961.

far as employment, salary and other working conditions are concerned."

So far we have dealt in this chapter with the skilled or semiskilled worker and the impression may have been given that the problem of unemployment in Southern Italy is either already solved or very near solution.[20] The opposite is in fact true—the number of unemployed is still high and the exact number, as we have seen, is difficult to evaluate. Furthermore any true compilation of statistics is also complicated by the fluctuating number of underemployed.

Theoretically, of course, the underemployed should be absorbed by the increased demands of the Common Market but most are unfitted for industrial life. Some, after years of physical privation, just do not have the necessary strength; most of them are illiterate and would be unable to read posters on factory walls, dials or numbers on machines, etc. It will be a long time before these people become productive, skilled workers like the other members of the Community. The important thing is to see that the new generation receives the basic education and training needed to equip them for the tasks ahead. Meanwhile, some of the unskilled mass may, despite their handicaps, be converted into semiskilled or skilled laborers. Others will help to fill the many menial jobs which will be available in the Community.[21]

---

[20] But, as a matter of fact, we find that, in 1960, "employment increased least in relation to output in Italy, where the very rapid rate of industrial expansion during the present boom has only moderately relieved the problem of chronic unemployment." ECE, *Economic Survey of Europe for 1960*, chap. I, p. 9. Furthermore, the moving of the larger firms to Southern Italy ". . . has been the cause of some concern, since the large, heavily automated plants, though they represent large investments and mean the introduction of an advanced technology, provide relatively few jobs." *Italy: an Economic Profile, op.cit.*

[21] "The development of intra-Community migrations has been accompanied by an important increase in immigration originating from countries outside the Community, at least towards two nations: France, which Spain and Portugal have furnished with more workers than Italy, and the Federal Republic of Germany, where the immigra-

142

Having thus seen how important the outlet of emigration is for the workers of the Italian South, we can realize that the provisions of the Treaty relating to freedom of movement are more important to them than to the workers of the other members of the Community. If, then, these articles referring to freedom of movement and establishment within the Common Market area are liberally applied, together with the other measures being taken to develop the Mezzogiorno, there is a good chance of gradually eliminating the unemployment that now characterizes these regions and of bringing them to a level comparable to that of the other parts of Italy.[22]

POSITION OF THE FRENCH WORKER

In France, the employment problem in the underdeveloped areas has different characteristics than that of Italy. It is not so much a question of too many people for too few jobs, but of unequal distribution of population, so that the underdeveloped regions suffer from lack of people to help develop them.[23] France, in fact, has in the past been a coun-

---

tion of Spanish and Greek workers has increased in higher proportions than the immigration of Italian workers. As the employment situation in Italy improves, it becomes more difficult for the partner countries, which are demanding labor, to find in the Italian labor market enough workers conforming to the professional criteria of selection. This evolution puts in rather sharp terms, on a Community level, the problem of the professional training of the Italian labor force which remains unemployed." CEE, *Exposé 1960*, p. 27.

[22] "It is . . . the most industrialized regions, as a rule, which have given proof until now of the greatest dynamism, which the current expansion interests most and benefits most, whereas the others, and particularly those where a large part of the active population is engaged in agriculture, seem only to enjoy reduced benefits. The case of Italy illustrates this assertion very well. It is indeed in the North-West of the country, and to a lesser degree in the North-East and in the Center, that the recent economic development has marked the greatest progress, and that the employment situation has improved in the highest degree." *Ibid.*, intro.

[23] "It is certain that inequalities of production and income correspond to the inequalities of natural conditions. But these inequalities

try where immigration of foreign workers has always exceeded the number of people leaving to settle either temporarily or permanently in French overseas possessions or in foreign countries. The phenomenon of the relative depopulation of France in respect to the rest of Europe is due to a variety of reasons, both of an economic and sociological nature, which cannot be fully analyzed here. Suffice it to say that this unfavorable trend has been reversed since World War II, and it seems that this will be a constant characteristic of French demography in the foreseeable future. From an excess of births over deaths of 298,000 in 1946, the figure rises to 332,000 in 1947 and 358,000 in 1948. And, in the following decade, there was still a considerable surplus of births over deaths.[24]

REDISTRIBUTION OF WORKERS IN FRANCE

It is stressed throughout this work that a laissez-faire economy in Europe would enhance the growth of the most industrialized regions, thus leaving the present underdeveloped areas ever further behind, so that, instead of being the poor regions of their own country, they would then become

---

may entail underdevelopment and an insufficient exploitation of the wealth of the less-favored regions; and it is this phenomenon that is observed more and more frequently in a large area of France, which stretches from the south to the west of a line passing through Saint-Malo, Nevers, St. Etienne, Briançon. It results in the average standard of living of the populations being subject to important differences, according to the *département* in which they live." CEE, *Rapport 1958*, p. 280.

[24] According to an *Etude de l'Evolution Démographique*, published by the Institut National de la Statistique, I.N.S.E.E. (Paris, 1964), as of December 31, 1963, the population of France was 48,133,000, compared with 47,573,000 the previous year. In eighteen years, the population has increased by more than eight million people. At present, the active population (from 20 to 64 years) represents 54.4% of the total population, with 26,219,000 persons, against 59.4% in 1946 with 23,847,000 persons. The under-twenty group, with 16,210,000 young people, represented, at the beginning of 1964, 33.7% of total population, against 30.5% in 1946. (*Passim*)

the poor regions of the new community. There will be a greater concentration than ever of people in the industrialized areas. Thus, in France there would be a tendency to move towards Paris, the North, and the East from the mainly agricultural area of the West and South-West, from Brittany, Corsica, and certain small pockets of underdevelopment.[25] Furthermore, technological improvements will bring about a great increase in productivity and a decrease in the number of workers deriving their income directly from the primary sector.[26] However, the absorption of these workers should not prove too difficult; actually, additional

---

[25] ". . . some grave problems of adjustment between supply and demand will come onto the labor scene. . . . Brittany, Normandy, the Loire region, Poitou, Charentes, Languedoc, will in any case have heavy surplus labor forces. Most of these regions traditionally direct their migratory movement towards Paris, which risks having an excessive influx of labor if these migrations continue the same trend." CEE: *Rapport 1958*, p. 282.

[26] Situation in the main French underdeveloped areas:

Region	Active Population	Agriculture No.	%	Industry No.	%	Services No.	%
West	3,369,500	1,496,730	44.4	995,071	29.4	877,699	26.2
Center	1,974,400	886,600	44.7	597,337	30.2	490,463	25.1
South-West	2,070,300	935,677	45.0	586,963	28.3	547,660	26.7

Source: Cassa, *Contributo alla Conoscenza dell'Agricoltura dei Paesi della Comunitá Europea* (Rome, 1961), I, p. 43.

It has been discovered that the exodus from the countryside in the last decade has been much greater in numbers than was thought. "Each year, 160,000 people engaged in agriculture in France leave the land; together with their children they represent an annual diminution in the total agricultural population of some 250,000—300,000 . . . these figures, which have come as a surprise to everyone in France, have just been revealed by the results of a census carried out last year. The general amazement springs not so much from the trend of the demographic movement, which was known to all, but from its volume, which no one had suspected. When, a few years ago, the Commissariat au Plan announced that the economy could count upon a rural exodus of 100,000 inhabitants a year, this was widely disputed. The actual movement has been three times as fast." *The Economist*, June 15, 1963.

145

workers from outside will probably be needed. The secret consists in a steadily expanding industrial production, for which the first years of operation of the Common Market augur well. And such expansion should continue in the foreseeable future, according to the forecast of most economists.

We have before us the very recent example set by the Federal Republic of Germany which has not only easily absorbed the twelve million refugees who have poured into its territory since the end of the war, but could also import, and still is importing, workers from abroad to satisfy the ever-increasing demands of its industry.[27] For France, therefore, the establishment of a Common Market of workers should only mean an importation of labor from abroad and a certain amount of internal readjustment of the working population.[28]

[27] The *New York Times* (Europe-Mideast Business Review) of January 10, 1964, reports: "The national manpower problem is still one of shortage. Some 821,000 foreign workers were recruited last year to meet the still unfulfilled demand. . . . There are predictions that, barring an economic reversal, the total number of migrant foreign workers in West Germany will reach two million. . . . At present there are . . . 286,000 Italians. Three years ago there were almost 350,000 Italians." This obviously means that the pool of unemployed labor in Italy, ready to expatriate in search of a job, is decreasing, and also means that many workers, after having obtained a specialization and made some money, prefer to go back to Italy.

[28] "It is on a regional level, rather than a national, that the evolution of the labor market should be analyzed if a faithful image of it is to be projected. This analysis would show that only the heavily industrialized regions situated to the east of a line running from the mouth of the Seine to that of the Rhône are experiencing a scarcity of labor, whereas in the regions situated to the west development persists in being insufficient to ensure a satisfactory degree of employment of local labor. Internal migrations partly remedy these imbalances. But these migrations, to which has to be added foreign immigration, tend to enlarge the gap between the levels of development of the different regions rather than to reduce it, and *only the enactment of a coordinated regional policy* [emphasis supplied] towards which it seems there is a strong tendency, can regulate this evolution, the most worrisome aspect of which remains the disproportionate growth of the conglomeration in the Paris area." CEE, *Exposé 1960*, p. 38.

Obstacles to Free Movement of Workers

It must be pointed out that the principle of free circulation of workers between Member States of the Community, assured by Article 48 *et seq.* of the Treaty, sharply contrasts with existing legislation in the nations of the Economic Community. Indeed, in all these States the immigration of foreign workers is strictly regulated, and in no case even approaches the freedom which is the final aim of the Treaty of Rome.

The general principle directing the immigration of foreign workers is that they be admitted only when they are needed and when all local workers are employed, unless they happen to have some special skill which cannot be found locally. However, in general, national workers must have priority over immigrants.[29] This law, written or unwritten, is sometimes tempered by humanitarian considerations (reuniting families, etc.). In France, which is of particular interest for our survey in view of the potential immigration to that nation of sizeable quantities of workers from the Mezzogiorno of Italy, the regulations referring to entry of foreign workers, in spite of its long tradition as a country of immigration, are somewhat strict.[30] Shortly after the end of World War II, on

[29] A very important agreement signed by the Council of Ministers on August 16, 1961, and which came into use on September 1, 1961, has fixed a time limit on this preference for nationals in the Member States of the Common Market. The offers of employment originally directed to nationals of the country of the requesting firm automatically become all-Community offers if they have not been taken up within three weeks; also a number of other provisions have been approved to ease the adaptation of foreign workers when they work in a country other than their own. See *Journal Officiel des Communautés Européennes*, IV Year, No. 57 of August 26, 1961, and No. 80 of December 13, 1961.

[30] For more information on this subject, see: Guy Chesne, *L'Etablissement des Etrangers en France et la Communauté Economique Européenne* (Paris: Librairie Generale de Droit et de Jurisprudence, 1962). As far as workers' migrations between France and Italy in particular are concerned, the communiqué issued at the end of the visit of the President of the Italian Republic, Signor Segni, to General de Gaulle in Paris, in February 1964, emphasizes among other things

November 2, 1945, the Ministry of Labor issued a decree in which Article 7 makes it necessary for all foreign workers who want to emigrate to France to obtain, previous to entering French territory, special authorization by the same Ministry. Upon entry into France, they must obtain a *carte de travail* without which they cannot start any paid activity. This document entails further limitations, because generally the new arrival is restricted in his movements (the card may only be valid for a certain area) and in his activity (only a certain paid activity is allowed), and a limit (generally one year) is put on the time the immigrant may work. However, the permits are renewable at the discretion of the police authority. As a rule, only after years of residence in France and of good conduct is a *carte permanente* finally granted. It must be said that these measures are justified, at least in part, because indiscriminate immigration is in nobody's interest.

Under the same decree mentioned above, Articles 29 and following assign to a newly created Immigration Office the task of acting as a central agency for the immigration of foreign workers. Further restrictions are established in the "Règlement de la Carte du Travail," Section II, Articles 64 and 172. The latter article also imposes stiff penalties for breaking the immigration laws in force. Last of all, it must be remembered that the Law of August 10, 1932, whereby maximum quotas of foreign workers allowed per single enterprise are established, is still actively applied. From all this, it is clear that, once all the bureaucratic formalities

---

that "The problems deriving from the exchange of labor between Italy and France have been examined. The emigration to France of Italian workers . . . creates certain problems: lodging, family reunions, social security, standard of living, education. The authorities of the two countries have observed the results obtained in these domains and follow attentively all these problems in order to adapt the Italian workers to the way of life of the neighboring country and to assure to them an ever increasing parity of treatment." Reprinted in *Le Monde* (Sélection Hebdomadaire), February 26, 1964.

148

have been observed and the worker finally starts his job, he is not automatically assimilated as a French worker. Noticeably, he does not benefit from certain Social Security provisions, though there is now a tendency to extend these to foreign workers.[31] But this progressive assimilation is the result of an extension of exceptions brought about by the necessity of attracting to France those workers she needs: discrimination is still the underlying guiding principle. Until now, international bilateral treaties have smoothed out some of these obstacles, especially the harsher dispositions. However, these treaties offer "conditions of reciprocity" which are more apparent than real, because the movement of workers is almost exclusively one way, from abroad (especially from Italy and Spain, now that normal relations with the East of Europe have been made nearly impossible) to France. Immigration treaties have actually often been dealt with in the broader context of general commercial agreements, where immigration advantages granted to one side have been balanced by concessions from the other side in a different field.

Even in the EEC Treaty itself we find limiting clauses; for instance, Article 48, paragraph 3, states that the right of free entry is subject to limitation for reasons of public order

[31] The Members of the Community are presently working towards integrating their social security systems. A comprehensive summary of this endeavor can be found in *Communauté Européenne*, No. 2, February 1963. The theme of the article is that "Freedom of circulation will not be in fact attained before the conditions that the working man finds in the different parts of the Community are aligned, at least to a certain point." Also the EEC Commission, at the beginning of a chapter on the Social Policy in the Community in *Memorandum de la Commission sur le Programme d'Action de la Communauté pendant la deuxième étape* (Brussels, SPCE, October 24, 1962), p. 53, thus expresses itself on the question: "Considering the ultimate goal envisaged by the Treaty, which is the ever closer union of the European peoples, there is no doubt that an advanced social policy would constitute an indispensable element in the Community endeavor, above all in view of giving a solid base to the European construction; this would be the effective adherence of the workers, i.e. of the vast majority of the people of our countries."

149

or public health and must, furthermore, be contingent on a real or effective offer of employment. Under this provision, it is obvious that a country can easily block any immigration of workers from other countries, or even certain categories of workers or those of a particular nationality. This is apart from deliberate bureaucratic slowness which can so delay and hinder the entry of a worker from abroad that in many cases the victim finally gives up the effort and abandons his original idea of emigrating.

The second and perhaps more obscure corollary to Article 48 is that employment must actually be offered. This, however, is subject to various interpretations: a restrictive one, for instance, is that a worker in, say, Sicily who intends to emigrate to Paris can do so only after some firm in Paris accepts him and sends him a valid contract. Only when he has this contract in his possession may he cross the border and settle in Paris. An extremely liberal interpretation of paragraph 3a of Article 48, on the other hand, accepts as a valid offer of employment an advertisement appearing in the "Help wanted" columns of a newspaper; in this case, the worker would have sufficient justification for crossing the border merely by showing the advertisement to the frontier police.

Problems of Emigrant Workers Abroad

There has always been traditional hostility on the part of local workers to their new colleagues from abroad, especially those coming from Southern Italy. Most of these workers are illiterate and downtrodden; in their own country they have accepted any conditions imposed upon them by unscrupulous employers simply in order to maintain some sort of job to keep themselves alive. Thus, when they emigrate, they are unaware of their rights as workers. They are forced to go abroad through sheer economic necessity and they will grasp at any job open to them. They are used to substandard living in their own country, so a low standard of life in their new home does not bother them excessively. The local workers see them as a threat to the conditions which they have gradually built up over the years through collective bargaining, etc. Furthermore, employers are liable to look upon uncontrolled immigration as a means of getting a constant supply of cheap labor.[32]

If a free movement of workers is to function efficiently, these people must first be prepared in their own country for their new responsibilities and privileges as members of the new Europe. They must have an educational program to help equip them to become skilled or semiskilled workers;[33] they must also be made aware of their dignity as workers and taught that they are not going abroad to beg for jobs at the mercy of all-powerful employers. The training program must be started in school, in order to change their whole

---

[32] In this connection, a survey conducted by the Coal and Steel Community shows that "the major part of the unions subordinate immigration to full employment of nationals, at least of the nationals who are liable to be working in those industries to which such foreign workers are admitted. At the same time, they insist that the immigration of foreign workers should not be a factor in depression of conditions of salary and work. The unions do not want immigration to damage in any way whatsoever the position of national workers on the economic level or on the subject of industrial relations." CEE, *Communauté Européenne du Charbon et de l'Acier* (Cahier No. 5, May 1961).

[33] "There are at present in the Community 600,000 unfilled offers of jobs. Does this mean that all the unemployed workers who could be interested by these offers do not have any professional qualification that would allow them to apply? To face this problem, the Council of Ministers of the Common Market has just taken a decision in principle that will permit the gradual attainment, in all the six countries, of a community policy of professional formation. . . . This decision in fact will allow the elaboration of programs of professional formation based on the exigencies of any of our countries and the realization of these programs by a joint or at least coordinated effort of the 'Six'." *Communauté Européenne*, No. 3, March 1963. "Questions of vocational guidance and training, occupational transfer and 're-cycling,' as well as those of placement, are being studied in increasing close connection with the problems of regional expansion. . . ." Economic and Social Council of the United Nations: *Report on Manpower Problems in Europe in 1963, op.cit.*

philosophy and rid them of their primitive ideas and superstitions.[34]

TRAINING OF WORKERS

Various programs have been set up by the Italian Government and other organizations within Italy for the training of unskilled and unemployed workers, for it is a fact that giving them a skill is practically equivalent to finding them a job, in Italy or elsewhere in the Community.[35]

One of the most important provisions in favor of the unemployed goes back to the pre-World War II period; the *Decreto Legge* No. 1380 of June 21, 1938, set up *Corsi per Disoccupati* (Courses for the Unemployed) and decreed that not only should these courses be free, but that workers admitted to them should actually be paid by the State, for they were preparing to take jobs of higher importance and benefit to the society and were therefore entitled to a kind of "advance" on their future productivity. The project was so successful that the new regime after the war did not suppress it but actually incorporated it in the general structure of provisions in favor of labor and even amplified it by Law No. 264 of April 29, 1949, and No. 456 of May 24, 1951.

There are two types of courses today: the general course for professional instruction (at the end of 1959 there were

[34] Danilo Dolci cited further examples of this ignorance in the aforementioned interview he gave to *Realités* in October 1961: "Tradition and superstition reign, with ignorance in their train. . . . We made a survey near Cammarata and found that, out of one hundred landowners who had suffered from avalanches, twenty blamed the erosion on magic invoked by their enemies. . . . Why should they want a dam? They've never seen one, they don't even know what the word means. How can you hope to make farmers stop burning their manure, if they do not understand its use and if they continue to believe that it 'soils the land'?"

[35] "The most eloquent commentary on the economic progress made by Italy is the reason generally given to explain why it has not been more rapid: Italian industry is held back by a shortage of skilled labor." *New York Times* (Annual Economic Supplement), January 9, 1962.

1,195 of these courses being carried on in the whole of Italy, with an enrolment of 25,084 unemployed; the total cost to the State was more than three billion lire); and the *Corsi per lavoratori emigrandi* (courses for emigrating workers) which have assumed special importance since the signature of the Common Market Treaties. Most of these courses are carried on in Southern Italy; the two main centers are in Messina, Sicily, and in Salerno, Campania. They are restricted to workers between 18 and 35 years of age, and are carried on under the auspices of the Ministry for Foreign Affairs, the Cassa per il Mezzogiorno, the Ministry for Public Education, and the Intergovernmental Committee for European Migration, in which all Member States of the Community are represented. The courses are concerned almost exclusively with teaching the building and factory trades since they offer most opportunities for Italian workers in the Community.

Another notable feature, and one that could perhaps be imitated in other countries where the same problem arises, is that of running retraining courses in the factories. These courses are set up when it is foreseen that dismissals may have to be made; the workers are trained in other skills while still working at their old jobs. Retraining courses take place after working hours and are financed partly by the State and partly by the workers themselves through a *Cassa di Integrazione dei Guadagni degli Operai dell'Industria* (Fund for the Integration of Wages of Industrial Workers), established by the aforementioned Law No. 264 of April 29, 1949 (Article 56 in particular).

The Cassa per il Mezzogiorno is developing a comprehensive program of professional training either directly or in cooperation with several large organizations, both public and private, like ENI, Fiat, Montecatini, the trade unions, etc. Particular care is devoted to the training of apprentices. The Ministry of Labor authorized, for the fiscal year 1959–60, an expenditure of 2,952 million lire for this cate-

153

gory of aspirant worker, of whom there were 304,431 divided among 11,743 courses. This scheme was made necessary in view of the new situation created by the enactment of the EEC Treaties. The Ministries of Labor and of Public Education will coordinate their activity so that the Member States of the Community will recognize the professional titles conferred on these apprentices and treat them accordingly.

OTHER FACTORS

Apart from the important obstacles to free movement already discussed, there are others that influence the situation. It is hard for the American reader to realize fully the many difficulties of various kinds involved in movements of people between European states. In this country, the differences between two towns in any part of the continent are often negligible, and actually a person who moves from one part of the country to another may do so without encountering any difficulties, apart from the usual ones directly connected with the moving. Common language, background, outlook, habits, culture, and history all contribute to making the change smooth and uneventful. But in Europe it is a different story. Even within the borders of the same nation, differences can be enormous. A Sicilian and a Milanese, or a Breton and a Corsican, although belonging to the same nation, are poles apart; they have different dialects, unintelligible outside the region of origin, different sets of values, habits, etc.

In the United States, what is morally acceptable in New York is also acceptable in San Francisco. But in Europe there may be a vast chasm between the values of Palermo and Turin, or Ajaccio and Paris. And we are still talking of national states.[36] If we go beyond the borders, then the

[36] Evidence of some of the enormous difficulties encountered in a free movement of workers even within the same nation can be found in a study published in 1956 by the Institut National d'Etudes Démo-

situation becomes worse as other difficulties are added, especially the difference in language which, of all obstacles, is probably the greatest and often prevents a complete assimilation into the new environment.

In regions where there is a history of emigration, as for instance throughout all Southern Italy, the departure of a member of the family or of a friend and neighbor is accepted with fatalistic resignation. From the time when their children are young, mothers are prepared for the fact that they will probably leave one day, and this has come to be accepted almost as the natural order of things. But in regions where this tradition does not exist, as is the case in the underdeveloped parts of France, the story is different. To individual reactions must be added those of the whole

---

graphiques, Paris: *Développement Economique et Mobilité des Travailleurs* (Etude realisée pour la Communauté du Charbon et de l'Acier), p. 14:

"In 1950, for various reasons, a crisis developed in the coal basins of the Centre-South. The result of this was a progressive diminution in the number of jobs available and partial unemployment.

"There is a remarkable difference in wealth between the deposits of the Centre-South and those of Lorraine, which give almost double the output of the former and have a much longer life. In view of this situation, the Directors of the Charbonnages du Midi (Coalmines of the South), anxious to avoid layoffs, envisaged—in agreement with the Charbonnages de France (Coalmines of France)—the transfer to Lorraine of 5,000 miners within a five-year period.

"As the first transfers, in October 1953, provoked a lively reaction, a system of volunteering was introduced in liaison with the Syndicats (Unions), Force Ouvrière, and Confédération Française des Travailleurs Chrétiens (French Confederation of Christian Workers). (The Confédération Général du Travail—General Confederation of Labor —remained hostile throughout to any displacement.) One billion francs was budgeted, to be shared equally by the C.S.G.I. and Charbonnages de France. In spite of the advantages offered (free move and travel, a new apartment guaranteed, seniority rights safeguarded, and premiums of 75,000 fr. for bachelors and 200,000 for family units), the results were disappointing, showing that the attachment of men to their environment has been much underestimated: from April 1954 to March 1955, only 186 volunteered, of whom 37 were French bachelors and 92 were foreigners, the balance being constituted by French families, most of them of large size. These figures are self-explanatory."

155

community in which the prospective immigrant lives. An intense propaganda and information effort is needed to overcome the opposition of the local community, which sometimes even goes so far as to organize against any emigration of its members. There then develops, as in the case of the miners, deep hostility to any displacement. In addition, the vested interests add their influence. The following excerpt is an interesting example of this:

A study conducted around the end of 1954 describes a veritable panic which overcame the tradespeople of a small mining town when the transfer of a considerable number of local miners and their families became a certainty. Nearly all rushed to sell, or try to sell, their shops and properties. However, there were practically no offers. After the first days of frenzy, the traders decided that the only thing they could do to safeguard their interests would be to impede the departure of the miners. They then organized a "regional committee for the defense of trade." Thus, the local pressure group went through the usual steps in these cases: approaching the Mayor, their Deputy, etc. The Confédération Général du Travail joined the fray and loudly proclaimed that "an appeal is made to all the workers to prevent our region from being transformed into a desert." Les Charbonnages de France (national) and the European Coal and Steel Community (supra-national) were both accused of dire intentions and of being tools of a vast number of people, classes and nations, ranging from American and indigenous capitalists to German *revanchists*, and cries were heard of "deportation" to a "strange" country (the bilingual character of Alsace-Lorraine being taken into account). The local priests, unwilling to see their flock dispersed, strongly supported the traders' viewpoint, as did the petty local bureaucracy, afraid to contemplate the sudden disappearance of their administrees and the consequent fadeout of their administration. Thus, eventually, the strange combination of Extreme Left with the Church and "la loi" helped to bring about the failure of the Government's project.[37]

In a policy of free movement of workers, we also run into such obstacles as a shortage of housing. Here again, this is especially true in France (it was also common in Italy in the postwar years, but has now been almost entirely corrected).[38] There exists in France the system of *droits acquis,* whereby the tenant and his family, who may have been living in the same place for generations, acquire a quasi-proprietorial status, while the real owner does nothing but collect a rent that has constantly been reduced since Napoleonic times in proportion to the cost of living. So long as the same tenant goes on living there, the rent cannot be increased, whereas if he moves into a new apartment of corresponding size, where rents are not controlled, he is liable to pay ten to fifteen times as much rent. A family of workers whose budget is very limited will think more than twice before giving up the privilege of cheap rent; in many cases, the extra money they would earn by moving to a better job elsewhere in the country or in the Community would be more than swallowed up by the increased rent they would have to pay for an uncontrolled apartment.

We can see from the preceding discussion that, while the principle of free movement of labor is one of the aims of the European Community, there are many obstacles to its practical application. Complete freedom of movement will only come about gradually, in line with economic expansion and changing exigencies within the Community. It would

[37] J. M. Abbertin, "Problèmes humaines et Aménagement du Territoire: les Mineurs d'Alès," *Economie et Humanisme,* No. 88, Nov.–Dec., 1954.

[38] "Some important social needs are not yet even moderately satisfied [in France]. The most important is that of housing. Building activity is insufficient to satisfy the demand for housing during the coming years." CEE, *Rapport 1958,* p. 262.

seem that traditional fears of a mass exodus from Southern Italy once the doors to free movement are unlocked are now receding. As we have seen, the economic integration of Europe is already bringing extremely beneficial results to the Italian economy so that it will be able to absorb a considerable number of its own excess labor.[39] And certainly the number of workers leaving Italy for other countries in the Community will not be more than those countries can absorb in their own expanding industry.

Articles 123–130 of the EEC Treaty contain two very original provisions: the first concerns the establishment of a "European Social Fund," and the rules governing it are covered in Articles 124–128, while Articles 129–130 are dedicated to provisions for setting up a "European Investment Bank." We shall examine these in some detail, as they are both very pertinent to the subject of this chapter, the first insofar as free movement of workers is concerned, and the second in connection with free movement in general.[40]

[39] The following data are supplied by Mr. Rosario Purpura, Director-General of the Ministry of Labor and Social Security: number of people holding jobs in Italy (month of April or May): 18,508,000 in 1958; 19,476,000 in 1959; 19,906,000 in 1960; 20,475,000 in 1961; 20,080,000 in 1962 (slight decrease). Unemployed: 1,096,000 in 1959; 655,000 in 1962; 426,000 in 1963. As reprinted in *Le Monde Diplomatique*, February 1964. However, the newly found prosperity is threatened by a mounting spiral of inflation, which provoked the following warning to Italy on the part of the Directorate-General for Economic and Financial Affairs of the European Economic Community: "Present price trends and the effect they are having on the balance of payments show that immediate and energetic countermeasures are called for." Reported in *New York Times* (Europe-Mideast Business Review), January 10, 1964.

[40] It must be pointed out that, even though completely independent from each other, they often work in close cooperation on particular projects. For instance, *Communauté Européenne*, No. 6, June 1961, states: "The Executive of the Common Market has authorized the Italian government to adopt certain measures of a temporary nature to safeguard a number of products (sulphur, lead, zinc, etc.). Such measures should allow a reconversion of several sectors of the Italian economy, with the aid, in particular, of the European Social Fund and of the European Investment Bank . . . particularly in Sicily and in Sardinia."

FREEDOM OF CIRCULATION

The European Social Fund

The Social Fund was inserted in the Treaty at the insistence of the Italian delegation; special economic conditions in that country required provisions along these lines in order to obtain financial help for unemployed labor in certain particular cases. It was created to improve occupational opportunities for the workers of the Common Market area, and to contribute to the improvement of their standard of living. As specified in Article 125, the Social Fund will endeavor to promote, within the Community, facilities for employment and the geographic and professional mobility of workers.[41]

At the time of the conclusion of the Treaty, one of the most serious ills of the Italian economy was chronic unemployment and underemployment that far exceeded anything to be found in the other countries of the Community. This problem was destined to become a problem for the whole European Economic Community, and the other five Members were therefore deeply interested in its solution. By the same token, they were interested in seeing a viable Italian

[41] The total contribution granted by the European Social Fund since it came into existence amounts to $19,853,275, involving about 263,500 workers, divided as follows:

West Germany: 38,500, plus 35,740 resettled Italian workers
Belgium: 2,400
France: 15,050
Italy: 167,200
Netherlands: 4,600

During 1963, the operations in which the Fund participated allowed about 80,500 workers to get new jobs after benefitting from a period of professional re-education or from a moving allowance. These workers are so divided:

West Germany: 18,528, plus 35,740 Italians
Belgium: 994
France: 5,304
Italy: 18,929
Netherlands: 1,016

Source: *Communauté Européenne*, No. 2, February 1964.

159

economy, essential to a smooth and well-balanced functioning of the Community once it is in full operation. Therefore their financial contribution to the Fund will offer them indirect returns, even if the main beneficiary in the first stage will be Italy.[42]

The envisaged freedom of movement of workers will contribute only partially to the solution of this problem; the technological preparation of a very high percentage of the workers from the South of Italy must also be improved so that lack of skill will not be added to the many other handicaps of migrant workers. Also, the demand for unskilled labor, due to technological progress, will be increasingly reduced and, of course, unskilled workers get the worst-paid and the least attractive jobs, those which the local workers do not want to fill. Furthermore, the realization of the Common Market will probably entail, in certain sectors and for a certain length of time—especially at the beginning of its period of full operation—an increase in unemployment in some industrial sectors. In order to face the increased competition, factories will have to discontinue or reduce production, or certain types of production, or they may modernize and, as a consequence of technological improvements, some of the workers hitherto employed will lose their jobs.

The Coal and Steel Community has already faced the same problem, but in the limited sector under its jurisdiction. The solution adopted is imperfect, at least as far as the particular situation in Italy is concerned, because the equivalent of the Social Fund instituted in that Treaty foresees only the granting of subsidies to workers in that sector who lose their jobs for reasons deriving from the establishment of the Coal and Steel Community and who are await-

[42] "The Common Market must not mean for any nation the opportunity to rid itself of its burdens at the expense of its partners; it must remain the means of solving, in common, the problems each country used to face by itself." George Elgozy, *La France devant le Marché Commun* (Paris: Flammarion, 1958), p. 126.

ing other jobs. A similar solution would certainly not have been adequate in solving the chronic Italian unemployment or underemployment problem. In fact, no unemployment compensation can constitute a lasting solution, especially in regions such as the Italian South. There the opportunities for new employment are practically nonexistent until new activities are created.[43]

Realistically enough, the drafters of the Treaty constantly kept in mind the question of unskilled labor. One of the reasons that industry is somewhat reluctant to set up new plants in the South is that it is extremely difficult to fill the skilled and highly skilled jobs available with locally re-cruited workers. Of course, it is a different matter in the case of unskilled labor of which, as we have seen, there is an abundant supply.

The Social Fund will endeavor to give professional skills to all the unemployed labor force without distinction be-tween unemployment deriving from the Common Market or from other reasons. (It would be practically impossible to differentiate between these.) In Article 125, the Treaty states that the country to which the unemployed workers belong and the Social Fund must each contribute 50 per cent toward the cost of retraining or teaching skills to unem-ployed workers.[44] Furthermore, they must share the burden of providing indemnities for workers transferred to another place. Possibly the contribution of the national state will be eliminated once political integration becomes a reality. In fact, if the free movement of workers within the Community proceeds unhampered, it would hardly be fair for a national

[43] "The backwardness of Italy is, essentially, that of its Southern regions, the weak industrialization of which meant, until a short time ago, a very mediocre degree of employment." CEE, *Exposé 1960*, intro.

[44] This provision has already been used repeatedly. For instance, "Italy will have recourse to the European Social Fund to cover 50 per cent of the expenditures for the professional retraining of redundant workers in Navy shipyards, for whom a program is now being elabo-rated." *Communauté Européenne*, Nos. 4–5, April–May 1961.

state to pay 50 per cent of the costs necessary to transform an unskilled into a skilled worker, in order to see the same worker, as soon as he has achieved some qualifications, migrate to another part of the Community. Of course the most common case of this kind is likely to be that of the Southern Italian worker, who will then migrate to France or Germany. The money so spent could be more efficiently employed in the development of the area.

The Social Fund also grants financial aid to enterprises which otherwise could not continue to pay the same salaries to their workers during a period of reconversion. In this case, the scope of the aid is not only to alleviate the difficulties of the workers who would be unemployed or who would have to accept a lower salary for a period of time, but also that of permitting the enterprises undergoing reconversion to keep their skilled workers, who otherwise could disperse, causing additional difficulties and waste in replacing them once the reconversion work is fully achieved.

Certain conditions and procedures are established for the administration of the Fund. These should last for the whole of the transition period (Article 125). Afterwards, the Council, in the light of past experience and of the new objectives of the Community, will determine whether the Fund must be continued as it is, modified, or abolished altogether.

The Social Fund is of the greatest importance. It could even become the nucleus around which a European system can evolve that guarantees economic security to workers, and could also give a certain degree of stability as far as labor is concerned to the enterprises undergoing modernization. If adroitly administered, the Fund could become one of the chief instruments in reconversion of the European economies and help to smooth the process of integration, which will undoubtedly cause difficulties of a temporary nature to some of the workers and enterprises involved.[45]

[45] Some students of European integration see even further into the future and maintain that the Social Fund, together with the Invest-

FREEDOM OF CIRCULATION

FREE MOVEMENT OF CAPITAL

One of the fundamental principles of a common market is the free circulation of capital; it is also perhaps the most difficult to regulate, compared to the freedom of circulation of people, merchandise, and services. The letter of the Treaty reflects this—it is less bold and precise in its wording in the articles concerning freedom of circulation of capital than in the corresponding articles relating to other aspects of the same question. In this case, the compromise resulting in the wording of the Treaty was particularly elaborate because, during the period when the Treaty was being written, the situation of the French franc and the continuous passivity of the French balance of payments caused the French representatives to fear a complete liberalization of circulation of capital.

The principle expressed in Article 67 entails the progressive suppression during the transition period of the restrictions on movements of capital belonging to residents of the Community and the abolition of all discrimination deriving from nationality, place of residence, or place of investment. However, in the same Article, it is specified that the liberalization is limited to the measures "necessary for a smooth operation of the Common Market." Thus this freedom is accepted almost more as a consequence of the existence of a common market, which could not operate without it, than as a premise of a common market, i.e., one of the fundamental conditions on which the European Economic Community is based.

---

ment Bank, are the beginning of the implementation, in practice and without admitting it, of a Plan on a European scale. Jean Boissonnat, for instance, in an article entitled "Seeking Ways for a European Plan," *Economie et Humanisme*, Nov.–Dec. 1961, writes: "The Social Fund and the European Investment Bank, if properly used, may lead to a Central European Planning Agency . . . to correct economic and regional disequilibrium—a result that can be achieved only by a global policy that derives from a planning effort on a European scale."

However, be this as it may, the importance of this freedom must be underlined, particularly for the purposes of our study. In fact, free circulation of capital will entail a greater supply of capital in all Member States and consequently stimulate keener competition. And, if all the hindrances to freedom of movement of capital from one Member State to another are removed, the way for a greater investment of "foreign" capital (from outside the national state, but from within the Community) in the underdeveloped regions of the Common Market is open. This is particularly important for the Italian market, in view of the paucity of national capital and of the high cost of money.[46] As we have pointed out, and will later explain in more detail, the Government, be it national or European, must play a principal role in attracting this capital, which will now be free to circulate within the Community.

The uncertainties that prevailed during the drafting of the Treaty are confirmed by the fact that, unlike the cases of the other "freedoms of circulation," there is no precise procedure setting the pace for the successive stages in the process of liberalization during the transition period. The Treaty leaves it to the Council, upon proposals of the Commission and after hearing the advice of the Monetary Committee (Article 69) to issue directives and regulations on the matter.[47] At the same time, together with the freeing of movements of capital, an attempt is being made to eliminate

[46] As the *New York Times*, March 9, 1964, puts it: "Money is tight in Italy. It is, according to the authorities (in Rome), the tightest in Europe. It is tight because the authorities—the Bank of Italy—make it so. It is tight because the country's economy is continuing to expand and its international payments are showing a substantial deficit. . . . One measure of the tightness is short-term interest rates for prime borrowers—6 and $6\frac{1}{2}$ per cent now, compared with $4\frac{1}{2}$ and 5 per cent in 1962."

[47] Attempts are being made continuously to bridge this important gap. For instance, *Communauté Européenne*, No. 12, December 1963, reports that "The Executive of the Common Market is preparing fresh directives that will permit the achievement of new progress in the domain of free movement of capital. . . ."

the control of exchanges which, if left to the authority of the national states, could cancel at least in part the beneficial results deriving from the Common Market. This is one of the most important powers in the hands of the individual countries, and its effective dismantling will be one of the most far-reaching achievements of the European Economic Community Treaty toward an effective unification of Europe.

Furthermore, the Treaty has gone far beyond the mere task of creating the conditions intended to bring about the elimination of exchange control by the national states. Thus, in Article 107, paragraph 1, it is prescribed that the national states must treat their policy on exchange rates as "a matter of common interest." And any Member States of the Community who, in spite of this regulation, persisted in an independent exchange policy which would twist and falsify the conditions for really free competition, would be practically quarantined, as the other states would be able to retaliate in the measure authorized by the appropriate organs of the Community (Article 107, paragraph 2).[48] This is one of the most serious violations of both the spirit and the letter of the Treaty, and one of those most liable to entail the disruption of the whole structure of the Community. It is therefore certain that particular care will be exercised by the Member States in standing by their commitments. If, however, an abnormal situation should arise, in which there is a "sudden crisis in the balance of payments" (Article 109), the national

[48] Some promising indications that the Six are now aiming at a closer monetary cooperation are reported in the *New York Times* of June 21, 1963: "The European Common Market Executive Commission has completed a new plan for strengthening and unifying the monetary systems of the Community's six member states . . . it proposes to accomplish the following: Create a council of central bankers from among the six member states. . . . This would assure formal monetary cooperation. . . . Provide for closer cooperation among the member states in international monetary matters. . . . Make consultation mandatory among the member states to maintain currency stability, particularly in the field of foreign exchange."

165

state is authorized, by a special emergency procedure, to take "strictly indispensable" appropriate measures of a temporary character under the control of the Council and of the Commission which may impose their modification, suspension, or suppression as seen fit.

To conclude, as in most other matters regulated by the Treaty, it is hoped that the reality of economic reason will, in the long run, bring about unifying forces that will triumph over the vagaries of special interests. Here also the will to reach positive results is paramount. The Treaty can only show the way, and it is up to the national states to follow it.

FACTORS OPPOSING THE MOVEMENT OF CAPITAL AND INDUSTRIES TOWARD THE UNDERDEVELOPED REGIONS

We have previously seen that capital and industry tend to cluster around areas which are already developed and industrially advanced and to shy away from those areas which are insufficiently developed. Furthermore, long-term investments, which tend to immobilize capital for a number of years, usually follow the same pattern, and stay in areas where there is a much greater guarantee of economic stability and where the possibility of reaping the benefits of the money invested is greater too. Short-term private investments of an essentially speculative character may be made from the advanced parts of a country to its underdeveloped regions but stay in the area only for the limited time necessary for the completion of a particular purpose and then return to the region of origin. In other words, they do not become part of the "permanent"—if it may be called that— amount of money available for investment in the underdeveloped region but, after they have served their purpose they are quickly withdrawn.

As far as industry is concerned, the same concept applies; it tends to concentrate around certain places. The original causes that gave rise to these regional aggregations may no longer be present, or may have lost much of their importance (for example, vicinity to a mine, now exhausted); the fact remains, however, that these industrialized areas exist and in general have a tendency to grow by attracting new industries and capital, which for a number of reasons prefer to congregate around them.

> Thereafter, the ever-increasing internal and external economies—interpreted in the widest sense of the word to include, for instance, a working population trained in various crafts, easy communications, the feeling of growth and elbow room and the spirit of new enterprise—fortified and sustained their continuous growth at the expense of other localities and regions where instead relative stagnation or regression became the pattern. It is easy to see how expansion in one locality has "backwash" effects in other localities. More specifically the movements of labour, capital, goods and services do not by themselves counteract the natural tendency to regional inequality. By themselves, migration, capital movements and trade are rather the media through which the cumulative process evolves—upwards in the lucky regions and downwards in the unlucky ones. In general, if they have positive results for the former, their effects on the latter are negative.[49]

The aggregation process, which embraces industrial production, credit, insurance, transportation, and all the non-economic activities that are, however, linked to a high standard of living (such as the arts, literature, education), will affect certain places and certain regions. This does not mean that only these privileged regions will produce geniuses and notables, or even technicians; it only means that, wherever they are born, they have to move to the privileged areas if they are to be successful. A Sicilian play-

---

[49] Gunnar Myrdal, *Economic Theory and Underdeveloped Regions* (London: Duckworth and Co. Ltd., 1957), p. 26.

wright will have much more chance of getting his plays produced in Milan than in Palermo or Catania. A brilliant journalist from Bari will find fame in Italy and abroad if he writes for the *Corriere della Sera* of Milan or *La Stampa* of Turin, while his readership will remain largely local should he write for any Meridionale paper.[50] A scientist from Ajaccio has no alternative but to go to Paris if he wants to benefit from the enormously better facilities that he can find there, or an artist from Aquitaine must move to Paris if he wants to make himself known and have a better chance of success.

Once more, we have the same phenomenon of the industrialized areas moving even further ahead, and the underdeveloped regions growing proportionally poorer in the larger market.[51] Not only this, but some of the regions that today are more or less halfway between wealth and poverty would be the first victims of the flight of capital towards the advanced, industrialized areas.

A high standard of living will affect all types of ancillary activity directly, indirectly, or even remotely connected with economic factors. A rich region will be able to afford good roads, schools, medical care, large public libraries, and all the amenities that a high level of living brings. Additional

[50] The following is an excerpt from a debate on this subject held on Italian TV on July 12, 1961: "Hon. Casalinuovo, M. P.: During the last few years, the Southern Italian communities have been *steadily losing* labor, not only unskilled labor, but skilled labor. And the same applies to the intellectuals and technicians; they systematically escape, attracted by the much better possibilities and conditions of the North." Summarized in *Mondo Economico*, No. 30, July 29, 1961.

[51] The same phenomenon, that of an increasing gap between rich and poor areas, is taking place on the international scene, where the heavily industrialized nations of North America, Western Europe, Japan, etc., are outdistancing more and more the underdeveloped countries. The reasons are essentially, but not exclusively, the same as those relating to regional underdevelopment within a state or economic union. Comprehensive data, referring especially to the evolution of the labor force in both groups of countries, are supplied by the International Labour Office in *Yearbook of Labour Statistics, 1963* (Geneva, 1964).

jobs will be created for such people as construction engineers, librarians, doctors, etc. Their families will need the normal necessities of life, therefore new demands will reach the market and the supply will consequently increase to satisfy them. In brief, the "reverberation" process will increase prosperity in the already rich regions, and conversely, will decrease it in the already poor regions.

Thus, the liberalization of capital, in the Common Market area, will produce utterly different results according to the degree of the State's intervention in correcting market forces which tend to congregate capital investment in certain areas or in the hands of certain rich individuals or organizations. If conditions are created in the underdeveloped areas for good, safe investments (by the many means at the disposal of the State, such as tax exemptions, transportation facilities, subsidies, etc.), there is no reason why capital—private capital—should not move to the underdeveloped areas.[52] However, as far as the infrastructure is concerned, the State will have no alternative but to take direct control of what has to be done.

COMMON CUSTOMS TARIFF AND FREEDOM OF MOVEMENT OF MERCHANDISE

A basic difference between a free trade area and a customs union is the establishment in the latter of a *common* customs tariff toward "outside" states and freedom of circulation within the union of all merchandise, even that originating in nonmember states. In a free trade area, each country keeps its own customs tariffs toward "outside" states, and the products originating in nonmember states generally cannot move freely within the area.

Therefore, the Treaty sets out in detail a gradual pro-

[52] "The role of the state . . . is to create an economic climate, market conditions within which private persons may act in the way most favourable to the general interest." Pierre Mendès-France and Gabriel Ardant, *Economics and Action* (New York: UNESCO and Columbia University Press, 1955), p. 50.

cedure for establishing a common tariff toward the outside world and decrees how customs barriers and quotas between Member States are to be abolished within the transition period.[53]

Parallel to the suppression of customs duties between Member States, a common external tariff wall will be established so that any inside reduction will bring a corresponding variation toward the outside world. This variation will entail a reduction in some Member States and an increase in others, according to the product. In general, France and Italy are countries with a high tariff protection, Germany and Benelux with a moderate one. Therefore the effects of a progressive reduction on one side of the tariff wall, and elevation on the other, will give rise to a variety of consequences and also produce a number of dangers. The final tariff wall toward the external world is to be based on the average of the tariffs in force in each Member State on January 1, 1957, that is one year before the Treaty came into being. However, numerous exceptions are established to protect certain products, a number of them originating in the underdeveloped areas, which are not in a position to stand competition in an open market with a reasonable chance of success. Several lists of these products have been compiled and attached to the Treaty; the best known is list "F"—certain products on which the external tariff, for imperative economic reasons in the country of origin, is already fixed, irrespective of the "average" tariff. List "G" also includes products whose tariffs will not be based on the averages prevailing in January 1957, but on which the final

[53] ". . . A customs union, which was the nineteenth century technique, is today not sufficient. This is because the main obstacles to the expansion of foreign trade are no longer tariffs, but either quantitative restrictions, such as quotas or, even more frequently, monetary restrictions. . . . Thus, economic union implies a complete free trade, that is, movement of goods, capital and persons inside the area, which requires the establishment of roughly similar levels of prices, wages, indirect taxation, etc. in order to avoid excessive disequilibrium and hardships." Alpert, *op.cit.*, p. 431.

tariff has not yet been fixed. A certain elasticity is permitted in the tariffs toward the outside world, the relations with which will now have to undergo profound changes after the formation of the Common Market[54]; the cases where exceptions are allowed are clearly stated. In case of emergency, a Member State will be able to act on its own initiative, but the Commission will then have to sanction its action. A traditional supply may be permitted from an outside country with little or no customs duties when there is no possibility of producing that item within the Community and when no Member State will be harmed. The Commission will also make final decisions as far as State monopolies are concerned.

Some of the effects on individual underdeveloped areas of the Community brought about through the removal of barriers to a free movement of merchandise between Member States are dealt with separately, under the appropriate headings.

The European Investment Bank

The second original creation of the EEC Treaty is the European Investment Bank; it was established, as Article 130 states, to "contribute . . . to the balanced and smooth development of the Common Market in the interest of the Community. For this purpose, it shall facilitate . . . the financing of the following projects in all sectors of the economy:

[54] "It is very evident that the prosperity of the entire world depends more and more on the level of production attained in Europe." OEEC, *L'Europe et l'Economie Mondiale*, p. 36. On November 16, 1964, a trade conference opened in Geneva, Switzerland, to settle tariff questions mainly between the United States and the Common Market. "The Kennedy Round, named for the late President because of his association with the Trade Expansion Act adopted by Congress, is widely regarded as the most important liberalization effort in modern history. The primary objective is to make simultaneous tariff cuts on all possible industrial products involved in world trade." *New York Times*, November 15, 1964.

(a) projects for developing less-developed regions;

(b) projects for modernizing or converting enterprises . . .

(c) projects of common interest to several Member States. . . ."

This Bank was also brought into being largely at the insistence of the Italian delegation; the need for a "risorgimento" (re-birth) of the Italian Mezzogiorno called for this kind of institution.

However, apart from considerations of self-interest, it is obvious that, if the Member States are to reach the degree of economic integration envisaged in Article 2, the problem of the underdeveloped areas must be faced and solved without delay.[55] An expanding economy, which the European Economic Community is and, it is hoped, will be for a long time to come, can ill afford the continual brake put on it by the existence of sizeable underdeveloped zones within it. The whole expansionist process will be slowed down. It is therefore in the interest not only of Italy but of the whole Community to bring the Mezzogiorno up to a level with the other regions. The same, of course, applies to France and her underdeveloped regions.[56]

[55] "All considered, it will no doubt be necessary to complete the (European) Planning Office by a European Accountancy system. It will be equally necessary to give to a Central Agency sufficient authority to proceed to a program of investments. At present, the European Investment Bank can do nothing durable and efficacious. To try to increase its means signifies, in fact, entering the institutional debate which gives rise to the second series of problems before Europe, and which are of a political nature." *Realités*, No. 161, June 1959.

[56] "The inequality of regional development constitutes a crucial problem for the Common Market. The philosophy that has inspired the Treaty is that, without deliberate action, the gap may become final, as is shown by the example of . . . France with the Paris region and above all of Italy with the difference between North and South. If certain basic conditions are assured, land improvement, creation of an infrastructure of ports, transportation means, power, improvement of hygiene and of technical training, then the initially less-developed regions may profit from the advantages they have: abundance of labor, and higher productivity for investments. The creation

However, financial help to underdeveloped regions does not constitute the only purpose of the European Investment Bank. It also plays an important role in the help it gives for reconversion of industrial plants—needs arising from the changing economic demands brought about by the Common Market. It is obvious that such aid may be very important to enterprises in the underdeveloped areas, wherever they may be, especially to small organizations which are often intrinsically weak and have limited credit facilities.

The aim of the European Investment Bank is to contribute to a smooth and uniform development of the Community through its own means and outside capital. Mainly, it purports to rectify, as much as possible, the unfavorable position of the underdeveloped regions of the European Economic Community in order to fill or at least narrow the gap which divides them from the more advanced areas.[57] The Statute of the Bank is contained in a separate protocol attached to the EEC Treaty. Members of the Bank are the Member States of the Community. It is interesting to note that profit-making is not within the scope of the Bank. This was done deliberately to forestall the dangerous possibility that it might prefer to invest money in some of the other activities contemplated in Article 130 (modernization and reconversion of industrial plants, etc.), which offer greater monetary rewards in a shorter time. We must also make this important observation: while the Bank, as a rule, contributes to only

---

of the European Investment Bank is the clearest evidence of the attention given to the problem." CECA: *Septième Rapport Général*, p. 54.

[57] "To be true, the problem of harmonized economic growth would have shown up sooner or later in Europe, and a solution to it would have had to be found, even if the Common Market had not been established. . . . Furthermore, by enlarging the market, it will open the way to economically more advantageous solutions. Finally, from an institutional viewpoint, the Treaty recognizes the legitimacy of the regional policy; in this matter, it gives precise competence and functions to the European Commission and to the European Investment Bank." CECA, *Premier Rapport Général*, p. 45.

173

those projects which, for certain reasons, cannot be financed *in toto* by the national governments, in the case of the under-developed regions financial contributions by the national governments are not required. Italy worked hard for the formation of the Bank and, in order to make it a success, has not hesitated to subscribe a greater share than her real possibilities warrant. However, it is Italy's hope that the European Investment Bank will be instrumental in the solution of the Southern Italian problem.

Contribution quotas have been established by taking into account the gross national product, the economic possibilities, and the population figures of the Member States. The Bank is endowed with a capital of one billion dollars, of which 25 per cent has been paid up. The participants contribute in the following proportion: France, 30 per cent; Germany, 30 per cent; Italy, 24 per cent; Belgium, 8.65 per cent; Netherlands, 7.15 per cent; and Luxembourg, 0.2 per cent. The Bank has procured the capital needed to finance its operations, in excess of the 25 per cent, on the financial markets. Most of this capital, but not all, is raised in Common Market countries. Public loans were floated in the Netherlands in 1961 and again in 1962, and in Italy in 1962. These loans have been very successful and show that in a relatively short time the Bank has acquired a solid reputation in financial circles. On January 1, 1963, the consolidated debts of the Bank reached 53.7 million dollars. The total amount of commitments was 254.3 million dollars, 24.3 million dollars more than its paid up capital. The Bank is empowered also to grant loans to enterprises belonging to countries outside the Common Market, provided the projects are situated inside the territories of the Community.

The most important limitation on the Bank's activities, (apart from pursuing ends of profit-making) is that the project to be supported must favor the smooth operation of the Common Market; therefore the approval of the Common Market Executive is mandatory, although the requirement is very elastic and can be stretched to include a variety

174

of things. Also, the governments of the recipient countries must approve the projects.

The Bank has enlarged its activities to cover new fields in addition to big industry: transportation, agriculture, and small and medium industry. As far as small enterprises are concerned, a "test" operation has been decided upon: 400 thousand dollars are being invested in Italian textile manufacture. In the agricultural field, the first intervention, amounting to 9.5 million dollars, consists in participation in the development and irrigation of the Bas-Rhône and Languedoc regions, together with the Compagnie Nationale d'Aménagement de la Région du Bas-Rhône et du Languedoc.

Up to January 1, 1963, the Bank had disbursed 254.3 million dollars in thirty-seven loans, which represent a total investment much larger than one billion dollars (the loans actually cover only an average of 20 per cent of the total cost of the projects). The distribution by country and by sector is as follows:[58]

Country	No. of Projects	Loans (million $)	Percentage
Belgium	1	4.8	2%
West Germany	2	27.4	11%
France	8	54.0	21%
Italy	25	164.1	64%
Luxembourg	1	4.0	2%
Total	37	254.3	100%
Sector			
Industry			
Steel	1	24.0	
Building Mat'ls.	3	9.1	
Paper pulp and paper	2	12.8	
Mechanical	3	11.2	
Chemical	9	71.9	
Food	4	4.8	
Other	3	1.2	
	25	135.0	53%
Agriculture	2	10.5	4%
Transport	4	66.2	26%
Power	6	42.6	17%
Total	37	254.3	100%

[58] *Communauté Européenne*, No. 6, June 1963.

The underdeveloped regions of the Community have benefitted from more than 90 per cent of these loans. In Italy the projects have included the financing of a petrochemical complex at Priolo in Sicily; the development of a lignite depot, with construction of a thermoelectric power station activated by the energy derived from the lignite; the construction of a dam in Sardinia, with three hydroelectric power stations producing 74.4 megawatts; and various loans to the Cassa per il Mezzogiorno. Also, the Bank has participated in the building of a large steelmill in Taranto, capable of supplying two million tons a year. In France, attention should be drawn to the building of a hydroelectric power station, producing 180 megawatts, at Oraison, in addition to participation in the development of the Bas-Rhône-Languedoc region mentioned earlier.

At present, the Bank gives its assistance only to projects of a certain financial momentum. Now, most companies of the Europe of the Six do not have enough financial strength to be able to turn directly to the Bank with a serious chance of success. In practice, the dossiers of application for credit from the small and very small enterprises should be assembled and collectively handled by specialized financial organs, with regional jurisdiction (such as the Sociétés de Développement Régional in France or the Istituto Regionale per il Finanziamento delle Industrie Siciliane in Italy, etc.). "It is in the common interest that these financial organizations be put in condition to communicate with the Bank, and to interest it in operations of a regional character, aiming at various objectives simultaneously."[59]

The Commission has expressed its intention to intensify the activities of the European Investment Bank. In particular, thorough studies will be prepared concerning the over-all economic and social structure of the underdeveloped regions of the Community. The Bank will base its future activities on the results of these studies. And these should, as

[59] *L'Economie*, No. 759, January 12, 1961.

is proper to the activities of the Bank, be essentially dictated by humane considerations; also, "close cooperation will be established with the six governments to establish provisional regional budgets and programs of action. These efforts will have the added advantage of giving in advance, whenever preventive action is possible, an idea of the insufficiencies in the economic and social infrastructure which will appear in the course of future years."[60]

[60] EEC Commission: *Memorandum*, p. 73.

CHAPTER IV

Agriculture

RECENT DEVELOPMENTS

Thus far the Common Market has gone through a number of minor "constitutional" crises and two major ones. Both major crises concerned agriculture—the creation, step by step, of an agricultural common market. Indeed, in both cases, the situation was tense and dramatic, and it looked at the time as if the whole European organization might collapse.[1] In fact, in both cases, the stakes were so high that the Ministers who represented the six Member States "had" to reach an agreement.[2] It is true that the French delegation forced the issue, playing a sort of "brinkmanship" policy, but was finally rewarded for being so persistent and adamant. In the words of Edgard Pisani, French Minister of Agriculture: "France has already twice—in December 1961 and December 1963—rendered an exceptional service to Europe, by insisting that the lag accumulated by agriculture over industry in the building of the Community be reduced."[3] Actually, the end result may be that the favorable solution given to the crises has indeed fortified the Common

[1] At the time of going to press, a third, and perhaps even more serious crisis, has been brilliantly solved. On December 15, 1964, a grain-price agreement has been achieved, creating a common market for cereals among all member states. The pact may have incalculable psychological and practical consequences, as exemplified by the reaction of Walter Hallstein: "Never in the course of our evolution have we taken a decision of such magnitude." De Gaulle called it: "A capital step." *Time*, December, 1964.

[2] "If the Common Market partners ever want to put an end to their cooperation, no treaty will compel them to stay united; if, however, they remain convinced of the high interest of their supreme objective, they will soon eliminate—by acting in common—the obstacles they will find before them." Elgozy, *op.cit.*, p. 117.

[3] *Le Monde Diplomatique*, January 1964.

178

Market, for as *The Economist* stated: ". . . The Christmas agreement has created a kind of inner compulsion to move forward from economic to political integration. . . . Unless things go astonishingly wrong it will in future be hard to conceive of any large food producer, least of all France, taking the decision to break the Market up."[4]

The agreements worked out cover almost 90 per cent of the agricultural production of the Member States, assuring to it, among other things, a progressively freer circulation within the territory of the Community. Details will not be discussed here; it is clear, however, that the agreements have a major impact on French and, to a smaller extent, on Italian agriculture, and consequently on their underdeveloped regions. A discussion of these questions follows.

FRANCE, AGRICULTURE, AND THE COMMON MARKET

The position of France in the agricultural community is very different from that of her partners and warrants special analysis.

It is generally believed that France, the nation with "a colossal potentiality of production in agriculture,"[5] and whose arable land is about equal to the arable land of all the other five Common Market partners together,[6] will necessarily derive great advantages from the agricultural Com-

[4] January 18, 1964.

[5] *Le Monde* (Sélection Hebdomadaire), August 1, 1962.

[6]
*Arable land in countries of
the Community*
(thousands of hectares)

West Germany	14,229
Belgium	1,750
France	39,131
Italy	20,874
Luxembourg	141
Netherlands	2,319
Total	78,444

Source: OECE, *Statistiques de l'Agriculture et de l'Alimentation* (Paris, 1956).

179

mon Market. However, while this is undeniably a distinct possibility, it should also be mentioned that many difficulties must be overcome before it materializes. In the first place the countries of the Community produce most of their own foodstuffs. The main exception is wheat, or, to be precise, certain types of wheat, of which the five partners of France have to import an average of 20 to 25 per cent a year.[7] Other imports are not essential in character.[8]

Another widespread belief is that the climate in France is extremely favorable to agriculture; this is a generally true, but it should not be forgotten that certain areas have a completely unfavorable climate and therefore a poor output. An all-important factor in a better understanding of the position of French agriculture within the Common Market is that, due to her central geographic position, France can produce within her boundaries all the commodities found in any of the other countries of the Community.[9] In other

[7] West Germany is the most important outlet for French wheat within the Community. "Unless both the West German support price and domestic output are reduced, it seems likely that higher French production and exports will further displace West German imports from third countries (mainly overseas) and thus produce still greater self-sufficiency in wheat within the EEC." ECE: *Economic Survey of Europe, 1960*, III, p. 34.

[8] Agricultural production in the Community covers 87 per cent of needs, on an average, but in many cases it exceeds the demand of the Common Market countries: if 100 = total needs in the Community, production is as follows—cereals 90, secondary cereals 80, potatoes 102, sugar 102, vegetables 202, fruit 85, beef 95, pork 102, eggs 92, butter 101, oil (olive etc.) 42. Total average food 87 out of 100. Of course, the figure 100 is not immobile, but will vary with the standard of living; it will go up for some items like meat, sugar, butter, etc., and down for others, like potatoes, cereals, etc. A good example of this change in consumption, determined by the evolving standard of living, is given by the fact that before World War II the countries of the Community were generally exporters of beef, eggs, and butter, whereas they are now importers, even though production has increased 28 per cent. Statistics from EEC, *Le Marché Commun Agricole* (Cahier No. 7).

[9] It should be noted here that, at least to some extent, the same considerations apply to Italy. "Back in 1885, (Minister) Stefano Iacini, at the conclusion of the Agricultural Inquiry, making a report on the results obtained, expressed the following thoughts: Agricultural

words, she does not specialize in certain crops, but, for each one she produces, she must face the competition of at least one of her partners. Furthermore, this great diversity is reflected in costs, which are influenced by the variety of crops produced,[10] each requiring separate expenditures of several kinds in order to find the needed outlets, etc. In sum, the advantages which France can expect from the Common Market are partially offset by the fact that this nation already possesses the whole gamut of products to be found throughout the Community. Each country will, of course, tend to specialize in those crops most suited to its climate, soil, etc., therefore lowering production costs on these items.[11] France will be unable to do likewise, due to the great variations in climate, soil, and other conditions, and will thus have to face competition from several sides on all her products.

Apart from the natural causes affecting French agriculture, those deriving from the action or, in certain cases, lack of action of man should also be mentioned. First of all, there is a certain reluctance and diffidence in taking full advantage of technological progress. In fact, "in France, only 20 per cent of the total agricultural area is worked mechanically."[12]

Italy is composed of such a variety of conditions that, far from constituting an economic unit, it is, more than any other of the great countries of Europe, the most varied as far as agricultural economy is concerned." Cassa, *Contributo*, I, p. 105.

[10] "With the exception of a few regions (Beauce, Brie, Nord), most French farms practice polyculture. Consequently, and also taking into account the family character of many of the farms, there is a high rate of consumption *in loco*, weak average productivity, and high average costs of production." François Visine, *L'Economie française face au Marché Commun* (Paris: Pichon, 1959), p. 49.

[11] "The Member States must agree on a limited number of products. It is probable that the regional division of work will constitute the main subject of discussion; and that full advantage will be taken of the fact that, from Sicily to Brittany, the spectrum of climates is logically varied." Bernard Oury, *L'Agriculture au seuil du Marché Commun* (Paris: Presses Universitaires de France, 1959), preface by Pierre Fromont.

[12] Cassa, *Contributo*, I, p. 49.

However, the pattern is not uniform, and lack of progress is mainly confined to the underdeveloped areas. One of the most serious basic deficiencies is the lack of agricultural schooling.[13] France has one agricultural instructor on an average for 1,500 farms, while the Netherlands has one for every 140, West Germany one for 900, and even Italy one for 960. France has less than fifty professional agricultural schools.[14]

Another weakness is the high cost of transport due to the peculiarity of the French road and railway systems which both radiate from Paris, causing longer routes and consequent waste of time and money. This problem becomes acute for most underdeveloped regions, in view of their peripheral position. In order for certain goods to be moved from one city to another only a few dozen miles away, they must often make a detour through Paris, lengthening the journey by hundreds of miles, and causing delays, damage to perishable goods, and price increases. We have already drawn attention[15] to the curious system practiced in France where nearly all produce must go through Paris to the great

[13] The Commissariat au Plan is now gradually trying to remedy this situation. In fact, "agricultural instruction has undergone profound modifications of structure since the application of Decree No: 59-531, of April 11, 1959. The public services are charged with the task of putting into effect, coordinating and controlling programs of instruction. Increased means are put at the disposal of professional organizations and, in minor measure of the public services with a view to developing such instruction." *Rapport annuel du Commissariat au Plan, 1960.*

[14] "The percentage of farmers who have received technical agricultural training reaches 36 per cent in the Netherlands and about 33 per cent in Luxembourg and West Germany; in France it is only 3.7 per cent and in Italy 1.1 per cent. According to estimates, the percentage of young farmers who have received technical training varies between 82 per cent in the Netherlands and 4 per cent in Italy. These differences between north and south of the Community have increased, rather than diminished in the last few years." From a report *Training and Cultural Life in the Rural Milieu*, presented to a Conference sponsored by the Executive of the EEC on the theme "Social Aspects of a Common Agricultural Policy." Paris, 1959.

[15] *Supra*, Chapter I.

182

market of Les Halles, and then be redistributed across the country.[16]

There is also (and this is common to Southern Italy as well) the problem of the middlemen between the producer and the consumer; their number must be sharply curtailed if prices are to be kept down.[17]

Though these two drawbacks, despite much criticism, can survive under a regime of strong protectionism,[18] this will not be the case when French agriculture, and the whole French productive process, for that matter, is open to competition from the other five members of the Common Market and prices must be kept in line. Furthermore, the cost of

[16] "The cost of transport to Les Halles from one of the Paris stations exceeds that from the most distant corner of Southern France to Paris; but tomato boxes from Cavaillon, lettuce from Perpignan, cabbage from Brittany, have not just to be sent *via* Paris, but to be put through this incredible bottleneck in the center of Paris, and to travel perhaps 1,500 miles and undergo five reloadings, from train to barrow and from barrow to truck before they get to market, from where they have to make their way back in the same way by another train, with all the wear and tear of the market behind them, only to end up at last in Bordeaux or Lille, perhaps only a few hundred miles from their place of origin." Luethy, *op.cit.*, p. 22. However, according to the objectives of the fourth Plan, the situation should improve in the future. "The measures provided . . . for modernizing distribution channels, particularly wholesale market centers for perishable foodstuffs (fruits and vegetables), are principally the creation of: 26 national markets . . . ; wholesale markets . . . to reduce the transport costs by grouping deliveries; and regional markets permitting the decentralization of the Paris Market (Les Halles)." Ambassade de France, New York: *France and Economic Planning*.

[17] "An element which contributes to the high costs to the consumers is the overemployment in the commercial sector still existing in some of the Member States like France and Italy. It is well known, indeed, that commerce, particularly small food retailing, offers relatively easy access and refuge to marginal operations." Cassa, *Contributo*, III, p. 77.

[18] "In France, state intervention in support of agricultural prices and agricultural income is sizeable. Price support is given to agricultural production in the measure of 72 per cent of its value, calculated on the basis of the price paid to the producers. . . . In Italy, on the contrary, state intervention in favor of this sector is rather limited: only 27 per cent in value of production results is financially supported." *Ibid.*, pp. 27, 30.

the means of production is higher than in the other Common Market countries.[19] Tractors are on an average 30 to 50 per cent more expensive, and certain special materials are about 100 per cent more expensive.

Now that all these weaknesses have been listed, let us mention an immense advantage enjoyed by French agriculture: the quantity of land at the disposal of each farmer is much larger than that of his colleagues in the other countries of the Community. The average number of hectares per farmer in the Community is as follows: France 8.3; Italy 3.5; Netherlands 4; Belgium 5; West Germany 5.9; Luxembourg 6.7.[20] Thus, the French farmer has more than double the land of the Italian or Dutch farmer, and more than the other farmers in the Community as well.[21]

Now, when barriers between Member States are definitely lowered, the elimination of obstacles to free circulation of agricultural products will benefit not only French producers but also farmers from the other countries of the Community; in other words, it will be a two-way traffic which will flow unhampered to and from France. Some marginal products that will not be able to withstand serious competition without protection will have to be replaced by certain other products more suited to the new, expanded market. This will entail a readjustment in several branches, but it should be possible to carry out successfully such a reorganization.[22]

[19] ". . . It is something absurdly trivial which stands between France and her own health . . . between France and Europe, and in the last resort between France and herself. At its crudest and most prosaic level, it is simply her costs of production." Luethy, *op.cit.*, p. 333.

[20] Pierre Fromont, "Problèmes de l'Agriculture," *Le Marché Commun et ses Problèmes*, Jacques Rueff *et al.*, (Paris: Sirey, 1958), p. 187.

[21] "It is only since the Common Market came into being, and comparison with the agricultural systems of their neighbors was made, that French farmers and the Government have finally realized that, with only 26 per cent of the active population of the Community, France has 50 per cent of the arable land." *Communauté Européenne*, Nos. 8–9, August–September 1961.

[22] "Certainly if such rationalization is to be achieved, extraordinary sacrifices will have to be made in some areas. The vested advantages

In the underdeveloped regions, where this process of replacement of one crop by another will present some difficulties, the farmers will be able to avail themselves of the European Agricultural Fund, which has particular provisions for underdeveloped areas. The Fund has been set up in order to achieve financially sound production, offering an equitable income to the farmers, and keeping in mind that, to ameliorate in a lasting way the present unfavorable income and the difficult conditions of life of a large fraction of the agricultural producers, it will be necessary to undertake an energetic program aimed at improving the regional structure.

One branch of the Fund will be considered here: *Le Fonds Européen d'Amélioration de la Structure Agricole.* This organization has a distinctive regional character and will complement in the agricultural sector the work of the European Investment Bank by granting financial help to public or private organizations or firms, with a view to reducing the interest rate or prolonging the period of amortization on Bank loans. However, "the resources of the Fund are only applicable to agricultural projects as part of a program of *regional economic development* and aimed at objectives conforming to the principles of a common agricultural policy."[23] The national governments will also have to contribute to this effort of reconversion.[24]

---

of particular economic groups, such as the agricultural producers, deriving from established economic and social policies of national governments, will have to be modified and the comparative advantages enjoyed by some areas over others will have to be foregone, at least in part, to raise the economic and social levels of less-favored regions." Zurcher, *op.cit.*, p. 184.

[23] EEC, Annex to *Le Calendrier du Marché Commun Agricole* (supplement to *Communauté Européenne*, Aug.–Sept., 1960).

[24] An entirely new approach to agricultural problems will henceforth guide the policy of the French Government. A comprehensive law was passed in 1962 by the Parliament by an overwhelming majority. As a result, "the systematic equality of aid by the public powers will be *corrected by the necessity of redressing the inequality of opportunity according to the regions.* The right of property will be *adapted* to the exigencies of the economy." (emphasis supplied) *Le Monde* (Sélection Hebdomadaire), July 5, 1962. A summary of the new law ap-

In conclusion, the outcome of the agricultural Common Market for France, as for the other Member States, is closely linked to the outcome of the Common Market as a whole.[25] If the standard of living of the people in the Community continues to improve (the results during the few years since the Treaty became valid are encouraging), there will be an increased demand for products that today are considered a luxury, such as meat, good wines, etc., and French farmers will be the first to benefit from this general improvement.[26]

peared in the *New York Times*, July 20, 1962: "Radical reforms in the pattern of farm ownership and use in France were voted by the National Assembly early this morning. The Deputies were up all night debating what specialists consider a revolution in French agriculture, the most conservative and traditionalist sector of the country's economic life. . . . The Government is sympathetic to the move to get young blood (young farmers with modern, aggressive ideas) into agriculture as part of the effort to modernize it and *to improve its competitive position in the European Common Market*. [emphasis supplied] The official attitude is that only long-range reform can solve the problems of French farmers who, in general, seek a larger share of the national revenue." It is, of course, obvious that "it is not just a coincidence that the complementary [agricultural] law was approved a few days before the coming into being of the agricultural Common Market. . . ." *Le Monde* (Sélection Hebdomadaire), August 1, 1962.

[25] "To give an idea of the profound changes entailed by the Common Market in the present agricultural legislation, we have to point out that the *Journal Officiel des Communautés Européennes* . . . is becoming the bedside book of the [French] farmer. . . ." *Le Monde* (Sélection Hebdomadaire), August 1, 1962. Of particular interest to the American reader is the following comment by Jean Boissonnat in *Le Monde Diplomatique* of June, 1963: "Everything concurs to favor French agriculture, provided the European Community be *one* agricultural market and not *a part* of the world market; in fact, in the latter case, our prices cease to be competitive and we are menaced by the American surpluses, which can be sold no matter where, or at what price, for it is not the customer but the [American] taxpayer who pays the American farmer."

[26] A theoretical calculation shows that "if each inhabitant of Benelux and West Germany would consume an average of 25 liters of wine per year (which is only a fraction of what the French and Italians consume), the EEC would need to produce 124 million hectoliters, whereas present average production in the total area up till now has been 114 million hectoliters. It is easy to see what prospects are open for increased sales of wine in the Common Market once barriers have

And, if, as is very probable, over-all demand increases by much more than the corresponding demographic increase in the territory of the Community, then the present problems of overproduction will be solved.[27] Not only this, but there will be a major need for a thorough reorganization of land ownership and systems of production in order to increase agricultural output in the now semidormant areas of the "désert français."[28] Let us now examine these areas and try to assess the impact of the agricultural Common Market on them.

BRITTANY

From the agricultural viewpoint, Brittany can be divided into two zones: a maritime and an inland zone. In the center of the region there are two plateaus, partly covered with

---

been abolished and wine becomes an everyday drink for the average German, Dutchman, or Belgian, instead of a de luxe beverage for special occasions. The consumption of wine is in effect limited in the countries of Benelux and in Germany by virtue of the imposition of high duties on alcoholic beverages. . . . At present, annual per capita consumption of wine in the EEC, in liters, is as follows: France, 155.4; Italy, 111.0; West Germany 9.2; Belgium, 6.1; Netherlands, 1.4; Luxembourg (not known)." Oury, *op.cit.* pp. 166–168.

[27] Jean Delau, president of the French Association of Wheat Producers and of the Committee of Professional Agricultural Organizations of the EEC, writes in *Le Monde Diplomatique* of January 1964: "We are persuaded that the growth in [agricultural] consumption in an economy in full activity will surpass the increase in production."

[28] French Minister of Agriculture, Edgard Pisani "estimates that in France there are too many fallow lands: 4,300,000 hectares, that is the [equivalent of the] area of eight *départements*. . . . He wishes that the State recover these fallow lands so as to enlarge the existing farms and to create new ones." *Le Monde* (Sélection Hebdomadaire), August 1, 1962. And *Time*, August 10, 1962, adds: "The new farm legislation creates a 'collectivization' agency—as traditionalists scoffingly call it—with power to buy and resell at reasonable prices all land that comes on the market, plus most of some 11 million idle acres whose ownership is in dispute (the new body is known as SEFER—Societé d'Etablissements Foncières et d'Economie Rurale): the Agency will have authority to designate maximum and minimum sizes for new farms, thus protecting peasants simultaneously against *cumulards* and *morcellement* (land-grabbers and pulverization of the land)."

landes (unproductive moorlands). Agriculture developed in the nineteenth century, when the country benefitted from an improvement in communications with the rest of France. Many *landes* were redeemed and used for cattle grazing. Cereals are extensively cultivated all over the region. The mild, maritime climate is highly favorable to the growth of fruits and vegetables of various kinds. One zone in the region is called the "Golden Belt" because of its fertility; but rational and technologically advanced methods of cultivation could improve the yield of many areas up to tenfold.[29] Gravier tells us that the

> experiment of the "fodder" revolution, realized near Loudéac, for instance, in the "poor" lands of interior Brittany, has given a more abundant yield than in Jutland or in the Low Countries. The very great possibilities for improvement offered by the climate apply also to lands subject to floods, which were formerly considered worthless. Thus, the Director of Agricultural Services of Nantes informs us that the "swamps" of the Lower Loire furnished two successive harvests during the "dry" periods of 1955 and 1956 . . . and experiments with beetroot have brought about a yield of 1,500 kilos per hectare. This technique brings the value of the yield per hectare from about 10,000 francs to 300,000 francs.[30]

However, before talking about increasing current production, which is easily feasible with technological improvements and more rational and modern methods of cultivation, the problem of finding outlets for this production must be solved.

[29] "Only modernization of the structures of European agriculture will allow the growth of productivity and will create favorable conditions for the application of the most recent technical advances and *for the development of the weakest economic regions.*" (emphasis supplied) CEE, *Où en est le Marché Commun?*, p. 15.

[30] Gravier, *op.cit.*, p. 250.

Agriculture is engaged at present in an evolution which begets cumulative effects, because it produces more and commercializes its products; as a consequence, it is capable, without increasing prices, of increasing its revenue. . . . However, whatever we do, if we are not capable of exporting, nothing will be realized: in the hierarchy of priorities, the conquest of outlets comes first.[31]

It is a fact that adequate outlets cannot be found within France itself,[32] and the great hope of Breton farmers is that when the agricultural Common Market is in full operation it will provide an opening for massive exports from Brittany.

When French agricultural problems and, at the same time, those deriving from insufficient development of a region are discussed, invariably the prime example is Brittany. This region, glorious in so many ways, land of many of the greatest French navigators and explorers, is a perpetual hotbed of unrest.[33] This is due partly to the character of the inhabitants but mainly to the economic organization of the region. "There is little industry in the area and experts feel that too many people are trying to live on small, uneconomical farms that average about 25 acres."[34] During the violent peasant demonstrations of June 1961, "the demonstrators accused the Government of not giving enough help in supporting prices for their produce, particu-

[31] *Le Figaro,* October 27, 1961. Report of speech made the previous day by M. Pisani to the French Senate.

[32] "If the results of national agricultural policies have not always been very satisfactory (the equilibrium between production and the possibilities of outlets is precarious and the income of the farmer has remained behind in relation to the other strata of the population) the cause is that no doubt these problems were *insoluble in the long range in the narrow framework of our small countries.*" (emphasis supplied) EEC, *L'Agriculture dans le Marché Commun.* (Cahier de Communauté Européenne.)

[33] *Le Monde* (Sélection Hebdomadaire), August 1, 1962, calls it: "Bretagne, région traditionnellement 'remuante.' " ("restless, active, always stirring"—*Petit Larousse Illustré*)

[34] *New York Times,* June 21, 1961.

larly when the crop is over-abundant, and of generally neglecting the Breton economy."[35]

An analysis of the agricultural problems of the region, in the framework of the Common Market, should start by emphasizing that they are closely related to the general condition of underdevelopment.[36] Furthermore, Brittany, contrary to the other underdeveloped regions of France, is overpopulated compared to its resources. Families, in the old peasant tradition, are generally large; its 3 million inhabitants represent a density of 95 per square kilometer compared to 73 for France as a whole (including Brittany). Since the region has little industry, most of its people base their source of income on activities directly or indirectly connected with agriculture or fishing, the other main activity of the region. But, even if agricultural production continues to rise, year after year, the number of people employed diminishes constantly due to technological improvements. This fact has been partly counterbalanced by intense emigration, but has also created a serious situation that continues to perplex the French Government, which is urgently seeking a solution to it.[37]

[35] *Loc. cit.*

[36] "Situated on the Atlantic tip of Europe, far away geographically and, more important, because of the insufficiency of its railroad and road infrastructure, and of its airlanes, from the great industrial axis of the Common Market, lacking in industries, Brittany could not be in the forefront of the European regions whose prosperity has been immediately stimulated by the first measures of application of the Rome Treaty. . . . But she has confidence in the progressive dispositions of the Treaty . . . Brittany is an [agricultural] exporter. One of her roles is that of being one of the great food supplying provinces of the Common Market." René Pleven, former French Premier, in *Communauté Européenne*, Nos. 8–9, Aug.–Sept. 1962.

[37] "The outflow of labor from agriculture—a prerequisite for viable farming in Western Europe—is not synonymous with migration to the big towns. Clearly a policy that creates alternative opportunities for employment—in industry and services—near the farm population which it is desired to shift into other occupations would greatly facilitate the adjustment and minimize many social costs. Such a regional policy could make possible more part-time farming supple-

Agricultural overproduction and lack of organization in the transportation system, due in part to the isolated geographical position of Brittany, are two of the greatest plights of the region; the representatives of the agricultural organizations now see very clearly that a real solution to these problems can only come about within the framework of the enlarged European market. In a speech made at Nantes, in Brittany, on November 8, 1960, M. André Raillet, dealing with the development of the whole Western part of France in the framework of the Common Market said:

> If the east of France is the only part to develop, there will not be any Common Market, because there will not be any viable internal market. It is in the interest of France that the west be developed and it is necessary for this to be done quickly. It is not possible to solve the problem of the west without framing it in the proper context. In this area of depression constituted by the west . . . why not interest some of the European countries, where great financial resources probably lie dormant, in a plan of investment which will spell the end of economic imbalance in France.[38]

Two of the important products of this region where grazing is widespread are milk and beef. At present production of these items increases constantly and at a much quicker pace than the natural increase of the French population. Therefore, the increasing supply tends to bring prices down in spite of the many measures taken by the French Government to counteract this trend. That is to say, prices threaten to go down for the farmer; the butchers and the many

mented by part-time jobs in forestry, tourism, fishing, or industry, although the remaining farmers would mainly occupy farms big enough to provide full-time employment (and a reasonable income without exceptional protection)." ECE, *Economic Survey of Europe,* 1960, III, p. 43.

[38] *Le Monde,* November 9, 1960.

middlemen see to it, however, that there are no reductions in price when the beef reaches the consumer.[39]

The problem of finding new outlets for beef in the Common Market is not complicated because it is a well-known fact that at present there is a pronounced underconsumption of meat in all the Common Market countries, and not only in their underdeveloped regions.[40] This potentially immense outlet would provoke an even greater increase in production once free circulation is attained, if cattle-raising did not entail immobilization of capital for a certain time. It is improbable that important amounts of capital could now be subjected to this immobilization since employing it in industrial activities within the Common Market (especially in view of the "boom" of the last few years) offers greater and quicker rewards. Therefore, the European Agricultural Fund should, by a system of loans, help farmers to face the first phase of the new situation deriving from the agricultural Common Market, until progress in the process of capital formation enables them to proceed by their own means.

As for milk, its direct sale on the European market pre-

[39] The President of the Chamber of Agriculture of the Blanc, in an interview granted to Raymond Cartier and published in *Paris-Match*, April 19, 1960, states: "He [the butcher] pays from 250 to 400 francs per kilo for our animals, and resells them from 450 fr. a kilo for the worst cuts to 1,200 for the best. This profit is unacceptable." The rapacity of the middlemen reaches impressive proportions in Brittany, in all sort of agricultural products: "Last year trucks full of Breton artichokes rolled all over the Paris streets. . . . Before this march of Breton farmers on the capital, artichokes sold for 0.02 to 0.05 NF. a kilo at Saint-Pol-de-Léon and were sold for 1.00 to 1.50 NF a kilo in Paris." B. Lambert, article entitled "La commercialisation des produits agricoles" in *L'Agriculture en France*, *p.* 60.

[40] Beef consumption in the Community, in kilos per capita per year is as follows: France 28.3; Belgium and Luxembourg 21.1; West Germany 17.8; Netherlands 17.3; Italy 11.2; Community average, 18.9. See CEE, *L'Agriculture dans le Marché Commun.* "As far as beef is concerned, there has never been any difficulty in selling it. Prices are comparable in the six countries and the prospects of outlets in the Community are very attractive. Consumption in the six countries is going to double from now until 1970." *Communauté Européenne*, No. 2, February 1964.

sents certain difficulties:[41] first, since it is a perishable commodity it faces a very serious handicap. In addition, the consumption of butter in the European market has reached a stalemate, showing little sign of increase in recent years. Therefore, most of the milk should find outlets in the Common Market in the form of evaporated or powdered milk, and of cheese. While the demand for milk in these forms is limited in Europe, the market for famous brands of French cheese is infinitely better, providing the producers know how to maintain quality and thus make them suitable for the foreign consumer. Numerous experiments, some successful, have been tried to sell some famous brands of cheese in Germany by packaging small portions in wooden boxes.[42]

Furthermore, Brittany could take advantage of her maritime position to ship her products by sea to the "Northern tier" of the Common Market: North Germany, Belgium, and Holland. At any rate, it would seem that the continuous increase in quantity, and the improvement in quality, of agricultural products, especially vegetables, dairy foods, and cattle, can contribute in a decisive way to increasing the standards of the region and turning it into a rich agricultural area, provided agriculture, together with fishing, does not remain the only important activity of Brittany.[43]

It is not true that there is no hope outside agriculture. There is no hope outside a well-balanced cooperation of

[41] Milk production in the countries of the Community reached 59 million tons (in weight) in 1957–58 against 48 million tons in 1950–51, which represents an annual increase of almost 3 per cent. According to estimates, milk production will be between 64 and 69 million tons a decade from now. Excess milk production will by then be about 3 million tons. CEE, *L'Agriculture dans le Marché Commun.*

[42] *Le Monde*, June 21, 1960.

[43] "The structural improvement of agriculture is incomplete in certain regions unless efforts are made simultaneously to create possibilities of employment in other sectors of activity for the rural population. In numerous cases, structural improvement will liberate a number of workers who could be employed elsewhere." CEE, *Situation de l'Agriculture dans le Marché Commun,* p. 27.

agriculture with industry . . . in particular, there is no purely agricultural solution to the Breton problem: the population pressure is too high in the peninsula and the land too poor and too limited. If a sufficient number of industrial "poles of development" are not implanted there between now and 1970 in order to furnish employment for the accumulating excess of manpower, in the next ten years hundreds of thousands of young emigrants will be added to the streams of jobless coming from the Creuse, the Massif Central, the South-West, and the provinces of the West, to go on inflating the Paris region and complete the process of transforming our beautiful France into a macrocephalic monster.[44]

It is therefore essential that a better balance between agriculture and industry be struck.[45] Progress will be more complete and long-lasting as the introduction of new activities helps the commercial and industrial spirit to penetrate well into the peninsula.

Experience shows that the evolution and adaptation of the farmers have been more rapid and spontaneous in the coastal areas, where maritime activities, and tourism as well, have contributed to breaking the homogeneity of the agricultural milieux. Already, a systematic effort at giving technical advise has been centered in the Loire-Atlantique area of Brittany. The Government has contributed financially to the redemption of about 200,000 hectares and to the setting up of some light industry, mainly canning, processing dairy products, and meat packing. However, these efforts, laudable as they are, will not settle the agricultural problem of Brittany.[46] A permanent, final solution can

[44] *Le Figaro*, August 11, 1961.

[45] "Parity of per capita income between industry and agriculture will be difficult to obtain. This is the reason why agriculture will have to be supported, at least in the next decades by industry." *Le Figaro*, November 18, 1961.

[46] Various protective measures have also been devised in favor of the small and medium farmer in this context. For instance, the *New*

only be found by the opening of large, new outlets for the output of the area once the agricultural Common Market becomes fully operative.[47]

LANGUEDOC

Any discussion of agriculture in Languedoc means essentially a discussion of vineyards. We have seen in Chapter I the overwhelming role played by this activity in the development of the region and the fact that its decline entailed the decline of practically all the economic activities of Languedoc. For this region, perhaps even more than in some other poor regions of France, the problem can be summed up in one single word: overproduction. The obvious remedies are two: (a) diversification of production on the one hand, so that the share left to viniculture will decrease; (b) the finding of new outlets in the larger European Common Market. But neither of these seems to present possibilities for a solution to the problem in the near future. Meanwhile, production continues to increase and the problem acquires intensity.[48]

York Times, July 21, 1962, reports that ". . . special authorization will be required for any company wishing to enter hog, chicken and egg production. This measure was taken to protect small family producers, notably in Brittany."

[47] "To make full use of its advantages in the Common Market, Brittany needs a number of important investments in order to create or modernize the basic infrastructure and equipment which will be indispensable to both its agriculture and to the industrialization which looms. The regulations of the Treaty of Rome creating a European Investment Bank, which indicates its role in favor of the peripheral, less economically developed areas of the Common Market, have suscitated there hopes which start to become realities." René Pleven, *Communauté Européenne,* Nos. 8–9, Aug.–Sept. 1962.

[48] *Revue de l'Economie Meridionale,* No. 40, Oct.–Dec. 1962, notes the following apropos the harvest of 1962: "The 1962 harvest, the second largest of the century, is much bigger than that of 1961. . . . Comparison with the average of the last decade confirms its exceptional character:

Of course, viniculture is not the only agricultural activity of the region. However, it is by far the most important, the one which will probably determine the position of Languedoc in respect to the other regions of France and of the Common Market.

Many of the other Mediterranean agricultural products find ideal climatic conditions in Languedoc and are also cultivated throughout the region: olives, almonds, figs, peaches, apricots, etc. Cereals are also grown in appreciable quantities, and grazing is widely practiced.[49]

A problem which has always beset the region is the scarcity of water. This is now well on the way to a solution, with the building of the Bas-Rhône-Languedoc Canal. Thus, "Languedoc, thanks to this canal, will soon *enjoy a considerable advantage over all the other regions of France.* Throughout its plains and its low hills, it has suddenly been offered a production tool of the 21st century, in a region much less affected than the rest of France by winter frosts. The 'North of the Loire,' traditionally quoted as much in advance in

Department	Harvest 1961 (*hectoliters*)	Harvest 1962 (*hectoliters*)	Increase	Average— 1952–61
Aude	5,543,424	8,500,458	53%	5,925,125
Gard	4,866,702	7,300,586	50%	5,035,066
Hérault	8,854,385	14,579,669	65%	9,363,958
Pyrénées-Orientales	2,191,952	3,090,554	41%	2,544,226
Total 4 Depts	21,456,463	33,471,267	56%	22,868,383
Total France	46,715,000	73,478,000	57%	55,499,000

In the meantime, the quantity of wine exported from the region went down by 11.5% (15% Aude; 6.5% Gard; 12% Hérault; 10.5% Pyrénées-Orientales).

[49] The importance of agriculture in the regional economy is evident once more as the income it produces represents:

	1956	1957
Pyrénées-Orientales	45%	50%
Hérault	30%	32%
Aude	33%	42%

For France as a whole the proportion was below 12% for agricultural income. Data from *Revue de l'Economie Meridionale*, No. 41, January-March, 1963.

agriculture, must face strong competition if the enormous possibilities of this irrigation, here more productive, thanks to the sunshine, are utilized in full and rapidly."[50]

Of course, the potentialities brought about by the newly distributed water supply must not be used to support new vineyards; instead, the Government, in cooperation with the Compagnie Nationale d'Aménagement de la Région du Bas-Rhône et du Languedoc and with the regional organizations, is trying to persuade the local farmers to switch to other products, taking advantage of the irrigation facilities.[51] But several factors oppose a quick conversion. Some of these are more of a psychological nature than others: for instance, a real "mystique de la vigne" has developed throughout the years in Languedoc and many farmers feel almost as though they would betray their heritage and their life purpose if vine-growing were abandoned. Also, new products would be subject to strong competition from the other Mediterranean partner of the Common Market, Italy, and the farmers of Languedoc do not feel that a change of culture would necessarily bring them financial advantages despite the Government's propaganda to the contrary.

AQUITAINE

In Aquitaine, as we have seen, historical events are at the root of the present state of underdevelopment, together with

[50] René Dumont in *L'Agriculture en France*, p. 81.

[51] *Le Monde*, April 8, 1960, has this to say: "The public effort should be directed to the reconversion of certain agricultural regions and to the modernization of the centers: to producing peaches instead of wine, or selected fruit and vegetables instead of cereals, or green vegetables instead of sugar beet. . . . Agricultural reconversion is as necessary as industrial reconversion and often an equally important amount of capital is necessary (one should bear in mind, for instance, the costs of the irrigation projects in the Bas-Rhône-Languedoc area). . . . It is not by turning the greatest part of its effort to traditional outlets and by making use of few workers that the state will orientate French agriculture towards renewed growth and thus prepare it to play its proper role in the Common Market." A decree approved by the Council of Ministers on August 21, 1963, actually promises monetary rewards to the farmers who agree to discontinue viniculture in certain particularly unfavorable areas.

197

reasons originating outside the region. Even more than the other regions, Aquitaine had lived, until a century and a half ago, as a closed economy since she produced practically all that was necessary for the support of her inhabitants. This relative stagnation was more or less common to every region before the industrial revolution, but the situation changed after it. In Aquitaine, however, it changed for the worst; her flourishing handicraft industry was almost killed by the new mechanized industries installed in other regions. Also, in the middle of the nineteenth century, Aquitaine underwent a series of agricultural crises (insufficient wheat production in certain years, requiring expensive imports; phylloxera) which contributed to the acceleration of her decadence. In the meantime, progress was being made rapidly in most other regions. Aquitaine did not keep pace, and a growing emigration followed. In the last eighty years, almost all the rural districts have lost more than one-third of their population. In 1954, the *département* of Lot had less than a half the population it had in 1850. Luckily for Aquitaine, this mass emigration from the region was partly compensated for by immigration, almost exclusively made up of Italians and Spaniards who, as they had no work in their own country, and were in any case used to a very low standard of living, accepted without complaint the new living conditions which, low as they were, at least gave them the assurance of satisfying their basic needs. In 1936, more than 10 per cent of the population was made up of these immigrants in certain *départements*, particularly in the Gers and Lot-et-Garonne.

The economy of the region is based largely on agricultural activities: a majority of its *départements* are almost exclusively agricultural. There is no equilibrium in the economy of South-West France; in contrast with France as a whole (where the figure is 27 per cent), the number of persons actively employed in agriculture reaches 45 per cent. Actually, in some *départements* it reaches and surpasses 60 per cent

198

(Lot, 60 per cent; Tarn-et-Garonne, 65 per cent; Gers, 70 per cent). The peasantry of Aquitaine has practically cut itself off from the rest of the country, following a policy of isolation which is certainly the shortest way to stagnation and decadence. The farms are generally small or medium-sized—50 per cent do not attain ten hectares in area; share-cropping is practiced extensively. These two factors combined are not conducive to agricultural progress. Lack of capital, lack of proper equipment, and lack of rational systems of cultivation are some of the by-products which derive from this situation. Productivity is consequently lower than the average for the country.

Fortunately, a great change has been brought about recently by the discovery of important deposits of natural gas at Lacq in 1954, of oil at Parentis, and also of other minor sources of energy. Around the factories, power stations, etc. which have acted as "poles of growth" the improvement has been general. This will increase in the future, it is hoped, when greater industrialization and modernization of the region will also entail a general agricultural improvement, the close connection between industrial and agricultural development of the region being evident. Consequently, this industrialization should put a stop to emigration or at least slow it down considerably and actually invite immigration. While technological progress is advancing, Aquitaine presents great possibilities for growth beyond the meager results thus far obtained. For example, the average wheat yield per hectare used to be 14 to 17 quintals, but now a certain selected strain (produced after repeated experiments) is reputed to be able to almost triple that yield, bringing it to an average of 30 to 40 quintals per hectare. Also, the introduction of some strains of hybrid corn has produced amazing results (up to 100 quintals per hectare, and sometimes more) in the areas with a maritime climate, and it might well be that the Adour basin will become the French equivalent of the American "corn belt."

199

These zones could therefore consequently be transformed into exporters of meat and poultry (the demand for which is high in the Community) and dairy products.[52]

Some of the *départements* of Aquitaine, particularly the Basque country (Hautes et Basses-Pyrénées) and Béarn, enjoy a very good climate, from the agricultural viewpoint, and, if more modern methods and more fertilizers were used, production would certainly increase noticeably. In the "Coteaux de Gascogne" soil erosion and irregularity of rainfall are obstacles to the growth of wheat and corn, and also to grazing, practiced on a large scale in the region. While the soil of the Causses is not suitable to intensive cultivation, some of the valleys of the Lot and Dordogne could grow special crops, such as walnuts, early strawberries, tobacco—products which are now rather sparse and of secondary importance.

Certain measures for development are already taking place; the capital involved is either public or at least mixed.[53] In the latter category, for instance, belong the companies entrusted with the development of the Landes de Gascogne and the redemption of the Landes Béarnaises (from 50,000 to 100,000 hectares). The European Investment Bank decided in 1961 to loan five million francs to the Aménagement des Landes de Gascogne, with the goal of exploiting the hitherto uncultivated land situated in the forest zones of

[52] The French Government is already orienting its policy in this sense. "The authorities hope to limit the need for support by encouraging the production of commodities such as beef, fruit and vegetables, for which domestic demand is more promising. . . ." ECE, *Economic Survey of Europe*, 1961, p. 35.

[53] "The structural conditions of agriculture, which are often quite unsatisfactory, limit, more than in the other sectors, the effects of capital investments. This puts a brake on any increase in productivity and improvement in the situation of the agricultural workers. It appears that a rational utilization of capital in many places makes a modification of the agricultural structure necessary, which in its turn necessitates in almost every case the financial support of the State." CEE, *L'Agriculture dans le Marché Commun.*

South-West France by creating rational and high-output agricultural entities.[54]

At the moment, there is a tendency to reduce the amount of land for corn-growing. The contrary is true for wheat, the output of which, as we have seen, is increasing. The same applies to wine, with reasonable prospects for exportation both within the Common Market and outside it.

The waters of the main rivers must be harnessed; in fact, periodic floods threaten the lands along the Garonne, Ariège, and Tarn. Conversely, the problem of lack of water is rather serious in other zones, in particular in the *département* of Gers. Another problem in parts of the region, and particularly in Gers and the Causses, is the scarcity of drinking water. In view of the configuration and sparse population centers, provision of a network supplying sufficient water presents great difficulty, and in addition is abnormally expensive. Obviously, drinking water is a necessity for development of these areas, and efforts are being made, often by *ad hoc* associations made up of administrations of neighboring towns and villages, to finance water systems, either locally or through the intervention of higher authorities when the expense would be too great. These efforts are particularly active in the *départements* of Ariège, Gers, and Lot. There are projects, some of which are already being implemented, for large irrigation works in the Coteaux de Gascogne, the valleys of Ariège, Lot, Dordogne, and more are contemplated. The most important are those carried out by the Société d'Aménagement des Coteaux de Gascogne.

The Gers and Basses-Pyrénées also have the problem of bringing electricity to many hamlets and isolated farms; modernization and extension work in the area served by old facilities is in progress in many parts of the region.

It is necessary for several reasons that reforestation be carried out on a larger scale than hitherto. For this purpose, the Fonds Forestier National, by direct subsidies, loans, or

[54] CEE, *Communauté Européenne*, Nos. 8–9, Aug.–Sept. 1961.

in other ways, renders valuable assistance. At present, the average annual area being brought back to forest is about 1,200 hectares for Tarn, 1,000 for Lot, 500 for Basses-Pyrénées, 500 for Ariège; these averages can certainly be improved if additional credits are supplied by the proper authorities.

Nonetheless, the fact remains that, out of 1,484,000 hectares, the total area subject to cultivation is only 245,000 hectares, most of which is extensively farmed. If, as the prospects for European outlets improve, the general situation so warrants,[55] the area could soon be increased to 300,000 or 400,000 hectares. It has been ascertained by agricultural experts that, not even allowing for the technological improvements certain to come about in the next few years, agricultural production in this region could easily be doubled and perhaps even tripled.[56] Such a development would be an incentive for the present inhabitants to stay in the region; moreover agricultural immigration would actually be encouraged. Naturally, the development effort should be a basic one, enbracing the whole region in all its economic activities, and coordinated to similar efforts in other regions. The European Agricultural Fund should help the national Government with financing and also help coordinate the agricultural policy of the six partners so that

[55] "On recent production figures, the expanded Community would still have to import considerable supplies of foodstuffs. But if the prices are fixed high enough to encourage European farmers—particularly in France—to increase output, the situation could change radically." *The Observer*, August 5, 1962.

[56] For instance, linked to the finding of outlets in the Common Market and elsewhere is the fruit production of the valley of the Garonne, which could easily be doubled in about a decade. The same applies to the production of vegetables in the same valley, for which soil and climatic conditions are particularly favorable. Another example is given by Serge Mallet in an article entitled "La Réforme de la Propriété Foncière" in *L'Agriculture en France*, in which he says "By modifying the orientation of its crops, the country of Blayais, north of Gironde, which was the most backward in the region from the viewpoint of agricultural income, is becoming the richest. . . ."

new outlets can be found to correspond to the gradual increases in production.

These possibilities of modernization, of increased production, and even of resettling of immigrants from other parts of the Community and from Algeria are indications that the European Economic Community can expect very positive results from Aquitaine, if it is decided to exploit to the maximum its great agricultural potential.[57]

CORSICA

One quarter of the island of Corsica is covered by forests; only about 2 per cent of the total area is cultivated, while the total arable land exceeds 20 per cent (190,000 hectares). But agriculture is chronically suffering from lack of labor, capital, and water. Therefore most of the land which could, with a rational irrigation system, be given over to the culture of various crops—particularly cereals, for which the climate and soil are well suited—is instead used for grazing. Mediterranean crops are grown (olives, grapes, fruits, cereals, tobaccos), and cattle are relatively common. An organization was established in 1958 to aid development of the region—the Société d'Economie Mixte de Mise en Valeur de la Corse (SOMIVAC). Its main task is the modernization and industrialization of the agricultural economy of Corsica. The results thus far obtained, without

[57] The connections between this region and the Common Market are becoming closer and closer, particularly since the conclusion of the agreements of December 1963, which might have very beneficial results for the agriculture of Aquitaine. For example, in *Communauté Européenne*, No. 2, February 1964, it is reported that "The first traveling exhibit on French agriculture within the context of the Common Market has been inaugurated at Bordeaux (Aquitaine). This exhibit, arranged by Jeune Europe and presented by the Centre National des Jeunes Agriculteurs, with the participation of the Service d'Information des Communautés Européennes, will permit farmers to see the concrete problems, the opportunities, and the disciplines of the agricultural Common Market. It will circulate first in the South-West and West of France."

203

being striking, are at least a start in the right direction. Lack of governmental credits, as well as other reasons, have helped to slow down the rather ambitious initial plans. One asset that may tend to accelerate the present pace of progress is the immigration to the island of thousands of farmers from North Africa, who have elected to reside there since the island's climate and other conditions are similar to those of the land they left behind. As a matter of fact, it seems that these refugees have been so favored by the Société that several protests have been raised by the islanders against the disparity of treatment.

Irrigation being one of the major problems in Corsican agriculture, SOMIVAC has naturally done some work in this field. It has however been demonstrated that very large sums would be necessary even for partial, local solutions. If a decision is finally made to carry out the projects now under consideration (the dams of Castirla and Sampolo, with a capacity of 30 million cubic meters, the reservoir of Alesani with 15 million cubic meters), the reasons would be political rather than economic. However, some achievements have been realized during the period of its existence by the Société; for instance, an important five-mile canal to bring to the plain of Chisonaccia the water of the Fium'Orbo. Another irrigation system is soon to be tried: the building of small, artificial lakes in hilly zones, which will form reservoirs with a capacity of millions of cubic meters of much-needed water. Two of these small lakes are already in the process of being built at Teppes-Rosses and at Alzitone. Furthermore, a number of natural wells have been discovered and some of the water is already being used for irrigation purposes, through a system of pumps.

Thus, all three major obstacles to rapid agricultural progress in the island—labor, capital, and water—have been attacked, but continue to act as the major brake on improvement of internal conditions. Furthermore, the insular position of Corsica is a serious handicap that threatens to cancel out any progress made by Corsican agriculture in the future. According to long-range forecasts by agricultural experts, thirty years from now the utilization of 50,000 additional hectares of good land will lead to a total production of 400,000 tons per year of agricultural crops. Since the quantity of these particular products consumed *in loco* was only 50,000 tons in 1961, it is clear that there will be an immense surplus. Therefore the vital need is to organize cheap and rapid transport to both France and the nearby Italian coast to partially overcome this severe drawback. Of course, the ideal solution would be to lower over-all costs by integrating the transportation systems of Corsica and Sardinia within the framework of the Common Market. With this in mind, there are now insistent demands for the building of a bridge linking the two islands across the Strait of St. Boniface.[58] Also, some agreements to regulate production should be concluded with those regions of Southern Italy and Southern France that produce similar crops. Of course, this will be much easier after the agricultural Common Market solidifies and a central agency is able to exercise a certain degree of authority over production in the Six.

THE MASSIF CENTRAL

In the area of the Massif Central, agricultural productivity is by no means uniform. Physical contrasts in the region are striking—in certain areas a relatively small acreage produces every type of crop grown in continental France. Unfortunately, this does not mean either quality or quantity production. Actually, with few exceptions, the productivity of the land is low and the climate is bad.[59]

[58] See *Prospettive Meridionali*, January 1963.

[59] "It should be observed that these plains and sunny valleys represent only a few oases in an immensity barren and hostile to man. We may remember the appalling poverty of certain areas where the *gross* revenue of a peasant family is no more than 25,000 francs a month [\$50] and the decline or the disappearance of several traditional industries isolated in the mountains. All this, which is a fact, seems to justify the very old currents of seasonal emigration (Versailles was built by masons from the Limousin), then the final exodus toward Paris, Lyon, etc." Gravier, *op. cit.*, p. 264.

However, the present situation could be considerably improved if a thorough plan of development could be devised that would encompass the whole region. As repeatedly stated in regard to the other underdeveloped regions, agricultural advance *per se* is practically impossible unless it is paralleled by industrial development—especially industrial development that utilizes local products, such as food processing and industries connected with wood and wood products—paper, furniture, etc.

In this region, uncultivated land (potentially subject to cultivation) and moorlands cover at least 850,000 hectares, i.e., 15.3 per cent of the territory; forests cover 822,000 hectares. The arable land and pastures give a very mediocre yield due in part to insufficient fertilization (fertilizer consumption reaches 2.5 per cent of the total fertilizers consumed in France, while the total area cultivated is 10.4 per cent of the cultivated land in France).

It has been estimated by various experts that to reach optimum efficiency, the area left to forestry should be in the neighborhood of 400,000 hectares—less than half its present area; the forest area would still be slightly above the national average (22 per cent as compared with 20 per cent). Several agricultural experiments have been tried in the area and most of them have produced very favorable results: for instance, in the high plateaux of the Mezenc (1,200 meters), a more reasonable system of fertilization has brought the yield from 28 to 114 quintals for irrigated fields, and from 32 to 82 quintals for dry fields, at the same time improving the quality of the crops. At the same altitude, in the Haut-Velay, the French record for producing potatoes has been reached: 70 metric tons per hectare at Fay sur-Lignon. But the technical instruction given to farmers must bring them up to date in modern techniques of cultivation, and also encourage them to direct their efforts towards production of fodder and certain very specialized crops in the "sheltered" high-altitude zones (strawberries, summer vegetables, etc.).

206

Perhaps the most interesting, and certainly the most compact of the *départements* of the Massif Central is the Aveyron, which corresponds exactly to historical Rouergue, one of the most ancient regions of France. It is essentially mountainous, with a harsh climate and land generally unsuitable for meaningful cultivation unless greatly helped by the use of fertilizers, etc. The population has decreased in recent decades, as in all the *départements* of the Massif Central, and a high percentage of those remaining derive their livelihood from agriculture (54 per cent). The geographical isolation and mountainous nature of Aveyron have kept it apart from the main cultural, technical, and commercial currents.

In conclusion, the development of agriculture in the Massif Central area does not require huge capital investment but only relatively small projects, plus varied technical instruction to the farmers of the area, whose antiquated methods constantly bring lower yields than need be.[60] On this point, prospects are encouraging.

THE ALPINE REGION

The northern part of this region is most suited to cultivation, except of course where the altitude or climate prohibit it, while the southern part is more rocky, arid, and barren. While the north has characteristics similar to the Swiss and Austrian valleys, the south resembles more a semifrozen desert, very sparsely populated and cultivated. However, the almost complete state of abandonment in which this southern region finds itself could be modified if enough de-

---

[60] "If farm productivity goes up, a surplus can be transferred to other growing sectors and the farmer will still be better off than he was. This gives him an incentive to produce more food. Prosperity also enables the farming population to provide a growing market for industrial goods. If the countryside is stagnant, the farmers cannot buy the new goods and the beneficent cycle of interdependent upward growth in both industry and agriculture cannot go forward. *If you do not change agriculture, you will not change the economy.*" (emphasis supplied) Barbara Ward, *The Rich Nations and the Poor Nations* (New York: Norton and Co., 1962), pp. 105–106.

207

mand from the Common Market partners were to guarantee a fair reward for the expenditures necessary to reconvert it.

Some suggestions as to how to counter the tendency to depopulation of this mountainous area are as follows:

(a) The agricultural, pastoral, and forestry possibilities of the mountain areas should not be neglected.

(b) The reception of urban populations during the vacation period is possible only if some of the agricultural population remains on the land, even in the poorest regions.

(c) The abandonment of vast territories hitherto inhabited and cultivated would create political problems linked to free circulation of people in the framework of the Common Market.

Grazing and cattle-raising, and consequently meat and dairy industries, could make of this region the "Little Switzerland" of the Community; the produce could be strikingly close to that of the neighboring country, whose climatic conditions and mountainous terrain are so similar. With this in mind, plans have been made with other Alpine regions of Europe for exchanges of information and for detailed and specialized studies on matters of common interest.

Some export currents are already operating, for instance, the traditional one towards Italy; however, the important problem is to improve the communications network, both by rail and road, so that full advantage may be taken of the geographical propinquity to Italy and, to a lesser extent, to Germany. Besides meat and dairy produce, certain types of fruit and vegetables could also be advantageously grown and exported, especially to the Northern states of the European Community where demand can be substantial.

The most active assistance in the field of forestry and pastoral economy comes from the Société d'Economie Alpestre de la Haute-Savoie et de la Savoie.

It can be said that the possibilities for agricultural development in this region are excellent, subject to a sustained demand by the partners of the Community.

Summary

It is now time to summarize the problems facing France, bearing in mind particularly the underdeveloped regions of the nation, vis-à-vis her partners of the Community. "There is only one way for French agriculture to get out of its present difficulties, that is through the Common Market," a former French Minister of Agriculture declared during a meeting in the *département* of Allier, one of the poorest areas around the Massif Central. "And," he added, "exchanges must take place within the framework of a solid organization, with controlled prices which will be entrusted to the appropriate bodies. The European framework is the only possibility for renewing French agriculture."[61] Until recently, the French peasants, especially those living in the underdeveloped regions where costs of production are often too high, benefitted relatively little from the existence of a Common Market.[62] Indeed, in these marginal regions, the situation has been deteriorating steadily for years, and has given rise to continuous peasant agitation, often degenerating into open revolt. The *New York Times*[63] described one of the periodical outbursts of violence in these regions thus:

The French farm revolt grew in size and violence today as it moved south from its point of origin in Brittany to the

[61] From a speech by M. Boscary-Monsservin, Deputé à l'Assemblée, former Minister of Agriculture, in the *département* of Allier, at a peasants' meeting. Reported in *Le Monde*, March 22, 1960.

[62] However, the situation is changing rapidly. On July 30, 1962, as the *New York Times* of that date dramatically put it ". . . probably the greatest crumbling of trade barriers in history took place. . . . For grains, poultry, eggs and pork, import quotas, minimum price regulations and tariffs disappeared. In their place, the customs o fficers began to apply only a single control—a so-called 'levy' that will be variable. Over the years ahead, millions of farmers inside and outside of Europe will almost surely feel the effects. . . . Internal price policy has not yet been fixed, but it is quite possible that in France, in particular, any sizeable increase over current price levels could bring forth a large increase in production."

[63] June 25, 1961.

regions of Bordeaux and Toulouse. Throughout the country, farmers are at the boiling point over the low prices they receive and their difficult marketing conditions. . . . Government efforts to cope with this change are lagging, notably in attempts to get France's European Common Market partners to lower barriers to trade in foodstuffs. Meanwhile, farm income has failed to keep up with other sectors of the economy. The anger that first boiled up in Brittany at the beginning of the month brought about 7,000 tractors out to block roads and besiege prefectures in south-western France today . . . at Montauban, 2,500 farmers swarmed around the Prefecture (departmental administrative headquarters), attempting to burn in effigy Premier Michel Debré and engaging in battles with security forces. . . . The police three times broke up demonstrations with tear-gas grenades only to have the farmers regroup and reply with stones, and with bottles picked off cafe tables.

In this connection, it is interesting to take note of the figures in Table 5 comparing the evolution of agricultural and non-agricultural income in France in the decade 1949–1958.

TABLE 5[64]
EVOLUTION OF AGRICULTURAL AND
NON-AGRICULTURAL INCOME
(1949 = 100)

	1949	*1950*	*1951*	*1952*	*1953*	*1954*	*1955*	*1956*	*1957*	*1958*
Agricultural income	100	101	94	92	99	99	101	99	107	104
Individual farmer's income	100	103	97	97	106	107	113	113	125	124
National product	100	108	110	113	119	125	132	140	149	152

[64] INSEE (Institut National de la Statistique et des Etudes Economiques), "L'Evolution des Revenues Agricoles," *Etudes et Conjoncture* (Paris: December 1959).

These figures are self-explanatory. Only a few words of comment are therefore necessary: first, it should be noted that income deriving from agriculture in the ten years under consideration has stagnated (100 to 104, while the national product has jumped from 100 to 152). Individual income for farmers is much higher—124—because the number of people engaged in agriculture has considerably decreased in the ten years covered.[65] However, the increase has been only about one-quarter in agriculture, and one-half in the other sectors. In the same study, a comparison is made between the real income of prewar (1938) agricultural and non-agricultural workers, and those of 1958. For the first group, the increase approximates 25 per cent, while the increase is 60 to 70 per cent for non-agricultural workers. We see, therefore, that the relative situation of the French agricultural worker (including all those deriving their income from agriculture, owner and non-owner alike) has deteriorated, compared to that of his colleagues in the secondary and tertiary sectors.[66] Now, with the Common Market and the consequent increased prosperity and higher wages of non-agricultural workers, the gap will keep widening, unless something is done to counteract this trend.[67]

[65] "The diminishing number of people active in agriculture has not, however, been uniform in all regions. This means that modern undertakings with a high degree of productivity could be created in certain regions, while in others certain undertakings, with much excess labor, could not fully apply modern agricultural techniques and were thus unable to increase their productivity." CEE, *L'Agriculture dans le Marché Commun.*

[66] "In France a strong imbalance remains nowadays between individual agricultural incomes and those deriving from other activities; the gap in the last few years has been about 40 per cent." Cassa, *Contributo,* III, p. 27.

[67] The French farmers continuously prod their government to help them overcome their lower economic state. Among other things, they are certainly endowed with vivid imaginations and their protests take the most varied forms. The *New York Times* of July 13, 1963, for instance, reports that "Hundreds of peasants in Southern France stormed the offices of their tax collector today, strewing about 30 tons of surplus potatoes, carrots and green beans through the building in a renewal of their campaign to get Government relief from their plight

The necessary measures must be taken first by the national government, then possibly by a European government; however, whichever it is, governmental intervention in agricultural matters will be necessary for an undetermined period because the economic structure of a modern industrialized state is such that agriculture inside that state must be heavily protected in order to avoid chaos and collapse.[68] Therefore, the French Government had no alternative but to try to impose its own views on the other members of the Common Market, a policy which, in essence, has been crowned by success, as we saw at the beginning of this chapter.[69]

---

of overproduction. . . . Plummeting prices of perishable produce in the last two weeks have brought to a climax the widespread feelings of frustration among farmers who fear being left behind in Western Europe's new prosperity."

[68] The French Government has been intervening actively in agriculture for some time. Among the most noteworthy forms of this intervention are: the Organization of the Agricultural Markets (Decree of September 30, 1953), which allows the Government to regulate directly the marketing of agricultural products; and the Fonds de Garantie Mutuelle et d'Orientation de la Production Agricole (Decree of May 20, 1955), which gives the State the power to orientate production according to existing or prospective outlets, internal and external, to promote the necessary adaptations and guarantee the quality of the produce. It is difficult to overestimate the political importance that the agricultural question has in France, because ". . . no government in history has ever successfully defied the French peasant." *Time*, August 10, 1962.

[69] This concept was stressed by Gen. de Gaulle, in his press conference of January 31, 1964: "We are an agricultural, as well as an industrial country. To place production of our factories in a European framework, while leaving aside that of our fields, would have meant provoking an unimaginable rupture in our economic, social and financial life. As far as we are concerned, it was absolutely necessary that the Community include agriculture, otherwise, as we had announced, we would have had to reassume our freedom of action and there would have been no more Common Market. We agree, it is true, that among the six States, we are the one most interested in this serious agricultural business; why, we supply most of the cereals, beef, milk, cheese, wine, and, with Italy, most of the vegetables and fruit; all of which impelled us, at Brussels, to be the most insistent." *Le Monde* (Sélection Hebdomadaire), February 5, 1964.

This, of course, is the present situation; it remains to be seen what will happen when improvements in technology and, most of all, when better utilization of the land in Aquitaine, the Massif Central, Languedoc, etc., add to this problem through a greatly increased agricultural output.[70] As far as the underdeveloped areas are concerned, conservative estimates foresee a doubling, a tripling, and even more of production in a relatively short number of years provided the necessary development work (in irrigation, better communications, etc.) is carried out. The opportunity for French agriculture which, as former Premier Debré repeatedly stated "will always remain the first of the national industries," resides in the particular position it will attain in the European Community.[71]

In sum, the problem of agriculture in the underdeveloped areas of France, in the European context, is so closely tied to the general problem of French agriculture that it is almost indistinguishable from it.[72] If new outlets are secured within

[70] Even now ". . . it is recognized that there may be substantial surpluses, notably of wheat and dairy produce, which can be exported only with the help of subsidies. (It is hoped to minimize these, however, by exploitation of the price advantage that many French producers should enjoy in the Common Market for agriculture, as internal barriers are progressively dismantled.)" ECE, *Economic Survey of Europe, 1961*, p. 34.

[71] "There is not a single point of French agricultural policy that might today be conceived or solved, without taking into account the necessities deriving from the Treaty of Rome." *Communauté Européenne*, Nos. 8–9, Aug.–Sept. 1961.

[72] ". . . the claims of French agriculture can be so summarized: to attain *economic parity* with the other categories of society . . . and *social parity*. . . . In 1961, agricultural income represented 8.9% of national income while the agricultural population was about 22% of the total active population. . . . A half of the peasants do not have running water in their dwellings and it is admitted that it will take 20 years before electricity can be extended throughout the nation." M. René Blondelle, President of the Assemblée Permanente des Présidents des Chambres d'Agriculture: speech delivered at UNESCO Headquarters in Paris on occasion of a convention of the Conseil National des Economies Régionales. Printed in *L'Economie*, March 14, 1963.

the Community, as seems certain after the Brussels agreements, then it will be possible to increase agricultural production, and the necessary attention, energy, and money will be dedicated to the agricultural development of these areas.

Thus, if all works out for the best, the underdeveloped regions of France will, within a few years, bring their contribution to the export drive of French agriculture in the Community.

ITALY, THE GENERAL SITUATION OF AGRICULTURE

On a national scale, agricultural progress in the century following Italian unification can be summarized as follows. In 1861, about 60 per cent of the national income originated from agriculture, and more than 60 per cent of the active population were engaged in it. Other activities—industry, commerce, services—were proportionally low, both in terms of income and numbers of workers engaged in them. Today, while the population has almost doubled (from 26 to 51 million people) and the national income has increased fivefold, agricultural income has not even doubled, whereas the income from non-agricultural activities has increased tenfold. Agriculture accounts for about 20 per cent of the national income.[73]

Agriculture has not only lost its position, but has gradually become the least progressive force in the Italian economy, particularly southern agriculture;[74] it engages a disproportionate number of workers, whose income is therefore

[73] Data from *Agricoltura*, No. 2, February 1961. It is also interesting to notice that "In the important sector of employment in agriculture, the first five years of existence of the Common Market have registered a result undoubtedly favorable to Italy. The number of people actively engaged in agriculture has decreased from 42% in 1951 to about 29% in 1962." P. Albertario in *Prospettive Meridionali*, January 1963, No. 1.

[74] ". . . In the Italian economic expansion, Southern agriculture seems destined to be the principal delaying factor." *24 Ore*, May 27, 1961.

correspondingly lower than that of their colleagues engaged in other activities, and still lower for agricultural workers of the Mezzogiorno. In recent years, the average annual income of a wage-earning agricultural worker in the North ranged from 450,000 lire to 650,000 lire, whereas in the South the range was from 300,000 lire to 450,000 lire.[75] Thus low agricultural income afflicts Italy as well as France; also, as in France, Italian agriculture, even that of the Mezzogiorno, is beginning to have trouble in finding suitable markets for its products. For instance, *24 Ore*[76] reported:

> At the recent convention on mechanical irrigation, organized by the Committee for Land Redemption of the Capitanata region [Apulia] on the occasion of the Exhibition held at Foggia, it was stressed that in those zones irrigation will quadruple output; however, some doubt has been expressed about finding the proper outlets for such large increases and actually it has been doubted that the farmers would derive much economic benefit from such an increase in production.

In Italy, again as in France, agriculture is trying to keep pace with the general economic advancement but is steadily losing ground.[77] It remains to be seen whether, now that national markets are about to give way to the much larger Common Market, this fact will completely cure the ills common to the agriculture of both countries. But, of course, the whole structure of both agricultural systems—the stabilization and organization of the Common Market, tariffs toward "outside" countries, relations with the overseas

[75] Cassa, *Contributo*, I, p. 109. Data compiled by the Istituto Attuariale (ISTAT).

[76] July 2, 1961.

[77] "Although the structure of Italian agriculture improved considerably between 1950 and 1962—production increased by 40 per cent and the labour force decreased by a third—this was offset by the widening gap between farm prices and those of other goods and services. The actual income from agriculture increased by a bare 1.5 per cent." *The Economist*, March 28, 1964.

territories, and free entry of their products into the territory of the Community—have to be settled.[78] In particular, production and trade will have to be regulated and coordinated between Southern Italy and Mediterranean France in order to avoid the excesses of a potential competition ruinous to the agricultural systems of both countries.[79]

It is a fact of contemporary economic development that the more industrialized a nation becomes, the more agriculture is relegated to a secondary position. The Mezzogiorno is no exception to this rule, although there is still a long way to go before this part of Italy can be considered "industrialized." We shall now examine the agricultural South of Italy in more detail.

AGRICULTURE IN THE MEZZOGIORNO

THE SOIL

As far as the nature of the soil is concerned, a detailed discussion will not be given here; it should, however, be

[78] "Among the new facts which have strongly affected the economic life of our country, there stands out, for its tremendous historic impact, the institution of the European Economic Community . . . the Cassa per il Mezzogiorno fully realizes that certain revisions of its agricultural program, at the territorial as well as at the sectoral level, have to be examined, and made in the light of a deeper knowledge of the implications that the coming into being of the European Common Market entails." Prof. G. Pescatore, President of the Cassa per il Mezzogiorno, in the introduction to *Contributo*, I.

[79] This is not only a potential danger, but a real one. *Le Monde* (Sélection Hebdomadaire), August 14, 1963, reports for instance that the Italian and French representatives at the EEC in Brussels have already clashed on the problem, involving the Commission in a rather bitter controversy. "But the reproaches of the Commission also concern a basic problem: the refund to the farmers of 50 per cent of the transportation costs of fruits and vegetables destined for export. Is this not, as we must also say of other kinds of support, of such a nature as to falsify conditions for free competition? The problem has been brought up by the Italians, our principal competitors in the fruit and vegetable market. They have been worried enough at seeing French producers export their peaches to the German market. . . . France can only renounce her support if the Italians also undertake the obligation of renouncing it . . ."

216

born in mind that there are great variations over such a vast area, which includes the islands. In general, in the poor areas, which constitute the great majority, the soil is essentially clay, which is unstable and rocky; the form of culture practiced in them is the extensive one. On the contrary, in the better areas, where cultivation is intensive, the soil is usually of volcanic origin, belonging to another geological period, and is more stable and fertile. These generalizations are not absolute, however, for intensive cultivation is sometimes practiced on poor and rugged land, while obviously fertile land may be cultivated extensively.

There are a few zones in Southern Italy that are among the most intensively cultivated in the country and provide an exception to the general state of backwardness and primitiveness. But even in these zones a state of disorganization of markets and of production prohibits the attainment of good results, as compared with the standards of the surrounding region. Actually, these intensively cultivated areas are also overpopulated, so that many of the advantages which would otherwise derive from their relative fertility are thus destroyed, the higher margin of profit having to be shared by a larger number of people. These areas include: parts of Campania (especially the zone around Naples, which might in time well become one of the most productive "gardens" of the Common Market); some areas in Sicily, particularly the Conca d'Oro (Bowl of Gold) region around Palermo; small parts of Apulia and Abruzzi; parts of the Calabrian strip between the Tyrrenian Sea and the Apennines; and even two small areas in Sardinia—the country around Sassari and the Campidano in Cagliari province.[80]

[80] While the zones of intensive cultivation in the Mezzogiorno occupy only 27 per cent of the surface, they engage 45 per cent of the population and contribute 44 per cent of gross production; those cultivated extensively, although occupying 46 per cent of the surface, engage 38 per cent of the population and contribute 37 per cent of the gross production. These figures applied to "latifondo contadino" (see footnote 91) become 42, 28, and 30 per cent, respectively.

AGRICULTURE

While the amount of rainfall in the winter months is fairly equally divided between North and South Italy, in the summer, on the contrary, there is a progressive diminution of rainfall as one goes from North to South. Whereas in the Alpine region the average rainfall is higher in the summer than in the winter, in the South it is completely inadequate for all but a few types of culture. With the exception of Campania, where the average rainfall reaches and sometimes surpasses 800–1,000 mm., the whole of the Mezzogiorno, including the islands, is characterized by a very low average rainfall—450–500 mm.; in certain zones the average is even lower. Furthermore, it is worth noting that, in the South, three-quarters of the rain falls from mid-October to mid-February, a four-month period, and the other quarter falls in an eight-month period. In addition, the pattern is very irregular and the rain falls in the form of summer thunderstorms, or violent downpours, so that its usefulness to agriculture is very doubtful; actually, in balance, it may be damaging. On the other hand, the long summer drought which afflicts Southern Italy is itself pernicious; temperature and solar irradiation reach a much higher degree in the South than in the North. In the summer, due to the extreme dryness, combined with the scorching sun, a long pause takes place in agricultural activities in the South.

Ideally, under conditions existing in the Mezzogiorno, grazing should be the only kind of agricultural activity undertaken in most of the region. Unfortunately, however, while both climate and soil were favorable to an extensive utilization of grazing land in Southern Italy, population pressure has made this impossible, and many different types of low-yield crops have been grown in order to provide at least a minimum subsistence to the population.

This tragic contradiction has dominated the history of the Mezzogiorno for centuries. Actually, while the population was growing, the only means of supporting it consisted in turning to crops for which the soil and climate were unsuited. And even after massive emigration started the process went on, since the population continued to grow. In order to feed himself, man had to increase the cultivation of wheat which, with some exceptions, is unsuitable to the climate and other conditions of the South. In fact, the climate is so irregular and unpredictable that the normal cycle from sowing to reaping is liable to be interrupted or disturbed in one way or another. However, these considerations could not be taken into account when it was a question of feeding the population. Fortunately, today great advances have been made in agricultural techniques and in improving methods of cultivation, so that much more rational systems of agriculture can be applied.[81]

IRRIGATION AND PRODUCTIVITY IN SOUTHERN ITALY

While irrigation is of considerable importance everywhere agriculture is practiced, it is much more important in lands like Southern Italy where the characteristics of climate and soil make it imperative to bring large amounts of water to the fields by artificial means to achieve even a mediocre level of productivity.

There seems to be agreement among agricultural experts that, other things being equal, irrigation in the Mezzogiorno and in the islands may in some cases attain results superior to those in Northern Italy. This is partly due to the longer growing season for certain types of produce. However, in spite of the increased usefulness of irrigation, securing pro-

[81] "By pushing the agricultural system to develop a greater capacity for competition, the participation of Italy in the Common Market will only accelerate the process of modification of the extant structures and above all will modify the types of crops to which her agriculture is dedicated. The ensuing specialization will lead first to abandoning the cultivation of cereals over a vast area, located especially in the Apennines and in the hills of the South. After the transfer of its population, this area will for the most part be dedicated exclusively to forestry and cattle-raising." CEE, *Rapport 1958*, p. 408.

portionally greater output and profit as well as making possible cultivation of crops not otherwise practicable, there is much less of it in the South and it is more costly. It is worthwhile to refer to a study by the Italian Ministry of Agriculture[82] to emphasize the tremendous difference that exists between the amount of irrigation in the North and South of Italy: "Of the national total of 2,778,424 hectares of irrigated land, 85.1 per cent are in Northern Italy, 14.9 per cent in the South (8.5 per cent in continental Southern Italy, 6.4 per cent in the islands). This represents 19.5 cent of all cultivable land for the North, and 4 per cent for the South.[83]

[82] Ministero di Agricoltura e Foreste: Dir. Gen. della Bonifica e della Colonizzazione, *Relazione sullo stato dell' Irrigazione in Italia* (Rome, 1961), *passim*.

[83] Further broken down, we have the following figures:

		Irrigated land (thousands of ha.)			
	Total	*North*	*Center*	*South*	*Islands*
1950	2,100,000 ha.	1,810	72	137	81
1956	2,526,500	2,020.3	174.15	210.95	121.10
1957	2,650,800	2,098.3	192.9	224.6	135
1959 (Jan.)	2,785,200	2,174.1	227.4	240.1	143.6

In eight years therefore the irrigated surface has increased about 685,200 ha., subdivided as follows: North 364,100; Center 155,400; South 103,100; Islands 62,600. The respective rates of increase have therefore been 32.63 per cent for the whole of Italy; 20.11 per cent for the North; 218.61 per cent for the Center; 73.33 per cent for the South; 77.28 per cent for the Islands. On a regional basis we have:

(Jan. 1959)	
Lombardy	695,825
Piedmont	508,700
Abruzzi	30,609
Campania	80,000
Apulia	21,157
Basilicata	10,300
Calabria	98,000
Sicily	122,591
Sardinia	21,033

In the South (contrary to the North, where financing operations are carried on according to normal criteria), irrigation works have an

Obviously such disequilibrium has heavy repercussions on the agricultural economy of the South. G. Fazio, one of the contemporary experts on Southern Italian agriculture, writes:

Irrigation represents the irreplaceable instrument for the development, the specialization and the economic localization of agricultural production in the Meridione and is the basic element that complements to the fullest the technical means which are employed to improve and spur production. For water, because of its direct action on the nutritive system of the plants, constitutes the best regulator of growth, development and per-unit output of the crops, of fodder and of pasture.[84]

Furthermore, irrigation ensures a constant supply of water, independent of the caprices of the weather, and consequently production also will assume a character of regularity thus far unknown. This consideration is very important for meeting the competition within the Community that is armed with equal weapons: it is easy to see that a purchaser in Hamburg or Brussels will turn to a producer who can secure a steady supply of his products in the appropriate season. Obviously, all other conditions being equal, the "regular" producer will be favored.[85]

---

emergency character in view of the plan to put them in suitable condition to play their role in the Common Market. They are entrusted to regionally or locally constituted bodies, like the Ente per lo Sviluppo dell'Irrigazione in Apulia and Basilicata, the Ente Autonomo per il Flumendosa in Sardinia, and various appropriate sections of the Cassa per il Mezzogiorno. If the growing demand of the Common Market is up to expectations and production can be increased noticeably without disrupting the market and with good possibilities that the crops, or most of them, will be absorbed by the needs of the Community, it is planned to greatly enlarge the surface of irrigated lands in the South, where this process is particularly necessary and urgent. *DVI*, No. 91, June 1959.

[84] Fazio, in *Prospettive Meridionali*, No. 6, June 1961.

[85] The following figures stress the importance of the irrigation problem in Southern Italy: "In a coastal zone, after rational irrigation,

Because of all these considerations, and because action must be taken soon before a full agricultural Common Market comes into effect,[86] the Italian Government has, after considerable discussion, approved the so-called *Piano Verde* (Green Plan).[87] According to this, under Article 22, a fund of 40 billion lire—8 billion a year for a period of five years—is established exclusively for irrigation work and land redemption, with absolute priority for those irrigation systems already started, and for direct utilization of water (from springs, rain, etc.) This section of the Plan should be completed in 1966.

In Article 11 of the same Plan, a total of 15 billion lire is allocated to the construction of artificial reservoirs and related irrigation canals and fertilizer plants. The action promoted by these two provisions of the Plan, for which the entire burden will be borne by the State, is aimed at stimulating private initiative in the agricultural field in the areas that will benefit from these provisions, and at helping the local farmers to face with confidence the competition of those of the other Common Market areas. Fortunately, the Italian Government seems to be fully aware of the importance of solving the irrigation problem in Southern Italy and

---

production rose from 264 to 426 units, income from 201 to 382, and the workdays produced by it from 87 to 295. In an interior, and consequently drier, area, the difference is even more noticeable: production rose from 166 to 555 units, income from 142 to 298 workdays from 233 to 452." Istituto di Economia Agraria, *Rapporto sulla situazione idrica nell'Italia Meridionale*, (Rome, 1959).

[86] Fazio recommends a maximum, concentrated effort now, before the new situation brought about by the agricultural Common Market takes clear shape. "It will indeed be difficult," he says, "to recover the place lost in the formative stage of the new, large market (new customers, establishment of new currents of exchange, etc.). It is always a difficult undertaking to win competition with firms already established in their relations with actual buyers, even if the conditions offered are equivalent. This, therefore, creates the necessity for the South to speed up its tempo in the relatively short time left before the market becomes a reality." Fazio, *loc. cit.*

[87] For details see Appendix II.

solving it quickly.[88] As the income deriving from a rapidly expanding rate of production in the last few years is increasing steadily, the Italian Government can now allocate greater amounts of money to the solution of this essential problem.[89]

One possible additional source of water for irrigation, though perhaps far in the future, is the sea water that surrounds Southern Italy; the use of atomic power for the energy needed in a de-salting process and in carrying water by means of irrigation canals and pumps could solve the irrigation problem in most of the area. Once an economical way of doing this is devised, then a complete transformation of the area can take place. However, if and when such a possibility materializes, huge investments of capital must then be made. The Italian South will not have, at least in the foreseeable future, the financial capability necessary for supplying the huge, steady amounts of capital such an enter-

[88] In a speech made to the 20th Congresso Nazionale delle Bonifiche in Naples in August, 1961, the Minister for the Cassa per il Mezzogiorno, the Hon. Pastore, said ". . . land redemption should be completed efficiently and speedily, as industrial activities in the South are already in a position to conveniently exploit the current land transformation. And they will be exploited more and more, while Southern agricultural produce will find its way not only into national markets but also into the international one, following the progressive liberalization of exchanges." *Il Popolo*, September 10, 1961.

[89] "Apart from State aid, the South is also making use of help from outside organizations and agencies. For instance, about 40 billion lire, originating from loans already agreed upon with the IBRD, have been granted for the partial financing of four important complexes in the Mezzogiorno. The first concerns the construction of a complex of hydraulic plants, designed to irrigate about 32,000 ha. in the Catania plain, with a total expenditure of 26 billion lire. In the Campidano plain of Cagliari in Sardinia, the realization of a notable complex to irrigate about 50,000 ha. with an expenditure of 33 billion lire is proceeding. The Consorzio di Bonifica of the Capitanata is in its turn executing the work for the irrigation of 66,000 ha. in the province of Foggia, with an expenditure budgeted at 11 billion 325 million lire. The fourth irrigation complex concerns 40,000 ha. of the area of the Lower Volturno, in the province of Caserta, with an expenditure of 8 billion 549 million lire." ANSA (Italian News Information Agency), April 11, 1961.

prise will require. It is only the Community as a whole that can furnish this.[90]

THE PROBLEM OF THE LATIFUNDIA

Another great hindrance to the development of agriculture in the South has been the system of latifundia.[91] The origins of this scourge are very ancient, in fact they go back to Roman times, when, victorious after the Punic Wars against Carthage, Rome had at its disposal all the land of Southern Italy. This land was actually taken over by the Roman Republic and the owners expelled; some of the estates were distributed among the soldiers, but most of them fell into the hands of Roman politicians who, as usually happens in such cases, obtained the biggest and best. They, of course, did not interrupt their political careers to live on their new land, but installed managers while they remained in Rome, where their income was now assured from these new sources. Thus originated the phenomenon

[90] "As in other regions, the most backward areas possess large potentialities for progress. This is linked, in the Mediterranean and sub-Mediterranean regions, to the problem of water, hence to the development of irrigation—thus necessitating important capital investments. These exist within the Community and elsewhere, and an observation of the facts shows that one of the characteristics of contemporary economy is that of *compelling the rich regions to develop the poor regions* [emphasis supplied] in order to elevate the purchasing power of the populations." Oury, *op. cit.*, p. 213.

[91] Not to be confused with latifundia is the so-called "latifondo contadino" (peasant latifundia) which is commonly found in Sicily, Calabria, Apulia, and Basilicata. In this, what originally were large units have through the centuries been subdivided and fragmented so much among the peasants that the various plots do not generally exceed a very few hectares, or even less. Here, by reason of their size, any form of mechanization is unknown, and so are any appreciable investments in modern forms of cultivation. The owner generally lives in a large village, far away from the field, because he has to be near the source of possible odd jobs to supplement his meager income from the field. This is one reason why it is derisively called "latifondo contadino"—the owner is indeed a sort of "absentee landlord" almost like those who own huge latifundia and live in the big cities instead of residing on their property.

of the absentee landlord, who did not really care about the land itself as long as he obtained some profit from it. In addition the land allocated to the soldiers often far exceeded the working capacities of the assignee and his family; some of the soldiers sold the land to neighbors or lost it to pay debts, etc., causing many fields of normal dimensions to become two or three times larger than they were originally. Consequently, there were two possible alternatives: to keep a part of the land unproductive, or to have it tilled by slaves. It was the latter solution that was generally adopted. Consequently, most of the land was worked by people who did not have any interest in it and gradually became less and less productive; centuries of this treatment brought about a profound change in the agricultural structure of the whole of Southern Italy.

A similar situation befell Sicily: first of all, the Roman conquerors, because of their own necessities, ordered the local populations to concentrate on what they, the Romans, needed most, i.e. cereals. The crops, once harvested, were either confiscated by the conquerors or paid for at very low rates. As a consequence, the cultivators, almost *en masse*, abandoned their fields, perhaps hoping that they would thus force the Romans to be more reasonable. On the contrary, Rome replied by sending her own veterans to till the land, giving a considerable tract to each of them. Ironically, at the same time, agricultural improvements—rotation of crops and better methods of cultivation—greatly increased agricultural production in the North, thus initiating the process of differentiation between agricultural production in the two parts of the country which is still clearly discernible in Italy today.

It is true, of course, that climate, scarcity of water, and poverty of the soil enter into and contribute to the sharp difference between agricultural conditions in the North and South of Italy. The work of man, however, has also played an important part in developing this imbalance between the two parts of the country. Actually, to go back once more to Roman times, the way the land was distributed in the first place bears much responsibility for successive developments. In the South, the Rome conquest had been mainly an enterprise of the bourgeoisie and of the Senate, and therefore reflected the views of these upper strata when victory was achieved: large estates, exploitation for profit alone, and a kind of absenteeism aggravated by the difficulties of traveling at that time. In the North on the contrary, the lands were, for the most part, distributed among the veterans. This was an established Roman policy which achieved a dual result: rewarding her soldiers, and at the same time having them strategically located among the local population and ready to take up arms again if necessary, asserting by their presence the rights of Rome over those regions. Also, the process of assimilation of the local inhabitants was naturally enhanced by the presence of the Romans among them. The land was therefore distributed in relatively small plots and was cultivated by the veteran and his family, who had a direct interest in the condition of the land. This process perpetuated itself throughout the centuries. Feudalism, of course, accentuated it; in the North the rise of a rich, industrious bourgeoisie in a relatively short period of time counteracted this feudal influence and commercial activities attracted some of the Northern nobility, but in the South the feudal seigneurs remained attached to the land since it provided the only available source of power, prestige, and money. And, even when they did not remain on their own land, but lived in Palermo, Naples, or even Rome, their greedy demands—often based not on any real appreciation of the situation but on their own rapacious needs— certainly contributed to a further deterioration of the land, irrationally exploited to the maximum. The Byzantines, the Normans, and the Spaniards, who successively dominated the unfortunate South of Italy, all strongly fostered and encouraged this phenomenon, from which they themselves also benefitted. Therefore a structure of land distribution and a way of productivity was created which, in spite of all the attempted reforms and the lapse of centuries, still persists today.[92]

RELATIONS BETWEEN INDUSTRY AND AGRICULTURE IN ITALY

As we have seen, the agricultural problem in Southern Italy must be considered the main influence in the present structure of the area. In fact, while the rest of Western Europe, with the exception of most of the Iberian peninsula, gradually evolved a mixed industrial and agricultural economy (and Northern Italy is included in this), the South of Italy, on the contrary, remained a region with a basically agricultural economy. It is undeniable that a certain amount of industrialization has taken place, but at a low level and very unequally distributed geographically; in addition to areas where there is a certain amount of industry (around Naples, for instance), there are entire regions (such as Basilicata) where industry is practically nonexistent.[93] With perhaps the exception of the province of Bari, where there is a certain amount of industry for processing agricultural products, there has been up till now little relation between local industry and the surrounding rural regions. In other words, industry—what little there is—and agriculture are two almost unrelated activities in Southern Italy. Perhaps the main reason for this phenomenon is to be found in the fact that Southern Italian agriculture, being disorganized

[92] Serious attempts at land reform have been made in the postwar years, and details of these will be found in Appendix III, Table XXXII.

[93] The situation is gradually changing. C. L. Sulzberger, correspondent of the *New York Times*, wrote from Italy: "North Italy, with its humming factories and electric power grids, gradually approaches industrial saturation. Therefore, encouraged by the Cassa's impact, big business is for the first time beginning to move South. Socially, this is of enormous significance. The traveler through the Southland can now for the first time see evidence of improvement . . . the situation has changed, and factories, roads, power plants at last are tying this region into the latter 20th century." *New York Times*, August 15, 1962.

227

and backward,[94] does not create a market for industry, and consequently does not foster those direct exchanges at a local level that are one of the basic prerequisites of industrial development everywhere. This is the reason that the core of the so-called "Questione Meridionale" can be reduced mainly to agricultural development.

Whereas in other localities it is possible to bring about development through better use of existing industrial resources or their modernization, this is not possible in Southern Italy. Industrial development cannot be synonymous with regional development since Southern Italy has no important raw materials for industry, is in a marginal geographic position away from the main currents of international traffic, and has very few important ports. In the Meridione, industrialization will come only when a profound agricultural transformation finally facilitates industrial development[95] by creating better and richer bases for the economic life of the region by creating a market, by stimulating new technical processes, etc. It must therefore be reiterated that the main manifestation of depression in Southern Italy may be considered this imbalance between industry and agriculture—itself poor and backward—and this situation threatens to perpetuate itself in spite of the measures already taken.

[94] The surest indication of this is the number of tractors employed in the Center-North and in the Mezzogiorno:

	1956	1957	1958	1959	1960
North	116,293	131,450	146,672	160,517	179,109
Center	25,173	27,457	29,216	31,077	33,574
South	17,967	19,484	21,063	22,407	24,208
Islands	8,874	9,656	10,380	11,223	12,094
Total	168,307	188,047	207,131	225,224	248,985

Source: *Prospettive Meridionali*, Nos. 4–5, April–May 1962.

[95] "It is a poetic and literary myth, which in the end can be very damaging, to talk of an exclusively industrialized South." *Ibid.*, No. 12, December 1963.

AGRICULTURE

Social Aspects of the Problem of Industrialization of Agriculture

Two conditions must be met in order to bring about any agricultural development in Southern Italy and before any progress can be made: (a) a really final solution will only be possible if a well-organized, carefully planned effort is made, in which both private and public enterprise participate at a sustained pace; (b) the social relations now existing, with a sharp gap separating the upper and lower strata of the population, must be completely overhauled if any development process is to take place.[96] As they are now, the forces supporting the ruling classes stand resolutely in the way of progress. And as such modification certainly cannot be brought about only by decree, a long job of persuasion and education is necessary to achieve it. Activities in land redemption and land reform, already being carried on or projected, can only alleviate but not solve the problem.[97]

---

[96] As Sulzberger says, *loc. cit.*, ". . . the increasing number of letters from those who have left bring an awareness of modern life and the potential of well-being. *The Southern peasant is no longer content to stay a Southern peasant.*" (emphasis supplied) G. Fazio, in an article entitled "Problemi sociali del mondo contadino", *Prospettive Meridionali*, No. 12, December 1962, says "The peasant of the Mezzogiorno has become a man, knows and is aware of having rights like those of other citizens, is aware of his own dignity which has to be respected by others, above all in according him a human and civil life."

[97] Since 1950, the Cassa per il Mezzogiorno has budgeted a sum oi 1,138 billion lire for the agricultural sector, of which 638 billion are for the execution of public works, 200 billion for financing privately executed land reform, 20 billion for agricultural credit and 280 billion as financial support for organizations presiding over land reform in the Mezzogiorno. At the end of the Cassa's activities, it is planned to have a total land redemption of more than 1,600,000 hectares, of which 350,000 will be irrigated. For details, see *Contributo*, I, p. 113.

All this investment is having positive results, as we see from the following: "As for the increase in agricultural production . . . after ten years of operation of the Cassa, which represents one of the surest criteria for the evaluation of the economic results of land redemption and transformation, the data obtained show increases that range from 40 per cent in the predominantly hilly and dry land to 400–500 per

In the process of a rapid industrialization of agriculture, sociological factors are very important. The rural society is based on values stemming from centuries and centuries of traditional life in the countryside, not subject to the changes and violent shocks of the city, particularly in the industrialization stage. Now, industrialization of agriculture will bring about similar developments in the traditional, deeply conservative agricultural society.[98]

In the final analysis, human problems are paramount in any kind of economic development. It is a peculiarity of rural areas, particularly poor rural areas, to express diffidence toward any form of change and to show reluctance to adopt any technological advance. This does not mean that progress will not finally extend to these areas, only that the process in human terms, as well as in technological and economic terms, is often painfully slow and frustrating. Therefore, whenever modifications of any substance take place, particularly in the depressed agricultural areas, it is necessary to bear in mind the human factor which is decisive in this field, and not take for granted that man will be a docile partner in any technological change.

Let us consider a phenomenon that is taking place in Italy—the "flight from the land." Within the space of a decade, more than two million people have abandoned the Italian countryside for the cities and the more prosperous

cent in valleys which have been irrigated. In the first, the value of gross agricultural production has increased between 20,000 and 80,000 lire per hectare; in the second, between 250,000 and 600,000 lire." Pescatore, *op. cit.*, p. 32.

[98] The Italian Government, for its part, is trying to accelerate this development. One of the many cases of such intervention is reported in the *New York Times* of February 20, 1964: "The Government said in a message to Parliament today that it wanted to pattern Italy's agriculture on the Western European and United States models. . . . The legislation, which represents a major political issue, would do away with ancient customs such as sharecropping and personal services of farmhands for landowners. The reform would profoundly influence the rural way of life, introducing industrial methods where a patriarchal and artisan attitude has survived."

regions.[99] There is no doubt that the shift from agriculture to industry and from the South to the North of available labor entails beneficial consequences for the expansion of the national economy as a whole. However, this movement sometimes assumes disorderly and irrational features so that certain areas suddenly find themselves deprived of needed agricultural labor (for instance, a new factory in a neighboring city has attracted many people formerly working on the land), where other areas continue to be plagued by a surplus of labor. It seems, however, in view of the natural reluctance of peasants to move too far from their place of habitual residence, there is not much to be done about this. Agriculture will have to bear some of the brunt for the industrialization of the Mezzogiorno.

But why is there this new trend to "fleeing" the countryside (and not only the countryside, for that matter) of the South? The reasons are easy to find: salaries are low, continuity of work is nonexistent, the general standard of living is very poor, professional instruction is not available, and social security is not remotely comparable to that enjoyed by the workers in other productive activities.

Therefore the incentives granted to agriculture in Southern Italy will have to be constantly revised, keeping in mind the opportunities deriving from the rapidly progressing integration in the larger agricultural market of the EEC. It is now clear that the agriculture of the Mezzogiorno is

[99] "According to reliable estimates, in Italy between 1951 and 1957 about 1.2 million workers quit agriculture, which corresponds to an average yearly flux of about 170,000 people; in the two following years, 1958 and 1959, the rural exodus increased, nearing 200,000 a year, a figure which, according to estimates, was surpassed in 1960. In 1961, it is reckoned that 350,000 abandoned agriculture for other activities, within and outside the country. Since 1957, that is in just four years, the annual volume of rural exodus has doubled, whereas for the whole period 1951–61 the phenomenon has concerned more than two million workers." Comitato dei Ministri per il Mezzogiorno, *Relazione*, p. 8. The figure for the period 1951–63 is 2,750,000 according to *The Economist*, March 28, 1964.

rapidly becoming a part of the agriculture of the Common Market and therefore, like that of the other parts of the Community, must be restructured accordingly.[100] Customs barriers, by their fall, will leave certain sectors of agricultural production in this region unprotected, and they should therefore undergo a process of modernization or reconversion. Agricultural activities, from the long-term view, will probably have to be more limited, both in the range of products and in the areas subject to cultivation.

The parallel restructuring of the agriculture of the other Member States to form the Agricultural Common Market will eventually result in a division of production among them, possibly regulated by some European agency.[101]

The increasing industrialization of the South, and the technological progress in agriculture, will result in the switching of hundreds of thousands of people, through the

[100] "The old, patriarchal European agriculture, the stronghold of economic and political conservatism and a thorn in the side of all governments because of its recurrent crises, has entered a revolutionary period." *Il Corriere della Sera*, January 22, 1962.

[101] It is interesting to compare production and consumption within the Common Market of the agricultural produce in which the Mezzogiorno specializes. Production and consumption of vegetables and fruit in certain countries of the EEC (1958–59):

Country	Total Production (in tons)	% of Self-sufficiency	Consumption (in tons)	Consumption per capita per year (in kg.)
(Vegetables)				
W. Germany	2,280,000	77.2	2,462,000	45.9
France	6,950,000	99.7	5,935,000	130.0
Italy	8,000,000	119.2	6,108,000	124.9
Netherlands	1,365,000	156.5	735,000	65.1
(Fruit)				
W. Germany	3,822,000	85.4	4,075,000	76.0
France	1,450,000	81.0	1,490,000	32.5
Italy	4,100,000	128.3	3,050,000	61.5
Netherlands	695,000	128.3	445,000	39.4

Source: *Prospettive Meridionali*, No. 1, January 1963.

years, from agriculture to industry and to services.[102] The race by the local population for the possession of a plot of land, however small, has already perceptibly slowed down. Land ownership, which for centuries had been the embodiment of security, is now being replaced by the possession of a skill and by a position in a factory or an office.[103]

Consequently, the population pressure on the land will undoubtedly slow down in the coming years and this will be an important factor in the stabilization of Southern Italian agriculture in the European context.[104]

[102] The figures for all Italy in the forecast of the *Interim Saraceno Report* [A Study of the Italian Economy in view of a Future Plan] (Rome, 1963), show that, by 1973, one million and a half workers will have left agriculture, a yearly rate of reduction of 3%. The percentage of the rural labor force by that year will be 18%.

[103] The possession of land, not only in Italy, but also in France and other European nations, was, from time immemorial, the way to assert oneself on the social ladder. "*To own property in the sun,* even if it were negligible in size, has represented for the serf, the villain, the land laborer of feudal times, the symbol of his accession to a higher social dignity. Because the possession of land modified the personal status of its purchaser by linking him to the land, it conferred citizenship upon him; by showing it to others, he could guarantee collective endeavors [the land could not be taken away]; by guaranteeing his material existence, he was sheltered by the land forever from having to knock at any door for his bread. . . . [Now however] the modern farmer has chosen his social function: he possesses an inalienable capital . . . his skill." Serge Mallet, *op.cit.*

[104] *The Economist,* March 28, 1964, writes: "Emigration is bound to continue. The only question is whether it points, as in the 1950s, to the north, to Lombardy, and Switzerland or the Common Market, or to the south itself, to the coastal plains and valleys that may be fit for development."

CHAPTER V

Other Main Economic Factors

TRANSPORTATION

TRANSPORTATION IN SOUTHERN ITALY

The transportation system in Southern Italy must be completely overhauled if this region is to participate in full in the activities of the Common Market. It should be not only equal to, but actually *better* than, that of most other regions of the Community in order to compensate in part for the peripheral position of the area from the center of the Common Market. Conversely, retaining a thoroughly inadequate transportation network will only aggravate the disadvantages deriving to Southern Italy from its unfavorable geographic position. In the United States serious problems of distance are overcome by an adequate network of roads, railways, airways and, in smaller measure, inland waterways. Refrigerated trucks and railroad cars, and some equipped to carry frozen food, cross the country continuously, enabling, for instance, New Yorkers to benefit from California oranges or Florida vegetables. There is no reason why, if a similar system, geared to a European—not Italian —scale is evolved, Southern Italy could not become the California or the Florida of Europe. An improvement in the transportation system also means advantages in respect to imported industrial and agricultural goods (more rapid distribution and, often, consequently cheaper prices). Tourism in the area would also be favorably affected. In sum, only with a well-developed system of communications can Southern Italy really become an integrated part of the Community. The following is an analysis of the situation as it is at present, and as it should and, it is hoped, will be, in relation to the rest of the Community.

234

Railroads

In Italy, as in the rest of Western Europe, the railroads belong, in the overwhelming majority, to the State. Consequently, it will be much easier to plan a basic scheme of development on a European scale within the Community, there being no private railroad interests to be taken into account. It is therefore possible to draft a program in this framework destined to accelerate the process of development of the area.[1]

In view of the particular geographic position of Southern Italy, transportation by rail in the European context will assume special importance. A few problems should therefore be considered: the initial extension of the rail network, the rolling stock available and needed, and the relation between the potential and the demand of traffic.

As far as the initial extension is concerned, the railroads of Southern Italy are in a position of grave disadvantage compared to those of the rest of Europe. This is of course the consequence of particular conditions and patterns of trade between the various localities at the time the railroads were built.[2] This legacy unfortunately continues to exist even though the situation is vastly different now in the era of the Common Market.[3] However, it must be added that the

[1] "In all countries of the Common Market, considerable projects are being undertaken, and vast plans are being prepared for future needs. . . . Only a coordinated investment policy, bearing in mind both the needs and the economics of the solutions proposed, will be able to solve the requirements of the country at a minimum cost for the Community." From an advertisement inserted by the Italian State Railroads in the *New York Times* (Europe-Mideast Business Review), January 10, 1964.

[2] "These problems . . . must be considered as a direct consequence of the predominantly nationalistic point of view which then underlay the transport policy of European countries. It is therefore obvious that the problems of modernization and rescaling of the infrastructures arise within every European country, and particularly so within EEC countries, in order to give a unified European character to the various national networks." *Ibid.*

[3] "Railroads were almost non-existent in the South at the time of integration; the Kingdom of the Two Sicilies, as the South was then

rugged character of the terrain, together with important technical considerations, make the construction of new tracks inadvisable, indicating rather a concentration on the building program for the construction of new highways and roads. Therefore, appreciable results should be obtained by improvement and better utilization of existing lines.

A concerted effort must be made by all the European railroads to evolve a European system (direct lines and connections) so that goods and passengers originating in the most distant regions can reach the important centers of the Community within a reasonably short time.

Very few new railroads have been built in the Mezzogiorno since the war. The management of the Ferrovie dello Stato (FFSS—Italian State Railroads) is presently concentrating on enlarging to normal size the gauge of practically all the so-called secondary railroads so that the area they serve can be directly integrated into the Italian and European network, thus eliminating all the wasted time, delays, and additional costs caused by having to unload and reload, wait for connections, etc. This is especially important in the transport of perishable products, such as

---

called, had only ninety-eight kilometers of railroads. Italy as a whole had only one-seventh the network of Britain, and one-fifth that of France." Saraceno, *Economic Development of the Mezzogiorno*, p. 5. The present disproportion in the amount of passengers and traffic between the railroads of the South and those of the North, is illustrated by the following data: "In the eleven years from 1951–1961 inclusive, the average amount of freight received for loading in Italian stations by the Italian State Railroads was almost 50 million tons a year. In the stations of the Mezzogiorno instead it was only 8.8 million tons, equal to 17.7% of the national total. . . . As an average, in the ten years 1951–60, about 73 million passengers purchased one-way trips—and proportional figure season tickets and round-trip tickets—in Southern and Insular Italy, against 292.4 million in the Center-North and 365.4 in the whole of Italy. The average percentage of the Mezzogiorno happens to be exactly 20.0%". Comitato dei Ministri per il Mezzogiorno: *Relazione sulla Attività di Coordinamento* (Rome: Istituto Poligrafico dello Stato, 1962).

fruit and vegetables, which are most likely to be shipped from these areas to the other regions of Western Europe.

Full advantage will also be taken of the pooling of part of their rolling stock by the Six. These cars are marked "Europe" and can be used interchangeably by any Member State in whose territory they happen to be when needed. Thus the necessity of returning them—often empty—to the country they came from is eliminated. To foster the export of perishable commodities, large numbers of refrigerator cars are urgently needed; the national government does not seem able to provide them in sufficient quantities.

It is evident that a well-devised system of progressive and preferential tariffs on a European scale[4] should counterbalance, at least in part, the disadvantages which most underdeveloped regions, be they Brittany or Sicily, Aquitaine or Apulia, owe to their peripheral geographic position. It must be added that the income deriving to the railroad from operations in these regions will often not cover expenses; it is, however, essential that they keep operating, even at a loss and without tariff hikes, in order to contribute to the development of these areas.[5]

The real problem to be faced by the management of the FFSS in the Mezzogiorno is that of making technical improvements in the now existing railroads. In fact, the time is not far away when, if adequate improvements are not made, the capacity of the network in Southern Italy will be saturated by the ever-increasing volume of traffic brought about by the European Economic Community. Traffic bottlenecks, delays, etc., will then be created and prove very

[4] Preferential tariffs for the underdeveloped South of Italy already exist and are part of the Italian Government's effort to develop the area.

[5] "Railroad tariffs in Italy are fixed on the same base for the whole national territory, independent of costs and the income from each line. Preferential tariffs, established for certain categories of products, mostly favor fruit and vegetables destined for export, as well as industrial equipment destined for the Mezzogiorno." CEE, *Rapport 1959*, p. 390.

damaging to the areas in question. Many new switches, side tracks, bridges to eliminate crossings, etc., must be added to greatly improve the rapidity of communication. It must be said to the credit of the FFSS that, for the past few years, and particularly since the formation of the Community, major efforts have been made to face this problem and to increase the traffic capacity of the railroads in the South. The maximum activity in the modernization plans of the Italian rail network is now constantly centered in the South. A few names deserve mention: the important Messina-Palermo and Messina-Catania lines in Sicily, and the Foggia-Bari and Pescara-Foggia lines on the lower Adriatic coast, have been electrified. The Battipaglia-Reggio line in Calabria is being converted to double track. This conversion presents many difficult engineering problems: the line was built in a very rugged, mountainous region, and the many bridges and tunnels, gauged to a single track, now have to be rebuilt or enlarged to accommodate two-way traffic. Substantial improvements have also taken place in many other lines, principal among them being the Reggio Calabria-Metaponto-Taranto, Catania- Bicocca, and Palermo-Fiumetato. The number of FFSS ferryboats (whereby whole trains are ferried between Villa S. Giovanni, Calabria, and Messina, Sicily) has also been noticeably increased.

It should finally be added that the Italian State Railroads are engaged in a Ten-Year Plan, running for the period 1962–1972. Law No. 211 of April 27, 1962, authorized the Italian State Railroads to draft ". . . a Ten-Year Plan for works and renewal, rescaling, modernization and improvement of the facilities, tracks and fixed installations of the network, to the amount of 1,500 billion lire, to be carried out in two stages, each of five years." Eight hundred billion lire are allocated to the stage running from the fiscal year 1962–63 to 1966–67, now being implemented, and 700 billion are to be spent in the second half of the program.

The breakdown of the 800 billion lire to be spent in the first stage is as follows:

	Re-scaling	Modern-ization & expansion (*billion lire*)	Total	% of Total
Fixed installations	171	304	475	60%
Rolling stock	178	142	320	40%
Shareholders participation	—	5	5	—
Totals	349	451	800	100

In agreement with the policy of development of the Mezzogiorno, Article 9 of the law directed that a minimum of 320 billion lire be invested in Southern Italy, either in fixed installations and tracks or as rolling stock, including spare parts, to be commissioned in Southern Italian factories.[6]

The present situation of the railroad network in the South is summarized as follows in a recent communiqué of the Ministry of Transport:[7] "The process of renewal of the Southern railroads should not be considered as definitely settled, because the continuous necessities of technological, economic and social progress may, in the not too distant future, lead to considering today's program as just a stage, even though a fundamental one. In the meanwhile, the first

---

[6] There is, however, little hope of bringing about in the near future the attainment of some of the objectives of the plan as they concern the South. In the words of the *Relazione Generale sulla Situazione Economica del Paese in 1962*, presented to Parliament by the Ministry of the Budget (Appendix 3, p. 267ff.): "As far as commissioning to the industries of the Center-South [of matériel destined to the railroads] is concerned, in accordance with the law, many difficulties have been encountered. . . . As for the manufacture of rolling stock, it should be noted that the factories of the Mezzogiorno are in no condition, in their present productive capacity, to satisfy the load of orders prescribed by law, which reserves for the industry of Southern and Insular Italy orders totalling at least 128 billion lire, equal to $\frac{2}{5}$ of the entire sum [320 billion] allocated to rolling stock." Hope is however expressed that the situation will soon improve.

[7] *Prospettive Meridionali*, No. 11, November 1963.

concrete results of the direct contribution of the orders from the Italian State Railroads to the industrialization of the Mezzogiorno, are seen in the recent surge, in some Southern localities, of important new factories for manufacturing railroad material."

In conclusion, the Italian State Railroads are engaged in the South in a vigorous financial and economic effort, the beneficial consequences of which will deeply affect the Southern economy as a whole and enhance its chances in the Common Market.

Roads

Whereas a large expansion of the present railroad system is not foreseen, a broad extension of the road network is not only possible but desirable and necessary.

The problem of rendering the Italian road network adequate for the continuous increase in traffic[8] and for the industrial development which the European Economic Community should help to bring about in Southern Italy is being tackled by the Ministry of Public Works, which is

[8] "At the end of 1959, it was estimated that 5,534,247 vehicles were using Italian roads and highways. Unofficial estimates for the end of 1960 revealed the number to be six million vehicles of all kinds, a figure that was initially contemplated for 1962–63. Should the volume of traffic continue to grow at the same speed, traffic using Italian roads will reach the surprisingly high figure of eleven million vehicles by 1970. It is also necessary to include vehicles used by tourists during visits to this country and, according to estimates made by the border police, tourist figures rose from three million in 1952 to ten million in 1958. Private motorists increased from 86,000 to 800,000 while motor cycles and other light vehicles jumped from 9,700 to 90,000." *Italian Affairs*, Vol. x, No. 1, Jan.– Feb. 1961. The trend is at present not only continuing but acquiring momentum. In a summary of the *Economic Survey of Europe in 1963* it is stated that in that year "The largest increase [in industrial output] was in passenger-car production, which rose by 19 per cent above the 1962 level in the four major producing countries taken together; and new registrations of passenger cars in Western Europe as a whole went up by some 16 per cent." Document ECE/98, April 7, 1964, Press Services, Office of Public Information, United Nations, New York.

responsible for it, through a Ten-Year Plan, approved by the Council of Ministers on December 2, 1960.[9] The program is certainly the most comprehensive to be launched so far and it foresees the construction of approximately 5,000 kilometers of superhighways, highways, second-class roads, and bypasses. However, while most of the new highways will be built directly by the State through ANAS (Azienda Nazionale Autonoma delle Strade), state participation in the balance of the mileage to be built under the program will also be heavy.[10] Indeed, most of this will be the responsibility of the IRI (Istituto di Ricostruzione Industriale), a public holding company which has already given a splendid performance in its new field of road construction by building, among others, the Autostrada del Sole (Highway of the Sun), between Milan and Naples. In its activities in Southern Italy it will be assisted by the Cassa per il Mezzogiorno. The program also foresees the handing over to the IRI, for a period of thirty years, of some toll highways already in existence, to compensate for the heavy deficits that building the new highways will certainly entail. The State will furthermore grant to IRI and to private firms willing to embark on highway construction certain fiscal exemptions (turnover tax, internal customs duties, registration tax, materials, etc.) and a contribution equal to 4 per cent of the total cost of the work over a period of thirty years. Such contribution may reach 4.5 per cent in certain cases. There are some places, practically all in the South, where the lack of traffic does not stimulate private investment in toll highways. This is one of the reasons why the State contribution

[9] For details of the Plan, see *Italian Affairs, ibid.*

[10] This intervention was frequently vocally advocated in the past. For instance, *Il Messaggero*, August 3, 1960, has this to say: "Intervention by the State for the roads in the South, either directly or indirectly, through the Cassa per il Mezzogiorno, becomes increasingly more urgent as the Common Market solidifies; the Mezzogiorno is in a disadvantageous position in regard to this because of its situation in respect to the geographic and economic center of the Community."

241

is so large; on the other hand, "it is a question of projects amounting to hundreds of billions of lire which, *without State intervention, could never take place* [emphasis supplied]. . . . The intervention of the State with the budgeting of one hundred billion lire for new highways has provoked investments of three hundred billion lire by private enterprise."[11]

The creation of a modern highway network, particularly in the South,[12] is very important from the viewpoint of the nation as a whole and its position within the Community. Many projects are presently under way along the Italian border—Ponte San Luigi and Mont Cenis with France, Simplon with Switzerland and Brenner with Austria (both to be used for road traffic between Italy and Germany)— and several tunnels have been completed or are projected.[13] Therefore the South must advance at least with the same speed, if it does not want to risk being further outdistanced.

[11] *DVI*, No. 107, October 1960.

[12] "The statistical indexes . . . in the case of roads in the Mezzogiorno make little sense. What does it mean that the number of roads per square kilometer in a region of the South compares favorably to that of a region of the North when their condition is so inferior to the average? Very often these roads can only be used by ox-carts and they are thoroughly inadequate for motorized traffic; most of them have not changed since the times of Joachim Murat . . ." *Il Messaggero*, August 3, 1960.

[13] The situation concerning road tunnels is thus summarized by *Communauté Européenne*, No. 12, December 1963: "The Italians want to cancel, within ten years, the barriers of the Alps by piercing half a dozen road tunnels, which will allow the establishment of lasting relations between Northern Italy, Switzerland, France and the rest of Europe. (The present state of works is:

> *Grand St. Bernard Tunnel*, linking Turin and Lausanne; completed in 1964; length 5.900 kms.
>
> *Mont-Blanc Tunnel*, the longest in the world (11.600 km.); completed in 1964; will link Geneva to Turin.

The other most advanced projects are:

> *Fréjus Tunnel*, running parallel to the railroad tunnel between Modane and Bardonecchia. It will exceed in length the Mont Blanc Tunnel (12.176 km.). Work on it is due to start in the near future.
>
> *Mercantour Tunnel*, will put Turin in direct contact with Nice and Marseille.)"

The Ten-Year Plan has been conceived to fit perfectly into the European Plan, drafted by the EEC Commission, and this fact has been publicly recognized and praised by the latter. The Community project, which has been planned by experts of all six Member States, will receive financial aid directly from the Governments concerned, and from the European Investment Bank.[14] This project envisages a long-range, organic development of transportation facilities between the Member States to cope with the heavier traffic resulting from the common economic growth, at an increasingly accelerated rate. The Italian Government and the EEC Commission plans have the same aims, each within its sphere, of making the transportation systems in the territories under their jurisdiction adequate for the more important purposes they will have to serve in the new economic community, these being "to insure to the European Community transportation which is at the same time cheaper, of better quality, more modern and efficient."[15]

The combined action of the State (through ANAS and the Cassa per il Mezzogiorno), mixed companies like IRI, and private enterprise should bring about positive results in the next decade.

The Ten-Year Plan for road network development runs until 1969. Eighty-eight per cent of the program should be completed by 1966 and the remaining 12 per cent by 1969.[16]

The program is an ambitious one and involves a high rate of investment in the period 1960–69. It will secure a high employment rate for that period (approximately 1.5 million units), and will considerably improve communications be-

[14] CEE, *Communauté Européenne*, No. 6, June 1961.

[15] *Ibid.*

[16] An interesting feature of the Ten-Year Plan is that ". . . all highways will be transferred to the State, without any additional expenditure, at the end of thirty years. Sums in excess of 5 per cent on net income from toll charges will be paid to the State. It is now estimated that execution of the program will produce an increase of 2,300 billion lire in national income between 1961 and 1972." *Italian Affairs*, No. 1, Jan.– Feb. 1961.

tween the South and the North of Italy and consequently between the South and the heart of the Community. Industry and related services will also greatly benefit from the program, and tourism will possibly reap the greatest advantages, with hundreds of thousands of additional visitors from all over the Community finding it easier to reach the beautiful resorts, places of archeological interest, etc. of the Mezzogiorno by means of their own cars (which most families throughout the Common Market area will eventually possess).[17] Since more traffic means more money and more activity, together with a quicker tempo of life, Southern Italy will indeed greatly benefit from the program of road improvement.

ANAS immediately understood the importance of developing the communications network—a (it is tempting to say "the") necessary prerequisite for the development of the whole area. More attention has been directed toward the great national superhighways which, together with the railroads, will form the arteries of the Community. By far the most important among them is the aforementioned Autostrada del Sole, 754 km. long, linking the South of Italy with Milan and, through Milan, with the heart of the Community. Construction began in 1956, and was completed in 1964. Its impact is already perceptible; it has received very favorable reaction abroad and will do more in the future to render distances shorter and bring Southern Italy completely into the Community.[18] Also, but still in the

[17] "In 1962, there was one car for every eight people in France and in Luxembourg, eleven in Belgium and Germany, nineteen in the Netherlands, twenty-four in Italy. In the United States, there was a car for every three inhabitants and in Great Britain for every eight." CEE, *La Communauté Européenne* (Paris: Bureau d'Information des Communautés Européennes, March 1963).

[18] An important new development in this connection is announced by the *New York Times* of June 13, 1963: "A syndicate of European bankers has negotiated the first issue ever arranged on the London market of dollar bonds to finance the building of Italian superhighways. . . . The bearer bonds, to the value of $15 million would

project stage, there will be undertaken in the coming years the construction of other highways, linking up with the Autostrada del Sole. This will benefit Apulia (Bari-Naples), Calabria (Reggio Calabria-Naples), and Sicily, which is linked to the continent by ferry and will, sometime in the future, also be linked by bridge (Catania-Palermo, Catania-Syracuse). A large road-building program is envisaged, which will be fed by the increased currents of traffic moving to and from the North and the heart of the Community. The roads will also increasingly have to supplement the rail network since, as already indicated, construction of new lines would be impractical.

Sardinia. Special transportation problems arise in the case of Sardinia. This is due, of course, to her insular position which is, unlike Sicily, far from the mainland. The difficulty is how goods, raw materials, etc. are to be carried to the island from all over the Common Market and vice versa. Even though air traffic in passengers and freight between Sardinia and the mainland has noticeably increased in the last decade or so, the solution of the problem lies with sea communications.

In the last few years "sea travel to the island of Sardinia, an increasingly popular stop in tourist itineraries, has been facilitated by the Tirrenia Line (affiliated with the I.R.I. Group). Ship connections are available from Civitavecchia (near Rome), Naples, Genoa, which stop at Cagliari, Olbia, and Porto Torres."[19] But these lines cater essentially to passengers.

---

be for the Concessioni e Costruzioni Autostrada SP. A., which is a wholly owned subsidiary of the I.R.I. group. . . . It is believed to be the first foreign borrowing made by IRI. Sources said IRI would guarantee the bonds. They are expected to help finance the completion of the Autostrada del Sole linking Milan with the South."

[19] *Tourist News from Italy;* a monthly supplement to *Economic News from Italy* (Italian Information Office, New York), Vol. 15, No. 8, August 1963.

The real problem for Sardinia in this important formative stage of the Common Market is that of freight. Sardinia's typical products and, particularly, perishable agricultural products, which face keen competition from the rest of Southern Italy and from Southern France, have two major difficulties to overcome before being channelled into the mainstream of traffic within the Economic Community.[20] These difficulties are waste of time and high costs. The second is much more serious than the loss of time, for with better organization, quicker loading and unloading operations and, when necessary, the addition of new ships, the disadvantageous effects consequent to the insular position of Sardinia will be reduced. However, higher costs deriving from loading and from transport by sea, can only be met—at least so say the Sardinian producers—by direct (subsidies) or indirect (absorption of loading expenditures) intervention by the State. Otherwise, they add, not only will the Common Market bring no benefit to Sardinia, but will actually damage it—a forecast to be taken with a grain of salt.

TRANSPORTATION IN FRANCE

In France as a whole, the number of people directly or indirectly engaged in public transportation reaches respectively 3.3 and 1.7 per cent of the active population. The aggregate value of all transport activities is equal to 6 per cent of the gross national product, of which 4 per cent is in the public sector.[21] These data give an idea of the importance of transportation in France in the framework of the economy of the nation. We shall examine how it will be affected by the Common Market and what the consequences will be for the underdeveloped regions of the country.

We have talked repeatedly of how, in the present system,

[20] Also, if conditions so warrant, Sardinia could open direct sea communications with Southern France, thus considerably lessening the costs of transportation to that part of the Common Market.

[21] Visine, *op.cit.*, p. 201.

both the road and railroad networks are centered in Paris and have seen how this phenomenon came about and how one of its most disastrous consequences has been the progressive state of neglect and abandonment of certain areas of France, particularly the Center, the South-West, and Brittany, whose links with Paris have been, and to a certain extent still are, poor and slow. The establishment of the European Economic Community will entail, as a consequence, the displacing of part of the economic activities of the nation; the flow of traffic must be redirected—from the provinces toward Paris, to Northeast, East, and Southeast France toward France's partners Benelux, Germany, and Italy respectively. The obvious danger for the area south and west of Paris is that of being pushed further into a peripheral position—peripheral not only relative to France but to the whole Community. The Government and the European Authority must therefore contribute to the establishment of a rational communications system, which will not only make possible an intensification of traffic between the most industrialized parts of the Community but also enable the geographically remote regions to participate in full in the advantages deriving from the large European market.[22] However, in order to achieve this, coordination between the national governments, even before a Federal Authority is established, must be much closer than it is at present. "Transportation policy being an essential element of the economic policy of the various States, the Common Market, in the absence of a common transportation policy, will never become a true economic unity."[23]

[22] This applies to all forms of communication, not only to railroads and roads. For instance, *Revue Juridique et Economique du Sud-Ouest*, No. 4, 1962, writes: "Our canals [of the South-West] carry only regional traffic and cannot be integrated into the general network of French river traffic and more so of European river traffic. . . . Three great regions, Languedoc, Midi-Pyrénées and Aquitaine are isolated from the rest of France. . . . They will also be isolated from Europe . . ."

[23] CEE, *Communauté Européenne*, No. 6, June 1961.

Railroads

We have already briefly described in Chapter I how the French railroad system developed, and the pernicious influence this development had on the regions of South-West and Central France, connected to the main trunks by slow and insufficient railroad connections, if at all. In the frenzy to build a "star-shaped" rail network around Paris, potentially extremely important lines (such as the Limoges-Bordeaux and Rennes-Nantes, linking respectively most of the Massif Central region to its natural seaport, and part of Brittany to its second important seaport) were left out and were added much later after the damage to these regions had been done. But, even in more recent times, this process of centralization has not slowed its pace. For example, until all the schedules, along with most other things, were blown up by the holocaust of World War II, a passenger spent less time on the train to go from a point along the river Garonne to a place on the river Rhône (in the South-West and South of France respectively) if he went via Paris (1,093 kilometers, 10 hours 50 minutes) than he did if he took the direct line (639 kilometers, 12 hours 5 minutes); or from Lille-Nancy, via Paris (611 kilometers, less than six hours, depending on the connection) and Lille-Nancy direct (386 kilometers, 6 hours 23 minutes).[24]

These examples give an idea of how this centralization of the railroad network in Paris contributed to the dislocation of old currents of traffic in France, to the progressive centralization of practically all economic activity around Paris, and to the pauperization of the provinces.

Even now, the situation has undergone only minor reforms, and, in a broad sense, it is as bad as it has always been. In the context of the Common Market, the Société Nationale des Chemins de Fer Français has planned, and is actually accomplishing, a broad program of modernization, electrifi-

[24] Gravier, *op.cit.*, p. 18.

cation, and replacement of steam locomotives. However, by far the majority of the current projects concern the Paris region and the Lille-Metz-Strasbourg area. Obviously these lines will improve the speed and the quality of service between the "Ville Lumière" and the densely industrialized regions of South Belgium and the Rhineland. This would be highly commendable, because it is in the interest not only of France but of the Community as a whole, if it did not mean that, as usual, the underprivileged areas of the south, west, and center have been almost completely left out. The results of a study made by the Société Nationale des Chemins de Fer Français, which analyzed the achievements of French railroads since World War II and gave a detailed sketch of the plans for the years ahead, were made public in *Le Monde*.[25] In all the projects presented, the names of the above-mentioned regions appear in very few cases.

From this plan, and from others, it seems that the attention of the Société Nationale des Chemins de Fer Français is, for the time being at least, mainly turned toward strengthening the links between the rich regions of France and the rich regions of some of her partners; the interests of the South-West and Center of France are not being sufficiently taken care of, nor is their integration in the mainstream of the Community being fostered as it should. Actually, upon scanning through the long list of works already started or planned, it is obvious that almost all those of major importance are to take place in the northeast, a few in the southeast, and a very few minor ones in the Massif Central and South-West France.[26] What is being done that will benefit

[25] November 22, 1959.

[26] For Brittany, the direct influence of the Executive of the Common Market is already being felt. "As far as transportation is concerned, it [the Executive] has, since June 1961, recommended to the French government the electrification of the railroad Le Mans-Rennes, and incited the administration of the French railroads to extend its effort in this domain to penetrate more deeply into the peninsula of Brittany. . . . The European Investment Bank has granted to the SNCF a loan of $16.2 million for modernization of the railroads in Brittany . . ." *Communauté Européenne*, Nos. 8–9, Aug.–Sept. 1962.

the whole system, irrespective of geographic position, is the gradual replacement of old, steam-driven locomotives with Diesel engines. The advantages deriving from this are many: in fact, a locomotive of the latter type, with the same power, represents a saving, translated into monetary terms, of about 40 per cent and a diminution in the weight of fuel in the relation of 1 to 5, oil being used instead of coal.

It is obvious that part of the savings thus obtained will go to improving the lines, from which the underdeveloped regions will also benefit. Actually, the work of replacement by Diesel is almost complete on some of the lines in these areas (notably Nantes-Bordeaux and in the so-called "Etoile de Capdenac" area of the Massif Central and Tours-Bordeaux). New types of locomotive have been destined for service in the mountainous areas of the Massif Central, Alps, and Pyrénées, with a traction force increased up to 1,650 metric tons, over a 10 per cent difference in grade. A remarkable result of the pooling of rolling stock by the railroads of the Six has been the sharp economy in matériel needed.

Placed under the double heading of economy and of the unification of matériel on a European level, the modernization of rolling stock has been equally oriented towards diversification as a function of the needs of the economy. The total amount of rolling stock available, which had suffered badly from the consequences of the war of 1939–45, has not been entirely reconstituted: 100,000 cars have had to be built. However in spite of the increase in traffic, which is more than double that of 1938, the present figure (375,000) is considerably lower than that before the war (508,000), which allows notable savings both in capital and in maintenance expenditures.[27]

[27] *Le Monde*, November 22, 1959. This preference for the powering and coordination of lines serving the richest and more central regions in respect to the rest of the Community, seems to be the approved policy for the time being. In fact, it seems that the Executive of the

Roads

The French road network is certainly dense enough (1.2 kilometers of road for every square kilometer of surface area; or fifteen meters of road per inhabitant),[28] but as France has for a long time had a first-rate network, there has been no incentive to add to it, build new routes, or improve on the ones already existing. The consequence is that, after the long stagnation and deterioration, the once more-than-adequate road system has become somewhat obsolete. "If the network of secondary roads is [still] particularly remarkable for its density and quality, certain of the more heavily used routes risk becoming insufficient."[29] The risk was well discerned by the former Minister, Jules Moch, who, in an article published in 1960,[30] wrote:

There is urgency; people from abroad may desert our roads. The Dutch and Belgian ports will soon be linked to the German super-highways. . . . This network will be linked to Italy through Switzerland. . . When it is possible to drive better and at less risk outside our borders, our tourism—a national industry—will only retain that fraction of tourists who come expressly to visit France, but not the "explorers" of Europe. The hotel industry,

Community, realizing the importance that the railroads will have in the integration of Western Europe, has decided to put its major efforts, for the time being, in the major industrial areas of these nations. Consequently, France, west and south of Paris, the whole Italian peninsula, and the eastern part of the Federal Republic of Germany are omitted from the over-all recommendations made to the national governments by the General Direction of Transport (one of the advisory bodies of the Executive of the Common Market).

[28] Visine, *op.cit.*, p. 214. "The following data on the national road network are also supplied: 80,000 km. of national routes; 270,000 km. of departmental routes; 370,000 km. of local roads; 700,000 km. of country roads. *Most of these routes converge on Paris.*" (emphasis supplied)

[29] *Ibid.*

[30] "Reflexions sur les Transports: Autoroutes, artères vitales," *Le Monde*, July 7, 1960.

garages, balance of payments and national Treasury will pay for our present lack of foresight. Our lag is severe; at the beginning of 1960 there were 2,525 kilometers of superhighways in West Germany, 838 in Italy, 720 in the Netherlands, 154 in Belgium, and only 106 in France, before the opening of the super-highway to the south from Paris. This lag is growing: in 1960, projects are taking place over 530 kilometers in Italy, 375 in Germany, and only 122 in France (including the 40 kilometers of the above-mentioned super-highway recently opened to traffic).

It is evident when looking at a road map of the Community that, proportionate to its size, the area containing fewer roads than any in the whole Community—even fewer than Southern Italy, now that the Autostrada del Sole has been opened to traffic—is the Center and the South-West of France, where only *one* superhighway, the Bordeaux-Toulouse-Marseille-Nice, is presently in operation.[31]

It is true that there are many plans to change this state of affairs. There is general agreement that the whole system must be overhauled and modernized, and there is also substantial agreement in Government circles on which routes should have priority. The main difficulty is that of obtaining adequate financing for the projects, skilled labor, etc. The *Rapport Annuel*[32] frankly admits that

At the end of 1959 the second Five-Year Program of Equipment of the national road network, which should have been finished by the end of 1961, was only 15 per cent under way. This lag has been one of the factors which have provoked new programming for the general development of the national road network and for construction of

[31] A comprehensive map of the road network in the Community appears in *Communauté Européenne*, No. 7, July 1960.

[32] *Rapport Annuel sur l'Exécution du Plan de Modernisation et d'Equipement, 1960*, p. 228.

super-highways, taking into account the foreseeable situation of road traffic in 1975.

The new orientation which will be given to the road network in France in the coming years will follow the broad lines set out in the general Plan for transportation in the Community.

While most of the proposed new roads will be in the central part of the Community, the "periphery" of France has not been completely forgotten. Thus, new superhighways should link Nantes, in Brittany, and Bordeaux, in South-West France, to Paris, where they should join the other numerous roads leading to the east and to the north of the Community.[33] As a matter of fact, parts of the prospective superhighways are already functioning; it will therefore be only a question of completing them. Another superhighway should connect La Rochelle (West France) to Lyon, thus

---

[33] At present, various projects are being carried out to fulfill the programs set forth by the French Government for the different regions. The most important of these sectional programs, as far as the underdeveloped areas are concerned, are the following:

"1) *Diverse road improvement works* . . . including the building of modern bridges, particularly over the Garonne river;

"2) Specific works of improvement, that is:

   (a) *Work on the main road arteries:* Paris-Toulouse (R.N. 20), Toulouse-Bayonne (R.N. 125, 117, 124) and particularly Bordeaux-Toulouse-Marseille (R.N. 113); this road must be studied in the perspective of a great national network;

   (b) *Roads penetrating into the Pyrénées* towards Spain and Andorra, among which the most important are: Bayonne-Hendaye (R.N. 10), Pau, Oloron-St. Marie Jaca (R.N. 134), Toulouse-Foix-Puigcerda (R.N. 20), Perpignan-Col du Perthus (R.N. 9) and Perpignan-Cerbère (R.N. 114; R.N. 15 in the Tech valley);

   (c) *Roads of entry to the Massif Central*, particularly towards Castres-Mazamet-Albi-Rodez (R.N. 88) and Millau (R.N. 111);

   (d) *Roads for tourist traffic* in the Pyrénées and in the Massif Central, particularly the final section of the Pyrénées route which will offer a first-class tourist circuit . . . another important project is the Lake Route between lakes Aumar, Aubat, and Orédon.

"Finally, of special note is the construction of a tourist road in the valley of the Aveyron and a projected mountain road in the Montagne Noire." *Journal Officiel, Région Midi-Pyrénées*, Paris 1959, pp. 88–89.

crossing the central-south area of France. In Lyon, it should then connect with the already existing highways, or super-highways, linking that city with Turin and the rest of Italy and with Luxembourg and West Germany via Dijon and Nancy.

Transportation being an integral and very important part of the economy, it is understandable that governments might hesitate to adopt certain measures that, particularly in a country with a partially planned economy like France, risk upsetting the economic balance.

> Aware of these difficulties, the Executive of the Common Market did not want to elaborate a system which is theoretically perfect, but unrealizable, nor rest content with fragmentary measures, adaptable to the regimes in power in the different countries. Its propositions form a system which is at the same time logical, coherent and reasonable and which has a very good chance of being adopted and realized.[34]

France now has to make good for an accumulation of delays in the last ten years.[35]

The requisites for an all-inclusive road-building program were explained in detail by M. Buron, then Minister of Public Works and Transportation in an official communiqué issued after a meeting of the Council of Ministers, presided over by President de Gaulle on March 30, 1960. In this, the

[34] CEE, *Communauté Européenne*, No. 6, June 1961.

[35] *Le Monde*, March 5, 1960, gives the following figures: only 70 per cent of road building and road improvement projects envisaged in the first Plan have been realized; and in the period 1957–Feb. 1960 of the second Plan, only 28 per cent of the projects foreseen for the whole period covered by the plan had materialized. This delay is mainly due to the lack of money allocated to the Special Fund for Road Investment (Law No. 53-1336 of December 31, 1953). A yearly allocation of 300 million new francs was foreseen in the Plan; however, only 40 million were allocated in 1958 and 107 million in 1959. The situation was much improved in 1960, but the 250 million allocated then are still 50 million short of the goal. It is estimated that about 800 million are needed to make up.

Minister, after admitting that the development of the road network in France has not kept pace with the increase in road traffic (about 10 per cent per year), estimates that modernization and remolding of the French road network, taking into account the new directions that will be given to traffic by the operation of the Common Market in the period until 1975, should comprise: 15,000 kilometers of modernization of existing roads, of which 6,000 are highways and 9,000 secondary roads. Furthermore, the construction of 2,000 kilometers of new superhighways is advisable. Now, as in past years, the program of road development is limited by lack of money (it is indeed common practice to divert money originally allocated to road and school construction to other projects when an unbudgeted need arises). The Minister foresees a dual system of financing, partly directly by the State, which will grant concessions for the exploitation of the new roads to mixed-economy companies for a number of years. These companies will then recover some of the money invested in building the new roads and, of course, profit from the investments by a system of tolls, as is commonly practiced in the United States.

It must be noted here that, as far as the underdeveloped regions are concerned, this system is not likely to be applied, because the scarcity of population, industry, and consequently traffic will not attract private investment for road building in these areas. The government will have to take complete charge of road building and maintenance in these regions, at least during the transition period foreseen by the Treaty, after which the European Executive should take charge of the whole system and proceed to a better integration of the French system with those of the other Member States.[36] And the present underdeveloped regions (which

[36] "Starting from six different national systems, we must arrive, by the end of the transition period, at a transportation market organized according to communal rules. This market must be suitable to respond to the growing needs of the Community and to assure the suppression of any discrimination based on nationality." M. Lambert Schaus,

by that time should be more developed) should participate fully in this.

Power

POWER IN SOUTHERN ITALY

It is a well-known fact that the local sources of power in Southern Italy are now, and have always been, scarce and utterly inadequate for industrial development. Indeed, this paucity of power has been one of the main causes of underdevelopment. In contrast, most of Western Europe and parts of Northern Italy have an abundance of energy *in loco* or within easy reach, and this has been essential to industrialization.[37] Fortunately for Southern Italy, conditions are now rapidly changing: in fact, not only is there an overabundance of energy in the industrialized parts of the world, but technological progress in transportation makes it easily available to areas with little local production so that in some cases they may actually be better served than areas nearer to the centers of production. Furthermore, in the near future, the use of atomic energy may become general, and geographic and geologic position will have very little relevance.[38]

Member of the EEC Commission, in a declaration to *Communauté Européenne*, No. 7, July 1962.

[37] "It is true that the peripheral regions of Europe have suffered very severely for the last century and a half because of their distance from the coal mines. But the authors of the Treaties of Paris and Rome have rightly reacted with vigor against the laissez-faire type of policy, knowing that it is not correct to think that the opening of customs barriers suffices to bring very different regions to the same level of well-being, even if they are as near to each other as Northern Italy and the Mezzogiorno." The late P. Malvestiti, Président de l'Haute Autorité de la CECA, *Les Sources d'Energie et les Révolutions Industrielles* (Paris, 1961).

[38] . . . the needs of the Europeans for energy grow with great momentum. . . . In 1980, the six countries of the European Community will need four times the quantity of energy available to them today: 900 billion kilowatt/hours instead of 230 billion in 1960." CEE, *Europe 235* (Cahier No. 4). ". . . Twenty-five per cent of this

Nuclear Energy and Electricity

In the framework of the European Atomic Energy Community (Euratom), Southern Italy is developing a relatively modest nuclear energy program. The contribution of the new nuclear plants to the areas where they are to be built will be important not only from a strictly economic viewpoint but also from a psychological viewpoint—reminding the people living there that they should make an effort to adapt themselves to the atomic era. Three atomic power plants have already been built with the financial participation of Euratom, two in Southern Italy and one on the border between Belgium and France. The two Southern Italian ones are:

(a) the plant at Garigliano, co-participation Euratom-Società Elettronucleare Nazionale (SENN), with a financial contribution of 35 million new francs by Euratom;

(b) The Latina plant, co-participation of Euratom-Società Italiana Meridionale Energia Atomica, with a financial contribution of 20 million new francs by Euratom.[39] The most recent information available about their performance is the following: "The Latina station, which is of natural uranium, graphite-gas type, reached its full capacity of 200,000 kw. in December and has already provided over 300,000,000 kwh of electricity in 1963; the Garigliano station which is of the boiling water type and has an installed capacity of 150,000 kw. has already fed electricity, experimentally, into the power line to Naples."[40]

Perhaps the main drawback to nuclear-produced electricity is that it is expensive; a more economical solution could be the construction of thermal plants using imported

energy will have to be supplied by the atom. That is, in 1980, nuclear energy will have to furnish the equivalent of the total amount of the European production of 1959, i.e., about 230 billion kilowatt/hours." CEE, *EURATOM* (Cahier No. 2).

[39] CEE, *Communauté Européenne*, No. 10, October 1961.
[40] *The Economist*, March 28, 1964.

fuel oil or liquefied natural gas from the Sahara. However, the disadvantage of the high cost will be more than compensated for by having a ready supply of electric energy available, which will foster and sustain the industrialization of Southern Italy.

An event of the greatest importance for the energy situation in Italy, and particularly in the Mezzogiorno, where the cost of electricity had hitherto been higher than in the North[41] is the nationalization of the electric industry, and the establishment of the National Electricity Board, ENEL (Ente Nazionale per l'Energia Elettrica). The Electricity Bill was approved by the Italian Chamber of Deputies on November 28, 1962, and became law after being published in *Gazzetta Ufficiale* of December 12, 1962, (Law No. 1643, entitled: "Creation of the National Electricity Board and the transfer to it of the various undertakings composing the electricity industry"). The new Board has taken over more than 500 private electricity companies. In the final text of the law, special provisions appear (article 4) in favor of certain local agencies in various parts of Southern Italy. The ENEL hopes to attain the maximum efficiency by, among other things, a regional division of operations, among its eight *compartimenti* (area boards), which will be in charge locally of construction and management of power gener-

[41]

Light Industry		
Region	Energy Sold (in kwh)	Average Price (in lire, per kwh)
North	3,040	19.05
South (Continental)	328	22.16
Islands	165	24.10
Total	3,533	

Private Consumption		
North	1,673	33.76
South (Continental)	305	39.57
Islands	170	42.24
Total	2,148	

Data supplied by the Società Meridionale di Elettricità to *Prospettive Meridionali*, No. 1–2, Jan.–Feb. 1961.

ation and transmission lines as directed and coordinated by the National Board. The division of jurisdiction is: three over Northern Italy; two over Central Italy; one over the continental Mezzogiorno; and one each for the islands of Sicily and Sardinia. A further administrative subdivision has been decided on: regional districts, composed of a number of operating units (zones).

The outcome of the nationalization of electric energy in Italy will be watched closely by the Executives of the European Communities, since it will have important repercussions on the price they eventually set as the common European price for electricity, as well as for other forms of energy, at the end of the transition period. Obviously this price will weigh heavily on the price formation of finished products, and one of the tasks of the Executives,[42] according

---

[42] The more the economies of the Six become interwoven, the more evident become the shortcomings of the three-Executive system, despite the formation of an inter-Executive Committee to try to coordinate policies. These discrepancies are far more visible in the field of energy. In principle, Euratom has exclusive competence in the nuclear sector, ECSC in coal and similar fuels, the EEC for oil and electricity (not atom-produced, otherwise it would fall under Euratom's competence), and other forms of energy. It is clear that, beside the waste and duplication common when two or more bodies encroach on each other's sphere of competence, as in most human endeavors each of the Executives tends to underline the importance of its own field of action to the detriment of the others. This is particularly evident in many ECSC reports and publications, where the importance of coal production against the continuous advance of oil and against the competition of North American coal is strenuously, if not always convincingly, defended. The direct consequence of this situation on Southern Italy could be deleterious; in fact, ECSC proposes limitations on the imports of coal and oil from outside the Community *and* a bringing-into-line of the price of these products—or at least of the reduced quantities imported—with the price of these commodities obtaining inside the Community (which means higher prices). Southern Italy, because of its geographic position, is advantageously situated for receiving fuel from abroad, such as Middle Eastern, or even Russian oil shipped directly into the area across short Mediterranean routes, through the seaports of Naples, Palermo, or Bari. Therefore, were the above suggestions to be adopted, Southern Italy's advantageous position would be annulled, and this difference between

to Article 3 of the EEC Treaty is "the establishment of a system ensuring that competition shall not be hampered in the Common Market."[43]

We shall now examine the primary sources of energy in the Mezzogiorno (by "primary" is meant energy-producing raw materials, such as coal, crude oil, etc.) and the various means for transforming and distributing it.

Coal

The only coal deposit of any importance in Italy is that of Sulcis, in Sardinia, where exploitation started more than a century ago, in 1853. Ever since then, the mines of Sulcis have constituted a problem for successive Italian governments. Depending on the circumstances, praised or criticized, the fact remains that, from a strictly monetary viewpoint, they have always been a liability. In the last decade, the Sardinian Regional Government, which administers them directly for want of private enterprises willing to do the job, has suffered an average loss of two and a half billion lire a year. In the recent past, the mines have undergone a

cheap and not-so-cheap fuel could have serious repercussions on the general development of the area.

However, now a very important decision has been taken by the Council of Ministers of the Six; in principle, and subject to ratification by the Parliaments of all the Member States, by January 1, 1967, the three Executives should be merged into one, possibly a decisive step towards an eventual supra-nationality. *Le Monde* (Sélection Hebdomadaire), February 26, 1964.

[43] However, the field of power is one where particular provisions apply. "Before a risk of oligopolistic and monopolistic evolution, the scientific advice is, without the shadow of a doubt, to proceed to general planning in the sector of power. This planning will, on one side, enable private economy to maintain the largest possible freedom of action and, on the other hand, assure that keen competition take place between national and foreign sources of power. . . . The general planning of the means of power delivery and transportation should have as a fundamental principle the duty to see to it that the users be able to choose as freely as possible between the different sources of power and that this freedom of choice be offered in as large as possible a number of points." Malvestiti, *op.cit.*, p. 44.

thorough process of rationalization: production has been voluntarily brought down from an average of over a million metric tons a year between 1947 and 1957 to the present 600,000–700,000 tons a year; the output per man has been notably increased; and the number of miners has been reduced.

These endeavors, however, are not enough to offset the causes (poor quality of coal extracted, difficulty of getting to the coal seams, etc.) which make the coal of Sulcis more expensive than that sold at world prices, particularly after the costs of transportation outside Sardinia—loading, unloading, and temporary storage—are added. The solution to this problem therefore is to be sought in trying to promote its consumption *in loco*, thus avoiding the additional costs. Such an over-all solution is at present being studied by the regional government, in cooperation with the central government and the Istituto Ricostruzione Industriale (IRI). Actually, a new thermoelectric station has been built in the Sulcis valley,[44] and is now generating electric power from coal. In fact, *all* the electric power produced in the island should be used there by moving in new industry. And in this, the European Economic Community can play a major role. Sardinia indeed enjoys many advantages, strategic and geographic, which makes the setting up of new industries there highly advisable.[45] Plants mainly financed by the capital of Community members could very well operate in the island. Other advantages are the availability of space, the warm, dry climate, and the propinquity by sea to Southern France, the Iberian peninsula, and Africa.

[44] Details of the project are to be found in *Prospettive Meridionali*, No. 10, October 1959.

[45] ". . . the profitability of production is to be seen in the function of a market that already embraces the whole of Europe. Luckily this task is facilitated by the fact that in many cases . . . the plants are new, and no reconversion therefore is required. It is thus possible to produce the items that are liable to have more possibility of sale in the Common Market." Pastore, *loc.cit.*

The Italian Government has approved by Law No. 588 of June 2, 1962, a "Piano di Rinascita," or Plan of Rebirth (Piano Straordinario per la rinascita economica e sociale della Sardegna). For this, 400 billion lire have been budgeted, to be spread over thirteen financial years, from 1962–63 to 1974–75. It will help to prepare the region for the tasks awaiting it in the Community. In the words of the Hon. Efisio Corrias, President of the Sardinian Regional Government:

> The problem of the *Rinascita* is a problem not only of a national, but of an international character. Our depression inevitably reverberates on the other regions of the continent [continental Italy] and of Europe. . . . Sardinia has an important role to play in the framework of a coordinated development of the Mediterranean and European economy. Following the favorable consequences brought about by the application of the Euratom and EEC Treaties, the *Piano di Rinascita* will make possible, for an area of 24,000 sq. kms., located in the center of the Mediterranean, the realization of its natural function of meeting point for economic activities of Mediterranean countries and of North Africa."[46]

Lignite

Two main deposits of lignite are extant in Southern Italy: in Mercure, near Potenza (Basilicata), with reserves of anything between 22 million and more than 100 million metric tons, and the Marcone basin, near Benevento (Campania), with reserves between 10 million and 30 million tons. While hitherto their exploitation has been of an irregular character because of the uneconomical prices involved, it now seems probable that, in the framework of the regional development of Basilicata, a thermoelectric power station will be built in the Mercure area to exploit the lignite there for the

[46] *Prospettive Meridionali*, No. 1, January 1963.

production of electricity, which the region will need in the future.

Hydroelectric Power

In view of the scarcity of water in Southern Italy, the exploitation of hydroelectric resources is negligible and has nearly reached the limit.

Oil and Natural Gas

Together with Italian companies, several foreign companies from inside the Community, particularly France and Germany, and from outside, especially America, are prospecting the Meridione and the Islands in search of oil and gas. Important deposits of natural gas have been discovered in various parts of Southern Italy; however, their exploitation up till now has been slow and irregular.

Up till March 31, 1960, thirty-eight full prospecting permits were granted for the continental part of Southern Italy, covering an area of 1,170,202 hectares; in the Islands, fifty-eight were granted, covering 1,347,704 hectares. Concessions for exploitation numbered three, all in Sicily, within an area of 59,307 hectares. Sicily is practically the only region in Southern Italy where oil has been discovered in commercial quantities and where it is presently being exploited. Almost all the Italian production of oil (1.8 million metric tons in 1962) comes from this region. The three concessions are: one in the provinces of Catania, Siracusa, and Ragusa (the "Ragusa"), one in Caltanissetta (the "Gela"), and one in Catania (the "Fontana Rossa."). A great drawback is that, due to its chemical composition, the crude oil extracted from these wells, if refined, will be priced higher than world prices, especially since prices have developed an apparently irreversible downward trend.[47]

The question of oil production at uneconomical prices

[47] A fuller explanation of this problem will be found in *Prospettive Meridionali*, No. 12, December 1960.

within the Community is a serious one. France has a strong interest in supplying most of the Community's oil from the Sahara; therefore, when at the end of the transition period, oil of French origin freely circulates within the Community, the future of Sicilian oil seems doomed. Possibly the only way to rescue it will be not to refine it, but use it crude for power stations to be built *in situ*. In this case, its price will be economical and promising sources of energy for regional development will not be destroyed.

Other areas worth mentioning in Southern Italy, where oil prospecting is presently going on are Pescara, L'Aquila, Chieti, Teramo in Abruzzi, and northern Campania. Commercial exploitation is still limited to negligible quantities, but "the discovery of gas fields in Lucania (Basilicata), Sicily, and Abruzzi coincides with the growth of new interest in the South on the part of Italian entrepreneurs, and with a growing determination on the part of the Government to use more drastic means than incentives to entice industry to the South."[48] This is a good omen for the future.

Another activity that will soon assume great importance for the Sicilian economy will be refining imported oil, since the price could be competitive with French and Dutch oil within the Community. *Italian Business*[49] reports:

> Esso Standard Italiana, in cooperation with RASIOM, will build near the Augusta, Sicily, refinery the largest European plant for the production of lubricants. This new plant, which will use processes developed by Esso Research and Engineering Co., will have a total annual production of 200,000 tons of selective lubricants for automotive and industrial uses. This quantity is about twice as large as the present Italian production of selective lubricants . . . its production will be sold largely in Italy

[48] *The Economist*, November 25, 1961.

[49] April 30, 1961. Distributed by the Italian Information Office, New York.

and partly to countries of the Mediterranean and Middle East.

Responsibility for all matters pertaining to oil and natural gas in Italy accrues to ENI (Ente Nazionale Idrocarburi), the National Hydrocarbon Board. As far as the South is concerned, ENI is contributing in a very remarkable way to the industrialization of the area. This action was initiated by the late Mr. Enrico Mattei, whose dynamism and exceptional personal qualities have been one of the main factors in the "Italian miracle."[50] ENI's greatest success thus far is no doubt the industrialization of the area around Gela, following the discovery of important oil deposits. Gela was once one of the poorest and dreariest places in Sicily. Now its plants for the extraction and the immediate industrial exploitation of oil are among the most modern and best equipped in the world. In 1963, a huge new complex was added to the others already existing in the region: the ANIC petrochemical plants. They employ more than 3,000 people and may process 4 million tons of crude oil per year. In addition these plants generated jobs in many different fields, mainly in building. Actually, in September 1961, there were 1,700 men employed in the building trade; 1,350 of these were working on the ANIC plant. Many of these workers were eventually retrained and absorbed by the new plants, on their completion.

ENI has several plants scattered all over the South. Factories already functioning can be found in Pignone Sud,

[50] In his own words: ". . . I have given to the Italians the least expensive energy in Europe. . . . I was very poor in my youth; at school I discovered that all Italians were very poor. And we were taught that poverty was the lot of Italy. . . . I have shown to my countrymen that they have been misinformed. . . . Now we do not export any more workers. I give work to my countrymen at home and we export Italian products. The Italians are not poor any more, and they must be reckoned with." Excerpts from an interview granted by the late Mr. Mattei to *Le Monde*. *Le Monde* (Sélection Hebdomadaire), December 6, 1961.

Bari, and in Nuovo Pignone, Vibo Valentia; many others are in an advanced stage of construction and will shortly be operating. Outstanding among these is the petrochemical plant situated in Pisticci, in the heart of Basilicata, which hitherto has been practically deprived of any major industry. This plant will employ about 2,000 people, and it is hoped that it will attract other industries to that desolate area. The same function as a "pole of growth" will apply to a huge new wool factory now being built in Foggia, which will employ at least 1,000 people. The builder is Lanerossi, a textile group affiliated with ENI.

POWER IN FRANCE

Coal

In France, coal production takes place mainly in three regions: the North (Pas-de-Calais); Lorraine; and the basins of the Center-South and West. The latter are widespread and irregular, and because of the peculiar quality of the coal extracted from them they need complicated and expensive machinery. The known reserves are 4.4 billion metric tons, of which 1.9 billion are in the Pas-de-Calais region, 1.5 in Lorraine, and 1 billion in the South and West. Coal consumption in France now averages 69 million tons a year, having reached a peak of 87 million tons in 1957. In 1960, total French consumption continued to grow in meeting the demands of the steel industry and industrial heating; it has remained stationary for domestic heating and has diminished for railroad consumption in view of the extensive new electrification of lines.[51]

---

[51] This upward trend is common to the whole Community. Indeed, "the sharp decline in consumption of solid fuels in Western Europe in 1958 and 1959 had come to a halt by the beginning of 1960. By the summer of 1960 consumption of solid fuels was some 5 per cent higher than a year before, although remaining below the 1958 level." ECE, *Economic Survey of Europe, 1960*, I, p. 11.

Adaptation to the New Situation

In the framework of action by the Coal and Steel Community aimed at rationalizing and generally improving production of coal within the Community, and working in close cooperation with it, French technicians have improved the output per worker per working day from 1,732 kilograms in 1959 to 1,815 in 1960 (in 1938 it was 1,229 kilograms). To help in this effort of modernization and rationalization, which should allow the French coal industry to survive and possibly to prosper in the Community,[52] the total amount spent by the French Government between 1946 and 1959 was 840 billion (old) francs.

In order to stabilize the situation, a plan was approved by the government in June 1960 to gradually diminish French coal output from the 59.8 million tons of 1959 to 52.95 in 1965. Table 6 shows how this is being achieved.

TABLE 6[53]
COAL OUTPUT IN FRANCE
(million tons)

	1938	1959	1960	1965
TOTAL (including lignite)	47.5	59.8	58.3	52.95
North (Pas-de-Calais)	28.2	29.2	28.9	28
Lorraine	6.7	15.1	14.1	13.50
Center-South West	11.8	14.3	13.4	11.45
Loire	3.3	3.3	3.0	2.48
Cévennes	2.4	2.9	2.5	2.22
Blanzy	2.6	2.7	2.6	2.50
Aquitaine	1.5	2.1	2.0	1.55
Provence	0.6	1.3	1.3	1.3
Auvergne	1.0	1.3	1.3	0.60
Dauphiné	0.4	0.7	0.7	0.80
Non-nationalized mines	0.8	—	—	—

[52] "It is estimated that the best means of insuring the long-term viability of the European coal mines consists in concentrating production in the basins where the possibilities of improving output are the greatest." OEEC, *L'Energie en Europe*, p. 47.

[53] Source of this table and all data for this section: *L'Economie française*, No. 778, June 1, 1961.

The mining area most affected by this reduction will be the Center-South, and the revised situation will impose many new problems of structural unemployment on this already economically weak zone. Plans have now been drawn up by the State-owned organizations dealing with coal-mining activities in France—Les Charbonnages de France and Les Huillières de Bassin—to minimize the social impact of this painful but unavoidable step.[54] Most of the marginal mines are located in the Center-South, particularly in Cévennes, Auvergne, and Aquitaine, rather than in the two other main coal basins.

Aid by the State to help overcome this transition period is contemplated in the form of (a) direct contributions in the range of 15–20 per cent in the case of conversion to industry, enlargement, or creation of new businesses, or (b) indirectly, through the Sociétés de Développement Régional, if the proposed project is considered "essential" for the industrial development of the region. In this case, the State may increase the amount of its participation up to a maximum of 35 per cent. In both cases, facilities of various kinds may be granted to the companies affected.

A special provision is foreseen for the workers of the five coal basins of the Center-South as they will be most likely to meet difficulties in securing new jobs in this underdeveloped area.[55] Upon loss of their job through no fault of their

[54] According to André Maurois, *op.cit.*, p. 86, ". . . certain secondary mines are no longer profitable. In a liberal economy, and also in a totalitarian regime, they would be closed. In our country, whenever a pit is shut, all the parties protest. The notary, the druggist, the village grocer, they all threaten to vote Communist. Big industry (profitable) defends the marginal industry (unprofitable) in order not to remain isolated before a hostile proletariat. What happens then? Some moribund enterprises are subsidized, while the wise thing would be to reinvigorate the many small industries or, better yet, to create new industries *sur place*."

[55] However, those who are willing to transfer are more or less assured of a new job. Indeed, "The ECSC has brought an almost revolutionary innovation in workers' conditions. In fact, the 'right to work' legislation of the European countries, up till 1952, only included

own, they receive a special bonus equal to three months' salary. Also, unemployment benefits may be extended for an additional year.

Another source of financial help is that extended by the European Coal and Steel Community which may, when particular difficulties arise, grant loans to promote new activities which will facilitate reclassification of workers who have lost their jobs.[56]

The Coal and Steel Community may also contribute by means of subsidies—which will, in certain cases be granted equally by the organization and the State—to the maintenance of unemployed workers, or even help workers whose salary in a new job is lower than that they formerly earned. The Community may also contribute to installation allowances and transportation expenses, and to professional retraining and rehabilitation of workers affected by the change. However, notwithstanding all these provisions, great difficulties are encountered when they are implemented. The case of the coal miners of Decazeville in the *département* of Aveyron has become a classic reaffirmation of the famous words of Pope Pius XII: "Capital cannot move man around like a ball to play with."[57]

---

certain regulations which could attenuate the inconveniences deriving to the workers from their lay-off and from unemployment. The ECSC has opened a new right to the miners and to the steel workers: the right to continuity of employment." CEE, *CECA* (Cahier No. 5), p. 15.

[56] "The number of unemployed [in the coal mines] has increased in France. . . . The social implications of the adaptation and the rehabilitation of the coal industry bestow upon the High Authority increased responsibilities in the domain of the *readaptation of the workers* and *of the industrial reconversion of the basins* [emphasis supplied] particularly hit by the layoffs. . . . As for reconversion, the High Authority has organized an intergovernmental conference . . . and, on the basis of the inventories and of the means available, the High Authority will elaborate proposals for Community action in this field. As for professional training, the High Authority will soon engage in a new stage of its program. . . ." CEE, *Communauté Européenne*, No. 3, March 1961.

[57] Reprinted in *Le Monde* (Sélection Hebdomadaire), January 10, 1962.

In the general framework of rationalization of the existing productive forces, the French government decided to:

> . . . close the mines in Decazeville. Production in these mines is so low as to make their continuous operation unprofitable under the highly competitive conditions of the Western European Coal and Steel Community. Decazeville has become a pointed example of the difficulties that many industries in France now have to face with the gradual lowering of barriers to outside competition. The government has gone to considerable efforts to cushion the shock in Decazeville . . . its plans have been rejected.[58]

The strike in the coal mines of Decazeville, which lasted for sixty-four days, took place around the end of 1961 and the beginning of 1962. It roused passionate interest in the whole French nation and also abroad, following the determination of the miners not to accept the government's proposals. Some of the features of the strike contributed to centering general attention on it: the original way it was carried on—the miners refused to leave the mine shafts where they spent most of the time for the long period the strike lasted; the continuous demonstrations by wives and children of the men involved; and the time of year it took place, during the Christmas and New Year festivities. The crux of the dispute was that the miners did not want to lose, even in part, the benefits they had accumulated in working for the nationalized mines. "The miners are to be transferred to private industry, which the government is trying to bring to the area. The miners are protesting against the decision to close the Government-run mines and against the threat of the lower standards of living they say they

[58] *New York Times*, December 29, 1961.

will sustain from their transfer to jobs with private employers."[59]

After a strike lasting more than two months, the miners obtained substantial satisfaction in most of their demands. One of the miners' conditions that the Government accepted before the end of the strike was [the Government]" . . . will undertake the task of finding a solution to the social problems of the area and of facilitating the implantation of new industries in the Center-South, and in particular in Aveyron."[60] Thus, it may be that acts of this kind, in the long run, will benefit the regions concerned, and consequently the economies of France and the Community as a whole, for they will oblige the government to take more care of the depressed areas, to introduce new industries in these regions, and to revitalize them—in other words to "save" them. The "human factors" in economics, which the economists too often have a tendency to underestimate in their plans, will now have to be taken into greater account by the "technocrats" of the French Plan. Raymond Aron, in an article written during the strike,[61] skillfully expressed the point of the dispute: "The miners of Decazeville, in certain respects, are comparable to the workers who broke the first machines, but in others they belong to our time and illustrate a present problem: how to give back to men the roots they have lost and without which they cannot live."

Coal Productivity

In the field of productivity, the European Coal and Steel Community, together with Les Charbonnages de France, plans to direct the production of coal and the rehabilitation of the unemployed. As we have just seen, the organization plans to aid the latter directly, in cooperation with national

[59] *Ibid.*, January 10, 1962.
[60] *Le Monde* (Sélection Hebdomadaire), February 28, 1962.
[61] "L'Enracinement," *Le Figaro*, December 29, 1961.

organizations. It has already been pointed out that optimum results in this field will unfortunately not be reached until a real policy of coordination of all forms of energy is reached by the Six. "It is now generally agreed that there cannot be a real Common Market without a common power policy."[62]

However, a certain amount of coordination among the three Executives already exists. This has allowed a slowing down in the closing of marginal mines and of layoffs, particularly in the Center and South-West. Thus, the Coal and Steel Community and the French organizations have more time for the relocation and rehabilitation of the workers in these mines.[63]

French Oil and Natural Gas

Due to the immense Sahara fields, for whose output special arrangements have been entered into with Algeria, and due in smaller measure to metropolitan oil produced primarily in Aquitaine (Parentis and other parts of the region), France will soon have a large surplus of oil and the consequent problem of finding outlets, now that world demand appears to be losing momentum compared to the rapidly growing supply. In any case, whatever the solution,

[62] CEE, *CECA* (Cahier No. 5). Furthermore, quoting M. Reynaud: "In fact, it is not sufficient to agree on certain principles and on certain fundamental exigencies such as the necessity of ensuring to industry cheap power, to avoid serious upsets in the European economies and social bodies or to guarantee to Europe a security of supply. *It is above all necessary that an authority be able to arbitrate interests;* [emphasis supplied] that orderly progress be devised and that, by precise scientific methods, the market trends which condition the action of the investors and of the public powers be made known."

[63] The method generally followed by the French is that of not engaging new workers in the coal industry, so that redundant workers can simply be absorbed by taking the place of those who retire in the normal course of events. *L'Economie*, No. 760, January 19, 1961, reports an advanced pension granted in 1960 to two thousand miners of the Center-South West who had a thirty-year work record. This region was obviously chosen because layoffs there assume the most serious proportions.

it is certain that Aquitaine will benefit from its newly found natural riches in oil.[64]

However, more than the oil of Parentis, the really great boost to the industrialization and modernization of the region will be—and actually already is—the exploitation of the wealth of natural gas at Lacq. It is estimated that more than four hundred billion cubic meters of methane gas are lying in strata between two and three miles underground in the Béarn region around Lacq.

Lacq is situated in the *département* of the Basses-Pyrénées, not far from its capital city, Pau. Until the discovery of natural gas, the area surrounding the village was of an almost exclusively agricultural character. The first discovery of natural gas goes back to 1951. In the three following years prospecting was intensified and finally, in 1954, massive exploitation started. The operation was initiated and carried on by the SNPA (Société Nationale des Pétroles d'Aquitaine), a regional branch of the BRP (Bureau de Recherches des Pétroles), a state company, with the cooperation of some of the most important companies in the nationalized sector of French industry: Gaz de France, Electricité de France, Régie Autonome des Pétroles. A new city of about 11,000, Mourenx-Ville Nouvelle, has been built for the 4,500 workers employed at Lacq and their families.

According to estimates, the fields should produce about thirty million cubic meters of gas per day by 1965. After

[64] The following figures show the evolution of production of crude oil in metropolitan France:

| | *(Thousands of metric tons)* | | | |
	1955	1958	1959	1960
Total met. France:	878.4	1,386.4	1,622.5	1,979.0
Of which—				
Parentis region:	576.5	1,203.0	1,232.0	1,345.0
Other parts of Aquitaine:	251.1	101.1	99.2	93.0

Source: *L'Economie*, No. 768, March 16, 1961.
From this table we can see the importance of the combined output of South-West France compared to the total production in metropolitan France.

273

refining, about twenty million cubic meters per day will be ready for use, a quantity which represents an annual equivalent of about eight million metric tons of coal (10 per cent of French consumption in 1957). A by-product of this process of refinement will be sulphur, the yearly output of which should be 1.6 million tons, placing France second in world production, following the United States.

Meanwhile, this new source of energy is having a great impact on the transformation of the area.

Gaz de France is now oriented towards the implementation of new techniques of production and, since the discovery of the natural gas deposit at Lacq, towards the massive utilization of this natural gas. Consequently, since the creation of Gaz de France, more than 450 factories producing gas from coke have been shut and the distribution hitherto served by them has been fed by other sources of gaseous energy . . . 12,000 kms. of high-pressure pipeline connect most of the regions with each other.[65]

Much of the gas produced is consumed in the South-West but the greatest share goes to other regions of France, as shown by the following figures:[66]

(in millions of cu.m. of refined gas per day)

South-West	5.2
West-Center	1.2
Center-East	3.4
Paris region	3.2
Total	13.0

The whole of South-West France is now served by the Société Nationale de Gaz du Sud-Ouest, and a thick net-

[65] *Ibid.*, February 28, 1964.
[66] *Revue Juridique et Economique du Sud-Ouest*, No. 4, 1962.

work of pipelines has been built or is in the process of building.[67]

In a number of years, Lacq gas production should be a very important factor in the energy sources of France, and consequently of the Community. Several industrial complexes (aluminum, petrochemicals, plastics, etc.), most of which plan to sell their products not only in France but in the Community as a whole, have built branches in the area between Orthez and Pau to take advantage of the cheaper gas rates offered.[68] Thus, Lacq is carrying out very well its important task of being the main pole of growth in Aquitaine.

INDUSTRY

INDUSTRIALIZATION IN SOUTHERN ITALY

In 1950, when the basic Plan for Development of the South (Cassa per il Mezzogiorno) was devised, from an industrial viewpoint the disequilibrium between the North and the South of Italy was tremendous. Thereafter, little by little, the Mezzogiorno has steadily improved its position, but the North has also progressed rapidly. Therefore, the gap which separates the two parts of the country is still large, even though it is the stated policy of the government to narrow and possibly to bridge it.[69]

[67] *Rapport Annuel sur l'Exécution du Plan de Modernisation et d'Equipement, 1960*, pp. 92ff.

[68] Among the industrial establishments using Lacq's natural gas are: The Compagnie Péchiney; the Société d'électro-chimie et d'électro-métallurgie d'Ugine at Lannemazen; the Société Pierrefitte at Pierrefitte (chemicals); the Office National Industriel de l'Azote at Toulouse (chemicals); the Etablissements Kuhlman at Bordeaux (chemicals); and the Compagnie de Saint-Golain at Bordeaux (chemicals). The gas is also used to produce electricity in some electric power stations, like Artix and Bordeaux-Ambès.

[69] According to *The Economist* of March 28, 1964: "In the 1950s the gap has actually grown. Though real income a head in the south has risen 55 per cent from 1951 to 1962, as a percentage of the northerner's income it still fell in the same period from 63 per cent to 55 per cent. Such comparisons may not be very useful: it is important that the south progressed faster than ever before in its history." This, of course, is very

What is the final aim of the national government in promoting the industrial advancement of this hitherto backward and stagnant part of the country? Certainly not that of transforming the area into another Ruhr basin, perhaps not even another Po Valley, but simply to furnish it with a balanced economy in all three sectors of economic activity—something which presently does not even remotely exist in Southern Italy.[70]

The overcrowding and the obsolete means and methods of production in Southern Italian agriculture would have made it impossible to compete in the Common Market unless a radical overhaul—modernization and rationalization—had been conducted in this sector too. One of the negative consequences of this process is that increasingly great masses of agricultural workers are being put out of work year after year, thus aggravating the labor situation. Emigration to the other countries of the Community would only be a palliative, and in any case it is politically suicidal and unethical for a government to urge its citizens to leave the country as a solution to their problems. Emigration to the north of Italy, as observed before, is only a partial solution.[71]

---

important for the future of the whole country. As the Minister for Southern Development, the Hon. Giulio Pastore, said: "A responsible national effort must be made to industrialize the Mezzogiorno, not only because this is imposed by the future prospects for development of the economy of the whole country, but also because it constitutes the test of democracy in our country: that is, it constitutes the only valid guarantee of the possibility of continuing in freedom the development of civil and social activities." *La Politica di Sviluppo nel Mezzogiorno* (Quaderno No. 39)

[70] It is generally agreed among students of economics that a well-balanced economy in an advanced country should consist of about 50 per cent industrial activities, 30 per cent from the tertiary sector—commerce, credit, tourism, transportation, and other services—and only 20 per cent agricultural and other activities in the primary sector. The predominance given to the secondary sector derives mainly from the fact that investments in this are in general more productive than those in the other sectors, particularly agriculture.

[71] The following data have been furnished by the Istituto Italiano di Statistica and printed in *Prospettive Meridionali*, No. 12, December 1963:

The aim of industrializing the area does not mean that a great effort will not also be made in the agricultural sector. Indeed, the Hon. Pastore, in a report to Parliament in April 1961, stated:

> The stressing of our efforts in the industrial sector does not imply a decrease in those in the agricultural sector which, on the contrary, will have to be integrated into an over-all concept for the development of the region, responding to the fundamental exigencies of creating areas of industrialization in which there is no serious imbalance between agriculture and industry. The choice of industrial areas, without taking into account the agricultural situation, would risk ending in the creation of industrial complexes surrounded by lands which are poor and economically passive, with little or no relation to the market. The agricultural investment taking place near the areas of industrialization also has the effect of limiting the exodus from the countryside, which generally increases whenever industries are born in the neighborhood. Furthermore, it reduces the difference in income and in the standard of living between those who work in the industrial sector and those who continue to be employed in pre-existing activities.[72]

Extending this declaration to a much larger area, to the whole nation, in fact, it is obvious that the approach to the solution of the problem of the Mezzogiorno must be a broad

---

"In the decade 1951–1960, the South and the islands have lost 1,766,859 inhabitants of which 972,781 emigrated to the North and 794,078 abroad. Furthermore, in the first seven months of 1963, the excess of immigration over emigration in the North was 162,826."

[72] Reprinted from the aforementioned Quaderno 39: *La Politica di Sviluppo nel Mezzogiorno*. In many cases there is also a direct interaction between industry and agriculture. For instance, *The Economist* of March 28, 1964, reports that, in the area of Gela (Sicily), "In order to ensure an adequate supply of water for the installation, [of new industrial plants] a dam has been built across the Dirillo river. This dam retains 21 million cubic meters of water and can therefore meet the demand for irrigating water over a vast area of agricultural land."

one, and that the whole national economy must be geared to promoting that solution.[73] This is also true of the relationship that will exist between the underdeveloped areas and the industrialized areas of the Community. The effort must be collective and be performed harmoniously by both categories if positive and lasting results are to be obtained. We quote the words of the Hon. Emilio Colombo, Minister of Industry and Commerce: "We are convinced that the possibilities of State intervention, the progress made by technology in every field, a more widespread consciousness of the urgency of the terms of the problem, enable us today to attain positive economic results both in agriculture and in industry especially, in a much shorter time than was needed in the past by other nations."[74] The government, as previously seen, is encouraging investments in many ways.[75] Companies of all sizes have numerous branches in the South, not only giants like Montecatini (private) and the Istituto Ricostruzione Industriale (IRI) (public), but also many medium sized and small firms have, or plan to have, a Southern branch.[76] Now let us examine the operations in Southern Italy of the two largest companies.

[73] "It is first of all necessary that, in the industrialized area, as well as in the South of Europe, expansion take place *without leaving any resources unexploited.*" OEEC, *L'Europe et l'Economie Mondiale*, p. 7.

[74] From a speech before the Chamber of Deputies, February 7, 1961. Reported in *Corriere della Sera*, February 8, 1961.

[75] Special government aid to the South during the past decade has amounted to the equivalent of about 3 billion dollars. This aid, plus the availability of special incentives, as well as the various legal and administrative measures taken to promote industrialization, resulted in a dramatic increase in annual investments in the South. In 1951, investments in the Mezzogiorno (for agriculture, industry, housing, transport, and public works) amounted to about 550 million dollars. In 1962, they exceeded 2 billion dollars. A key feature of the investment picture is that in 1960, for the first time, more funds were invested in industry than in agriculture. The trend became more marked in 1961 and 1962 when a veritable explosion of industrial investments occurred and hit an annual figure of 700 million dollars. See *Italy—An Economic Profile, op.cit.*

[76] "To make up for the delay in development of the Mezzogiorno, it will above all be necessary to attempt to extend to the South the same

At the beginning of 1950, IRI had only 10 per cent of its personnel actually working in factories in the South, even though the total percentage, including administrative personnel, etc. was slightly higher, 15 per cent. However, after the plan for developing the Mezzogiorno had been adopted by the Government, investments in the South greatly increased and, between 1951 and 1960, the industrial investments of IRI in the Meridione reached about one-third of its total industrial investments. Actually the amount of investments follows a steep progression, being 35.5 billion lire for the eight-year period 1951–57, 55.5 for the years 1958–59, and 74 billion for 1960.

Naturally, this great increase in investments has brought about a large increase in employment, despite technological improvements and the rationalization of existing plants. The number of employees has jumped from 25,000 to 42,000, showing an increase of more than two-thirds. Today, more than 20 per cent of IRI's employees are working in the Southern branches of the industrial group. The main new installations are factories at Taranto (Apulia)[77] and Bagnoli (Campania), a thermoelectric power plant at Napoli Levante, railway workshops at Reggio Calabria, etc.

---

industrial equipment as for the rest of the country. Thus, it will be possible to correct the effects deriving from the tendency of industrial investments to concentrate in the already industrialized regions . . ." CEE, *Rapport 1958*, p. 409.

[77] *The Observer* of February 9, 1964, has the following comment concerning the Taranto plant: ". . . at Taranto, Italsider (an I.R.I. subsidiary), the giant of Italian steel, has already convulsed local conditions with the building of an £180 million integrated plant. It rises straight out of flat, olive-strewn farmland. . . . Whether Italy, economically speaking, needed a steel plant in the undeveloped South, 1,000 miles from Milan, is another matter. *I.R.I. state ownership helped to ensure that depressed Taranto was chosen.* [emphasis supplied] The plant will double the province's income . . . Taranto should work out. It will be the most modern, low-cost plant in Europe, living entirely off imported coal and ore . . . sucking in labour off the farms." Adds *Time*, October 16, 1964: "by early 1965 (the Taranto plant) will be producing steel at the rate of 2,200,000 tons a year and employing 4,500 workers."

The programs for the years 1961–64 accelerate this expansion: 536 billion lire have been invested in the South, at the rate of 134 billion lire a year. This average is three times that of the decade 1951–60 and almost double that of 1960 itself. The total number of employees increased by 10,000. And the repercussions on the economy of the Mezzogiorno will be considerable, because these new factories will be poles of growth around which new industrial zones will congregate.[78] The factories have been located in certain strategic positions, so that they respond to the general scheme of IRI to facilitate the inclusion of the Mezzogiorno in the new entity constituted by the Common Market.[79]

An interesting feature of the program of development carried on by the IRI in the Mezzogiorno concerns a new method of increasing the skills of its Southern workers: they send them, at company expense, to work for short periods in the factories in the North, so that afterwards they return to the factories of the South with new skills. The scarcity of skilled labor in the area has always been one of the factors that retarded its development. IRI has also opened a school of technical instruction in Taranto for its prospective and present employees, which is in addition to the one already existing in Naples. Not only IRI workers, but also those belonging to other firms, may benefit from these schools so

[78] On the importance and irreplaceability of the poles of growth in the underdeveloped areas, the Hon. Malvestiti writes: "The influence of *poles of growth* is not replaced in any appreciable manner by the phenomenon of *reverberation* that certain authors have thought to discover. Such concentrations have only distant and indirect effects on the peripheral regions; these stay poor and I should even add that they become relatively poorer." *Op.cit.*, p. 10.

[79] And the EEC, for its part, will help. Under the title: "Towards the Development of the Mezzogiorno," *Communauté Européenne*, No. 11, November 1962, writes that "The Executive of the Common Market has decided to take over the promotion of a pole of industrial development in the most unfavored region of the Community: the Italian Mezzogiorno. It has ordered the study of a complex founded on production and transformation of steel, in the provinces of Taranto and Bari, which will permit the integration of certain projects already being realized into a coherent ensemble, capable of developing by market play without the intervention of public powers."

that the task of producing technicians for the new factories of the South will be furthered.

The new role assumed by IRI in road-building must also be emphasized; apart from the Rome-Naples sector of the Autostrada del Sole, work has started on the new highways Porto d'Ascoli-Canosa and Naples-Canosa-Bari. Lastly, true to its purpose of extending its contribution to the industrialization of the South, IRI also participates in a different capacity: in fact, a subsidiary organization, the Istituto per lo Sviluppo delle Attività Produttive (ISAP) fosters the creation and development of small and medium firms, and plays an important role in this field when the size of the firms does not justify direct intervention on the part of IRI. Its help is generally financial, technical, and organizational. To stress the fact that ISAP wants to be of help to private enterprise, but does not aim at replacing it, a constant practice followed whenever financial participation in a venture is decided upon is to confine this participation to less than 50 per cent of the capital of the firm, so that the private entrepreneur continues to control the majority of the shares and therefore the administration of the enterprise. And to keep control of his enterprise is particularly important for him, for "unlike the committee-minded U.S. businessman, the Italian chief executive is a freewheeling autocrat who bases his decisions far more on intuition than on the promptings of scientific management."[80]

The colossus of private enterprise in Italy, Montecatini, is by no means new to investing and operating in Southern Italy; however, in view of the new development of the area by the Government, its participation in the economy of the region, particularly now that the Mezzogiorno must be prepared to play its role in the European Economic Community, will increase considerably.[81] While in the whole period

[80] *Time,* January 12, 1962.

[81] There are today "ample possibilities for industry in the South, and not at all of a parasitic nature; actually, taking into account the present reality of the labor market, in Italy and in Europe, the progress achieved in transportation of the techniques of production and dis-

281

from the end of World War II to 1960 the sum invested reached the equivalent of about 370 billion lire (in today's value), further investments of 200 billion lire are now contemplated for the next few years, of which 100 billion are for a gigantic new petrochemical complex at Brindisi (Apulia), which should be the largest in Italy and one of the largest in the European Community.[82]

This new industrial complex will completely transform the economy of the whole zone, which is precisely the result hoped for in this kind of operation. The seaport of Brindisi, accounting hitherto for a very limited volume of traffic (80,000 tons a year), will increase its volume many times over—according to recent estimates, it should reach one and a half million tons a year.

The second large plant built by the Montecatini concern is located at Ferrandina in Basilicata, where a few years ago a sizeable deposit of natural gas was found. The selection of the site responds to the desires of the local inhabitants to exploit this precious power in the region.[83] Chemical prod-

---

tribution, it seems that the convenience of localizing new investments and new industries in the South is considerably increased. . . . Numerous indications to this effect can also be found in international documents which give prominence to Italian problems, and in reports of the ECE and OEEC." Compagna, *op. cit.*, p. 47.

[82] Italy now has a tradition that the preponderant share of industrial output is in chemical products. The addition of this large plant will help to perpetuate this even in the larger European market, by taking advantage of the untapped resources, human and others, of Southern Italy.

[83] The inhabitants of the area had a rather forceful way of making their desires known! "When a large natural gas deposit was found in the hills at Ferrandina in 1959, there were riots in the surrounding villages for fear the gas might be piped elsewhere. For months the villagers set up a permanent guard around the derricks to prevent anyone laying the hated pipelines; and visitors were liable to be abducted by grim men with shotguns until they could prove their purposes were not that technical." At any rate, the industrialization of the area will certainly have beneficial repercussions on the local mores. "Two years ago at Ferrandina, a town of 10,000 inhabitants in Lucania, the average sale of tooth-brushes was forty a year." Both quotations from *The Economist*, March 28, 1964.

ucts are in great demand throughout the Community, therefore there should not be any difficulty concerning their sale.

The action taken by Montecatini in the South is perhaps the best example of cooperation between private and public enterprise, for not only do they not threaten or oppose each other's interests, but actually complement each other, with benefits deriving principally to that so-often-forgotten "king" of the market, the consumer. This has already been repeatedly demonstrated in the North, for even where government intervention is strongest, North Italy's private industry manages to flourish.

Among others, the well-known Motta sweets and candy concern has inaugurated a large complex near Naples, taking advantage of the many facilities and exemptions granted by the government. The plant is intended to serve the needs of the whole South. The total amount invested in this enterprise is 1,500 million lire, of which 550 million have been advanced by ISVEIMER.

> This sector of the economy is quickly expanding, either in order to increase exports to the other European countries following the progressive liberalization of exchanges within the Common Market, or to increase internal consumption, which is rising more rapidly in the South than in the North. Furthermore, the sweet-making industry is another positive element in the economy of the South, in that it uses the products of southern agriculture for its needs.[84]

More than 1,000 Italian firms have opened branches, or moved south, lured by the incentives offered to them, in the last decade or so. Actually, the movement has been considerably accelerated in the last few years. Furthermore, at least fifty foreign companies, of which about half are American, have also established branches in the Mezzogiorno. The

[84] *Il Popolo*, September 10, 1961.

range of activities covered is very wide: ceramics, canneries, transistors, pharmaceuticals, chemicals, plastics, refineries, textiles, etc. The role played by private enterprise in the development of the South, after the notable improvements brought to the infrastructure by the actions of the State, is acquiring momentum. As a matter of fact, according to estimates, "nearly 80 per cent of all industrial investment in the 'Mezzogiorno' now comes from private firms."[85]

It is perhaps worth mentioning some of the other principal private firms, Italian and foreign, that are prominent in the industrialization of the South: Marzotto, Fabbri, Fiat, Olivetti, Pirelli, Lepetit, Saint Gobain, Willy, Pfizer, Abbott, Monsanto, Union Carbide, Standard Triumph, Litton, Gulf, Goodyear, Remington Rand, and American Cyanamid.

An intense propaganda effort is being carried out to lure foreign capital into the area, particularly by means of advertising the many advantages accruing to the investor in Southern Italy. For instance, the *New York Times*[86] carried the following advertisement, inserted by the Institute for Assistance to the Development of Southern Italy:

Southern Italy represents the key location from which to seize the unmatched business opportunities provided by the mounting affluence of the Common Market nations and the economic growth of the new, fast developing countries of North Africa and the Middle East. Other good reasons for putting your plant in Southern Italy: more labor available here than anywhere in the Common Market; cheap and plentiful supply of natural gas and other raw materials; cash grants, tax rebates and other inducements, including a 10-year corporate income-tax exemption; a local market of 19 million people whose incomes are increasing at one of Europe's fastest rates.[87]

[85] *Italy, an Economic Profile, op.cit.*

[86] (Europe-Mideast Business Review), January 10, 1964.

[87] There is no doubt that the advantages offered are very real. For instance, *Italy, an Economic Profile* reports: "The value of this basket of

Before concluding, mention should be made of a financial institution, particularly successful in Sicily: SOFIS (Società Finanziaria Siciliana per Azioni), founded by the Regional Government of Sicily in 1957. Its main purpose is the promotion of the development of Sicilian industry; its main activity is investment in stocks of industrial firms. Its participation depends upon the following criteria: (a) the exploitation of oil and gas deposits and their derivatives; (b) the construction, expansion, or modernizing of industrial plants; and (c) the construction and administration of drydocks. SOFIS can, however, carry out financing operations in other fields; the only condition being that they benefit the public welfare. It generally participates up to no more than 25 per cent in the various industrial activities it choses to support.

INDUSTRY IN FRENCH UNDERDEVELOPED REGIONS

Brittany

Industry in Brittany is little developed, and most of it is in processing plants concerned with the canning or preparation in other ways of the chief products of the region—agricultural products and fish. It is true that this is not the only industrial activity in Brittany; heavy industry now has a few footholds, for example, at Rennes, Saint-Brieuc and

---

incentives and facilities is also impressive. It is reported, for example, that one American businessman ready to invest $340,000 in a printing plant in Southern Italy found that, by making use of all available concessions and incentives, he had to put up only $90,000 in cash." Another case in point is reported in the *New York Times* of March 6, 1964: "Litton-Italia . . . got the following for its $1.5 million plant: a 13-year loan of $1 million, partly at 3 per cent and partly at 4 per cent, with three years' grace to start; tariff exemption on purchases of foreign equipment, 10 years' exemption from the national income tax on profits; and cut rates on the national turnover tax on construction materials, the county income tax and the registration tax on the land purchase. Litton will also qualify for a pure cash subsidy, calculated on the costs of the building and its plumbing and other fixed installations. This payment may come to more than $200,000. Rich as these incentives may sound, they are not unusual and they are not even the maximum that a Company might qualify to get."

Ploërmel. However, the peripheral geographic position of Brittany is a severe handicap to the establishment of industry on a large scale because of the many difficulties involved. One of the chief difficulties, though not the only one, is that all raw materials must be imported from outside the area, and this means higher costs. These disadvantages could be partially counteracted by saving transportation costs on the finished products—in other words, they should be sold in the region. A vast range of opportunities exist in the manufacture of tools for fishing and agriculture, and in other types of light industry which do not suffer disadvantages due to distance, i.e., the manufacture of small electric gadgets and similar kinds of tools. Moreover, these industries do not necessitate heavy investments and the region does not have much capital to invest.

Brittany has another, perhaps more important, problem to overcome: the region has a scarcity of businessmen who might initiate the setting up of new industries since almost all the economic efforts made hitherto have been directed to agriculture, to fishing, or to small commercial activities and very few people are really competent in the industrial field. Consequently, these businessmen must come from outside the region, or be brought in to operate local branches of industries having their headquarters elsewhere.[88]

We have already considered the agricultural problem of Brittany, and seen how technological progress is turning increasing numbers of workers out of jobs. These new unemployed are eventually compelled, in large part, to emigrate elsewhere where jobs can be found, thus adding to the already rather heavy movement of population out of the region. This overabundance of labor, which is a rather unusual phenomenon in France—and throughout the Com-

[88] However, it seems that "there is a strong desire on the part of the numerous Breton executives scattered throughout France, to return to Brittany if suitable conditions are offered to them." *Le Monde* (Sélection Hebdomadaire), May 9, 1962.

munity for that matter (with the notable exception of Southern Italy)—is not always necessarily a disadvantage. Actually, the more severe the labor shortage becomes in "Little Europe," the more industry will turn to places unaffected by it.[89] So the chances for regions like Brittany, or Southern Italy, brighten considerably. And not only are new industries from within the Community liable to be placed in regions that have no labor shortage but also those from outside the Community, particularly from the United States. For instance, at the end of 1961 it was announced that:

The Goodyear International Corporation, a subsidiary of the Goodyear Tire and Rubber Co., will build its first plant for the production of synthetic rubber outside the United States near Le Havre, France. Richard V. Thomas, President of Goodyear International, said," . . . The rapidly expanding markets for specialty man-made rubber products, particularly in the European Common Market, guided our decision to build a plant in France at this time." He said "the Le Havre site was chosen because of the ready source of low-cost raw materials, primarily butadiene, and *because of the adequate labor supply*. Machinery and construction materials for the new plant would be purchased in Western Europe, and *raw chemical materials would be obtained locally*, where possible."[90] (emphasis supplied)

Other industries may follow the same line of reasoning. When freedom of establishment anywhere within the Community is in effect, there will be many advantages for indus-

[89] "Regional policy is already assuming a wider importance for economic growth. As Western Europe approaches full employment, the remaining patches of idle labour are to be found mainly in a few backward or depressed areas. In a speech on January 22, M. Marjolin, of the European Commission, emphasized that steady growth would increasingly depend on making use of such resources." *The Economist*, March 3, 1962.

[90] *New York Times*, December 19, 1961.

try, both foreign and domestic, to establish branches in such areas. Thus, a huge new Citroën factory has been installed in Rennes, the capital of Brittany. Professional and skilled labor has been recruited in the technical centers of the region and the cadres of the new organization have been formed in the first of the Citroën factories already in operation in Rennes.[91]

It is rewarding to note that the local authorities have for some time recognized the necessity of orienting the youth of Brittany towards a technical education, and the results now being obtained are very satisfactory. Indeed, considering that Brittany is a region with an essentially agricultural tradition (apart from a long and glorious seafaring past, of course), the fact that the average number of young people under twenty who go to technical schools is higher than the average for the whole of France[92] is almost astonishing. This is indeed evidence that the people of Brittany have fully grasped the situation and are aware of the fact that large numbers of them must have this indispensable technical knowledge if the region is to be saved. Otherwise, the new industries would by-pass it for lack of suitable personnel, and emigration would continue unabated, with deleterious consequences which are easy to foresee.

Fortunately, in view of the foregoing, this does not seem to be the case. In addition, the French Government seems intent on increasing its aid to the region as a whole: Brittany is top on the list of three regions which, according to the IVth Plan, will benefit from "*massive* [governmental] *intervention* where the State cannot just stand by waiting for private enterprise to act."[93] Therefore, a combination of local and State initiative and goodwill will eventually put Brittany

[91] And, of course, new industries congregate around this pole of growth. For instance, *L'Economie*, April 18, 1963, reports that ". . . in the photographic sector, we must note the construction by Eastman Kodak of a factory at Rennes for the development of colored pictures."

[92] 35 per cent, compared to 32 per cent. *Le Monde*, June 12, 1960.

[93] *Le Monde* (Sélection Hebdomadaire), January 10, 1962.

in a position to overcome the disadvantages deriving to it from its peripheral position in the Europe of the Six.

In addition to Rennes, the other main cities of Brittany must also serve as "poles of growth" if an equilibrium is to be achieved in the development of the region as a whole. Nantes and Lorient may become important commercial centers for the distribution of the industrial and agricultural products of their hinterlands. Brest, as well as other Atlantic ports, could profit from an intensification of the traffic between the Common Market and North America. "Brest traditionally lives on the sea; its port is the second French naval base and its shipyards constitute, if not the only one, at least the most important by far, of its industries. The problem of Brest today is that at the same time that its population is growing at a fast rate, the traffic of the port is decreasing and naval construction is threatened."[94] The essential factor in a recovery of Brest is a liberalization of trade between the Common Market and the United States. Brest could take advantage of its very favorable geographic position in this respect, and become one of the most important springboards for such traffic, but certain basic improvements must first be made in the network of transportation linking it not only with Paris, but with the entire North-West of France and the other regions of the Community it would serve. As it stands now transportation is completely inadequate and would be unable to handle any large volume of traffic between Brest and the hinterland. Furthermore the whole region should be more industrialized, enabling it to participate actively in this new trade with its own goods (or through processing products destined for export or others just imported).

The development of the main "poles of growth" at Rennes and at Brest, besides a few more secondary bases, would foster a regionally balanced economy. As Citroën has done

[94] *Le Monde,* June 29, 1960.

for Rennes, so the installation of a second pole of growth at Brest would favor the development of the whole of Brittany.[95]

These activities will perhaps not eliminate the problems of underemployment and underdevelopment from Brittany as quickly as might be wished, but, in this region especially, *industrialization is an agricultural necessity*, and a good start is essential. Thus, Brittany's economy will probably remain, even in the Common Market, basically an agricultural one, with an industrial superstructure.[96]

The Massif Central

As already seen, the depopulation process has gravely affected the Massif Central in the past century or so. An industrial renaissance is, however, possible and is indeed necessary if this region is to integrate fully with the Community and discontinue the present trend which is turning large sections of it into part of the so-called "désert français." This industrialization process, together with agricultural

[95] Former French Premier René Pleven looks into the future and writes: "One of the most characteristic features of the Bretons is imagination. The Bretons already visualize a Common Market enlarged to include Great Britain and Spain. An enormous share of the merchant fleets of the world pass through waters near Brest, one of the best natural harbors in the world. . . . In the acceleration of exchanges with the United Kingdom and with Spain, which would follow their adherence to the Common Market, Brittany knows that she would be admirably situated . . . and this fact already focuses the thoughts of continental industrialists who see far into the future." *Communauté Européenne*, Nos. 8–9, Aug.–Sept. 1962.

[96] It must be borne in mind in fact that "the principal obstacles to the industrialization of Brittany—high cost of energy and high cost of transportation (in which, incidentally, the infrastructure is deficient)— are still there. Perhaps they will become even more serious if the new rail tariffs are applied without modifications, as is presently envisaged." *Le Monde* (Sélection Hebdomadaire), May 9, 1962. However, according to the *New York Times*, August 18, 1963, the situation will change radically in a few years, as far as energy is concerned. "A dam to harness ocean tides for electricity is well under construction in Brittany. . . . [It] is expected to start producing electricity in 1966. . . . An expanded plant that may be built later would push the annual output up to more than one-third of France's total consumption."

and tourist development, should give the region the long-awaited boost it needs.

The industrial nuclei of the Massif Central have created, even in a mountainous and rugged area, a number of potential bases for new industrial zones. For instance, there are foundries at Ancizes (Puy-de-Dôme) and at Saint-Chély-d'Apcher (Lozère); aluminum factories at Ussel (Cantal); chemical and drug manufacturing plants at Vertolaye (Dore Valley); and other minor enterprises. Comparatively, this is very little in relation to the size of the area.

On the other hand, the rational exploitation of the mineral wealth of the Massif Central means also the creation of small, but promising, poles of development around which a certain amount of industry is bound to grow. A new activity, for the moment still at the prospecting stage, is the extraction of uranium, with good possibilities in the zones of the Haut-Rouergue, Mergeride, and Haut-Velay, where numerous deposits have been found. EURATOM is apparently keenly interested in the results of these endeavors. In one deposit at Bessines-sur-Gartempe (Haute-Vienne), the exploiting and refining of mineral ore containing uranium have already been going on for some time. The whole area, even though it has not been prospected very thoroughly, holds considerable promise of mineral wealth—lead, zinc, wolfram, etc.

If agricultural development proceeds apace with industrial development, then industries for processing agricultural products (canning, etc.), for manufacturing and repairing agricultural machines and tools, and for producing chemical fertilizers, etc., are bound to be established in the area. The paper industry will necessarily expand, since the local forests can be much better exploited than at present and furnish a sizeable share of the raw material needed to meet the great demand for paper which will probably arise in the Community. Also, other items using wood as the base can be manufactured in much larger quantities, if the

291

demand increases and warrants the investment necessary for new equipment. There is little doubt that French furniture, which is already well-known, will be in demand in the Community and that a number of places in the Massif Central will benefit from this.

Its central geographic position may also prove relevant in the industrialization of the region. Improved communications with Paris, Clermont-Ferrand, Montluçon and Lyons are already having favorable repercussions on the economy of the area: factories have been built by Lyonnaise companies in the Ardèche and Haute-Loire region. Some Parisian industries have started decentralizing by establishing branches in the Ardèche region, in Aveyron, in Creuse, and in Hérault. In the near future, with the expected improvement in railroads and roads, and with the higher demand produced by the large European market, the Massif Central will have good a chance for satisfactory development, thus reversing the depopulation process which has been afflicting it for decades. However, at least for a long period, it seems improbable that this region will reach the high level of the most advanced regions of the Community.

Aquitaine

This region of South-West France is still far behind in respect to the degree of industrialization reached by the rest of the country. As a matter of fact, the underdevelopment extends to practically all sectors of economic activity, from agriculture to services, etc. We have dealt briefly with the causes of this phenomenon. Let us now examine the present industrial situation of the area.

Aquitaine has the dubious honor of being the second major underdeveloped area of the Community (the first, by far, is Southern Italy). The first impression that a visitor to Aquitaine has is generally that of a region reminding him of the past when local production satisfied all or almost all the demand, and contacts with the rest of France were very scarce and irregular. This is partially due to the peripheral position of the area which, through the centuries, has always kept it somewhat detached from developments affecting other parts of France.[97] Fatalism and nonchalance seem to dominate the philosophy of life of the inhabitants; this, however, is not unusual in underdeveloped regions and countries. A massive propaganda campaign should be carried on among the local inhabitants pointing out the advantages deriving from a change in attitude, as well as the feasibility of improving conditions. One of the beneficial results of the establishment of the European Economic Community has been that of the *coup de fouet* necessary to awaken entire regions, industries, and enterprises from their lethargy. Until now they have remained dormant, securely protected by tariff walls, or otherwise they have become so used to their state that no incentive or desire to progress existed.[98] And, if the local populations did not care, neither did the national governments, absorbed as they were by a variety of problems that left little time and energy, not to mention money, for the underdeveloped areas. But now they will soon have to assert their position in the European Community: they must take their legitimate place and share in

[97] "The French economy does not suffer from faulty integration but from an excess of centralization. The hypertrophy of the Paris region has often been described and condemned. It has impeded the development of a sufficient number of regional metropolises which alone could put a stop to the exodus of the inhabitants of the provinces toward Paris, and it has contributed to slowing down the progress of the regional economies." *Rapport 1958*, p. 280.

[98] "The Frenchman felt more that he was the master of his own destiny in the days of craftmanship than he does now in the era of big industry. Hence, his sentimental attitude towards the small enterprise, property of the family, the hereditary rich, etc. It is the lament for a golden age. The Americans and the Russians do not remember happier times: they expect much from the future. France sees herself, against her instincts, catapulted into a world where all becomes collective. She is capable of adapting to it, and . . . her successes will be stupendous, but she will do it, for a long time to come, without enthusiasm." Maurois, *op.cit.*, p. 24.

the common prosperity if they do not want to fall farther behind the industrialized regions.

A very serious blow to the economy of Aquitaine came in the middle of the nineteenth century, when a disastrous series of agricultural crises (first the great phylloxera epidemics which almost wiped out the vineyards) left it in such a state of prostration that it never recovered. The agricultural crises came in a period when the first timid attempts to industrialize the region were being made and prompted their abandonment. A massive emigration to other regions took place, especially by the young people who could see no future in the land of their fathers. Some industrialization did, however, take place, either through regional efforts or external pressure. In the first category belong certain traditional light industries, some prospering in the midst of otherwise general apathy. Thus, several small factories of a semi-artisan type operate in the central Pyrénées region, powered by electricity generated by the Compagnie du Midi; these include: the textile industries of Lavelanet and Laroque d'Olmes; the two metallurgical centers of Pamiers and Tarascon (almost 3,000 workers for both); the paper industry in the Salat valley; the food industry of Montauban; the metal works in Castelsarrasin; and the rubber plant in Moissac. (The last three, by extending industry to the *département* of Tarn-et-Garonne, have given rise to slow but continuous demographic growth in the areas concerned.) There are also important sandal and shoe-making industries at Pau, Mauléon, Hasparren, Bayonne, and Tarbes.

As far as the second industrial category is concerned, in 1936 strategic considerations impelled the scattering of the French aeronautical industry to the provinces from the Paris region where it was concentrated. One of the safest places in all France from the point of view of probable air-raids was the region around the Pyrénées. Thus, an important share of the total productive capacity of the nation in this field was transferred to Toulouse, Bordeaux, and Bayonne, and has subsequently spread to smaller localities, while some of the original factories have been abandoned. At present great aircraft factories are located at Toulouse, where the "Sud Aviation" produces the famous "Caravelle" jet plane, Bordeaux-Merignac, Tarbes, Ossun; various subsidiary plants also exist at Figéac, Villemur, Aire-sur-Adour, Oloron-Ste.Marie, etc. The Société Turbomeca, which manufactures aircraft engines among other things, is located at Bordes, near Pau.

However, most industry is of an essentially local character, geared to catering to regional demand, and not particularly concerned with the possibilities of export markets within the rest of the Community.

The real breakthrough for the region may have been the discovery of important deposits of oil in the Parentis region and great quantities of natural gas at Lacq. We have seen what they mean to the economy of the region and no doubt these discoveries will be the prime factor in promoting the industrialization of the whole area, and will fully absolve the functions, naturally bestowed upon them, of "poles of growth."

For a few years now a process of industrialization has been going on in the area between Orthez and Pau, where the proximity to the new energy sources is bringing great bene-fits. Thus factories of various types have been set up—a desulphurization plant, an aluminum factory, and several chemical and petrochemical plants. On the other hand, apart from the establishment of new industries, practically all the pre-existing factories have undergone processes of modernization and transformation to make the best possible use of the newly found sources of energy; this applies to the chemical plants and the ceramic factories of the Hautes-Pyrénées, to the cellulose industry of Landes, to the cement factories of Boussens, and so forth.

However, these basic industries will not suffice to insure

the industrial growth of Aquitaine. They can only supply the needed "poles of growth" around which the bulk of the medium and small industry, mostly ancillary to them, will be built. Actually, some very encouraging signs may already be detected. Thus, various companies of a regional character have been constituted by private investors to conduct financial operations especially directed toward investing in new industries. Furthermore, in the years following the discovery of the new energy sources of Lacq and Parentis, there have been several examples of industrial dynamism. Worthy of mention are the new factories producing synthetic rubber at Moissac and Coutras-les-Eglisottes, shoes at Pau, Dax, Vallée de l'Ile, Nontron, agricultural machines at Miranda and Layrac, and electric gadgets at Brives and Montauban.[99]

A great number of processing plants should be oriented toward the areas best suited to receive them, taking into account all the preceding factors. Some areas still have a considerable surplus of labor, which however, cannot be immediately utilized because of the agricultural origin and lack of skills of the workers. The industrialization of the region must therefore be accompanied by a serious effort at reconverting these workers by teaching them a skill enabling them to find employment in the new industries.[100] Projecting

[99] Considerable efforts are also being made to attract foreign industry to the region. For instance, an advertisement which appeared in the *Wall Street Journal* of January 24, 1963, under the headline: "European Expansion—Development Opportunity in Southwestern France for American Industries," stated: "If opportunities presented by the rapidly expanding European Economic Community have interested you as they have us, you'll want to know more about the facts we have gathered concerning the Basses Pyrénées Province of Southwestern France. This area meets all our plant site criteria. It may meet yours as well. Some of the natural and human resources there are listed . . . Excellent transportation facilities. Many raw materials in abundance. Prospective manpower pool of 15,000 covering all categories from unskilled to professional. French government is actively supporting entry of industry to the area, offering tax and other inducements . . ."

[100] "The progress from which the less-favored workers must benefit should be more rapid, it being understood in any case that the improve-

this into the future, good technical instruction must now be given in the schools to those who will be entering the labor market when the need for special skills is greatest. Thus emigration to other regions will be curtailed and these skilled young people will enhance the development of their native area.

A great refinery for using the crude oil of Parentis has been built at Bec d'Ambès, and this will perhaps be the starting point for a new industrial conglomeration (petrochemical industries, etc.). Furthermore, it now seems certain—there have already been some minor discoveries—that the whole area of the Aquitaine basin has more oil deposits waiting to be discovered and exploited. Extensive findings would, of course, completely change the character of the region. The bulk of these products are exportable commodities, with good prospects of sale in the Community. The creation of new currents of traffic with the various regions of the Common Market will strengthen the bonds—at present rather tenuous—which unite Aquitaine with the rest of the Community outside France. The increased volume of traffic will inevitably reflect on the general economic situation of the region, lifting the standard of living of the local population.

The Alpine Region

One of the advantages possessed by this zone over other underdeveloped areas is its abundance of water. In 1950, Electricité de France began construction of a dam in a particularly high area called Serre-Ponçon (this dam is the tallest in the world, 450 feet, and the lake formed by it is 2,800 hectares in area); the dam is now completed, and it brings immense benefits to the whole area bounded by the Southern Alps on the one side and the sea on the other.[101]

---

ments must take place within the limits of the general economic equilibrium." CECA, *Septième Rapport-Général*, p. 295.

[101] This splendid achievement of French engineering is not as widely known inside France as it deserves, according to *The Observer*, Novem-

Electric power stations have been built, or are being built, to utilize the water of this dam at Curbans, Sisteron, Aubisnosc, Oraison, Manosque, and Beaumont. Other dams will be built in the near future at Serres on the Buech, and at Ste. Croix-du-Verdon. In all, the Durance basin, after completion of the projects now under way, will produce eleven billion kilowatt hours of electricity yearly, and the Var basin four billions. So this river which because of its irregularity and disastrous floods, had hitherto been called the "scourge of Provence" is now in the process of becoming one of its major sources of wealth. Its waters are now channeled and used for irrigation purposes. And, by producing enormous quantities of electric power in a region hitherto almost desert, it promises to draw into it industries which will gradually bring about the development of the whole area.

Actually, two medium-sized factories, the Péchiney of Argentière (aluminum) and of Saint-Auban, already existed in the area, before the Serre-Ponçon dam was built. Now these factories can benefit from the electric power generated by this dam, and have acted as catalysts for a cluster of small factories, at Digne (industrial carpentry), Sisteron (chemicals), Veynes (electrical gadgets), Gap (radios), Embrun (dynamos), etc.

The main change which will be brought by the Common Market to the region is that ". . . the central artery of the Common Market will displace to the region's advantage certain currents of circulation today centered on Paris and, consequently, will attract some industrial or tertiary activities, a tendency which is already apparent."[102]

Languedoc

In spite of the coal mines and other minerals found throughout the region, industrialization, even if very diversi-

---

ber 5, 1961. "The man in the Paris street [is not] likely to know that the dam and reservoir of Serre-Ponçon, with a capacity of 1,200 million cubic meters, is the most grandiose in Europe."

[102] Gravier, *op.cit.*, p. 295.

fied, is still a secondary economic activity. This region is essentially agricultural and the income deriving from industry in its *départements* never exceeds 20 per cent, whereas agricultural income is never lower than 30 per cent and in certain areas reaches 50 per cent.[103]

The most important industrial activities of the region are concentrated in certain "specialized" conglomerations.[104] Actually, in spite of the fact that many industrial activities such as chemicals and metallic ore mining are found in some places, a few activities are paramount: coal mining, construction, leather, and textiles. The low state of industrialization of the region is confirmed by the distribution of the active population: 41 per cent in agriculture, 26 per cent in industry, and 33 per cent in the tertiary sector. Thus, the number of people in the region deriving their income directly from industry is smaller than that of the other two sectors.

Also, most of the industrial establishments of the region are too small and obsolete, and have definite characteristics of marginality, with all the consequences that this entails. Numerous industries represent the bare survival of once prosperous activities whose fortunes have been steadily declining due to a variety of reasons; for instance, the leather industries at Millau, Nîmes, and in the valley of Aude, the

---

[103] *Revue de l'Economie Meridionale*, No. 41, January–March 1963, gives the following figures referring to four *départements* of the region; these clearly show how the average for their inhabitants is much lower than that of France as a whole:

		Comparison of financial resources per person				
		P.O.	Hérault	Aude	Lozère	France
Population (thousands)*		230.3	471.4	268.4	82.5	44,091.
Resources per person (in thousands of F. fr.)	1956	268.9	291.7	241.2	221.5	346.7
	1957	342.8	337.0	331.2	245.8	382.6
Index (France = 100)	1956		84.1	69.4	63.6	100.
	1957		88.0	81.2	64.2	100.

* Départment: 1954 census, France: estimates 1956–57.

[104] See Carrère et Dugrand: *La Région Méditerranéenne; la France de demain* (Presses Universitaires de France, Paris), p. 43.

woolen industry in Lodevois, hat-making in Aude, textiles and silk in the valleys of the Cévennes.

In contrast with the industrialized regions of France, Languedoc has seen its industrial activities pushed farther back in the last few decades. This decadence is due to structural reasons and there is no chance of recovery unless the State increases its intervention. Just as it does in many other regions in France, the Common Market entails a further shift away from the axis of industrial activities. Paris will look more and more towards the East (the Ruhr) and the North-East (Belgium, Holland), and Languedoc will continue to decline from an industrial viewpoint. Another drawback is the lack of an important industrial center to act as a "pole of growth."[105] The change must therefore be structural; the most promising activity in this respect is provided for the time being by the works in progress in the Rhône basin, which could eventually assure continuity between the Mediterranean regions and those of the North and of the East. This alone will allow considerable increase in interregional exchanges and a harmonization of regional expansion.

Both light and heavy industry are found throughout Languedoc-Roussillon. Particularly important among others are Péchiney of Salindres (aluminum, sulphuric acids); Pétro-Fouga of Béziers; a metal-work factory in Cameron (specializing in sluices); shipyards at Sète; chemicals at Thau; rubber products at Société Meridionale du Caout-

---

[105] "The economy of the region is a dependent economy. In fact, the region has its decision-making nerves outside its territory. Oil and chemicals . . . depend upon Marseille or Paris and even sometimes on London and New York. Regional financial markets are practically non-existent. . . . All the important works depend on decisions made in Paris." *Cahiers de l'Exagone*, April 1962. And *Population* (Revue de l'Institut National d'Etudes Démographiques), in its issue of April–June 1963: "The localities which exercise a central function, as everybody knows, have a strong demographic attraction, this function entailing the creation of numerous jobs, particularly in the tertiary sector."

chouc in the Aude. Also, some well-known sandal and toy factories in the Pyrénées-Orientales, and shoe making at Graissessac and in the Aude.[106]

In particular, it seems that attention is now increasingly being directed toward the Common Market partners in order to increase the possibilities of export or to counteract the increased competition deriving from it. Thus "an attempt at prospection has been made abroad by the hatters of the Aude, particularly in West Germany. . . . The first results are very favorable and numerous orders have been placed." Also "certain factories [in the agricultural machinery industry], after scouting the different countries of the Common Market, seem to have found the prospects for the future encouraging." Finally, in the rather important sector of wool industries: "Activity in this branch has been good during the past quarter . . . it seems that competition from the various countries of the Common Market is felt in a less worrying way than was feared a few months ago."[107]

TOURISM

TOURISM AND THE COMMON MARKET IN SOUTHERN ITALY

For climatic reasons, for the beauty of many of its panoramas, for the length of its coastline, and for the picturesqueness of its scenery, the Mezzogiorno is one of the parts of the Community destined to be the new "vacationland of Europe." The area has already been "discovered" by increasingly large numbers of European and other vacationers. But, whereas most overseas tourists hurriedly follow the usual "Grand Tour" circuits—Florence, Rome, Venice, etc., with at most a side trip to Naples and a one-day excursion to the island of Capri or the ruins of Pompeii—increas-

---

[106] A large new preserves factory will soon be built in the region by the American company, Libby, McNeill and Libby; this decision will have a great impact on the industrial development of the area where it will be located. *L'Economie*, April 18, 1963.

[107] All quotations from *Revue de l'Economie Meridionale*, No. 40, October–December 1962.

ing numbers of tourists from Northern Italy and the rest of Europe are spending extended periods in Southern Italy and the islands and benefitting from all they have to offer.

Several factors contribute to the growing attractiveness of Southern Italy as a tourist mecca: (a) The increasing standard of living, also derived from the progressive economic integration of Europe, which allows more and more people from the Community to take their vacations abroad, and many Northern Italians to vacation in the South of the country.[108] (b) The popularity of auto travel, which enables people to move around freely without being bound by train and bus schedules. It is not unusual to see long lines of Renaults, Volkswagens, and Fiats on secondary roads used mainly until only a few years ago by peasants and their ox-carts, or by cattle going to pasture. (c) A simplification of bureaucratic formalities towards the other members of the Community (passports, visas, declarations to the police, etc.).[109] (d) Improvements in the facilities of the area in general: more and better hotels, new roads, hygienic measures, shopping facilities, and better organization.

There are already established in Southern Italy certain tourist villages, in which members of the various European Clubs de Vacances spend their holidays. Of special note is the French "Club de la Mediterranée," whose *Village polynésien* in Palinuro has brought thousands of vacationers to that locality, with highly beneficial consequences, not only economic but social. More villages of this type are planned:

Construction of a tourist city at Manacore, on the Gargano peninsula (Apulia) is being undertaken by Compagnia Italiana Turismo Europeo. Heavily forested,

[108] For statistics, see Appendix III, Table XXXIII.

[109] "Without having completely disappeared, at the present stage of the Common Market border controls for travellers between the different states of the Community have greatly decreased during the last few years. In fact, our six countries have granted more and more facilities to travellers . . ." *Communauté Européenne*, No. 3, March 1964.

302

little-known Gargano is the spur of the Italian boot, and the tourist city will comprise 5,000 fully-equipped villas, nine hotels, with an aggregate capacity of 25,000–30,000 guests, bars, restaurants, shops, churches, swimming pools, etc. Zoning regulations will be strictly enforced and will include a ban on neon signs. Manacore, on the shores of the Adriatic, is about 260 miles from Rome and 174 miles from Naples. It is also the locale of the well-known novel *La Loi*.[110]

The effect of such an enterprise on the mores and on the economic progress of this region will be great, for this is indeed one of the poorest and most backward areas of Southern Italy.[111]

A mass of 175 million people in the Community, almost half of whom live in regions where the climatic conditions of the Mediterranean are never found, constitute a great potential market for Southern Italy. Several organizations are interested in the speedy development of the area to encourage tourism, and it would obviously be advantageous and conducive to higher efficiency if their efforts could be coordinated. Apart from the Italian Government, the European Investment Bank and the Social Fund constituted by the EEC Treaty should also help to improve the tourist facilities of the area; this is clearly in the common European interest. In addition to substantial contributions by local private initiative, contributions by private initiative from the other parts of the Community should be not only welcomed but invited; this will be of particular benefit to the development of the area as a tourist center. Some of the great European industrial, commercial, and banking concerns might make a contract for accommodations for their employees to take advantage of a few weeks of blue skies and

---

[110] *Tourist News from Italy*, Vol. XIII, No. 9, September 1961.

[111] The income of the Gargano area is one of the lowest in Italy: 131,997 lire per capita in 1953; 165,402 lire in 1959. *Mondo Economico*, Nos. 31–32, August 5–12, 1961.

sunshine each year. There would then be a need for new hotels, holiday villages, campsites, youth hostels, etc. Their construction, financed by both the national government and a Common Market agency, specifically concerned with tourism, would substantially help the general development of the whole area.

The facilities for tourists have made vast strides since World War II, before which they were, with some notable exceptions, practically nonexistent. The figures divided by region are given in Table 7.

TABLE 7
TOURIST ACCOMMODATIONS IN SOUTHERN ITALY[112]

	Hotels and Pensions	Board-ing Houses	Total	Beds	Rooms	Baths
Campania	611	540	1,151	31,290	17,445	7,725
Abruzzi and Molise	185	259	444	8,434	5,091	1,205
Apulia	127	155	282	7,716	4,726	1,349
Basilicata	33	240	272	2,562	1,460	273
Calabria	131	259	390	6,742	3,896	880
Sicily	403	641	1,044	21,888	12,654	3,879
Sardinia	101	150	251	4,881	2,955	935
North Italy	10,794	11,350	22,144	502,077	289,502	71,769
Central Italy	3,231	1,398	4,629	133,739	77,619	27,792
South Italy	1,087	1,453	2,540	56,744	32,618	11,432
Islands	504	791	1,295	26,769	15,609	4,814
Total Italy	15,616	14,992	30,608	719,329	415,348	115,807

A concentrated effort by the Ministry for Tourism and Recreation, the Cassa per il Mezzogiorno, the autonomous regions of Sicily and Sardinia, and the Enti Provinciali per il Turismo, operating together with private initiative, has directly contributed to the touristic rebirth of the area.[113]

[112] Statistica del Turismo, Nos. 41–42, August 1960.

[113] A remarkable example of coordination between public and private enterprise is the policy followed by the Autonomous Government of Sardinia, where many of the new hotels have been built by a

How tourism can benefit the over-all development of the Mezzogiorno is apparent from the fact that "for each person employed in the tourist business, five more find work in collateral activities."[114] And, apart from the direct economic benefit deriving from tourist activities of various kinds, important social consequences ensue; in fact, the local populations become accustomed to people who are different and have more advanced ways of life, and consequently imitate at least some of their customs and behavior—tourists contribute to the advancement of a backward and isolated area.

To promote tourist activity in the South it is necessary to greatly improve the number and quality of personnel: hotel employees, guides, tourist agents, interpreters, etc. A few schools to train such personnel are already operating, but their number is completely inadequate to meet demand in

private financial group, CIATSA, taking advantage of the low-interest, long-term loans granted by the local government to that effect. Conversely, in places suitable for development, but where private initiative has been deficient, the government has proceeded directly to the building of new hotels, through the ESIT (Ente Sardo Industrie Turistiche). Furthermore, the same Ente has undertaken another activity which, by its nature, did not attract private enterprise: the building of camping sites, youth hostels, etc., to cater to the thousands of young people, particularly students, who come from all over Europe to spend their summer vacations in Sardinia and who, by definition, are generally impecunious. The result of this combined action is that the number of foreign tourists has greatly increased over the "fifties . . . from only 5,400 in 1951 to 187,000 people last year." The Regional Government has formalized a ten-year plan to increase to 25,000 from the current 9,000 the number of beds available in Sardinian hotels and inns. Meanwhile big foreign financial groups have bought an extensive site along the coast to make it into one of the world's most luxurious residential areas." *Economic News from Italy*, No. 157, June 24, 1962. Exact figures are:

	1951	*1956*	*1961*
Italians:	226,419	387,754	571,826
Foreigners:	5,414	45,959	186,666
Total	231,833	443,713	758,592

Source: *Prospettive Meridionali*, No. 1, January 1963.

[114] From an article by the Hon. Alberto Folchi, Minister for Tourism and Recreation, *Il Popolo*, September 10, 1961.

the coming years.[115] Some of the many so-called "intellectuals," who are unemployed and would not otherwise benefit from the Common Market, may be absorbed into such tourist activities as guiding, interpreting, hotel administration, travel agencies, etc.

A very intensive publicity campaign must be carried on, both by the offices of the ENIT (Ente Nazionale Italiano per il Turismo), and by regional bodies, especially in the largest cities of the Community. When a politically unified Europe becomes a fact, the Europeans will want to know, or to know better, their "new" country, and they will thus travel throughout the Common Market area in great numbers. It is now up to the Southern Italians to "sell" their country to the other Members, so that it may become one of the "musts" for any good European. The proportion of foreign tourists who ventured to the South in 1960 was only 11.04 per cent of the number for the whole country; the percentage is even lower for the number of nights spent in hotels, 9.32 per cent; and the percentages for tourists who spent the night in places other than hotels (rooming houses, camping) are respectively 6.91 and 7.83.[116]

Part of this disproportion is due to the fact that the facilities in the South are definitely antiquated and inadequate to handle masses of tourists who might wish to go there but who refrain for several reasons. There is not a good network of roads and this is obviously deleterious to the tourist business in the South.[117] This limits the wanderlust of many thousands of people from neighboring countries who would otherwise tour the Italian South; they know the roads and

[115] There are three professional hotel schools in the South: in Naples, Porto d'Ischia, and Palermo. These schools have as their aim the cultural, technical, and professional training of hotel personnel.

[116] *Tourist News from Italy*, No. 9, September 1961.

[117] The *New York Times*, February 25, 1962, in an article entitled "Sicily, Isle of History and Beauty," gives its readers this warning: "Until the autostrada from Naples to Reggio di Calabria is completed, the tourist with an automobile is advised to put both it and himself aboard the boat at Naples and sail to Palermo."

other installations are inadequate. In view of the increasing rate of motorization in Italy and throughout the Community, and the consequent use of cars by many tourists, the islands have, until now, remained somewhat inaccessible to them. To counteract this situation, convenient ferry service has now been instituted during the tourist season.

Government Aid

In spite of the fact that the tourist situation in Southern Italy has noticeably improved in the last few years, much still remains to be done. "One cannot expect miracles from the Government's action," wrote the Minister for Tourism;[118] the gradualness of intervention derives from this same logic. The Government must rely heavily on the cooperation of local administrations and private initiative. An inter-Ministerial commission has been created especially for the study of problems connected with tourism in the Mezzogiorno.[119]

In the period 1949–1960, the number of hotels, pensions, and boardinghouses in Southern Italy has increased from 2,997 to 3,971; rooms from 26,862 to 52,651; beds from 48,603 to 91,145; baths from 4,324 to 19,366. In other words, there has been an increase of 33.3 per cent in the number of tourist installations: 96 per cent in the number of rooms, 87.5 per cent in beds, and 347.8 per cent in baths.[120] The last figure is remarkable, because it is indicative of a real effort being made to improve the quality of the accommodations available. This progress has been made possible through combined financing by the State (directly or through the Cassa) and private enterprise. Law No. 691 of August 4,

[118] Hon. Folchi, *loc.cit.*

[119] Particularly in view of the new situation brought about by closer links between the Western European States following the creation of the EEC, and by the ever-increasing number of European and overseas visitors to Italy, a structural reorganization of the agencies concerned with tourism was ordered by Law No. 617, published in the *Gazzetta Ufficiale*, August 14, 1959. This law institutes a new Ministry of Tourism and Recreation to deal specifically with these problems.

[120] *Statistica del Turismo*, No. 44, March 1961.

1955, authorized direct appropriations by the State for improving hotel facilities in the South. Up to December 31, 1960, 220 projects, totalling 5 billion 124 million lire, had been undertaken, and 5,650 new rooms had been built.[121]

However, it is a fact that:

> . . . Although the funds appropriated by the State do not amount to much, the Mezzogiorno could have derived many more benefits from them had private enterprise been more agile and sensitive. Action by the State should, in fact, only be an incentive and stimulus to local possibilities. . . . The responsible departments must orientate private initiative towards the most useful and productive investments. It will therefore be necessary to proceed according to an organic plan for gradual and harmonious development. . . . An efficient and responsible tourist policy for the Mezzogiorno cannot be elaborated without a development plan that will have to be studied and put into practice swiftly. The plan must point up the best solution to the problems of the area.[122]

Indeed, it is fully realized that the moment to "launch" Southern Italy into the Community has come and has to be taken advantage of quickly, before tourist traffic sets a pattern directed too steadily toward other parts of the Mediterranean not within the Community (Greece and Yugoslavia, for instance). To do this, the basic structure of the area must be greatly improved; otherwise the tourists will continue to shy away from Southern Italy and a perpetuation of the present imbalance in the Italian tourist business will continue. The Cassa has taken this enormous imbalance into account in elaborating its plans and has acted both to strengthen the general infrastructure and tourist facilities, concentrating on particular aspects of the tourist trade

[121] *Il Popolo*, September 10, 1961.
[122] Hon. Folchi, *loc.cit.*

(mainly roads leading to monuments, churches, ruins, and places of panoramic interest formerly very difficult to reach). As a start, the Cassa intervened in the already known tourist zones, but has progressively enlarged its actions to include other areas of potential tourist interest which are internationally little known or totally unknown.

To sum up:

It would certainly be an exaggeration to presume that the increase in tourism might, on its own, constitute the determining factor in the development of the Mezzogiorno; however, in the framework of the present policy, it assumes a place of particular importance, especially if due account is taken of its high occupational contribution. It is therefore desirable that larger amounts be destined to developing the touristic structure of the Mezzogiorno, to increase its reception equipment and make it more economically profitable.[123]

TOURISM AND THE COMMON MARKET IN THE UNDERDEVELOPED REGIONS OF FRANCE

Aquitaine

Recent trends in the tourist trade point to the development of "transit tourism" in Aquitaine.[124] Tourists travel in the region, generally on their way to or from Spain, and stop in one place for only a few days. Simultaneously, camping is becoming increasingly popular. In the summer of 1962, all the areas reserved for camping were filled 90 to 100 per cent of capacity, in spite of the fact that the size of such areas had been greatly enlarged after the 1961 season.

In the 1962 season there was a general decline in the number of *foreign* tourists (for instance, in Gironde 57 per cent less British, 18 per cent less Swiss), but nevertheless the number of tourists coming from the main Common Market countries

---

[123] *Bilancio 1959–1960*, p. 170.
[124] See *Revue Juridique et Economique du Sud-Ouest*, No. 1, 1963.

has increased: Italians by 11 per cent, Germans by 7 per cent, Belgians by 5 per cent.

In the region of Adour (Hautes-et Basses-Pyrénées) tourism has been a de luxe trade for a long time, particularly centered around the spas of Eaux-Bonnes, Saint-Sauveur, Cauteret, Barège, Bagnères-de-bigorre, etc., in addition, of course, to Pau and the world-renowned Biarritz. Naturally pilgrims from all over the world have been attracted by the creation of the shrine at Lourdes, which is visited by over a million faithful every year.

The famous Gorges du Tarn[125] may also attract visitors from abroad to the region, as may also such prehistoric grottos as Lascaux.

However, the greatest asset of this area for the attraction of tourists are the Pyrénées and the possibility of their developing into a great winter sports playground—skiing having become more and more popular in Europe.[126] The old winter sports areas are overcrowded and the possibilities offered by the Pyrénées are infinite. Prices would have to be kept low in order to compensate for the greater distance from the other countries of the Community, and also to attract those people who, up till now, have spent their winter vacations in the Alps. Some of the old watering places, taking into account changing tourist preferences, are reconverting their facilities for winter sports, and such places as Barège, Eaux-Bonnes, Mongie, Saint-Lary, Gourette, Saquet, and others

---

[125] In a "Classification of *départements* according to their touristic importance" (Ministère des Travaux Publics et des Transports: *Le Tourisme en France*, Commissariat Général au Tourisme, Paris, 1962), the *département* Tarn-et-Garonne has the dubious distinction of being the very last in France, accounting for only 0.5 per thousand of the tourist traffic in France.

[126] However, there is a long way to go before the Pyrénées winter resorts have reached a position comparable to that of those in the Alps. The most important *département* for winter sports on the Aquitaine side of this range (the Hautes-Pyrénées) is last, together with the Jura, in a list of the most developed *départements* for winter sports, accounting for only 1 per cent of the number of overnight stays in the area by skiers. *Loc. cit.*, p. 27.

are being so equipped. "In the Basses-Pyrénées, the two winter resorts which have finally been provided with improved equipment and better communications, are readying themselves to welcome a great many tourists and winter sports fans during the coming winter season."[127]

The French Government is now enacting a program that was first put forward a few years ago as a study in the *Journal Officiel*.[128] It is carrying on an intensive campaign of hotel building and construction of camping sites and various other types of accommodation to attract popular tourism in the *départements* of Ariège, Gers, and Lot, and is also building or enlarging many small hotels in the valleys of the Hautes-et Basses-Pyrénées. A big tourism campaign, both in France and abroad, is being carried on by each *département*. In Dordogne, the creation of a new chain of hotels is envisaged to accommodate the influx of new tourists expected to arrive as a result of the intensification of the advertising campaign by movies, press, radio, television, etc.

The potentialities of Aquitaine are good, and should overcome the drawback of being rather far from the main lines of communication within the Community. On the other hand, it is a well-known fact that being "off-the-beaten-track" offers advantages too—peace, tranquility, and also the satisfaction of man's curiosity and thirst for the "unknown."

Brittany

The tourist possibilities of this region, as far as the Community is concerned, are somewhat limited because of its rather remote geographic position from the Member States of the Community. However, if the facilities now existing are greatly improved and if the attractions of the region are properly promoted, a number of tourists will certainly brave the distance and spend a vacation in Brittany, perhaps com-

[127] *Revue Juridique et Economique du Sud-Ouest*, No. 1, 1963.
[128] *Journal Officiel: Région Midi-Pyrénées*, Paris, 1959, especially pp. 93–94.

bining a stay there with a tour of the neighboring regions, such as Normandy and Vendée, etc. Furthermore, a number of picturesque fishing villages and good beaches (those of Morbihan, the island of Noirmoutier, etc.) should make a stay in these regions particularly agreeable and worthwhile.

Surrounded by the sea on its longest sides, Brittany, which well deserves its definition of peninsula, is also an incomparable reserve of health, fresh air, and natural beauties for the people of the large human conglomerations of the Common Market. The stimulation to travel this gives to Europeans throughout the whole Community assures for tourism in Brittany possibilities of expansion and renovation practically untapped until now.[129]

The Massif Central

The Massif Central has certain attractions for mass tourism. It has the advantage that its geographic position in relation to the great population centers of France and the other Member States of the Common Market is not so remote as that of Brittany and Aquitaine.

As far as winter sports are concerned, numerous places could be advantageously equipped as winter resorts, even if they could not attain the excellence of the Alpine regions. The low prices they could offer would perhaps compensate for the inferior quality of amenities offered. The custom of sending whole classes of children, with their teachers, to mountain resorts to alternate regular schooling with skiing is now spreading in Europe. The experiment has been highly successful in France, and is now being extended, particularly to Italy and Germany.[130] The Massif Central should

[129] *Communauté Européenne*, Nos. 8–9, Aug.–Sept. 1962.

[130] "France has accomplished, in the last few years, very important progress. . . . The 'classes on the snow' are more and more numerous. 22,000 children have participated in 1962. In 1963 it is believed that the number will reach 28 or 30,000. Most of them are young Parisians (about 50%)—therefore the importance of the vicinity to the Massif Central. In Italy, in the mountainous regions, 'classes on the snow' are

offer many advantages for this type of winter sports. The reasonable prices offered and the relative easiness of the ski runs are the principal ones. Moreover students from other European countries would have the advantage of conversing in French *in loco* and also of seeing something of the country, the habits of her people, etc., from experience instead of from books. Places like the Hautes Cévennes, Margeride, Aubrac, Cantal, etc. would meet most of these requirements. The presence throughout the winter of several thousand students and their teachers would of course help to lift these areas out of the isolation and abandonment in which they now find themselves.

In the summer, the numerous dams in the region offer well over fifty artificial lakes; these could be used for aquatic sports, if properly equipped, similar to those practiced on the lakes in the Tennessee Valley Authority area. The areas around these artificial lakes could be furnished with small hotels, bungalows, camping sites, motels etc., so as to attract large masses of tourists. Something like this has already been done in the lake areas of Vassivière, Neuvic, and Bort in the Haut-Limousin. Also, many potentially important spas exist in the region and need only through an economic effort be equipped and made to serve the whole Community (Chaudes-Aguès may in time become one of the most important health resorts in the country).[131]

---

practiced systematically . . . in Germany, they are widespread. . . . In conclusion, it seems that a good start has been made in the Europe of the Six and that, soon, all its young citizens will benefit equally from the advantages of the mountains." *Communauté Européenne*, No. 2, February 1963.

[131] These attractions by no means exhaust the touristic possibilities of the Massif Central region. The fact is that scarcity of suitable transportation, combined with lack of promotion, have contributed to keep several parts practically unknown, even in France, let alone in the Community. For instance, *Le Monde* (Sélection Hebdomadaire), June 14, 1962, writes thus about one of the *départements* of the Massif Central: "Ardèche is one of the least-known *départements* of France, despite the fact that it can offer so many amenities to the tourist who manages to

313

Languedoc

With proper development, this region, endowed with many miles of beautiful natural beaches and hilly areas, has the capacity to become one of the main vacation resorts in all France, serving especially as a complement to the Riviera. It is expected that, in a few years, the Côte d'Azur will be quite inadequate to cope with the ever-increasing masses of people from every country of the Community and indeed from all over the world who spend their summer vacations in the beautiful resorts along the Riviera. Their number will increase as a consequence of the general prosperity, and since people will soon have longer vacations they will stay longer. Apart from the fact that it will be physically very difficult to accommodate the crowds, some vacationers will not wish to spend their time in the over-crowded, garish places some of these resorts are now becoming.

Up till now, there have been very few facilities for tourists along the Languedoc coast, despite the presence of the many beautiful, wide, sandy beaches that stretch almost uninterrupted between Camargue and the Spanish border. However, with the near saturation of the French and Italian Rivieras, the authorities, both local and national, have realized the possibilities for development of the Languedoc coast and are making plans accordingly.[132] Six summer resorts are to be created in four *départements* of the South-West. In the Hérault, a large strip of land, now mostly

---

escape the beaten track. What views, what panoramas, what souvenirs of history. . . !"

[132] "This possibility of creating within our developing regions a cumulative process of enrichment has been well understood by the administration, which has decided to launch a program of tourist investment along the coast of Languedoc, strengthened in this idea by the very probable saturation of the Côte d'Azur, which will be about complete by 1970 and which will therefore entail the creation of new seaside resorts." *Revue de l'Economie Méridionale*, No. 41, January–March 1963.

swamp, will be converted into a beach and will benefit from its closeness to Nîmes and Montpellier. Agde, another summer resort in the hills near Béziers, will be developed. A small town will also be built at the delta of the Aude, including a small port for yachts and pleasure boats in general. Two more resorts will be inaugurated in the Pyrénées-Orientales at Barcarès and Saint-Cyprien, situated in the neighborhood of Perpignan. Finally, Gruissan, near Narbonne, will become a most important beach resort, for it is naturally endowed with a beach several miles long. "These various programs will be coordinated under a comprehensive plan for laying-out the whole coastline. It is not a question, in fact, of building tourist resorts independent from each other, but a series of complementary beaches, connected by one great road which, coming from Avignon and the Rhône valley, leads to Bordeaux and Toulouse on one side and to Perpignan on the other."[133]

A number of important works are envisaged, such as draining of swamps, reforestation, construction of dikes, etc., as well as building roads to connect the new beaches with each other and with the nearest cities of a certain size. A serious attempt will be made to rid the area of the mosquitoes which, because of their great numbers, have in the past made it unattractive to tourists.

Thanks to the new communications facilities, tourists will be able to move with ease from one point to another of this section of the coast, and therefore take full advantage of the numerous activities which will be offered in the various resorts, from hunting to horse-racing, from golf to water-skiing.

The State will, for a number of years, underwrite most of the expenses, but later mixed-economy Societies will be formed. First estimates foresee appropriations of at least 800 million new francs for these projects to materialize.

Until now a great deal of potential tourist income has

[133] *Le Monde* (Sélection Hebdomadaire), May 8, 1963.

shied away from this region due to lack of tourist facilities;[134] people have only passed through and not looked upon it as a resort area. The main aim, then, of this new long-range operation is to lure into prolonged stays some of the hundreds of thousands of tourists (from France and Central and Southern Europe) who yearly pass through this part of Languedoc on their way to the Costa Brava, and also, as we have already explained, to provide an "annex" to the Riviera to accommodate its overflow.

Even in the winter, it would be possible to attract a certain number of tourists to these regions if some of the areas capable of being transformed into winter resorts were properly equipped. Such areas include, for example, the Canigou, Puignal, Capcir, and Cambre d'Azé.

Along with the actual physical development must go hand-in-hand a widespread publicity campaign to make the area known to the millions of potential tourists within the countries of the Community and rest of Europe.[135] If this

---

[134] A more precise idea of the present disparity between the two extremes of the Mediterranean coast of France can be obtained by comparing some data referring to the *départements* of Pyrénées-Orientales and Alpes-Maritimes, which contain respectively the sea-coast of Roussillon and the Côte d'Azur:

	Alpes-Maritimes	*Pyrénées-Orientales*
Hotels	1,016, of which—	146, of which—
	13 de luxe	0 de luxe
	46 first category	1 first category
Hotel Rooms	28,626	4,150
Overnight stays (June–Sept.)	3,912,000	190,000
% of all French sea resorts *départements*	42.5	2.1

Source: *Le Tourisme en France, passim* (figures updated to January 1, 1962)

[135] On the question of publicity, Mr. Robert Buron, former Minister of Public Works, wrote: "Why should we be reluctant to consider tourism as a national industry, the same as metallurgy or the manufacture of macaroni? . . . Tourism represents for France 200 billion francs in foreign currency a year." *Le Monde*, June 23, 1960. The same theme is reiterated by M. Pierre Dumas, Secretary of State: "Tourism

is done, there is no reason why, within a decade or so, this coast should not become as popular as the Riviera.[136]

Corsica

Corsica has recently been "discovered" by the currents of international tourism, and a number of holiday-makers from continental France and Italy, and especially from Germany, have had the pleasure of spending their vacations in this island, which combines the picturesque with the wilderness, the warmth of its climate, and its magnificent sea. Corsica has every possibility of duplicating the success of the Côte d'Azur; being an island, however, it does offer certain difficulties as far as transportation is concerned, especially for people who want to take their cars with them during their vacations to "explore" the island and get to know it.[137] Improved travel facilities, by sea and by air, which are

---

is one of the main national industries; let us have therefore the mentality of industrialists who do not manufacture whatever they would like, but what the consumers wish and have the means to purchase." *Le Monde* (Sélection Hebdomadaire), July 24, 1963.

[136] *Revue de L'Economie meridionale*, No. 44, 4th quarter, 1963, states the problem thus: "Our Mediterranean shores, to a growing number of Frenchmen and foreigners, seem outstanding places for tourism and for vacations. Paradoxically, the French Mediterranean coast is built, equipped and known by tourists only in less than a half of its length, from Menton to Martigues. The rest of this coast, despite the large stretches of fine sandy beaches . . . is only frequented by a limited number of people, mainly local." Proposals for the development of the Roussillon-Languedoc part of the French Mediterranean coast have been made by an inter-ministerial commission created *ad hoc* by decree of June 18, 1963, to do research work for the Delegué à l'Aménagement du Territoire. Its findings are published in the same issue of the *Revue*.

[137] But, on the other hand, there is the considerable advantage of enjoying peace and calm. "*Ici, c'est la tranquillité.* . . . There are many great efforts to be made, however, a whole structure to build. Also, the higher costs deriving from insularity should somehow be countered. [The island] could receive so many people! . . . Unfortunately, life is still hard for the Corsicans. Some villages, in spite of the many springs and rivers, have in the summer only ten minutes of running water a day." *Le Figaro*, August 11, 1961.

already being introduced will reduce these difficulties as far as possible, and will help to bring additional numbers of tourists to the "Isle of Beauty."

The Alpine Region

The Southern part of the Alps is not developed as it should be in comparison to the attractions it can offer to tourists. Not only is the area an ideal place for winter sports, but also in the summer its resorts offer optimum climatic conditions, away from the heat of the cities and the industrial zones.

It is strange that the southern part of the Alps has not reached a level of development comparable to the northern part. The reasons for this state of underdevelopment are several: paucity of communications, distance from the main centers, etc. The fact however remains that the whole area has been utterly neglected, and some capital and much initiative is needed to redress the situation. To promote winter sports and summer resorts, one of the first facilities to be offered to the international clientele should be a substantial number of ski-lifts, chair-lifts, and all kinds of mechanical equipment essential to these activities. Perhaps no other European region can boast at the same time of such a wonderful, clear climate and such a profusion of possibilities for mountain sports, both in winter and summer. The distance from the main centers of traffic has often been exaggerated; Briançon, the heart of the region, is only about 70 miles from Turin, 140 from Milan, and a comparable distance from many French cities, Grenoble, Lyon, etc. It is a fact however that the present network of communications is entirely inadequate to support the increased traffic which the development of the area as an Alpine resort for the Community would bring.

A new development will greatly enhance tourist and sports activities in the northern part of the region and, at the same time, improve the link-up with the Italian side of the Alps. "After years of debate, the Government has set aside the Massif de la Vanoise area in the Savoy Alps as a nature preserve. It will be France's first national park. A chain of chalets is being constructed for cross-country skiers and mountaineers near the highest peak, the Grande-Casse, which is 12,668 feet high. . . . Almost the entire park area lies above 6,500 feet. To the east it extends to the Italian frontier, joining Italy's Grand Paradise National Park."[138]

To conclude, it would be advisable, perhaps indispensable, to create a regional agency for the development of tourism, keeping in mind the new exigencies deriving from the fact that the area is destined to cater to a mass of people such as the Community can furnish. So, hotels should not only be built, but equipped to cater to an international clientele (multilingual staffs, etc.). The program of development should be spread over a number of years until it becomes self-financing.

[138] *New York Times*, July 22, 1963.

319

CHAPTER VI

Risks Inherent in Integration between Developed and Underdeveloped Regions

HISTORICAL EXAMPLES

We turn now to an analysis of the unification of Italy in 1861 and the reunification of the United States following the Civil War.[1] These two famous examples illustrate clearly that economic and political unification do not necessarily mean general and equal improvement for all the integrated parts if not paralleled by adequate government action. Moreover, if economic forces are given free play, some of the integrated parts actually suffer a retrogression, or at least a slowing down in the rate of development they enjoyed before integration.

Italian unification will be described at length since many of the problems also apply to the time when the South of Italy, together with the rest of the nation, will feel the full impact of the European Common Market. The transition period is nearing completion and the time for full implementation of the Treaty is not far off. The lessons learned from what happened a century ago when the barriers between the two parts of Italy were suddenly removed, should illuminate and guide those who are working for the new, much larger unification. However, history shows us

[1] On this subject, Professor M. Florinsky writes thus: "Prior to Italian unification, the standards of industrial efficiency in her Southern provinces were, broadly speaking, not inferior to those in the North. . . . The marked difference in wages and other conditions of work between the South and the North of the United States, which has persisted for decades, indicates that common sovereignty and the absence of legal barriers are not enough to assure the integration of the labor market." *Integrated Europe?* (New York: Macmillan, 1955), pp. 30,32.

many examples of mistakes being repeated over and over again, and the dangers of a century ago are ever-present. Moreover the situation now is more complex due to tremendous advances in technology and to the much larger framework in which the operation will take place.

A brief analysis of the reunification of the United States will also be given to support the contention that the unifying process, without pronounced governmental intervention, can be detrimental when great disparity exists between different parts of a country—the poorer area may actually be so badly affected that decades of effort can do little to improve the situation.

THE STORY OF THE MEZZOGIORNO

It is not pertinent to this analysis to go into the history of Italian unification, and the handing over of Southern Italy to King Victor Emmanuel II of Savoy by Garibaldi, after his amazing conquest of the country with his "One Thousand Red Shirts." It need only be pointed out that one of the assumptions of the Piedmontese ruling circles before 1861 was that Southern Italy was a rich country *per se*, and that only the appalling ineptitude of the Bourbon administration had hampered economic development more in line with the potential wealth of the country. Only after a number of years was harsh reality accepted when the Italian Government finally realized that Southern Italy was for a number of reasons—climate, scarcity of water and raw materials, lack of communications, etc.—a poor country.

The idea, currently so familiar, that in working toward economic integration there should be special provisions in favor of the weakest sectors had no part in the policies of the new Italian State. In accordance with a concept which, as a matter of fact, prevailed until quite recently, the Government assumed a position of almost total passivity with regard to any development taking place in the

321

economy of the various regions. Therefore its attention and particularly its investments were concentrated in the North, where industrialization had already started and where opportunities were more immediately apparent.[2]

The barely viable industries of the South were destroyed almost immediately, whereas industry in the North took advantage of the enlarged market to strengthen itself and to replace what small hold industry had gained in the Mezzogiorno.

It is important to point out here that some economic experts and intellectuals from the South, who, incidentally, were not against unification but had for the most part conspired to bring it about, were rather skeptical of an immediate and unqualified unification under the House of Savoy. They would have preferred a federation that allowed a great degree of autonomy in economic and other matters, thus avoiding the dangers inherent in a sudden elimination of barriers between North and South.

While Garibaldi and his Mille had aroused hope and enthusiasm among the people (they were idolized throughout the South of Italy), the attitude toward the Piedmontese Monarchy had been somewhat more reserved. When it became evident that the function of the House of Savoy was principally that of maintaining the status quo and protecting the landlords and the upper classes, the peasants did not wait long to rise in revolt against those very northern soldiers who only a few months before had been hailed as liberators.[3] This revolt of the peasants was courageous and spontaneous, but disorganized. They felt they had been betrayed and denied the benefits deriving from the change

[2] Saraceno, *Economic Development of the Mezzogiorno*, p. 5.

[3] "Soon after 1860, the phenomenon of brigandage assumed gigantic proportions in the South; it became a political weapon of the Bourbons in exile and of the clerics, who were inciting the people to pillage and robbery in the name of the throne and of the Altar." C. Barbagallo, *Cento Anni di Vita Italiana* (Milan, 1948).

of regime. The bourgeoisie had won its new place in the sun, but not the common people. No land reform or other progressive changes had been made; the peasants had even less protection in dealings with the feudal "signori" than before. At least the paternalistic government of the Bourbons had assured a certain amount of justice. What came to be called the "War of Brigandage" (little is known about this war either inside or outside of Italy) lasted for several years and in fact had periodic recurrences.[4] This war, which could easily have been avoided by the enactment of a few progressive measures (taking into account the rights, the aspirations, and the different background of the southern Italians) soon took the form of a real colonial repression. The consequences are apparent today in the hatred most southern Italians feel for the central Government, which they consider the oppressor, the exploiter, and the embodiment of northern domination.[5]

With the crushing of the sporadic armed resistance of the peasants, the new Government found no further obstacle to "Piedmontizing" the whole of Italy. In this, the Government was helped by the fact that for political reasons the Bourbon administration had prevented the formation of adequate "cadres" trained in modern methods of government. The formation of a progressive, enlightened bureaucracy could have been a serious threat to the rule of the monarchy. Thus the Piedmontese system prevailed throughout the new administration, and little of the brilliant juridical and bureaucratic tradition of the South was maintained. Unification came to be not the merger of two different sys-

---

[4] "In twenty months, from 1865 to 1866, 2,413 'cafoni' died fighting, and 1,038 were shot; 2,768 were jailed. And this does not take into account the 'guerilla' casualties in Sicily." G. d'Alessandro, *La Questione Meridionale* (Rome: Edizioni della Bussola, 1946), p. 14.

[5] "The War of Brigandage assumed all the appearances of a colonial war. And it was a war to conquer a country that had recently given 6,000 political prisoners to the cause of independence and national unity." C. Scarfoglio, *op.cit.*, p. 43.

323

tems, with a synthesis of the best aspects of each, but the imposition of one system upon the other.

The different economic structure of the two parts of Italy, the industrial development of one and the essentially agrarian economy of the other, was bound to produce a profound disequilibrium when the two parts merged: the formation of a common national market would be detrimental to the weaker side since the economy would be less able to adjust to a greater intensity of economic exchanges.

In all of this, the fiscal policy of the new government was unlikely to remedy the situation. The principal, if not the only, source of income in the South was agriculture, and even this was extremely poor in comparison with other European states. Industry and handicrafts were limited and were protected by a tariff wall about four times higher than that of the rest of the country. What little industry there was, was in the hands of either foreigners or the Bourbon state, and methods of trade and banking were primitive, as were communications.

In accordance with the laissez-faire theories prevalent at the time, the newly formed Italian state, instead of intervening to bolster the weakest sectors of the economy and the Mezzogiorno as a whole, simply assumed a hands-off attitude; therefore private investments logically went to the North, where profits were liable to be larger, surer, and made more quickly.

In the South, the Italian Government decided to sell the lands formerly belonging to the Bourbons and to the Church, mainly in order to acquire new revenue and new sources of taxation. But this move proved to be a fatal miscalculation: small Southern landowners and peasants alike rushed to buy the land, in large or small parcels, and contracted heavy debts while not retaining enough money to invest in tools, irrigation, etc. for the newly acquired lands, which were generally barely productive and required large investments and a great deal of hard work before yielding a sizeable output.[6] Thus, the land became a liability instead of an asset to the new proprietors. Needless to say, almost all of the income deriving to the State from the sales was spent in various ways in the North. Not only the small landowners of the South, but also the middle-class bourgeoisie, the majority of whom had advocated immediate unification, manifested their discontent. They did not use force, but agitated in Parliament against the Government of the "Destra Storica," which was finally thrown out of office in 1876. But the consequences of this "parliamentary revolution" were not what could have been legitimately expected. The new governments, with many Southerners in their ranks, and sometimes even headed by Southerners, did not cater to the problems of the South with the necessary energy and perseverance. It must be said in their defense that they were occupied with the overwhelming problem of organizing a new, financially weak state and dealing with a variety of interests on a national scale. Moreover, certain economists thought that the best way to protect the interests of the South would be to strengthen the North first; when the North was strong and prosperous enough, it would soon elevate the South to the same standing. This proved to be an unhappy illusion.

Under the continuous pressure of the northern industrialists, threatened by competition from other European countries, the Italian Government abandoned the hitherto liberal policy of almost free importation of goods from abroad and inaugurated a strict protectionist policy. The Law of 1887 establishing protective tariffs in favor of industry (then existing almost exclusively in the North), and the denunciation in 1888 of the Treaty with France, followed by almost complete cessation of southern agricultural ex-

---

[6] "It was really a race for the conquest of a great fortune . . . but to own the lands did not mean to be able to exploit them, as it was to be many years before the expensive and toilsome operation could give positive results." Barbagallo, *La Questione Meridionale*, p. 69.

ports to that country, were two formidable blows to the economic status of the South.[7]

The result of these two new factors on the Italian economy was that, as the impact of competition from abroad was greatly reduced, the prices of northern manufactured products increased. On the other hand, the purchasing power of the Southerners decreased and consequently more expensive goods had to be bought by an increasingly impoverished population. "We have to admit," says Scarfoglio, "that the general conditions of the Mezzogiorno were much better under the Bourbon regime than after unification, which only meant for the South a continuous regression from the level reached—however unsatisfactory it may have been— by the previous regime."[8] One of the worst crises in the history of the South began, and in addition to economic instability, social stability was strained to the limit. The population gradually lost hope and seized the only opportunity left open to them, i.e., emigration. There was no future for them if they stayed in their country; within the span of a few decades, entire regions saw millions of people leave; they lost some of their most productive people, adding desolation to desolation.

Administrative differences. From the purely administrative viewpoint, as we have already seen in part, there was a clash between the two systems; this was due in part to the rigidity of the Piedmontese administration, which should have taken the particular local conditions of Southern Italy much more into account. It is true that this would have entailed some delay and confusion, but it would have given the South more time to absorb the changes and make its own contribution to the new entity.

[7] "We do not believe that in the countryside around Naples there has ever existed a time when the financial disasters of the landowners have been so great and numerous as those which have recently happened here." A. Barraco: *I Demani Comunali dell' Antico Regno di Napoli* (Naples, 1894), p. 46.

[8] Scarfoglio, *op.cit.*, p. 134.

One of the most damaging blows to the South brought about by unification was the extension to the whole country, without modification or attenuation, of the taxation system then in force in Piedmont. Francesco Saverio Nitti called it" . . . a taxation system not only different, but almost opposite to the one until then in force; within a few years, one after another, taxes hitherto unknown were put into effect: income taxes, registration taxes, judicial taxes, taxes of succession, building taxes, and so forth; everything was changed and upset."[9]

In sum, shortly after unification there appeared, in all its magnitude, a reciprocal state of unpreparedness for merger in both parts of Italy. The South knew very little of what was going on in the rest of the country and was completely unable to offer any organic solution regarding the structure of the newly unified country; as for the rest of Italy, the North knew about the South only what anti-Bourbon propaganda had told it. Subsequently, in spite of a certain amount of good will on the part of the Piedmontese rulers, it was very difficult for them to make a distinction between temporary backwardness due to the "ancien régime" and the "organic diseases" of the South; the question of Southern Italy was simply a manifestation of the imbalance following annexation, and, at the same time, an indication of the absence of a Southern elite, ready to "Italianize" itself rapidly and simultaneously impose observance of the spiritual, legal, and economic traditions of Southern Italy on the Government.

AMERICAN RECONSTRUCTION AT THE END
OF THE CIVIL WAR

The "Reconstruction" of the Union offers more evidence that unification of two or more regions or parts of a country, whose economic disparity is great enough, does not necessarily imply a tendency of the parts to converge toward a

[9] F. S. Nitti, *Nord e Sud* (Turin: Roux, 1900), p. 49.

common economic average; on the contrary, it may mean that the already existing gap between them is maintained or even widened.

Of course, the problems posed by reunion in the United States presented several unique features, and in many ways cannot be compared to the problems posed by the present European union nor to Italian union a century ago. For instance, these unions have no race problem, nor are they—at least the former—the result of military conquest. However, the general theme recurs; thus the United States Government, aware of the economic needs of the conquered South, which also entailed a restoration of free trade and transport, removed restrictions on the exchange of commodities between North and South, completing this process a few weeks after the surrender at Appomattox. Soon afterwards, the railroads were given back to their former Southern owners. But the South, exhausted by the war, needed capital much more than markets and the means to reach them. Nevertheless, instead of importing the massive amount of capital it needed, the South had to pour out sizeable sums to satisfy the demands of the Federal Government. Some agents plundered the Southern states more for their personal benefit than for that of the Government. The latter realized only $34,000,000, and this sum was eventually returned to the legitimate former owners of the confiscated property. But a much larger amount had been appropriated by some of the Government agents, and it was never returned. After this bad start, the situation was further aggravated by the imposition of a tax on cotton, together with a variety of new taxes. The cotton tax in the three years 1865–68 produced $68,000,000, most of which was lost from the South.

Physical confiscation and confiscatory taxation contributed much to impeding a serious reconstruction effort by the people of the Southern states; worse, they fostered apathy and pessimism, which became a part of the general southern philosophy. Also, they discouraged the capital

328

formation process in the former rebel states, and southern capital, instead of being invested in the area, began to move North.

In order to meet the payments on mortgages contracted before the war, many farmers were compelled to sell some or all of their lands; also, to counteract the scarcity of money in circulation throughout the South, they devised the share-cropper system, which actually was one of the aftermaths of the abolition of slavery, whereby landowners and laborers combined to raise a crop which they would eventually share. This future crop was also used as security and, being such a risky proposition, the merchants who supplied the needed items (fertilizers, clothing, tools, etc., and land credit as well) had to charge very high prices which further impoverished the southern farmer. The lack of capital thus became chronic, potential investments from outside stayed away, and the South lagged behind the rest of the nation even several decades after the end of the Civil War. Fifty years after Reconstruction, the South had the highest illiteracy rate among white people in the United States, and if Negroes were included the rate would rise even higher.

Various attempts to industrialize the South were started a few years after the Civil War. However, in spite of some industrial growth, and also in spite of the fact that cotton is a southern product, all the Southern states together ranked only seventh in cotton textile production in 1880, below six *individual* states in the North. It became popular in the late 'nineties, to speak of the "New South," which was supposed to be progressive and industrialized. However, at the turn of the century, the "New South" accounted for a smaller proportion of the total national industrial output than the "Old South" in the year before the Civil War started. Also, in 1900, in the state of South Carolina, only 4 per cent of the population was employed in industry, while 70 per cent was still engaged in agriculture; similar ratios were common to all the Southern states. The following year, the discovery of

329

oil in Texas attracted huge amounts of capital from the North, part of which had originally been destined to be invested in other parts of the South. This was another heavy blow to the rest of the former rebel states, where the hoped-for outpouring of capital from the North failed once more to materialize; furthermore, differentials in transportation, banking policies, and tariffs, contributed to lowering the level of the South compared to the rest of the nation.

It was not until the beginning of World War II and afterwards that the process of industrialization in the South, first taking advantage of wartime needs, then sharing in the general boom, made much headway, and even now it remains behind the rest of the nation.

The Tennessee Valley Authority

Finally, it is appropriate to discuss briefly the highly successful Tennessee Valley Authority (TVA) which, thirty years after its creation, is very important to our study because it is still the model, par excellence, for other projects of regional development.

The creation, by Act of Congress, May 18, 1933, of the TVA—"A corporation clothed with the power of government, but possessed of the flexibility and initiative of a private enterprise"—was one of the most successful ventures ever to take place in the South. It provided for the development of the Tennessee Valley basin as a whole, that is, on a regional basis. It covers an area of more than 40,000 square miles with a population of about three million people, and was authorized to carry on a variety of activities, ranging from the building of dams to flood control, navigation improvements, soil conservation, reforestation, the encouragement and promotion of agricultural activities, industrial expansion, and the overseeing of social and economic activities in general, in the whole region. "The Tennessee Valley at this time was one of the most impoverished and backward areas of the nation. Under TVA, the valley blossomed into a rich farming and industrial region. TVA itself became a yardstick for the performance of the private power industry."[10]

Practically all agencies for regional development, particularly in Western Europe, give profound study to the experience of the TVA; this has been especially true of the French agencies for regional development and of the Cassa per il Mezzogiorno. The TVA is invariably quoted as an example to follow in any project designed to deal with underdevelopment and it is a very good argument in support of the theory that, in certain situations, only massive intervention by the State in economic matters can achieve a positive solution to the problem which has to be faced.

LESSONS

It is of interest now to extract a few lessons which can be learned from the foregoing examples.

(a) A thorough knowledge of the region concerned is required before proceeding to an organic inventory of its possibilities and needs preliminary to drawing up plans for its recovery. It is not only that a region's wealth and potentialities can be overestimated, as happened in the case of Southern Italy at the time of unification, but that actually the discovery of certain mines or deposits of oil can completely change the economy of a region, as in various Middle Eastern or South American states. Thus more thorough exploration and prospecting is advisable; this task, which entails great outlays of money, will be much easier to perform in a large market, with a concentration of technicians, capital, and effort otherwise impossible to find in the limited national markets. The French, who discovered and are now exploiting the Saharan oil and the natural gas of Lacq, and the Italians, whose ENI (Ente Nazionale Idrocarburi) has brought Italy rapidly into the limelight of the international

[10] William Miller, *A History of the United States* (New York: Dell Publishing Co., 1958), p. 415.

oil scene, can supply much of the know-how and organizational skill required, and all the nations of the European Economic Community could easily contribute the capital necessary for the formation of these task forces. There is no doubt that, until now, prospecting work in some of the underdeveloped regions of France and Italy has been largely insufficient. Even so, as we have seen, oil and natural gas have been found in Aquitaine, Sicily, and other places, and are now being exploited. However, it is certain that much more mineral wealth is hidden deep under the ground, and perhaps one day Common Market teams will help bring it to the surface.

(b) The State (and this will also apply to the Federal European State) cannot stand still and allow economic forces free play, because this can only mean an aggravation of the problem and the most unfavored regions tend to be pushed further into the background in this way. Only decisive intervention by the State, foreseeing a long-range solution of the problems to be faced, can help solve them. When the structure is built, then private capital, attracted also by other incentives, can be expected to be permanently invested in substantial quantities in the region.

(c) A certain diversity in taxation, salary, and administrative systems and scales must be maintained, taking into account local exigencies, traditions, and institutions peculiar to certain regions. Also, greater administrative autonomy and the responsibility which goes with it must be granted to local administrative entities. It would be thoroughly unrealistic to push the centralization process too far and have the people of, say, Thuringia, Sicily, and Brittany governed by the same laws and by the same administrative systems.[11]

---

[11] In this connection, M. Raymond Cartier, in a speech on French TV, stated: "To make Europe is the equivalent, in the definitive, of delegating to a federal European state some of the great attributions that the present-day nations exercise with more and more difficulty: general organization of the economy, money, diplomacy, defense. All the rest—administration, education, legislation, police—everything

Even national governments have recognized this fact of regional diversity: regions like Sicily and Sardinia now have their own administratively independent governments, and some measures of decentralization have also been adopted in France—much autonomous action, for instance, is left to the already mentioned Companies for Regional Development.

(d) A European Government will have more chance of success in curtailing the power of special interests and classes, such as the latifundia-owning nobility in Southern Italy, whose influence in an all-European Government will be proportionally much weaker than in the present national governments.[12]

(e) A careful credit policy must be devised in favor of the small landowner so as to give him the financial means to carry out and extend the development of his own piece of land. What is the use, for instance, of spending a huge sum of money on bringing water to a certain patch of land if the owner, a small proprietor, is then not given the financial

---

which directly concerns our everyday life, will remain under the jurisdiction of the national governments. . . . Our variety is part of our wealth. We do not want either to suppress it or even to alter it. No, it is not the case, and I hope it will never be the case, to have the same kind of justice at Palermo and Hammerfest, the same primary school at Galway and at Fribourg-en-Brisgau, the same holidays at Concarneau and at Salonica. Europe of tomorrow will be federal. . . . This means that every nation will continue to organize its particular life in the way it likes." Reprinted in *Communauté Européenne*, Nos. 8–9, August–September 1961.

[12] European integration will of course gradually speed up the process of social mobility which is much slower in the Western European nations than in the USA. It is interesting to note the following data given in Allais, *op. cit.*, p. 41. He summarizes the results of an enquiry made some time ago by the magazine *Population* whereby present-day Western society is divided into eight groups. "The chances for a child of a manual worker to end up in one of the first two groups are respectively 2.6 per cent in Italy, 4.1 per cent in France, and 7.3 per cent in the USA. Therefore social mobility is about 1.5 times greater in France than in Italy and 1.7 times greater in the USA than in France."

means to acquire mechanized equipment, chemical fertilizers, etc. to properly cultivate the irrigated land?

(f) The TVA has shown that much can be accomplished by a regional development agency, and that similar agencies formed in the various underdeveloped regions of the European Community could tackle their problems on an over-all scale with good chances of success. This example, as we have said, has already inspired a number of projects in Italy and France.

Transfers to Underdeveloped Areas as a Punishment

We have dealt mainly with economic factors in the development of the most important of the present backward regions of the Community. It must be added, however, that in France, and even more in Italy, these regions are generally considered a kind of limbo, to which sinners should be sent to expiate their sins—administratively speaking. Both nations have a long tradition of considering the transfer of an employee from the big city to certain regions, or vice versa, as a very effective administrative punishment, or reward; this is true particularly for government workers, whose careers develop in such a way that it would be strongly inadvisable for them to resign, thereby losing their seniority and pension rights, etc.

Whereas this phenomenon is not exclusively common to these countries, it is here that it assumes particular connotations. In France, most people's dream is to live in Paris; in Italy, the right direction is South-North and, of course, the wrong is North-South. As stated, certain poor areas are considered almost places of exile within the nation.[13] It must be

[13] The Fascist regime used to get rid of its opponents who had committed "crimes" which were not grave enough to send them to prison, by "confining" them to forced residence in some hamlet in the poorest parts of Southern Italy. Carlo Levi, the author of *Christ Stopped at Eboli*, is a case in point; the description of his exile is the subject of the novel.

sincerely hoped that this psychological tendency to consider the underdeveloped areas of France and Italy as an administrative equivalent of Devil's Island, will eventually be eliminated by the increased, and more balanced, standard of living which the Common Market is bringing to its Member States. The European union is also having portentous consequences in the field of communications: air and land travel, radio and television (where Eurovision, and now Telstar, link-ups common to the whole of Western Europe and to North America are more and more frequent). This will greatly contribute to eliminating that sense of isolation and nonparticipation hitherto common to most underdeveloped areas and will help bring them in line with the other regions of the Community—filling the deep gap that still separates one from the other.[14]

DANGERS OF REGIONAL IMBALANCE IN THE COMMUNITY

We now have a fairly good idea of the magnitude of the problems to be faced by any prospective European Government in giving a certain degree of homogeneity to standards of living among the various component regions (it must be emphasized that we refer to *regions*, not *states*). It is indeed an intolerable situation that there are regions within the European Community in which the average per capita income differs sharply from that of other regions—a differential of four or five times in some instances. If such disparities should persist, or even become more pronounced,

[14] "The Common Market, to become a reality, should remodel the economic map of Europe to be *absolutely free of the political borders* [emphasis supplied] which have provoked the artificial separation of complementary regions. After the 'Europe des Patries' it would be appropriate to resuscitate a 'Europe des Régions', such as already existed in the Middle Ages in an epoch precisely when Europe constituted a spiritual unity. If the regionalization of Europe is not for tomorrow, some—particularly the Italians—had hoped for a clearer affirmation of the *Europeanization* of regional problems. Their preoccupation is understandable, so great is the task that they must accomplish in the Mezzogiorno." *Le Monde*, December 10, 1961.

335

social unrest and political insecurity would play a strong role in the European Community; such forces, together with many other disruptive tendencies, particularly nationalism which is now much in evidence, would not augur well for the continuity and solidity of the new union. These dangers are always present and, in the case of Europe, will probably take a long time before they are overcome. Western Europe, besides its ethnic and historical diversity, has a long tradition of enmities and bloody, internecine wars which cannot suddenly be erased by the signature of a treaty. Therefore, the dangers deriving from centrifugal forces will persist for many years.

ROLE OF THE EUROPEAN GOVERNMENT IN THE EUROPEAN ECONOMIC COMMUNITY

What the underdeveloped regions of the Community essentially need is capital, ". . . capital for large-scale investment in public utilities: railroads and highways, electric power stations, irrigation, port facilities and the like. With the possible exception of electricity, these are not usually profit-making enterprises and they will have to be owned and operated by the State or public authorities."[15]

TABLE 8[16]

	Sq. mi.		*Sq. mi.*
Belgium	11,799	USSR	8,600,000 (app.)
Fed. Rep. of Germany*	95,913	United States**	3,615,211
France	212,659	China	3,800,000 (app.)
Italy	116,224	Brazil	3,270,223
Luxembourg	1,706	India***	1,270,000 (app.)
Netherlands	15,765	Canada	3,845,774
Total Community	454,046	Common Market	454,046

* including West Berlin   ** including possessions, etc.
*** including Kashmir

[15] Gunnar Myrdal, *An International Economy* (New York: Harper Bros., 1956), p. 108.
[16] Elaboration of data from *Statesman's Yearbook, 1961–62*, and *The Columbia Lippincott Gazetteer of the World* (New York: Columbia University Press, 1952).

Furthermore, in the European Economic Community, there is a basic problem, i.e. it is much smaller in size than the present industrial colossi, the United States and the Union of Soviet Socialist Republics, or even future colossi such as Canada, China, Brazil, or India. Table 8 gives comparative areas of the countries of the Community and the others mentioned. Therefore, and also in view of the natural demographic increase, Europe cannot afford to "waste" vast areas whose state of underdevelopment will detract substantially from the general welfare of the Community. And less industrial might will also mean less defensive might, which certainly does not conform to the concepts of the very important place Europe must occupy in the international scene in the future, ". . . a Europe united and strong - speaking with a common voice - acting with a common will - a world power capable of meeting world problems as a full and equal partner."[17]

In the case of Italy, the South will have to undergo drastic changes in order to reach the level of the other regions of Europe, including Northern Italy.[18] However, as repeatedly stated, such development is possible only if economic activity in these regions is promoted directly by the State, for otherwise:

> . . . the play of forces in the market normally tends to increase, rather than to decrease, the inequalities between regions. If things were left to market forces unhampered by any policy interferences, industrial production, com-

[17] President Kennedy, Frankfurt address, *New York Times*, June 26, 1963.

[18] In this connection, the Economic Commission for Europe states: "Industrial progress, hastened by the liberalization of imports, has placed Italy among the leading industrial nations of the world. Yet notwithstanding the policies of developing the south and modernizing agriculture, the fruits of this progress have been unevenly distributed. Industrial development has drawn labour and capital to the northern provinces, where a nucleus of industry already existed, and this has resulted in some respects even in a *widening of regional and other disparities.*" (emphasis supplied) UN: *Economic Survey of Europe, 1961*, Chap. I, p. 32.

337

merce, banking, insurance, shipping, and, indeed, almost all those economic activities which in a developing economy tend to give a bigger-than-average return—and, in addition, science, art, literature, education and higher culture generally—would cluster in certain localities and regions, leaving the rest of the country more or less in a backwater.[19]

To sum up, in order to insure a balanced, steady, and sustained rhythm of growth, the Executive of the Common Market will have to exercise a powerful influence on the economy of the Community. This is practically the only way to assure the necessary help to the regions that have been left behind in recovering lost ground and reaching a level comparable to that of the other parts of the Community. Myrdal states:

> Even in such countries as the United States or Sweden, where in the last century business enterprise has been able to exploit a particularly favourable situation as regards natural resources, and where other unusually advantageous conditions for economic growth have also been present, not least in the general cultural situation, developments have not been such as to draw the whole country into a more or less equal and simultaneous expansion process.[20]

While it is felt that the system of relations between the central and national governments of the European Economic Community should, taking into account national peculiarities, approximate a compromise between the Swiss-cantonal and the federal-state relationship in the United States, the role given to the central or federal government of the United States of Europe should be much more important than the role the government of the United States plays

[19] Gunnar Myrdal, *Economic Theory and Underdeveloped Regions*, p. 26.
[20] *Ibid.*, p. 32.

in the conduct of economic affairs. In Europe, to begin with, the degree of participation by the state in the national economies is already far greater. Vast sectors in the economic life of the Member States of the Community are nationalized or under the control of the state.[21] Nevertheless, state intervention in the economic activities of the nation, also usually very pronounced in the social welfare field, does not by any means imply that the liberty of its citizens is threatened or diminished. The freedoms enjoyed in states where this process is most advanced, such as Britain or Sweden, are certainly not inferior to those enjoyed in any other country.[22]

[21] In Western Europe, particularly in the States in which we are most interested—France and Italy—the Government's direct participation in the economy of the nation is very important. Thus, in Italy, for instance, government-controlled companies produce 85% of coal, 80% of lignite, 65% of mercury, 30% of zinc, 15% of lead, 80% of pig iron, 65% of steel, 80% of ship construction, and all the electric power. They manage 80% of the telephone service, 40% of all transportation by water, not to mention the many enterprises in which the control of the State is so preponderant that they almost "belong" to it. The two most powerful giants of public enterprise are the Istituto Ricostruzione Industriale and the Ente Nazionale Idrocarburi, well-known also in the United States. (In view of the foregoing, it is not difficult to agree with *Time*, June 29, 1962, that "nowhere in the Western world, save Cuba, does a government own and run so many businesses as in Italy.")

As far as France is concerned, the following activities are nationalized: the coal industry, almost all the production of gas and electricity, the Bank of France, and the thirty-four largest insurance companies; the Renault automobile company, most of the aeronautical construction industry, and several branches of the chemical industry.

In both countries, postal, telegraph, telephone, radio and television communications are operated by the Government; also road networks and railroads (with few exceptions), the airlines, the main steamship companies, etc. Tobacco production is a State monopoly, and so also are a few other commodities. The whole educational system, from kindergarten to university, is run by the State, and even some of the major press agencies, like "France-Presse."

[22] Barbara Ward, in an article entitled "Now the Challenge of an Economic Sputnik," *New York Times* (Magazine Section), February 8, 1959, stated: ". . . only in America is there quite so ideological a terror of Government activity or Government ability to help shape the broad pattern of economic development. . . . It is hard to argue that Britain is less essentially free than America; yet a Conservative Govern-

339

To see in state intervention in economic matters a threat to freedom recalls to mind the gloomy forecasts about loss of freedom that were made at the time the income tax and social security were introduced. Once more to quote Myrdal:

> Capital movements tend to have an effect of increasing inequality. In the centres of expansion increased demand will spur investment, which in its turn will increase incomes and demand and cause a second round of investment, and so on. Saving will increase as a result of higher incomes but will tend to lag behind investment in the sense that the supply of capital will steadily meet a brisk demand for it. In the other regions the lack of new expansionary momentum has the implication that the demand for capital for investment remains relatively weak, even compared to the supply of savings which will be low as incomes are low and tending to fall. Studies in many countries have shown how the banking system, if not regulated to act differently, tends to become an instrument for siphoning off the savings from the poorer regions to the richer and more progressive ones where returns on capital are high and secure. . . . [In Italy] the process was conditioned and encouraged by the liquidation of the political and administrative centres in Southern Italy, while those in Northern Italy, which at that time more than now were tools in the hands of the industrial interests there, gained hegemony over the whole country.[23]

It is improbable, however, that a laissez-faire economy will ever reappear in Western Europe; on the other hand, the predominant role of the state in certain fields is now generally accepted, not only by the left and center of the political spectrum, but even by moderately rightist forces

ment there cheerfully discusses the scale of public and private investment that is needed to 'double the standard of living in a generation.' "

[23] Myrdal, *Economic Theory and Underdeveloped Regions*, p. 28.

like the Conservative Party in Great Britain. In this connection, *Le Monde*[24] writes:

> Far from having attained its final structure, the State budget continues to evolve in favor of non-traditional tasks for public powers. This progressive sliding mirrors faithfully the profound change in the State, which, from policeman and diplomat, becomes each year a little more of an entrepreneur, teacher, builder and helper. This growing socialization of the national economy is not peculiar to our country, even if it attains a higher degree here than elsewhere. It comes in fact in the nature of things, and reflects the necessity for modern countries of a growing intervention by the economic "orchestra leader."

Necessity of a European Plan to Counter Regional Underdevelopment

We have already seen that, in order to make a going concern of a unified Europe, it is not enough to lower barriers and controls and let each State behave as it sees fit. "It is clear that the multifarious and deep changes that are taking place in our economic structures following the Common Market . . . cannot, must not, develop in chaotic fashion. In all cases, they must be carefully followed, often stimulated, and sometimes limited, slowed down, guided."[25] The building of a harmonious, balanced Europe can only be achieved according to a plan; the question is how far this plan can be allowed to encroach on the domain of private enterprise. It must be conceived in such a way as to allow the relatively rapid transformation and integration of separate national economies into a continental economy. The central Authority charged with its enactment must be capable of setting up the plan and of enforcing it against the

[24] *Sélection Hebdomadaire*, November 30, 1961.

[25] Robert Marjolin, "Is a European Plan Necessary?", *Communauté Européenne*, No. 6, June 1962.

inevitable opposition of national interests.[26] This is essential particularly from the viewpoint of regional development. An economy of European dimensions cannot be the sum total of several different sectionally controlled economies, i.e. economies controlled by the national governments in each separate State, maintaining what is still called "sovereignty."[27]

On the other hand, a centralized form of control, if too strictly applied, risks degenerating into a totalitarian form, upheld by a totalitarian state, with all the ensuing consequences. Once again, the question is one of common sense, and a system must be elaborated whereby power cannot easily be concentrated in one man, or in a few men, without adequate checks. In this, the United States of Europe can benefit from the example set by the United States of America. It is furthermore impractical, for reasons of efficiency, to push centralization too far.[28]

[26] ". . . in a period of depression, of grave economic crisis, it would probably happen that each national government would react its own way, export unemployment to its neighbor, take measures of intervention and protection that would perhaps attenuate its own difficulties, but aggravate those of the neighbor. It is easy to see that the Community could not survive such an ordeal. It is because the risk of disintegration of the Community cannot be dismissed that I believe sooner or later a European government will have to be formed which will be able to carry out a European economic policy." Pierre Pflimlin, reported in *Communauté Européenne*, Nos. 8–9, Aug.– Sept. 1962.

[27] The reluctance of the Member States, or at least some of them, to give up the essential attributes of this "sovereignty" is the basic cause of the malaise that is today found in the Community. Edwin Dale, in the article "Europe's Crisis of Sovereignty," *New York Times* (Magazine Section), July 7, 1963, writes: "The latent contradictions in the United Europe movement were really there all the time. They come down to a single, overwhelming fact: these are still very much sovereign nations with different interests and different foreign policies and different views of the world."

[28] "Thus, it would be utopian to try to fix, on a European scale, definite objectives for each industrial branch; conversely, it is quite feasible to try to determine the maximum possible expansion of production over the next five or ten years, taking into account the necessary reduction of working hours and the share of each of the basic sectors—industry, agriculture, services—in this general expansion." Marjolin, *loc.cit.*

As far as practical realizations are concerned, a concrete five-year plan was announced in 1963 on behalf of the EEC Commission by Robert Marjolin, who is the driving force behind the idea of European planning.

The program is scheduled to take effect January 1, 1966. Its purpose is to set basic guidelines for the economic growth during the following five years of the European Economic Community, or Common Market. . . . Mr. Marjolin repeatedly stressed that the proposed five-year plan was not intended to interfere with free enterprise or private competition in the Common Market. The main purpose of the five-year plan will be to coordinate government programs of the six member states with the balanced growth objectives of the community as a whole. Mr. Marjolin said no rigid goals for community growth would be specified in the first five-year program.[29]

If this plan is adopted, production should increase throughout the Community; consequently, standards of living should steadily improve and the underdeveloped regions, under the impulse of a plan covering the whole area, should finally catch up with the rest, or at least greatly reduce the gap that separates them.[30]

[29] *New York Times*, August 1, 1963.

[30] This point has been quickly grasped by the trade union members of the ICCTU (International Confederation of Christian Trade Unions) who, in their Convention held in Rome in May 1962, expressed their views on the subject in a final communiqué: "The Christian Trade Unions stress the desirability of a European Planning Office, based on Commissions each operating for a specific activity, which should include representatives of the administrations, of management, and of the workers. In particular, this office would *facilitate a policy of regional expansion.* [emphasis supplied] The ICCTU is in favor of social and economic programs on a European scale and of European collective contracts." *Communauté Européenne*, No. 6, June, 1962. For the time being, however, many *individual* European States will partially plan their economy, even if ". . . many men in the business establishment around the Continent are against such government interference—but they have more or less lost the battle. France's *le Plan* now is being widely copied throughout Europe." *Time*, September 6, 1963.

A United States of Europe, with its huge industrial and agricultural capacity, with its abundance of skill and great traditions behind it, with a consumer market able to absorb what it produces, with plenty of rich, or potentially rich, associated overseas territories, has the power to attain a very high degree of prosperity.

As it stands, the EEC Treaty results in a compromise between a variety of interests, and does not give entire satisfaction to any. The "Europeanists" had been hoping for a central organ similar to the High Authority of the Coal and Steel Community and furnished with even stronger powers; but this, in face of reality, was obviously impossible after the rejection by the French National Assembly in 1954 of the European Defense Treaty. After that, the concept of supranationality between the Six gave way to one of economic cooperation and functionalism. Political integration became a distant aim, although it was always, as it is now, the powerful factor underlying the whole construction.[31]

However, if the supporters of European integration were not satisfied, the "nationalists" were even less so. In both France and Italy many voices were raised against what they feared would be the possible formation of a few over-industrialized areas in Europe, particularly in the regions contiguous to the Rhine and in most of Northern Italy, so that the underdeveloped regions of France and Italy would be completely cut off from these industrial concentrations.

[31] As Pierre Pflimlin puts it (*loc. cit.*): "It will be necessary, sooner or later, to have a European government, to prevent nationalistic reactions, in the face of possible economic, social or monetary difficulties, from causing a parting of the ways which will make the Community collapse!" And another former French Premier, Michel Debré, in an interview given to the French magazine *Entreprise*, September 30, 1961, stated: "The problem of Europe is political. Certainly, economics are important, but we may remain satisfied with some good commercial treaties, complemented by agreements or investments, and even the repartition of markets. The real necessity is elsewhere: it consists in asserting . . . the necessity of union, expression of a profound political solidarity. . . . There is the key to Europe. . . ."

These "nationalist" circles, together with some sincere Europeanists, especially those from the regions concerned, were afraid that, as the Treaty now stands, the advantages of integration would bring far greater benefits to the more advanced regions, leaving behind the other areas. Unfortunately, this danger was and still is real and experience shows that the prosperity brought to the Six by integration has thus far favored the industrialized regions more than the poorer ones.[32] One hope is that, with the wider diffusion of atomic energy at economical prices, greater industrial decentralization will be possible within a certain number of years.

Several escape clauses are incorporated in the Treaty to smooth the way to the integration of the economies of the Six Member Nations during the transition period. The weakest economic sectors and the poorest regions will reap most benefit from this protection. In the first place, they will have time to modernize so as to be more fitted, at the end of the transition period, to face the full brunt of competition from other Members of the Community; and secondly, they may take advantage of the transition period to decrease, even if not to entirely eliminate, the disadvantages weighing on them at the time the Treaty was signed.

There are also important psychological advantages: if the people of those regions see the possibility of concrete advances in the future, they will participate with enthusiasm and confidence in the efforts aimed at improving their lot. A long period of poverty and underdevelopment has tended to make them passive and unable to take the initiative to

[32] "The authors of the Treaty of Rome have seen very clearly that a rational and dynamic regional policy is an indispensable factor of European unification. The Treaty underlines the necessity of an harmonious economic development of the Community, narrowing as much as possible the gaps between the various regions, and the backwardness of the less-favored ones. But it is pertinent to remember that, conversely, the Common Market, founded on the principle of competition, risks aggravating regional disequilibrium." Chaban-Delmas, *Quelle est cette Europe?*

345

help themselves, but "the growth of a regional economy is a collective work. The first people responsible for it are those who live in the area or derive their income from it."[33] And, obviously, the advanced regions welcome the prospect of higher standards of living and industrialization in the under-developed regions since a wealthy market is, of course, much more receptive to trade than a poor one.

[33] M. E. Danvin and L. Degeer, *Dynamique Economique de la Région Liègeoise* (Liège: Editions de l'A.S.B.L., 1959), intro. Yves Lacoste, in *Les Pays Sous-Dévéloppés* (Paris: Presses Universitaires de France, 1959), p. 11, states: "The fundamental problem is not, as is commonly believed, an insufficiency of production compared to needs, but too great a poverty which prevents the population from satisfying their needs."

CONCLUSIONS

Southern Italy

It can be said that conditions in the South of Italy are steadily improving, but there is still a long, hard struggle to be waged before a satisfactory level can be reached. The solution of the "Questione Meridionale" will certainly be one of the major problems facing the Community. In the last analysis, as we have pointed out, the local population must help itself, for the time arrives in such cases when prolonged economic assistance becomes a kind of charity accepted by the recipient as a right while at the same time all manner of ulterior motives are attributed to the donors. We have so many examples of this under the present foreign aid policy of the United States that it is superfluous to go into details. However, it must be noted that, when the recipient is an organized, advanced nation or group of nations, eager to recover and progress, as was the case with the Marshall Plan and Western Europe after World War II, the money received is then really put to good use and extraordinary results can be reached in a relatively short time. On the other hand, we have had the painful experience of seeing comparatively large amounts of money squandered in foreign aid because of bad administration or corruption in the recipient country.

We already have seen numerous examples of the reluctance of the local population in the South of Italy to avail itself of anything new or different from the traditional. An example of this is reported in *Le Monde*:[1]

The plain of Gela (Sicily) is scattered with nice little houses, in picturesque colors, but most of them are used

[1] *Sélection Hebdomadaire*, October 5, 1961.

only as warehouses or are just abandoned. The inhabitants of Gela prefer to continue living near their churches, in their one-room apartments, without windows, together with their mule, rather than scattered around the country. Nevertheless, some new garden-houses, which perhaps will never be inhabited, are being built even now, and the billions of lire spent by the State . . . continue to melt under the inexorable sun of the Mezzogiorno.

It should be noted that these houses being built by the Government have a very low rent, and it is therefore not the cost that prevents people from occupying them.[2]

One of the most familiar phrases in the South is "non mi fido" (I do not trust), applied to everybody and everything, including oneself. This innate diffidence, especially towards everything new and "foreign"—meaning from the North as well as from abroad—must be overcome if really effective results are to be reached and the whole area is to be prevented from becoming a millstone around the neck not only of Italian progress but of European progress as a whole. While progress presently being made by the whole country is promising, we must remember that "Italy still has almost 40 per cent of her people living in the South, Sicily and Sardinia in conditions often close to poverty. Over-all, she will have to grow for another decade at the present rate to catch up with the present level of incomes and living standards of the rest of industrialized Europe."[3]

[2] Further evidence of this aspect of the Sicilian character is given by Giuseppe Tomasi, Prince of Lampedusa. He writes: "In Sicily, it doesn't matter whether things are done well or done badly; the sin which we Sicilians never forgive is simply that of 'doing' at all. . . . Sleep, sleep, that is what Sicilians want, and they will always hate anyone who tries to wake them, even in order to bring them the most wonderful gifts." *The Leopard* (New York: Signet Books, 1961), p. 182.

[3] *New York Times*, September 18, 1961. However, according to *Prospettive Meridionali*, No. 12, December 1962, per capita income has been increasingly lately at a faster rate in the South than in the North.

CONCLUSIONS

Through European integration, the Mezzogiorno will perhaps be able to attain what it could not achieve through the national market alone.[4] The abolition of customs barriers should provide a powerful stimulus to the Italian South, which, of course, will also benefit, like any other region of the Community, from the more rational organization of productivity and distribution brought about by the Common Market. Furthermore, the European Economic Community will enhance the possibilities of migration throughout the whole area for Southern Italian workers. But most of all the principle of liberty, which is basic throughout the EEC Treaty, should stimulate the evolution of social life in the South and compel the upper classes to use completely different approaches and ideas, and to modernize their

Net per capita income in 1961 (thousands of lire)

Region	Amount	Average (1 = 100)	% variation between 1960 & 1961
North	408,855	128.1	+ 6.7
Center	328,149	102.8	+ 7.9
South	203,619	63.8	+12.2
Islands	210,038	65.8	+12.0
N-C	385,257	120.7	+ 7.0
S-I	205,736	64.5	+12.1
Italy	319,199	100.0	+ 8.2

---

[4] "The development in the South of Europe interests all the countries of the continent. The elevation of the standard of living is desirable, not only for the region itself, but for the large markets that could be opened up to the products of the various nations." Olhin and Byé, *Les Aspects Sociaux de la Coopération Européenne* (Geneva: Bureau International du Travail, 1956), p. 20. Those in responsible positions are well aware of the close interconnection between European integration and the development of Southern Italy. For instance, on the occasion of the Congress on the ideological foundations of the Christian Democratic Party, held at San Pellegrino in September 1961, Professor Saraceno stated: "This process of economic rebalancing and of social transformation must now proceed apace with the process of European integration in which Italy is engaged by the Treaty of Rome. . . . Internal equilibrium and European integration do not form two different commitments: they converge in a process aimed at attaining a maximum of economic homogeneity both inside the country and with other European countries which are economically more advanced." *Mondo Economico*, No. 38, September 23, 1961.

structure, if they do not want to be replaced by more active elements of the Community; in other words, the Common Market will project into European dimensions the often parochial views of these classes. If it succeeds in this process of renovation and rejuvenation, the South will face the new situation brought about by the European Common Market with confidence, certain that it will hold its own and benefit from the common prosperity. This social renewal is a basic condition of the region's progress in the Community; if it does not take place with the necessary thoroughness and speed, the lack of this essential prerequisite will hamper the progress of the South in Western Europe, of which it will then be the most backward area—an anomaly in an otherwise prosperous and advanced European Community (including Northern Italy).[5]

Not all the attributes of the Mezzogiorno, however, are disadvantageous. Actually, it has certain advantages which are peculiar to it. Perhaps more emphasis should be put on these, in principle, than on trying to over-industrialize and implant activities which, being more economically viable in other regions of the Common Market, are liable to remain unprofitable and marginal for a long time to come when introduced into Southern Italy. The climate, although unfavorable for certain activities, may, if proper provisions are made, become an asset for other activities. It is certainly no hotter or drier than that of Southern California or Arizona. In the tourist trade, for instance, the climate of Southern Italy is definitely an asset, in the winter as well as in the summer. It could also be used to advantage in agri-

[5] "It appears that in the North of Italy, the most industrialized region of the country, the standard approaches that of [the other five members] the Community." CEE, *Exposé 1960*, p. 88. And, on the same theme, "Italy is a 'dualistic' country. One-third has reached a mature stage of development and is second to none by any continental standard. The remaining two-thirds are in the tedious process of development (and in certain areas still on the very first steps of an effort to uplift themselves)." *Mondo Economico*, No. 39, September 30, 1961

culture, as we have seen, if appropriate irrigation facilities are made available. Southern Italy has the potential to be transformed, in a relatively short time, into the garden of the Community.[6]

In view of European unification, the problem of Southern Italy now becomes a European problem, and, in the same way, the other problems of the Community become Italian problems.[7] There are hopeful signs that the other Member States of the Community are well aware of the fact that the Questione Meridionale is also going to affect them, and that they are concerned about the necessity of contributing to its solution. Apart from the individual Member States, Community organizations seem to be fully aware of this, and are acting accordingly.

A certain amount of industrialization is today necessary, in fact, indispensable, in Southern Italy. However, the optimum solution of the problem of the Italian Mezzogiorno will be found in a well-balanced agricultural and industrial economy, with stress perhaps put on the former sector. The idea that "development" is synonymous with "heavy industry" is incorrect when applied to a region that forms part of a greater economic ensemble. The "corn belt" in the United

[6] In order to achieve this result, however, it is imperative to proceed to immediate basic changes in the agricultural structure. ". . . The rural community is being thrown into a turmoil by the decline in agricultural incomes. All the weaknesses of the land reform—which was conceived primarily to produce a crop of Christian Democrat votes— have come to the surface." *The Economist*, July 22, 1961.

[7] ". . . (the Common Market) is based on two things: one, the acceptance of the people in Europe and the countries of Europe that their problems are common, so that to deal with them we have common institutions; so we are not dealing any more with national problems, we are dealing with common problems; and, at the same time as we have done that, we realize that no one of us could solve our problems, or its problems, by ourselves." Jean Monnet, from the transcript of an intercontinenal TV debate, telecast via Telstar relay satellite by the Columbia Broadcasting System on July 10, 1963. Title of program: "Town Meeting of the World"; participants: Dwight D. Eisenhower, Jean Monnet, Lord Avon (Anthony Eden), and the late Heinrich von Brentano.

351

States is an outstanding example of this assertion. In agriculture and related activities, such as cattle-raising and processing of agricultural products (food canning, etc.), the South of Italy is perhaps in the most favorable position in the Common Market. An advanced, mechanized, rationalized agricultural system in the Mezzogiorno should be able to compete favorably with those of North and Central Europe in the products for which there is competition, and complement them in those in which Southern Italy is the main producer in the Community. Not only is the mechanization of the means of production essential for this, but also the development of the processing industries, so that prices throughout the Community of agricultural products originating in Southern Italy will be favorably affected by the fact that they have been processed *in loco*, thereby eliminating all the overhead represented by transportation expenses, deterioration of the fresh product, etc.[8]

A geographically well-balanced distribution of medium and heavy industry throughout Southern Italy (qualitatively and quantitatively), cheaper power from local and imported sources, greatly increased tourist activities, all of which we have already discussed in detail, should complete the framework of what promises to be a thorough renaissance of the Mezzogiorno. The European Economic Community offers perhaps a unique opportunity to break with the past and look toward a promising future as an integral part of the new Europe . . . "for even in the destitute, backward, uncultured Mezzogiorno, the West and its spirit

[8] This is to say that Southern Italy should eventually join the rest of Western Europe in evolving, in the sense that ". . . farming in Europe *is in the process of becoming a business*—and a quite highly capitalized business. Modernization and mechanization have operated to expand the productivity of many crops, along with a reduction in the number of farm workers, *at an unprecedented speed*. While agricultural employment was shrinking, more labor has been employed in industry on behalf of agriculture, to produce the increased quantities of fertilizers, fuels and tractors needed by farmers." *New York Times*, Oct. 5, 1961.

352

of freedom, its culture, its economic and social order are present."[9]

In a speech before Parliament, the then-Prime Minister, Amintore Fanfani, outlining the program for his administration, said:

The imbalances (zonal, sectoral and human) which accompanied economic development . . . warn us that the multi-annual programs covering sectors and areas up till now enacted do not suffice. The *Meridionalistica* policy has taught us that it cannot be continued as a policy exclusively concerning this area, and entrusted to one particular agency, even if it is flexible, richly endowed, competent and active like the Cassa per il Mezzogiorno. The policy towards the Mezzogiorno must instead be prominent in the selective number of supreme objectives which the whole policy—and I expressly do not say only economic policy—of our country must pursue and systematically follow. Only in this way shall we eventually thoroughly overcome the disequilibrium that still afflicts Southern Italy. . . . The Ministry of Industry, together with that of State Participations and with the Cassa per il Mezzogiorno will continue the policy of industrialization of the South.[10]

These same principles are being followed by successive governments which have adopted a frontal attack on the problem of regional imbalance between the North and the South of Italy as one of the principal points in their programs.

FRENCH UNDERDEVELOPED REGIONS

As stated in the Introduction, it is difficult to give a general appraisal of the French underdeveloped regions. Indeed, their scattered geographical position and the diversity of

[9] Ugo La Malfa, "Il Mezzogiorno nell'Occidente," *Nord e Sud*, No. 1, December 1954.
[10] Speech reported in *Corriere della Sera*, March 3, 1962.

their particular problems, which range from overpopulation and agricultural overproduction in Brittany to under-population in the Massif Central, or to technological unemployment of coal miners in the Central and Southern basins, do not allow for the kind of relative homogeneity which characterizes the problems of underdevelopment in the Mezzogiorno. However, the large degree of imbalance between the regions of France is still there, in spite of the provisions of the French Government aimed at counteracting it.[11] The Common Market, by creating new patterns of trade and production, risks accentuating this disequilibrium by promoting a further concentration around the "overdeveloped" Paris region and the eastern and northern parts of the country, thus creating a relative pauperization of the present underdeveloped area.[12] However, this does not mean that the existing industrial activities must be immediately decentralized and factories transferred to the underdeveloped regions from the industrialized zones until a fair balance is reached. This would obviously be impractical—it would create enormous human problems and would only result in economic

[11] "One-half of France is in practice excluded from the modern economy and makes no appearance in the contemporary market either as producer or consumer. More than half the French national income is concentrated in nine *départements*, or one-tenth of the country, with the Paris region as its center of gravity; for more than a century these same nine *départements* have accounted for all the increase in the French population, including immigrants, while, since the middle of the nineteenth century a slow process of depopulation has been taking place in the remaining nine-tenths of the country" Luethy, *op.cit.*, p. 21.

[12] "In relation to the all-French average (100) the index of income per person is 182 for the Seine, 130 for the Rhône, 126 for the Nord, 30 for Corsica, 64 for Vendée, Mayenne, Côtes-du-Nord, and Ardèche. While the national economy is in full expansion, there are troublespots where unemployment occurs. . . . Numerous measures have been taken during the last few years to reduce the congestion of the Paris agglomeration and to come to the aid of the underdeveloped zones. It is probable that they will have to be reinforced in the next decade, taking into account the foreseeable imbalance between regional increases in the active population and the regional possibilities of employment." CEE, *Rapport 1958*, p. 281.

chaos. Only in very exceptional cases can existing factories be transferred to other areas. What the French Plan is trying to promote is the implantation of *new* industries in the depressed areas, thus countering the trend of migrations from these regions to the Paris zone and to the industrialized part of France. Careful studies of demographic and technological progress in the next decade or so will be made, and will help in the over-all planning of the industrialization of these areas.[13] In any case, there is a definite trend against moving workers to places where jobs can be found, and towards the implanting of new industries in areas where labor is plentiful. However, this problem is by no means confined only to the industrial sector of the economy, and powerful forces oppose many of the "optimum" solutions of the questions related to underdevelopment.[14]

Having briefly illustrated these aspects of the problem, let us now examine what the French government is doing at present during the life-span of the IVth Plan. The South-

[13] "As of now, it is possible to know, with a good margin of approximation, the number of job applications which will be made in each region in a certain number of years. In order to attain full employment, these applications will have to be balanced by a corresponding number of offers, either in the region where they appear or in other regions." *Ibid.* Similarly, "the expansion of automation should provide the growth of production in the same establishment, with somewhat of a diminution in the numbers of personnel, and it is possible that this mechanization, pushed more and more ahead, together with automatic control, will make possible a certain decentralization of industrial establishments; quicker communications should greatly facilitate the task of the management, operating from distant headquarters, in deciding any important questions." Maillet, *op. cit.*, p. 11.

[14] As far as the agricultural sector is concerned, for instance, in its Annual Review of the French Economy, *Le Monde* (Sélection Hebdomadaire), January 3, 1962, states "Agriculture can only adapt itself slowly and laboriously to the industrial evolution. Among the farmers, are side by side, conservative forces which seek safety in State support and guarantees of prices and income, and progressive forces which prepare the necessary reforms of the structures and the methods of work. If the latter do not win, the general progress would be hindered *and the European union would run the risk of exploding or fading out.*" (emphasis supplied)

West is being aided by action of a "general character" and emphasis is being switched to the assets which augur well for "natural development."[15] In Aquitaine, the accent is put on modernization and transformation of agriculture and on a better organization of the markets.

In Languedoc, the State plans to intervene directly with only limited amounts of money, but to work more through incentives and facilities of various kinds to entice private enterprise. Priority is given to tourism. Conversely, in Brittany and in parts of the Massif Central, massive intervention is taking place. Brittany seems to be held in particularly high regard by the planners, and to be a kind of "test area" for regional development experiments. Special account has certainly been taken of the main characteristic which differentiates this area from the other depressed zones of France: that of overpopulation. Also, the new situation created by the agricultural agreements of December 1963 between the Six, and the potential powerful boost thus given to the important agricultural activities of the region, have certainly contributed to the first priority accorded this area and to serious attempts on the part of the French Government to face the problem. The recurrent peasants' "revolts" of 1960 and following years may also have played a role.

In the Massif Central the objectives are: encouragement to agriculture; implantation of new industry around the "poles of growth" of Clermont-Ferrand and Saint-Etienne; creation of an industrial infrastructure; improvement of communications. In the Southern part of the Massif, provisions have been made to assimilate thousands of Europeans who have returned from Algeria.

Innovations of the present Plan directly concerning the underdeveloped regions are: (a) the creation and promotion

[15] "But, after all these collective initiatives, private initiative will have to multiply, as eventually it is mainly on this that the development of the South-West and the improvement in the average income of the farmers, the industrial workers, the artisans and the traders, depend." *Journal Officiel, Région Midi-Pyrénées*, p. 114.

of so-called "dam-cities" (villes-barrage) for the purpose of acting as a dam between the depressed areas and Paris, that is, they would gradually absorb the masses of labor that usually move from these areas to the Paris region; (b) factories built directly by the State in the underdeveloped areas and rented on particularly favorable conditions to those enterprises which agree to decentralize their plants and move into the area. A large increase in other incentives of various kinds to attract private enterprise to the underdeveloped areas is also foreseen.[16] "If it be added that in numerous cases private firms will be charged by the Committee for Development with applying the regional policy set by the Plan, then this explains the large degree of 'understanding' shown by private enterprise towards the regional policy of the Fourth Plan."[17]

But, if these general provisions are now being applied by the French Government to combat the state of underdevelopment of the depressed regions of France, thus preparing them, by implication, for their new position in the European Community, the French economy as a whole must also gear itself to the new situation—a much larger market and infinitely keener competition *inside* as well as outside France. In this connection, a phenomenal adaptation by the French industry is already taking place.[18]

[16] The *Journal Officiel* of February 15, 1963, confirms that, in spite of the various incentives, private industry is still rather reluctant to move away from the great concentrations. ". . . in 1961, ten French *départements*, the wealthiest, have benefited from more than one-third of the new industrial plants and the large cities have attracted almost three-quarters of the new plants of their *départements*. . . . The attempts at decentralization of administrative services or of public industrial establishments owned by the state have had limited results."

[17] *Le Monde* (Sélection Hebdomadaire), January 10, 1962.

[18] *Le Monde* (Sélection Hebdomadaire), January 17, 1962, puts it this way: "In sum, the Common Market has already brought us a triple improvement: our suppliers, like most French industrialists, have endeavored to modernize their enterprises; we have been able to import cheaper merchandise; in the face of this competition, the national manufacturers have readjusted their prices. . . . [Therefore]

The same industrialists who were bitterly resisting the Common Market are busily defending it now. Today, the *Patronat* (the association of French employers) is educating its members on the need for a further step towards free trade. . . . The change in everyday attitudes, even in small firms, is remarkable. French businessmen are travelling more; they have a new "window on the world."[19]

There is no doubt that today the French economy, along with the economies of all the Common Market countries, is booming. Some clouds—a shortage of skilled labor and inflation—appear here and there, but the over-all picture is still bright. It can be summarized in the words of General de Gaulle:

Since 1958, and up till the end of 1963, the total earnings of France have increased 30 per cent, her income growing on average 5.5 per cent from the previous year. . . . In

---

the Common Market has allowed the importation of numerous items from abroad cheaper than the French products and, consequently, provoked a lowering in the price of the equivalent French products. . . . For them [the consumers] the beneficial effects are undeniable; and they call for a new effort of coordination of purchasing and manufacturing by business, leading to *a degree of European planning* [emphasis supplied]. . . . Otherwise, we shall not be able to avoid the saturation of the markets and all the consequences that this fact entails. The following are a few examples of what the establishment of the Common Market has meant to the prices of certain products in France [prices given in new francs]:

Product	Exporting country	Price of imported article in France	Price of equivalent article made in France
Blouse, linen	Holland	15	25
Twin-set, Orlon	Italy	50	70
Nylon raincoat	Italy	50	80
Handkerchiefs	Italy	1	2
Sewing machines	Italy	340	425
Chair	Italy	25	35
China service	Germany	130	175
Small cloak	Germany	25	35
Camera	Germany	300	470
Electric train	Italy	20	50"

[19] *The Economist*, May 20, 1961.

fact, during the same period, this level [the French standard of living] has increased 21 per cent, that is on average at least 4 per cent a year. . . . Thus, in the last five years, the income of our farmers, taking into account the decrease in their number, has gone up on an average by 5 per cent per capita a year, while their admission, finally attained, to the free market of the European Economic Community, can open up vast new perspectives for their production, their sales, their profits. Also, old-age pensions have increased, in five years, at least 25 per cent for all and 46 per cent for those who had paid Social Security. . . . In 1958, we were building on an average 793 apartments a day. This year, we shall build 1,000. In five years, credits allocated for public health have increased 57 per cent, for scientific research 100 per cent, for national education 136 per cent, for youth and sports 139 per cent.[20]

It can therefore be expected that the French expansion will continue at a substantially high rate for years to come; also, more and more favorable developments are expected in the French economy when the last remaining barriers between the Six collapse and French industry and agriculture push ahead with their exceptional performance in the Common Market, encouraged by the success thus far obtained. Again, no one can express better than General de Gaulle France's future tasks:

The French Republic appears as the outstanding example of political stability among so many countries which are prey to troubles, agitations, incertitudes. . . . We are, by the creation of our first atomic weapons and by the modernization of our armed forces, taking back into our hands our own destiny, which has been controlled, since 1940, by others. It is a fact that . . . by striving to make

[20] Speech reported in *Le Monde* (Sélection Hebdomadaire), April 22, 1964.

the European Economic Community a real community, really European . . . we have brought an important contribution to the building of the Common Market and, by that, to clearing the way that leads to a United Europe. . . . France, because she can do it, because everything invites her to do it, because she is France, must carry out in the world a policy which should be of world-wide dimensions. All through the coming year, we shall then work around the three great objectives that we have assigned to ourselves: unity of Europe, implying as soon as possible a regular and organized cooperation between Germany, Italy, Holland, Belgium, Luxembourg and France, in the domains of politics, of defense and of culture, besides, of course, economics; progress of the developing countries; finally, contribution to maintaining the peace.[21]

FINAL APPRAISAL

We have seen how even the most backward parts of the Community, helped by their own national governments, are being prepared to take their rightful place in the new entity. If this process of State support, guidance, and vigilance continues while the national states are still all-powerful, and is then gradually taken up by the Federal Government of the new Europe, these underdeveloped regions should gradually gather needed self-assurance and experience; their advancement will become steadier and more rapid, until such time as they can keep pace with, instead of lagging behind, the other regions of the Community. Otherwise, the present situation will be prolonged, whereby "The backward regions bring too small a contribution to the national product and they act like a brake on the expansion of the richer regions. . . . The insufficient development of part of the

[21] *Le Monde* (Sélection Hebdomadaire), January 8, 1964. Year-end report to the nation, televised on December 31, 1963.

Community consequently constitutes an economic liability which must be borne by the Community as a whole."[22]

Naturally, as far as evaluation goes, not all the same rules and criteria are applicable to each of the underdeveloped areas of the Community, or at least not in the same measure. The surplus of labor, common to Southern Italy and to Brittany, may induce new industries to establish themselves in the region, taking advantage of this "commodity"; there is already a substantial shortage of labor throughout the rest of the Community.[23] This means that the national governments must prepare the workers for their new tasks by helping them learn skills that are indispensable in today's rapidly advancing technology. This will not be easy in some of the cases in question; there are also psychological obstacles to be overcome.[24] For example, the young agricultural worker whose family has owned the same plot of land for generations and who is torn between continuing the family

[22] *Communauté Européenne*, No. 7, July 1963.

[23] "The general situation with regard to employment and manpower in Europe in 1963 may be summarized as follows. The level of employment remains very high in western Europe. . . . The level of unemployment remained relatively low. . . . Pressures were therefore not relieved, and in some sectors labour shortages, especially of skilled manpower, were aggravated." ECE of the United Nations, *Report on Manpower in Europe in 1963, op. cit.*, p. 2. *Time*, October 23, 1964, supplies the following figures: "West Germany has 681,000 vacant jobs for its 103,000 unemployed persons, many of whom are unemployable. Britain has 334,000 jobs going begging, The Netherlands 150,000, France at least 50,000, and Sweden 48,000."

[24] However, the adjustment is often made rapidly and without apparent effort; for instance, in this case, reported by the *Observer*, February 9, 1964: "[In] the backward, poverty-stricken South, the Mezzogiorno, in a little town near Naples, one I.R.I. company has a brilliantly designed factory, complete with swimming pool, where 320 young girls are making telephones and breaking clean away from the low consumption habits and male-dominated traditions of the place. It will be hard to keep them down on the farm once they have seen £8 ($23) a week." And *Time*, October 16, 1964: "The most profound change in *Il Mezzogiorno* has been the slow development of an 'industrial mentality' among people who had never known anything but manual work."

361

tradition or abandoning it and acquiring skills to admit him to industry; or the young, carefree, semi-illiterate Southern Italians, who are not prepared by temperament or habit for the strict discipline and precision required by factory life. If really effective training programs, aimed at turning these unexploited sources of labor into skilled and semiskilled workers, produce good results, enterprises from all over the Community and also from outside will certainly take advantage of this availability of labor to open branches *in loco*. This can be advantageous to these firms in strictly economic terms since it would be less expensive for them than bringing workers (and their families), all the way to, say, Germany, or to Eastern France, etc. Furthermore, new prosperity and increased purchasing power brought to the area concerned will help develop local markets and a good chance of selling at least some of the products locally.

A consideration of the utmost importance is that, parallel to the rapid advance of science and technology, and to the improved transportation facilities, a power revolution, directly affecting the underdeveloped parts of the Community, is taking place. This is due (a) to the discovery and exploitation of sources of power within these areas, such as in Lacq and Parentis (South-West France), Sicily, etc.; (b) to the greatly diminished costs of importing coal by sea from abroad to supply the coastal areas; and (c) to the development of atomic energy, although its large-scale industrial application is still in the future. However, when it does fully arrive, the underdeveloped regions, through EURATOM, will then benefit from the use of this form of energy under exactly the same conditions as the most industrialized areas, without any additional overhead due to transportation, etc.[25]

[25] Very encouraging information in this connection has recently been furnished by the Executive of EURATOM. "Nuclear-power plants under construction today could be producing competitively-priced industrial energy in four to six years, the Euratom Commission has predicted. The forecast indicates that eventually there will be within

Another important advantage possessed by the under-developed regions is that, having very few industrial plants at present, they can build new plants without encountering the problems posed by how to dispose of the old, amortization of costs, etc. The situation is similar in some ways to that existing in Germany soon after the end of World War II, when it became necessary to reconstruct the industrial might of Germany practically from scratch. This was made possible mainly through a massive outpouring of American capital and, in a comparatively short time, the new German plants were disseminating throughout the world less expensive and often better quality products than those of some of the conquering powers, particularly of France and Britain, with their old, overworked, and obsolete plants. It is evident that, if similar results, even on a minor scale, are to be attained in the underdeveloped regions of the Community, a massive quantity of capital is needed. Perhaps, ironically enough, Germany will be the foremost contributor of this capital.

When, a few years after the war, France and Italy, with the creation of the Sociétés de Développement Régional and the Cassa per il Mezzogiorno respectively, decided on a policy of development of their underdeveloped regions, these policies were geared to strictly national needs, and were therefore not coordinated in any way. But now, with the

---

reach unlimited local sources of energy to support the European Community's economic expansion. . . . The commission's report said that atomic energy offered a better long-term solution to the European Community's energy problems than any other energy source. . . . 'Large-scale nuclear power stations will therefore be economically justifiable in 1968 or 1970 on the basis of a 6,000 kilowatt hour a year load factor,' the Euratom report said." Finally the report continues with an affirmation which, if it materializes, will weigh very heavily on the economic developments of the last quarter of this century: " 'From the beginning of the next decades [meaning from 1975 onwards] it will be more economical to equip power stations with nuclear reactors than with fuel oil or high quality coal-fired boilers.' " *New York Times*, April 27, 1964.

creation of the Common Market, there should be a gradual shift toward a general European program of advancement for the underdeveloped regions of the Community.[26] "*The creation of the Common Market has had as a consequence the partial discharge by each State, to the advantage of the whole Community, of the mission of eliminating regional economic differences and of facilitating the development of backward regions or sectors.*"[27] The greatly enhanced economic possibilities of these areas and their higher degree of sophistication will naturally considerably increase the intercourse with the already advanced parts of the Community. Currents of traffic within this area will be invigorated and will follow the paths opened up by the new exigencies and possibilities; and the ever-increasing mobility of the inhabitants of the Community will accomany and support this process.[28]

It is clear, therefore, that the end of underdevelopment in the Community will benefit not only the regions at present directly affected by it, but Western Europe as a whole.[29]

[26] "It will not be easy to obtain a minimum of coherence between the European regions, and in the expansionist effort. The disequilibriums are such that they will make planning—very detailed planning—indispensable." M. Jean Boissonnat in *Communauté Européenne*, No. 7, July 1962. Steps are already being taken to this effect. *Communauté Européenne*, No. 3, March 1963, under the title: "Aid to the Less-Developed Regions," writes that "In order to achieve one of the objectives of the Common Market, that of securing benefits deriving from economic development to all the regions of the Community, the Executive has just created three Committees, which will study certain aspects of the program of regional development. To prepare the Community action in this domain, the Committees will examine: (1) Means to accelerate economic development in the less-developed zones; (2) Means to restore the development of the industrial zones whose activities have slowed down; (3) Methods destined to facilitate the establishment of the new industry in these regions."

[27] *Communauté Européenne*, No. 6, June 1963.

[28] "Furthermore, free movement constitutes a first stage of that *European citizenship* that could become, in the not too distant future, a reality." *Ibid.*, No. 7, July 1962.

[29] "It is evidently in the interest of the backward regions that they be given the means to modernize their economic structures and to arrest the deterioration of their demographic structures. But it is also

Particular care should be exercised by the Governments in fostering a regionally balanced economy, and to this end their task will be particularly important in the formative stage, when the various economies first come into contact (though the danger is attenuated in the Community by the gradualness of the process); we have seen how easy it is to increase the imbalance of the economy as the result of integration between regions having different levels of development. We have also seen how difficult it is to redress the situation, once it has been allowed to arise. On the other hand, if the public authorities take care to avoid this danger, this does not mean that, at a certain stage, once the pre-industrialization and industrialization phases are completed, the economies of the hitherto underdeveloped regions are to be abandoned to the laws of the market, which will probably push at least some of them back to the previous state of underdevelopment. Apart from purely economic interests (particularly if they refer only to certain groups and not to the bulk of the population), other values are also paramount among the aims of the State; the welfare of the citizens of certain regions may require continuous surveillance by the State. But vigilance is different from tutelage; therefore the task of the Federal Government will not be an indefinite period of support for the developing regions, but an awareness of their peculiar situation and a readiness to step in and redress the situation whenever it is deemed necessary.

This will be even more true in a European Federation, where so many national and economic interests will clash and where potentially disruptive forces will threaten the newly achieved unity for a long time before complete integration is attained. But the process of unification must pro-

in the interest of the more advanced regions, certain of which already suffer from the economic and social inconveniences deriving from their overdevelopment: too large concentrations of population in too small a space, high cost of land, scarcity of living quarters and difficulties in adapting the collective available equipment to rapidly increasing needs." CEE: *Exposé 1961*, intro.

365

ceed, or recede;[30] and political unification must follow economic unification, otherwise the whole edifice will collapse and the disruptive forces will finally prevail, breaking up the painfully arrived at European construction. However, this extreme hypothesis, although not impossible, seems remote, in view of the splendid performance of the Common Market thus far and therefore of the obvious mutual interest in furthering its success.

If the precautions described are taken, great advantages may derive to the developing regions of the Community from the merger of economies of the Six. The Brussels agreements concerning agricultural products will certainly greatly benefit most of the underdeveloped regions, enabling them to take full advantage of the immense opportunities afforded by the large European market. Capital, know-how, technicians, entrepreneurs, etc., which should circulate freely within the Community, normally would shy away from the underdeveloped regions because they offer fewer opportunities for profit; the incentives and pressures of the State must be such as to lure private capital into the economically backward regions, not only for short-term investments of an essentially speculative character, but also for long-range ones. This will mean, with time, that investments in these areas will become quite normal and not of an erratic character, as is now the case.[31]

---

[30] For, as Ortega y Gasset says: "A nation is always either in the making or in the unmaking; *tertium non datur.*" José Ortega y Gasset, *La Rebelión de las Masas* (Madrid: Revista de Occidente, 1956), p. 247. And a British expert on the Zollverein: "Customs unions . . . can seldom be regarded as a permanent arrangement. Its members must sooner or later decide if they are to go backwards or forwards." W. O. Henderson, *The Zollverein* (Cambridge University Press, 1939), p. 343.

[31] *L'Economie*, March 14, 1963, stresses the role to be played by the regional banks in this connection: "It is indispensable that some funds remain in the province and be put at the disposal of the regional economy. The essential mark of regional banks is that the funds they receive from their customers are reinvested in the region. . . . Thanks to the regional banks, a financial decentralization is therefore realized.

CONCLUSIONS

Two of the main economic objectives of the EEC Treaty—the liberalization of exchanges and harmonization within the Community—have been treated extensively, particularly in relation to the main underdeveloped areas of the Common Market. While the final aim of harmonization is far from being attained, in spite of the efforts made to standardize legislation in the Member States, the liberalization is proceeding with surprising speed and success;[32] in fact, it has been accelerated and the world echoes with reports of the "European miracle."[33]

It will efficiently help in the development of regional activities which, in their turn, will generate new capital."

[32] The EEC Commission, in its Program of Action (*Memorandum*, p. 14) thus expresses itself on this extremely important subject: "[If certain conditions are met] the Commission will foresee in its proposals the complete elimination of the internal customs duties by January 1, 1967. This means that . . . the internal customs duties which were still in existence on January 1, 1962, and which represent 50% of the basic duties, should be abolished in four and a half years." Normally, they should be abolished by January 1, 1970. An even more optimistic view is held by Mr. Hallstein, who, in his capacity as President of the Executive of the Common Market, ". . . put forth a suggestion to accelerate the dismantling of customs between the Six, which would bring about the total suppression of customs duties at the end of next year (1965). It was on the occasion of the presentation by the German Government of a working program for 1964 that Mr. Hallstein made this suggestion. . . . The customs union would then be completely achieved four years in advance of the schedule foreseen by the Treaty of Rome." *Communauté Européenne*, No. 3, March 1964.

[33] "During the last four years, the Community has had the quickest growth of all the great economic regions of the Western World. In the years following the creation of the Common Market from 1958 to 1962, the gross national product of the Community has increased 21.5% against 11% in Great Britain and 18% in the United States. In the ten years from 1960 to 1970, it is believed that the increase will amount to between 53 and 60%. In four years, industrial production of the Community has increased 37% against 14% in Great Britain and 28% in the United States. . . . The economic growth of the Community has been achieved without any difficulty in the balance of payments. Reserves have increased in the six countries: they reached 16,855 million dollars at the end of 1962 compared with 7,773 on January 1, 1958. Exchanges between the 'Six' have increased 98% since the creation of the Common Market. They have passed from

367

The regional problems of underdevelopment in the Community are clearly identifiable and it is imperative that they be solved. Otherwise, as we have seen, the whole construction risks collapse, with the inevitable widening of the gap between the rich and the poor regions. This discrepancy would be contrary to the spirit and the letter of the Treaty of Rome, which in article 2 stresses the ". . . harmonious development . . . of the entire Community," not only of certain regions. The fact is, however, that in most cases even if the situation in the underdeveloped areas considered in this book is improving, this improvement is comparatively slower than the rate of growth in the developed parts of the Community.[34] The problem, therefore, is how to reconcile the concepts "harmonious development, balanced expansion, increased stability" with this growing imbalance. The Treaty itself makes provision for applying several measures with the coordinated action of the Member States. Article 3, for instance, mentions the coordination of the economic policies of the Member States, the standardization of national legislation, etc. Also, a common policy in the areas of agriculture and transportation is foreseen; and, of course, very relevant to our subject, the establishment of the Social Fund and the European Investment Bank. The Bank is endowed with sufficient capital (one billion dollars) to carry on a program of regional development in the Community. And it may engage itself up to 2.5 billion dollars. It is true

---

6,864 million dollars in 1958 to 13,562 million in 1962. . . . From 1958 to 1962, exports have increased 30%, reaching 20,638 million dollars, and imports 38% (22,327 million dollars)." Communauté Européenne, *La Communauté Européenne.*

[34] "However, if great progress has been accomplished during the last few years about the understanding of the problems [of the underdeveloped regions] it must be recognized that results are coming along rather slowly, even in countries like Italy and France, where the attention of the authorities has been focussed on them for a long time. It is certainly normal that it be so, as it is a question of running counter to centuries-long processes, which continue to condition development in an extremely powerful manner." CEE, *Exposé 1961*, intro.

that, as of now, a regional policy on a European scale risks encroaching on the authority of the national governments, and it is therefore a matter of common sense to try to find a balance between the two authorities.

Even in the era of great markets, the concept of region (from the economic viewpoint) is still very important. There are agricultural, industrialized, or underdeveloped regions, as well as regions where certain products are much in demand, others where they are not, etc. Consequently, the study of their characteristics will be the object of the market researchers of the big industrial and agricultural organizations that are rapidly coming to the fore in the Community. Also, the labor market, for example, is to a large extent regional, because most of the demand and the supply takes place on the local level. And, as there is often no equilibrium between supply and demand, the various regional employment offices should keep in close contact, to enable them to respond quickly to various requests. "Estimates of availability of labor will have to be drawn up, to allow the spotting of regional disequilibriums with sufficient precision and in time for efficient action; such estimates will foresee the development of supply and demand of labor in each region (and eventually each regional section)."[35] It is obvious, indeed, that on a national scale this whole process is cumbersome and slow. A vaguely formulated request for 100 Italian carpenters to go to Germany would be much less speedily fulfilled than a request for 100 carpenters by the regional employment office of, say, Bavaria made *directly* to that of Sicily.[36]

[35] EEC Commission, *Memorandum*, p. 72.

[36] "Artificial barriers to the movement of workers are to be torn down as quickly as possible by Europeanizing the employment agencies on the one hand and by stimulating the training of migrants on the other, so as to enable them to take advantage of gaps in the labor force of another member state. A whole nexus of new agencies is to be created to this end. The Commission itself is told to take the initiative through a European Bureau of Coordination. . . . Member governments are to help by setting up special agencies to collect and dis-

CONCLUSIONS

The more a region is underdeveloped, as a rule, the more exchanges etc. take place on a regional and local basis. This explains how one of the tasks of the French Sociétés de Développement Régional is that of promoting and fostering inter-regional exchanges in the underdeveloped regions. They are also encouraging the growth of the traditional local institutions and the formation of organized bodies for regional development.

On a European level, the Study Committee of the EEC Commission has tentatively divided the territory of the Community into fifty-four regions easily recognizable for their historical, geographical, and economic features. Some of these regions are those considered in the present work, and the fact that the EEC Commission is carrying out thorough research on them is heartening. The needs and the potentialities of the underdeveloped regions will then be considered on a European scale, by the European authorities. These authorities will act in close cooperation with the national governments first and then possibly directly with the regional development agencies.[37] Whereas these regional subdivisions, for the time being, respect national boundaries, the Commission proposes to re-draw them in a second stage, irrespective of statelines.

It must also be noted that, in order to foster the development of the economically weak regions of the Community

seminate information about vacancies. These central services are to be *supplemented by regional ones* [emphasis supplied] which are to be encouraged to get into direct contact with each other in order to promote mobility. And where the migrants lack the necessary skills, they are to be given access to concentrated courses of technical training whose provision the Bureau is to stimulate." *New Statesman*, December 22, 1961.

[37] This concept is so expressed by the EEC Commission in the aforementioned *Memorandum:* "The programming . . . will have, as much as possible, to be detailed region by region; the Commission will recommend to the governments, whenever these have not yet done so, to prepare action programs for the great socio-economic regions of the Community; these programs will constitute in particular a guide for the operation of the European Investment Bank." p. 72.

on a European scale, and to a certain extent independently of the national governments, the Commission has issued to the European Investment Bank strict directives that financial priority be given to the less-developed areas, and the Bank has complied.

It is obvious that a great deal of cooperation will have to take place between the Executive of the Common Market and the institutions of the national governments concerned with regional development, such as the Cassa per il Mezzogiorno or the Sociétés de Développement Régional. There will be common projects for geographically contiguous regions (roughly the equivalent of inter-state projects in the United States). At other times, this coordination may take place according to economic divisions, with little emphasis on geographical considerations. For instance, a plan elaborated by the Central Authority of the Community for marginal coalmines may at the same time concern the mines of Sulcis in Sardinia, those of Borinage in Belgium, and some in Central and Southern France.

It is, however, indispensable to the achievement of positive results that close cooperation be maintained at all levels between the supra-national, national, regional, and local authorities with, as far as possible, a clear definition of their spheres of action and responsibilities. It will take some time to attain reasonably good results; it will also depend heavily on what degree of amalgamation will be reached by the economies of the Member States and on how the political power is distributed.

During the transition period, and even later until a European Authority with (it is hoped) effective supranational power is formed, it is unavoidable that there be clashes between the European Executives and the national governments. Actually, these conflicts will continue unless a super-centralized, authoritarian United States of Europe arises. Perhaps the best solution is not to suppress these conflicts artificially, but to devise mechanisms that will work

371

smoothly enough to solve them peacefully. In this field, the experience and example of the United States, with the relations between Federal and State Governments, the Supreme Court, etc., will help considerably; to a large extent the success or failure of the whole European construction will depend upon the establishment of a smoothly functioning European Supreme Court.[38]

From a practical viewpoint, complete coordination between the authorities of three different echelons—regional, national, and European—will allow a much deeper and more thorough knowledge of the various sectors of the economy of the Community and facilitate the elaboration of a program of development for the various underdeveloped regions as facets of a single problem: that of territorial development of the whole Community.

In sum, the European Community will have to take on the role played in the past by the national state in economic matters, and to ensure a fair distribution of riches and opportunities between regions as well as between individuals:[39] it is indeed likely that economic and political developments will greatly increase government intervention in economic matters.

It should be reiterated, then, that integrating Europe does not mean simply opening the borders and giving free-play to economic forces, hoping that all will then be for the best in the best of all possible worlds. As already stressed, the economy of the new Europe will not be just the result of blending the various economies of the Member States—they

[38] In fact, a European Supreme Court in embryo already exists—the Court of Justice—whose functions, however, are limited essentially to questions of an economic character, inherent to the interpretation of the Common Market Treaties, of which the Court is one of the institutions.

[39] "Regional policy means action by all the Community in favor of parts thereof. This expresses the solidarity extant among members of the Community and in the Community as a whole." *Communauté Européenne*, No. 7, July 1963.

must be harmonized and streamlined according to the social needs of the Community.[40]

The task of correcting regional imbalances within the Community will be an important stage in the formation of an effective European economic union that after a number of years can lead *only* to political union. "The cause of Western Europe is based on logic and common sense. It is based on moral and political truths. It is based on sound moral and economic principles. And it moves with the tide of history."[41]

There is perhaps no more fitting conclusion to our work than to quote the words of the late Pope John XXIII:

Among citizens of the same political community there often exists marked economic and social inequality due for the most part to the fact that some live and work in areas that are economically more developed, while others live and work in areas that are economically underdeveloped. When this situation obtains, justice and equity demand that the public authorities should try to eliminate

[40] Mr. Levi-Sandri, Member of the Executive Commission of the EEC, declared that "the evaluation concerning the action of the Executive of the Common Market in social matters may not be limited to ascertaining that a certain number of specified instruments have been put to work: there is a still more important factor, that is, the birth of a resolutely social conception of the European construction in its entirety." *Communauté Européenne*, No. 7, July 1962.

[41] President Kennedy, speech at N.A.T.O. Naples Headquarters, *New York Times*, July 3, 1963.

The Commission of the EEC thus evaluates the situation: "The European Economic Community is not just a purely economic enterprise that should now be paralleled by a political enterprise. To the contrary, it may be affirmed that with the Community political integration has already started in an essential domain, while other domains—cultural policy, most of the foreign policy, defense policy—still remain in the hands of the member states." *Memorandum*, p. 8.

Finally, Antonio Segni, President of Italy, in an address to a joint session of Congress, January 15, 1964: "But if Europe wants to be strengthened, if it wants to maintain its role and be equal to its tasks in the times in which we live, it must also unite politically: a divided Europe would rapidly become anachronistic and outdated." *The Atlantic Community*, Spring 1964.

or reduce such inequality. To accomplish this end, the public authorities should see to it that in the underdeveloped areas essential public services are assured, which should be in the form and in the extent suggested or required by the surroundings and corresponding usually to the average standard of life that obtains in the national communities.

Furthermore, it is necessary to develop a suitable economic and social policy regarding the supply of labor and the dislocation of population, wages, taxes, interest, investments, with special attention to expanding industries. In short, a policy capable of promoting complete employment on the labor force, of stimulating enterprising initiative, and of exploiting the natural resources of the place. But governmental action along these lines must always be justified by the demands of the common good, which requires that all three areas of production, agriculture, industry and public services, be developed gradually, simultaneously, harmoniously, to obtain unity on the national level. Special effort must be made that the citizens of the less developed regions take an active part, insofar as circumstances allow, in their economic betterment. Finally, it is necessary to remember that even private enterprise must contribute to effect economic and social balance among the different zones of the same country. And, indeed, public authorities, in accordance with the principle of subsidiarity, must encourage and help private enterprise, entrusting to it, as far as efficiently possible, the continuation of the economic development.[42]

---

[42] Encyclical *Mater et Magistra*, reprinted in the *New York Times*, July 15, 1961.

APPENDIX I

A Short History of European Unification

It is easy to see that the unity of Europe is a unity of civilization; despite all the differences among European peoples and within the European nations (a Sicilian is far different from a Venetian, and a Breton from a Corsican), the links that unite all the European peoples are so strong that the oneness of European civilization is indisputable.[1] During the millennia of European history, the borders have changed many times, great powers have become small powers and vice versa, and wars, which now appear internecine, have been fought almost continuously. It is only a very short time, from an historical viewpoint, since the bloodiest war of our history ended, and we already begin to think of Frenchmen shooting Germans or Italians with a certain sense of detachment—bygone history that no longer affects us. The peoples of Europe recognize that the period of "civil" wars in Europe is gone forever, that a new and challenging future is in store for the European nations, and that unity is the only alternative to vassalage and decadence.[2]

The process of unification is moving on, even if irregularly. It is possible to believe that in a few years the intra-European wars will seem in retrospect as outdated as the wars of ages gone by, the Armagnacs versus the Burgundians

[1] "It is only by uniting ourselves that we Europeans may protect our common heritage of freedom and reaffirm the spiritual values of our civilization. . . . For the time being, only the Western Nations are free to cooperate. But eventually the New Europe must comprehend the East as well as the West." From a speech made by Mr. Duncan Sandys to the Association of Anglo-Saxon Press, Paris, December 1, 1948.

[2] "Just as, at the apogee of European power, the European states were tempted to quarrel among themselves over the spoils, so eclipse has forced them to recognize what they have in common." *Economist*, August 19, 1961.

or the Genovese against the Venetians.[3] As we have just seen, in addition to the political, humanitarian, and other effects, unity will bring immense advantages of a strictly economic nature to all the participants in this process. It now seems that the pursuit of this goal is irreversible, and that any step backward would be nonsensical and increasingly difficult to take from a strictly technical viewpoint as the national economies become more and more intertwined and geared to cater to a market much larger than that limited by narrow national boundaries.[4]

Since the essential unity of the European peoples was felt, although in a vague, unformed way, even in remote times, the first plans to bring about some kind of unification go back many centuries. It is true that they all remained mere academic exercises until very recently, for times and circumstances were not ripe for such a development. The fact, however, that these plans were formulated, even if not enacted, suggests that a certain feeling of belonging together has always been present in the European peoples, even in the midst of the bloodiest struggles and enmities.

From the Roman empire, to the Carolingian empire, to the fiction of the Holy Roman Empire, this feeling of unity was always manifest. The Popes and Napoleon, Charles V and Louis XIV, wittingly or unwittingly, repeat the same theme. And the poets, politicians, philosophers, all elaborated schemes putting forth the same aspiration: Dante in his *De Monarchia*, the Duc de Sully with his project of "Association between European Nations," the Abbé de

[3] "Now for the Europeans comes the time when Europe can be converted to the national idea. And it is much less utopian to believe this today than it would have been to forecast in the eleventh century, say, the unity of Spain and France. The more the national state of the West is faithful to its real substance, the more will it become one gigantic continental state." José Ortega y Gasset, *op.cit.*, p. 250.

[4] Luethy, *op.cit.*, p. 521, states: ". . . what is taking place is not so much an overcoming of national sovereignties as a decay of national sovereignties; it is the disorganization of an old order rather than the creation of a higher order."

Saint-Pierre with his "Perpetual Peace," Victor Hugo who foresaw the United States of Europe more than a century ago; all had the same basic idea—Europe is a unity, therefore must unite. It was only after World War I, however, that the idea of European unification began to move, even if very slowly, from the domain of pure speculation to that of possible realization. In other words, more and more people started to think about it, although the group was limited to a certain number of intellectuals and, more important, to certain politicians who were, or had been, in positions of responsibility.[5] Outstanding among them, and showing an almost incredible foresight, was Count Coudenhove-Kalergi, the father and prophet of the modern movement for European unification. In 1923, with the publication of his *Pan-Europa*, he clearly outlined his plan for what he wished to become the United States of Europe. He wrote:

> The cause of the decadence of Europe is political, not biological; Europe is not dying of old age, but because its inhabitants kill each other and ruin themselves by taking advantage of all the resources that modern technique puts at their disposal. . . . Europe is still, qualitatively, the world's most fertile reservoir of men. . . . It is not the European peoples who have been affected by senility; it is their political systems.[6]

Committees were formed throughout Europe, and the idea began to be debated; it was taken up by the French

[5] It is interesting to quote the words of Altiero Spinelli, apropos of those who will spearhead the construction of the new Europe. He writes: "I am convinced that the European federation will be made by the political classes or will not be made at all. Notwithstanding the fact that the peoples are interested in its realization and may even be very sympathetic towards it, they may not feel aroused by the myth of federation, because federation . . . is the cold, sober and intellectual solution of a difficult problem." Altiero Spinelli, *Dagli Stati Sovrani agli Stati Uniti d'Europa* (Florence: La Nuova Italia, Collana "Orientamenti," 1950), intro.

[6] Quoted in Edouard Bonnefous, *L'Idée Européenne et sa Réalisation* (Paris: Ed. du Grand Siècle, 1953), p. 62.

Minister of Foreign Affairs, Aristide Briand, who tried without success to promote concrete measures to bring about some constructive move in that direction. "Briand, no doubt, acted too late (1930). The favorable moment of 1926–27 had elapsed. The economic crises had made utopian an operation that could perhaps have been accomplished in the midst of euphoria a few years before."[7] Then came the phenomenon of Nazism and finally World War II to smash any dream of European unification. But, amid the disaster and destruction that it caused, the War also perhaps had a salutary effect upon the European nations, inasmuch as they finally became aware of the fact that they were dwarfs in a world of giants and of the utter inability of relatively small national states to play any prominent role on the world scene.[8] Also, their economies, paralyzed by the war, could not keep pace with the requirements of a rapidly advancing world, and the once great and powerful European States could well have followed Greece and the Roman Empire into obscurity and decadence. "A new and broader basis for nationalist feeling was necessary to revive its appeal. Thus the ideal of European union became, for a great part of the youth in many countries of Western Europe, but particularly in France, an objective that stimulated their enthusiasm and appealed to their sense of a common destiny of all the nations of the area."[9]

This time, the statesmen of the leading nations of Western

[7] *Ibid.*, p. 69.

[8] "There is, as already suggested, Western Europe's continuing fear of the Soviet Union and the desire to counter that power with something more than a mere military alliance. There is also growing fear of the United States and perhaps some jealousy of the stature and influence of that federation in the contemporary world. More specifically, there is the fear that America's contemporary leadership may lead the world astray. It is a fear that impresses few Americans but it allegedly influences Europeans. Europe, in their opinion, must become a power in order to provide some checkrein for American policy." Arnold J. Zurcher, *op.cit.*, p. 177.

[9] Paul Alpert, *op.cit.*, p. 436.

Europe seriously considered the question. The United States discreetly pushed the process, first by the magnificent conception and enactment of the Marshall Plan, then through the Organization for European Economic Cooperation and other media.[10] A complex of favorable circumstances helped: the three leading statesmen of continental Western Europe, Adenauer, Schuman, and De Gasperi, all happened to be Christian Democrats, strong Pan-Europeanists, imbued with very similar conceptions of political philosophy and moral values, and all spoke the same language (German). A detailed description of the events that led to the signature of the Treaties of Rome would exceed our purpose; they were the result of patient negotiations, of ups and downs that covered the dozen years immediately following the end of the War. A first gigantic step in the direction of unification had been accomplished with the signing and then the ratification in 1951–52 of the European Coal and Steel Community Treaty. A drawback that threatened the whole construction was the failure of the European Defense Community Treaty to be ratified in 1954. A number of more or less ineffectual agencies and associations had been created to help bring about a European union of some sort, but actually nothing of any relevance was accomplished until, after very thorough and patient preparation, the representatives of "Little Europe" (Belgium, Federal Republic of Germany, France, Italy, Luxembourg, and the Netherlands) met in the spring of 1957 and, in a relatively short time, produced the Treaty which, it is hoped, will be one of the outstanding documents in the history of mankind.

On March 25, 1957, the Treaties instituting the European Economic Community and the European Atomic Energy Community (EURATOM) were signed in Rome and were

---

[10] "Americans might be said to have believed in European Union before Europe did, and sometimes America's championship of the cause has been somewhat embarrassing to the Europeans." Zurcher, *op.cit.*, p. 206.

soon ratified by the legislatures of the respective Member States.[11] Thus, what is generally referred to as the "Common Market" came into being. The Treaties have produced excellent results thus far, but they are necessarily limited in scope and cannot bring about, *ipso facto*, the political or even *real* economic unification of Western Europe. Such unification cannot be achieved outside a central, directing power, and the establishment of such an agency is not foreseen in the Treaties.[12] The aim of the Rome Treaties is that of liberalizing exchanges between the Six and evolving a common customs tariff towards the rest of the world. However, the underlying feeling is that "whatever happens, the European Economic Community is not a free-trade area or an area of preferential tariffs. It must be more than a stage in an integration that, as well as being progressive, will be total and affirm the weight of a unity that, although economic, will eventually be political. The Community is more than a Common Market."[13] Cooperation among the Member States is foreseen particularly in the fields of agriculture and transport, and the ensuing results are expected to be an increase in the general standard of living of all the people of the area, a continuous and well-balanced economic expansion, and "closer relations between Member States." What these closer relations will be is not specified.

[11] The legislatures of the Six ratified the Treaty of Rome as follows: Germany, unaminous, July 5, 1957; France, 345 to 234, July 9, 1957; Italy, 311 to 144, July 30, 1957; Netherlands, 114 to 12, October 4, 1957; Belgium, 174 to 4, November 19, 1957; Luxembourg, 46 to 3, November 26, 1957. See CEE, *L'Europe a Dix Ans* ("Les Cahiers de Communauté Européenne," No. 3; Paris: Service d'Information des Communautés Européennes, 1960).

[12] "The common Institutions do not have means proportionate to their task. Only a [common] government will be able to eliminate the weaknesses of present Europe and reinforce its foundations. If this great step is not accomplished one day . . . Europe will be condemned to remain what it is today: an entanglement of interests, a Franco-German summit dialogue." *Réalités*, No. 161, June, 1959.

[13] Jacques Duhamel, General Director of the (French) Centre National du Commerce Extérieur, in *Communauté Européenne*, No. 3 (March 1961).

The wording of the Treaties is very cautious, since the rejection by the French National Assembly in 1954 of the European Defense Community Treaty showed that the time was not yet ripe for even partial abandonment of the most jealously treasured prerogative of any state, that of sovereignty. Nevertheless,

> Despite the failures that have been encountered in the case of some of the efforts, failures that in the case of the European Defense Community and allied projects were particularly grave and that it may take years to repair, there can be no doubt that what has already been accomplished in developing centripetal European institutions has permanently changed the political face of that continent and significantly altered its economy.[14]

The Treaty of April 18, 1951, establishing a Coal and Steel Community, had created what was intended to be a strong central authority, having supra-national characteristics, with a somewhat imposing name: the High Authority. But, in practice, the supra-national character was quietly pushed more and more into the background and the important decisions were made by the representatives of the Member States as such in the Council of the Community and not by the High Authority as a sovereign body.

It is clear that a will to reach eventual integration of Europe underlies the writing of the Rome Treaties; the methodology followed is that of bringing the Member States so closely together, of making their economies so complementary to each other, and their interests so interlinked, that political integration will finally become inevitable and will perhaps come about almost naturally, progressively, and without great upheavals. A European authority or government will then be formed, with powers of decision-making and of enforcing those decisions. To quote Zurcher once more:

[14] Zurcher, *op.cit.*, p. 165.

United Europe is thus no longer an idealist's dream but a practical goal of politics. It is one of the profoundly revolutionary ideals that is currently influencing opinion and institutional developments in one of the most important regions of the world. In time, the European Movement could bring about a renaissance of Europe's world position, a position currently being eclipsed as a result of relative economic decline, the dynamics of contemporary world politics, the growing role of the so-called non-European super powers, and the impact of the colonial revolution. . . . What will supplant that system (the national state system), moreover, is clear. The European Movement has supplied or will supply the alternative in Europe. The future of political organization in Western Europe lies with the concept of regional and continental integration fostered by that movement.[15]

[15] Zurcher, *op.cit.*, p. 208.

APPENDIX II

THE COMMON MARKET TREATIES

The Common Market covers a variety of economic activities such as free movement of merchandise, capital, and people in the area of the Member States, agriculture, some forms of energy, relations with overseas territories, and so forth. These are by no means exhaustive of the possibilities for economic cooperation between the Six; some of these possibilities indeed are not covered at all, others are imperfectly elaborated.[16]

We shall first examine separately and summarily the two other treaties, each covering a specialized sector which, together with the EEC Treaty, form what is generally known as the Common Market.

SYNOPSIS OF THE TREATIES ESTABLISHING A EUROPEAN COAL AND STEEL COMMUNITY AND EUROPEAN ATOMIC ENERGY COMMUNITY (EURATOM)

These two Treaties, together with the EEC Treaty, form what is known as the European Common Market and, consequently, are two of the three mainstays on which it is based.

The European Coal and Steel Community—The ECSC Treaty is very important, especially because it is the first concrete realization of European economic integration. It helped to define the area encompassing the Member States and it

[16] ". . . The Common Market Treaty has numerous and grave omissions, which are essentially related to a weakness in the supranational character of the Institutions and to the general economic policy. . . . But, even if they can be explained, the omissions in the Treaty are still there and it can be affirmed that, unless common political power is created with enough authority to fill the gap in conformity with the general objectives of the Treaty, they will prove to be decisive obstacles to any real and substantial progress." M. Allais, *L'Europe unie*, pp. 183–184.

sought to strive for European economic and, eventually, political union through a functional approach. The Treaty is also an endeavor to inject into the Community the idea of supra-nationality—an attempt that perhaps has not yet given the expected results.

The European Coal and Steel Community originated through a declaration made by M. Robert Schuman, then French Minister for Foreign Affairs, on May 9, 1950, in which he urged the necessity of a united Europe. In his opinion, such a revolutionary idea could be implemented stage by stage, according to specified functions and not according to a predetermined plan. Above all, the removal of mistrust and enmity between France and Germany was one of the main aims of the Treaty. In fact, he foresaw that the essential coal and steel industries would become so intimately interrelated that any hostility between France and Germany would become practically impossible. In Mr. Schuman's words: "By pooling basic production and by setting up a new High Authority, whose decisions will be binding . . . these proposals will build the first concrete foundation of the European Federation which is indispensable to the preservation of peace."[17]

In June of the same year, West Germany, Italy, Belgium, Holland, and Luxembourg all agreed to the declaration and soon their delegations sat down to draft a Treaty which was eventually signed in Paris on April 18, 1951, and came into force on July 25, 1952.

The European Coal and Steel Community aims at rationalizing the system of production between the Member States, thereby increasing production and consequently raising the living standards of the people of the Community. Also, an increase in the number (except in the coal industry) and security of jobs is contemplated. But the principal purpose is of a political, not economic, nature: to help bring about the United States of Europe.

[17] From the Schuman Declaration of May 9, 1950. Reproduced in *L'Europe a Dix Ans*, p. 3.

Economic unification in the fields proper to the European Coal and Steel Community (coal, steel, iron, and scrap iron) is sought by various means: abolition of customs duties and quantitative restrictions between Member States, while an external barrier is raised against the outside world; suppression of discrimination based on national origin; and the protection of free competition, particularly difficult in this field, where trusts and cartels are the rule, rather than the exception.[18]

A transition period of five years helped to smooth the passage of the Treaty.

A turning point of decisive importance was reached with the coming into force of the Coal and Steel Community. For the first time in its history, concepts of supra-nationality in Europe were put into operation, over and above national interests.

The High Authority, which is the executive body of the ECSC, taxes the industries of the Member States directly (it finances itself thus, not through direct contributions of the Member States). This is the first example of a *European* tax. The Authority also has the power to fine and to some extent to control the activities of the various enterprises involved.

The High Authority is answerable to the European Assembly, as a national government is to its own parliament, and it is subject to the decisions of the Court of Justice, the relationship being roughly that of a national government to its own Supreme Court. As we have pointed out, supra-nationality is much more pronounced here than in the subsequent Treaties of Rome.

As far as the operations of the High Authority are con-

---

[18] A certain tolerance has developed, through the experience accumulated over the years, by the High Authority towards trusts, cartels etc. In the parlance of the ECSC's technocrats, the "ententes" are defined as "good ententes" and "bad ententes." The former are represented by "those agreements that . . . can be found to promote a good economic purpose" (*New York Times*, June 14, 1962); the opposite is true of the latter.

cerned, some of its achievements are closely related to our subject: for instance, in March 1954, the High Authority decided to assist financially in the transfer of miners from Central and Southern France to Lorraine. Also in December of the same year, funds were appropriated to finance the reconversion of the unemployed miners in certain regions of the Community to other types of work. The same financial backing in analogous circumstances was extended to the miners of Sulcis in Sardinia. Also under the auspices of the High Authority, a European Labor Card has been issued, entitling its holder to work anywhere in the Community. Finally, upon the insistence of the Italian delegation, after the disaster of Marcinelle in Belgium in which several Italians lost their lives, a permanent Safety Commission for Mines was established.[19]

The European Atomic Energy Community (EURATOM)— Very few words are necessary to describe the scope and purpose of the Atomic Energy Community. The Treaty setting up this Agency was signed on March 25, 1957, together with the Treaty setting up a European Economic Community. They both came into force on January 1, 1958. The main principles of the Treaty are that nuclear materials shall be put into free circulation within the Community, and tariff walls erected against the outside world.

This Agency is important to our study because atomic energy will sometime in the future give some of the under-developed regions the power they so sorely need; the lack of

[19] It is interesting to note a few of the concrete achievements of the ECSC during the transition period. Coal production increased by 3.8%, coke by 23.7%, iron ore by 33.8%, pig-iron by 30% and steel by 43%. Trade has increased by equal or even more remarkable figures. Within the Community, trade in steel products rose by 157%, scrap by 175%, coal by 21%, coke by nearly 15%, and iron ore by 25.5%. Imports of coal rose by 97.3%, of iron ore by 81.4%, and scrap by 822%. Exports rose by 45.5% for steel products, 66.6% for iron ore and 13.6% for coal. Transport costs have been notably reduced. Source: *Europe Yearbook* (London: Europa Publications, 1960), Vol. I, p. 40.

power is now one of the main causes of their backwardness. It may, therefore, revolutionize the whole industrial organization of these regions. Some plants, as we have seen, have already been built in those areas.

SYNOPSIS OF THE EUROPEAN ECONOMIC COMMUNITY TREATY

Principles—The aims of the Treaty are those envisaged in Article 2: ". . . to promote throughout the Community the harmonious development of economic activities, continuous and balanced expansion, increased stability, a more rapid improvement in the standard of living and closer relations between its Member States." To attain these objectives, the Community will:

(a) Progressively eliminate all customs barriers and quota restrictions between Member States

(b) Set up a common customs tariff and a common commercial policy towards third countries

(c) Grant free movement, at least in principle, of people, capital, and services, and the right to establish commercial activities anywhere

(d) Endeavor to bring social legislation in the different countries into line

(e) Establish a common agricultural policy

(f) Establish a common transport policy

(g) Coordinate the economic policies of the Member States

(h) Create a European Social Fund to assist the workers and improve their living and working conditions

(i) Establish a European Investment Bank to facilitate the economic activities of the Community and to furnish aid to its underdeveloped areas

(j) Allow the association, for a period of five years, of the overseas territories of the Member States. (Upon expiration of the period foreseen, such association has been renewed.)

387

The Common Market shall finally come into being in its full extent after a period of from twelve to fifteen years, and on completion of three stages, each of a minimum period of four years.

Any discrimination on the ground of nationality is forbidden.

Although it was not spelt out openly, the underlying over-all purpose of the Treaty is to bring about political unification of some kind, through economic integration. Article 2, quoted above, states ". . . to promote . . . closer relations between its Member States." It does not go into details. This, however, is as far as the Treaty could go at the time.

AGRICULTURE

Title II, Articles 38–47, are dedicated to Agriculture. Article 39 states the final objectives of a common agricultural policy. The agricultural activities of the Six are among the most complicated to regulate, covering as they do such an extensive range of products, originating in vastly different regions and grown under different conditions. At the time the Treaty was written, there was a great deal of controversy as to whether agriculture should be included at all. A positive decision was finally reached because it was realized that agriculture is an essential part of the economy of a nation and must therefore be included in a Treaty of this type.

In the words of the Treaty: "A common agricultural policy shall be established at the end of the transition period." Furthermore, the influence of agricultural prices on salaries and wages, and consequently on a very important price-formation factor, is considerable, and the whole competitive process would be distorted should agriculture be omitted. Finally, the advantages of an enlarged market appeared evident to many agricultural organizations, which naturally did not then wish to be excluded from its benefits.

It also appeared clear, for these reasons, that agriculture

388

could not be subject to the same general rules and evolve at the same rhythm as other activities. Consequently, since even a gradual suppression of the existing agricultural barriers threatens to produce many harmful consequences if it is not paced by a parallel organization of the European Common Market, special precautions and dispositions concerning agriculture are embodied in the text of the Treaty. Thus, the general rules incorporated in the Treaty to promote freer competition are not applicable to agriculture (Article 42). Actually, some aid, financial and other, may be authorized by the Council for the protection of those areas which for some reason are underdeveloped, or otherwise put in an unfavorable position (lack of adequate transportation or storage facilities, etc.).

The achievement by the agricultural organizations of the objectives contemplated is specifically based on three provisions which should contribute to stabilizing agricultural activities throughout the Community. These provisions are:

(a) The "minimum price" clause defined in Article 44, according to which any Member State is permitted to apply to certain products a minimum price, below which any importation will be forbidden. Only products originating from abroad whose price is higher than the minimum may be allowed in.

(b) The so-called "long-term contracts," which have been devised to foster and promote the exchange of agricultural products among Member States. In fact, before facing the expenditure involved in mechanization, modernization in general, irrigation, etc., it is often necessary for the farmer to be assured that his crops will find outlets in the various agricultural markets for years to come. Such assurance can only be given by long-term contracts. However, the contracts are not signed by the individual farmers. To be able to benefit from long-term contracts, a product is subject to certain conditions: (i) there must be a surplus in the country of exportation; (ii) there must be a deficit in the

389

country of importation; (iii) the national production of the importing country must be protected by its own national government.

These long-term contracts involve, as stated, the development of exchanges, but they must be applied very carefully in order not to upset the traditional patterns of trade too abruptly. In fact, for years to come, there will be differences in the price of agricultural produce between Member States. However, in the long run this type of contract should prove a favorable factor in the alignment of "European" prices with the prices obtaining inside the national markets.

(c) Finally the Treaty foresees the creation of new agricultural organizations common to the whole EEC area and the coordination of the already existing organizations. These organizations should each be responsible for a certain product or products, rather than constituted on a national or regional basis. As differences in specialization and prices are particularly profound in agriculture, it has been agreed that any decision will require unanimity during the first two stages, and then a qualified majority. However, a special provision enables the countries in the minority to appeal to the Court of Justice, and the decision will be annulled if the Court recognizes that it imperils any of the fundamentals of the agricultural Common Market. As can be seen, there is a large margin of elasticity. It could not have been otherwise in view of the delicacy of agricultural relations between the Six. And success in the agricultural sector is a basic condition for the success of the Common Market as a whole.[20]

FREE MOVEMENT

No common market could really exist unless, besides the free circulation of goods, such freedom of movement were also assured to people, capital, and services. However, al-

[20] "The Common Market cannot achieve economic integration if agricultural policy remains a national matter." *New York Times*, October 28, 1964.

though these may be laudable objectives for the time when the Treaty is fully applied, the matter is fraught with danger, either on a social or on an economic level. The drafters of the Treaty have been very careful to scale down the provisions regarding free circulation so that they would not unduly upset the market. This is why so many escape clauses appear in the Treaty in the articles dealing with this matter.

Free Movement of Goods

Of note is Article 9 of the Treaty: "The Community is based upon a customs union covering the exchange of all goods and comprising both the abolition, as between Member States, of customs duties on imports and exports and all taxes with equivalent effect, and also the adoption of a common customs tariff in their relations with outside countries." Article 32 reads: "In their trade with each other, Member States shall refrain from increasing the restrictive effects of quotas or other measures having equivalent effect in existence at the date of entry into force of the present Treaty. Such quotas shall be abolished by, at latest, the end of the transition period."

To reach this objective various provisions are laid down. Thus, first of all, no new customs duties or quotas can be introduced among the Member States. But complete freedom is left to them to carry out the reductions foreseen by the Treaty, or to abolish any restriction on imports from any other country of the Community more rapidly if they so desire (subject to certain conditions). The common customs tariff shall be, in principle, equal to the arithmetic average of the duties applied in the four customs territories (France, Germany, Italy and Benelux) one year before the Treaty came into existence, i.e. on January 1, 1957. Certain exceptions are foreseen, notably for Italy, especially to protect products coming from the Mezzogiorno.

The maximum limit for the application of a common customs tariff is the end of the transition period.

The Member States shall progressively adjust their State commercial monopolies in such a way that they cannot be detrimental to private interests. The obligations incumbent on Member States can be modified by the international agreements existing at the time the Treaty came into existence. A notable exception is foreseen for certain goods, on which a fiscal tax is levied.

Free Circulation of People

By the end of the transition period, the workers of any Member State of the European Economic Community shall be free, in principle, to reside and work anywhere they choose in the rest of the Community, under the same conditions as local workers. All discrimination based on nationality shall be abolished, when it exists, and this applies to remuneration, employment, and other conditions of work. The only exception, for understandable reasons, is employment in public administration. Social Security benefits already accumulated in the home country will not be lost when the worker moves to another Member State but will be retained in the new country.

Right of Establishment

With certain exceptions and subject to well-determined procedural rules, restrictions on the right of establishment of nationals of a Member State in the territory of another Member State will be progressively suppressed during the transition period. The same principle extends to any restriction on the creation of Agencies, Branch Offices, and the like, and to the starting of noncommercial enterprises. Also, during the transition period the Council will issue regulations aimed at a mutual recognition of diplomas and certificates so that the "professions" may be exercised in any country the person chooses.

Similar regulations concern activities such as insurance, banking, etc., and it is important to note that special restrictions aim at avoiding a concentration of these activities in certain favored regions, to the detriment of the poor, underdeveloped areas.

Free Movement of Capital

The restrictions on the movement of capital existing between the Member States at the time the Treaty went into effect shall be progressively removed during the transition period, provided that this does not hamper the smooth functioning of the Common Market. Discrimination of any kind, based on the nationality or place of residence of the parties or on the place in which such capital is invested, is abolished.

TRANSPORT

The subject of transport requires careful control, because it would not be difficult, by applying discriminatory tariffs, to falsify and distort the provisions of the Treaty tending to liberalize the economy between the Member States.

PROTECTION OF FREE COMPETITION

Trusts, Cartels, and Monopolies

Competition should be free, meaning by that as free as is possible under present circumstances. The action of the Treaty is aimed at assuring that the free market forces are unhampered by the various forms of "ententes" that deny free competition to develop.

It would be extremely difficult to try to break up the already existing monopolies, and it would also be unrealistic. Therefore, what the Treaty purports to do is to *control* their activities in a way compatible with the interest of the Community. In fact, the enlargement of the market can be a strong incentive to some enterprises to enter into agreements to fix the price of their products, or to share the territories of sales and supply, or control the quantity of production or investments. Even if "ententes" are as a rule forbidden, the realities of industrial life are not forgotten. Thus many

393

exceptions and very elastic methods of application are prescribed.

Dumping

If, during the transition period, the Commission discovers the existence of "dumping" practices inside the Community, it must intervene and order the State which is carrying on this practice to refrain from it. If it should continue, however, the State or States affected by it can be authorized by the Commission to take appropriate defensive measures.

Aid and Subventions

Aid and subventions, direct or indirect (such as tax facilities, special transport rates, etc.) favoring certain activities or enterprises are forbidden because they may hamper free competition. However, certain exceptions are allowed by the Treaty: (a) when they are destined *to aid underdeveloped regions;* (b) when they aim at the realization of projects of a *common European interest;* (c) when they aid the growth *of certain activities or of certain economic regions* (poles of growth). These exceptions are very relevant to our study.

Rapprochement of Fiscal Legislation

As a rule, Member States are free as far as fiscal matters are concerned. However, a certain amount of coordination and certain limitations have seemed necessary to assure efficient functioning of the Common Market. The Council is charged with issuing directives to this purpose.

A COMMON POLICY

Social Policy

Equality in progress is the objective of the Common Market as far as conditions of the workers are concerned. In other words, the conditions of working people in any Member State must be progressively brought to the level of better conditions in force in any other Member State.

Each Government of the Six is bound to assure the application of the principle of equality between salaries for men and women for equal work. Also, overtime pay and length of paid vacations should be standardized between the various States of the Community.

Economic Policy

It should be observed that a certain "laissez-faire" spirit is found in the Treaty in the legislation concerning strictly economic matters; it is hoped, in fact, that the operation of a large market will *by necessity* bring about a harmonization and coordination in these matters between the Member States.

A number of escape clauses, the gradual and elastic application of several rules, and the creation of the European Investment Bank and the European Social Fund are all directed to correcting these free market forces, *so that insufficiently developed regions will not have to suffer because of them.*

Once the initial disparities have been corrected, the rational development of economic activities inside the Community is to be based on the existence of a *common external tariff* towards the outside world. This will be supplemented by a common commercial policy, by the observance of procedures of consultation and coordination, and by common aims concerning investments and payments outside the Community.

Monetary Policy

If the Treaty brings the Member States into close association as far as commercial intercourse is concerned, their autonomy in the strictly financial sphere is much more extended; in particular, each State is to keep its national money and is exclusively responsible for its own budget and for its balance of payments. It should be pointed out, however, that, to assure smooth functioning of the Common Market, a certain amount of coordination of monetary policies is necessary. The Treaty, however, only points to vague objectives of stability and equilibrium. This is a focal point pertaining to the degree of integration the Common Market nations can achieve. In effect, the adoption of a common monetary policy and finally of a common money can very well be the decisive factor in the development of the European Economic Community. No integration can be complete without a common money. Conversely, a common money can exercise not only a powerful economic, but also psychological, influence on bringing about a real integration of the area.[21]

However, the realization of this ideal presents many delicate problems. The Treaty only prescribes coordination of economic policies between Member States, and the establishment of cooperation between their financial administrations and their central banks. Furthermore, it sets up a consultative Monetary Committee which will constantly follow the financial and monetary situation of the Member States and keep the competent institutions of the Community informed on this.

Assistance to a Member State by its partners in case of serious difficulties is foreseen by the Treaty. Also, in case of emergency, any State threatened by a sudden imbalance can take special measures. Subsequent approval of the emergency measures by the competent institution is however required.

Permanent consultation is also prescribed by the Treaty between the various institutions in view of obtaining better

[21] The latest developments in this field are encouraging. "The European Common Market made a vitally important first move today toward the creation of a common money market. . . . This was described as a necessary preliminary step to uniting the six largely isolated, and often contradictory, national capital markets into a single fluid market for the whole community. On this platform, the Common Market then will proceed to construct a single money market mechanism, including the substitution of a common currency for the six separate national currencies." *New York Times*, October 27, 1964.

coordination of financial and monetary policy. However, the Treaty cannot for the time being go further than this.

OVERSEAS TERRITORIES

France and Italy, together with Belgium and Holland, have overseas territories or have special relations with certain independent nations, and these overseas territories have had to be brought into the Common Market, also for practical reasons.

The basic principles governing this matter are: (a) Member States should in their commercial exchanges with these countries apply the same rules which they apply among themselves; (b) they should *all* contribute to the investments required for the progressive development of these territories.

INSTITUTIONS

THE COUNCIL

The most striking aspect of the Executive of the European Economic Community is the much less-extended character of supra-nationality it presents compared to the High Authority of the European Coal and Steel Community. It is understandable, however, that following the failure of the European Defense Community Treaty in 1954, a certain caution prevented the writers of the Treaty of Rome from running the same risk by going too far along the road leading to supra-nationality. Even the name adopted by the Executive Council is much less resounding and imposing than "High Authority." This Council of Ministers is composed of a representative of each Member State, generally its Foreign Minister. Its function is that of coordinating the economic policies of the Member States with that of the Community as a whole.

In most cases, and in all the important ones, the Council can only make decisions on questions brought up by the Commission (whose function is explained below). The pur-

397

pose of this system, which is one of the most original features of the Treaty, is that of allowing the Commission, an organ with supra-national character (whereas the Council is clearly an inter-governmental body), to initiate and promote the projects on which the representatives of the Member States will deliberate.

Conversely, in certain cases, the Council may go so far as to reverse the decisions of the Commission.

The decisions of the Council are taken unanimously in the first two stages and generally in the most important economic and political matters. But the Treaty tends to promote the habit of making decisions by qualified majorities. A total of seventeen votes is allowed thus: four votes each to the Big Three—Italy, France and Germany, two to Belgium and Holland, and one to Luxembourg. But a qualified majority is generally fixed at twelve, i.e., slightly more than two-thirds. This means that, if the Big Three agree, this agreement is sufficient to carry the decision. On the other hand, if two agree and one is against, the two have to seek the agreement of both Belgium and Holland.

THE COMMISSION

The Commission is composed of nine members, of whom no more than two can be nationals of the same State. They are named by their Government for a period of four years, but, once they have assumed their functions, they are supposed to report exclusively to the Community, over whose collective interest they preside. So, at least theoretically, they are independent and do not represent their national government. Contrary to those of the Council, the decisions of the Commission are taken by a simple majority.

The Commission is the organ of enforcement of the proper execution of the Treaty, and of the decisions taken by the Executive. The Commission also represents the Community before the Assembly, in judicial matters and generally in all relations between the Community and the outside world.

Whereas the power of decision, in major questions, belongs to the Council, the Commission has its own power of decision, in a variety of cases. And, as said apropos of the Council, the Commission participates in the power of decision of the Council by its "right of proposition."

THE ECONOMIC AND SOCIAL COMMITTEE

This body is composed of representatives of various economic activities, unions, etc., named by the Council upon request of the States. It includes two specialized sections for agriculture and transport, i.e., two activities where many of the final decisions remain to be taken during the transition period by the Common Market Executive. The Committee has only consultative powers, but its consultation is obligatory in certain cases.

THE ASSEMBLY

The Assembly is the organ with political control over the Executive of the Community. It is composed of representatives originating from the national parliaments and designated by them. The Assembly may put questions before the Commission, which must submit an annual report to it. It also has the power, which up till now has never been used, to overthrow the Commission by means of a vote of censure. Plans are being made to transform it into the Assembly of the Peoples of the European Economic Community, by means of direct popular election of the representatives.

THE COURT OF JUSTICE

The judiciary organ of the Common Market is composed of seven judges, nominated unanimously by the Member States. The Court is empowered with the enforcement of the law in the Community—for instance, between Member States, between Member States and organs of the Community, etc.

399

INSTITUTIONS OF THE EUROPEAN COMMON MARKET

Council of Ministers

Membership: 1 from each of 6 countries

Decisions: Majority vote or unanimity as provided in Treaty

Functions: Coordinate general economic policies of members and decide important issues arising in establishing and maintaining Common Market

Assembly

Membership: 142 delegates chosen by Parliaments of Six

Functions: Review and debate problems of Community; can force resignation of Commission by two-thirds vote of censure

Economic and Social Committee

Membership: 101 representatives of all major economic groups in each of Six countries, appointed by Council

Functions: Advise Council and Commission as provided in Treaty

Monetary Committee

Membership: Member States and Commission each appoint 2 financial experts

Functions: Advise Council and Commission on financial matters

Commission

Membership: 9, no 3 of which shall have same nationality

Decisions: Majority vote

Functions: Administrative organ of Community; recommends action to Council and takes decisions itself as provided in Treaty

European Social Fund

Administration: by Commission advised by Committee of representatives of governments, employers, and trade unions

Functions: Provide financial assistance to Member States for retraining and relocation of workers

Court of Justice

Membership: 7 judges appointed by agreement among Six Governments.

Functions: Adjudication of disputes arising under Treaty

European Investment Bank

Board of Governors: Finance Ministers of Six Member States

Board of Directors: 12 appointed by Governors on nominations from each Member State

Decisions: Majority vote or unanimity as specified in Treaty

Function: Raise capital and make loans for purposes specified in Treaty

THE ITALIAN PLAN FOR AGRICULTURAL
DEVELOPMENT (GREEN PLAN)

The law authorizing a five-year Plan for the Development of Agriculture concerns all of Italy; therefore the agricultural problems of Southern Italy are not specifically mentioned but treated as part of the whole, except when particular questions of coordination with the Cassa per il Mezzogiorno or others arise. Therefore, only a brief resumé of its provisions will be given, but it must be mentioned because it will be of profound importance in the development of agriculture in Italy in the next few years.

The period covered by the Plan is from 1960–61 to 1964–65, and the total amount allocated by the State is 550 billion lire. The Plan has three basic concepts: (a) it is integral, and applies to the whole territory of Italy, without regional or sectoral character; (b) it is organic, as it follows production through all phases from research to final utilization of the products obtained; (c) it is an elastic plan as it clearly provides for an annual revision in the allocation of the amounts foreseen, so that they may easily be transferred to meet new exigencies and situations.

Whereas a great number of interventions are specifically contemplated as far as Southern Italy in particular is concerned, it should also be noted that (a) the section of the budget destined to "facilitate and accelerate the execution of public works for land redemption and development" is almost in its entirety—with the exception of a few zones in Lazio and Tuscany—concerned with Southern Italy. In fact, in view of the economic weakness of these areas, the State has devised a system of loans to farmers, which will be used to pay for the improvements carried out and which will be reimbursed over 15-year periods at a 2 per cent interest rate; (b) in order to avoid clashing with the plans of the Cassa per il Mezzogiorno, a sum of 30 billion lire has been allocated under the Plan to this body, which will be responsible for the work carried on in its geographic sector.

Private investors and private capital will contribute to the total financing of the Plan in the proportion of about 1 to 3— 550 billion lire by the State and 1,650 billion by private enterprise.

The function of the State will also extend to a series of guarantees and participation in credit-granting by the private financial institutes.

Other interesting features of the Plan are that "an article in the Bill also contemplates subsidies up to 75 per cent of total expenditure, *87.5 per cent in the Southern underdeveloped areas,* for water and power mains and the purchase of electrical plants." Also, under the provision of "dealing with improvements to crops and the development of livestock breeding and widespread mechanization," the Plan foresees in various articles the expenditure of 14 billion lire—about one-third of the total in this sector, or *as high as 38 per cent*— towards the improvement and expansion, in Southern Italy, of particularly valuable crops such as citrus, olives, and other fruits.

APPENDIX III

Comparative Weights and Measures

U.S. dollar   —Italian lire (about) 625
U.S. dollar   —French francs (about) 4.95 (NF: New francs-
                       rate was 495 old francs)
1 pound (lb.)—kilograms   0.45359
1 ton   —kilograms   1,016.05
1 foot   —meters   0.3048
1 yard   —meters   0.9144
1 mile   —meters   1,609.34
100 hectares —1 sq. kilometer   0.386103 sq mi.

TABLE I
ITALIAN UNDERDEVELOPED REGIONS

Region	Area (sq. mi.)	Population 1951	Population 1961
ABRUZZI & MOLISE (L'Aquila, Campobasso, Chieti, Pescara Teramo)	5,883	1,686,546	1,584,777
CAMPANIA (Naples, Avellino, Benevento, Caserta, Salerno)	5,250	4,338,699	4,756,094
APULIA (Bari, Brindisi, Foggia, Ionio, Lecce)	7,469	3,214,854	3,409,687
BASILICATA (Potenza, Matera)	3,856	628,197	648,085
CALABRIA (Reggio Calabria, Cosenza, Catanzaro)	5,823	2,042,690	2,045,215
SICILIA (Palermo, Agrigento, Caltanissetta, Catania, Enna, Messina, Ragusa, Siracusa, Trapani)	9,815	4,462,220	4,711,783
SARDINIA (Cagliari, Nuoro, Sassari)	9,302	1,276,023	1,413,289

Source: Istituto Centrale di Statistica, *Bollettino Mensile di Statistica*, [Special supplement] (Rome: November 1961).

TABLE II
FRENCH UNDERDEVELOPED REGIONS

Region	Departments and Capital	Area (sq. mi.)	Population 1936	Population 1946	Population 1954	Population 1961
BRITTANY	Ille-et-Vilaine (Rennes)	2,697	565,766	578,246	586,812	609,850
	Côtes-du-Nord (St. Brieuc)	2,786	531,840	526,955	503,178	497,852
	Finistère (Quimper)	2,729	756,793	724,735	727,847	739,309
	Morbihan (Vannes)	2,738	542,248	506,884	520,978	527,432
	Loire-Inférieure (Nantes)	2,693	659,428	665,064	733,575	794,296
CORSICA	Corse (Ajaccio)	3,367	322,854	367,873	246,995	275,563
AQUITAINE (Béarn, Angoumois)	Ariège (Foix)	1,892	155,134	145,956	140,010	135,121
	Hautes-Pyrénées (Tarbes)	1,750	188,604	201,954	203,544	212,051
	Gers (Auch)	2,428	192,451	190,431	185,111	179,520
	Tarn-et-Garonne (Montauban)	1,440	164,629	167,664	172,379	174,559
	Lot (Cahors)	2,017	162,572	154,897	147,754	148,562
	Dordogne (Périgueux)	3,550	386,963	387,643	377,870	370,425
	Lot-et-Garonne (Agen)	2,078	252,761	265,449	265,549	271,506
	Gironde (Bordeaux)	4,140	850,567	858,381	896,517	936,056
	Landes (Mont-de-Marsan)	3,604	251,436	248,395	248,943	260,047
	Basses-Pyrénées (Pau)	2,977	413,411	415,797	420,019	469,455
	Charente (Angoulême)	2,305	309,279	311,137	313,635	324,752

404

TABLE II (*Continued*)

Region	Departments and Capital	Area (sq. mi.)	Population 1936	1946	1954	1961
MASSIF CENTRAL (Auvergne, Limousin, Quercy, Périgord, Nivernais)	Allier (Moulins)	2,848	368,778	373,481	372,689	379,024
	Puy-de-Dôme (Clermont-Ferrand)	3,090	486,103	478,876	481,380	509,240
	Cantal (Aurillac)	2,229	190,888	186,843	177,065	170,877
	Haute-Loire (Le Puy)	1,930	245,271	228,076	215,577	209,623
	Haute-Vienne (Limoges)	2,119	333,589	336,313	324,429	329,435
	Creuse (Gueret)	2,163	201,844	188,669	172,702	162,507
	Corrèze (Tulle)	2,272	262,773	254,574	242,798	238,733
	Nièvre (Nevers)	2,658	249,673	248,559	240,078	242,720
	Ardèche (Privas)	2,144	272,698	254,598	249,077	245,597
	Lozère (Mende)	1,996	98,480	90,523	82,391	80,891
	Aveyron (Rodez)	3,385	314,682	307,717	292,727	287,144
SAVOY	Savoie (Chambéry)	2,388	239,010	235,939	252,192	265,827
	Haute-Savoie (Annecy)	1,775	259,961	270,565	293,852	332,624
LANGUEDOC (Roussillon)	Gard (Nîmes)	2,270	395,299	380,837	396,742	433,030
	Hérault (Montpellier)	2,402	502,043	461,100	471,429	512,538
	Aude (Carcassonne)	2,448	285,115	268,889	268,254	267,905
	Tarn (Albi)	2,231	297,871	298,117	308,197	318,361
	Haute-Garonne (Toulouse)	2,457	458,647	512,260	525,669	592,071
	Pyrénées-Orientales (Perpignan)	1,598	233,347	228,776	230,285	252,105

Source: Elaboration of data from *Statesman's Yearbook*, *Lippincott Gazetteer* and *Journal Officiel* of November 15, 1962.

Basic Statistics and Comparative Standards of Living
in the European Economic Community*
TABLES III–XVIII

TABLE III

	Surface Area		Population Density
	(Sq. km.)	(Sq. mi.)	(No. per sq. km.)
Belgium............	30,500	11,779	300
Federal Republic of Germany........	248,000	95,913	215
France.............	551,600	212,659	83
Italy..............	301,200	116,224	164
Luxembourg.......	2,600	1,706	121
Netherlands........	32,500	15,765	300
Total area	1,166,400	454,046	

TABLE IV
POPULATION
(in thousands)

	1960	Estimated 1976
Belgium.............................	9,154	9,943
Federal Republic of Germany...........	55,960	60,540
France...............................	45,540	50,788
Italy.................................	49,259	53,920
Luxembourg..........................	314	345
Netherlands..........................	11,480	13,309
Total	171,707	188,845

* Source for Tables III–XVIII: *Communauté Européenne*, No. 3, March, 1962.

TABLE V
GROSS NATIONAL PRODUCT IN 1960
(millions of new francs)

Federal Republic of Germany..........	275.5
France.............................	207
Italy................................	141.25
Belgium............................	52.43
Netherlands.........................	46.48
Luxembourg.........................	1.98

TABLE VI
PERCENTAGE BREAKDOWN OF GROSS NATIONAL
PRODUCT IN 1960
(%)

	Agriculture	Industry	Services
Federal Republic of Germany	8.00	50.8	41.2
France	12.5	44.2	43.3
Italy	18.7	42.0	39.3
Belgium	7.5	48.1	44.4
Netherlands	10.1	42.6	47.3
Luxembourg	8.6	52.2	39.2

TABLE VII
GROWTH OF NATIONAL PRODUCT
(1953 = 100)

	1960
Federal Republic	161
Italy	149
Netherlands	142
France	136
Belgium	122
Luxembourg	118 (1959)

TABLE VIII
STEEL CONSUMPTION
PER PERSON IN 1959
(in kgs.)

Federal Republic of Germany	444
Belgium-Luxembourg	280
France	253
Netherlands	238
Italy	143
United States	491
United Kingdom	332
USSR	276

TABLE IX
CONSTRUCTION OF
DWELLINGS IN 1960
(per 1,000 inhabitants)

Federal Republic of Germany	10.3
Netherlands	7.4
France	7.0
Italy	5.4
Belgium	5.1
Luxembourg	3.2
United Kingdom	5.9
United States	7.1
USSR	13.9

TABLE X
GROWTH OF HOURLY
WAGES IN INDUSTRY
(1958 = 100)

	1959	*1960*
Belgium..........	102	—
Italy..............	102	107
Netherlands.......	102	111
Federal Republic...	105	115
France...........	106	113

TABLE XI
CALORIE CONSUMPTION
PER HEAD PER DAY
(Average 1958–59)

Netherlands............	2,947
Federal Republic of Germany............	2,943
France.................	2,923
Belgium, Luxembourg....	2,917
Italy.................	2,667
United Kingdom........	3,100
United States...........	3,300

TABLE XII
MEAT CONSUMPTION
PER HEAD PER YEAR
(in kgs.)
Average 1957–59

Italy..................	23.3
Netherlands............	42.8
Federal Republic of Germany............	52.0
Belgium, Luxembourg....	56.3
France.................	70.0
United Kingdom........	65.5
United States...........	86.5

TABLE XIII
NO. OF INHABITANTS
FOR ONE CAR
(1960)

Luxembourg...........	8
France.................	8
Belgium...............	11.6
Federal Republic........	12.0
Netherlands............	21.0
Italy..................	24.0
United States...........	3
United Kingdom........	10
USSR.................	333

TABLE XIV
PERCENTAGE OF DWELLINGS

	With Running Water (1959)	*With Bath* (1959)
Italy..............................	35.9	10.7
Belgium...........................	48.4	7.1
France............................	53.4	10.4
Federal Republic...................	87.3	42.3
Netherlands.......................	89.5	30.3
Luxembourg.......................	90.5	16.7
United Kingdom...................	81.4	62.4
United States.....................	82.8	73.2

408

TABLE XV	
NO. OF PEOPLE	
PER ROOM	
(1960)	
Belgium................	0.7
Luxembourg............	0.8
Netherlands.............	0.8
France.................	1.0
Federal Republic.........	1.1
Italy..................	1.3
United Kingdom.........	0.8
United States............	0.7
USSR.................	1.5

TABLE XVI	
DOCTORS PER 1,000	
INHABITANTS	
(1959)	
Luxembourg.............	93
France..................	99
Netherlands..............	111
Belgium.................	125
Federal Republic..........	137
Italy...................	162
United Kingdom..........	97
United States............	132
USSR...................	180

TABLE XVII	
NO. OF INHABITANTS	
PER T.V. SET	
(1960)	
Federal Republic.........	11.5
Netherlands............	14
Belgium...............	15
Italy.................	23
France...............	24
Luxembourg...........	42
United Kingdom........	5
United States...........	3
USSR.................	52

TABLE XVIII	
NO. OF TELEPHONES	
PER 1,000 INHABITANTS	
(1960)	
Netherlands..............	131
Belgium.................	118
Luxembourg.............	114
Federal Republic..........	104
France..................	90
Italy...................	68
United States............	399
United Kingdom..........	150
USSR..................	12

TABLE XIX
COMPARATIVE COSTS OF LABOR
(Wages, social charges, etc.)
(France = 100)

	France	West Germany	Benelux	Italy
Cotton industry	100	89	100	74
Shoe manufacture	100	92	88	66
Machine tools	100	73	95	65
Radio and electric	100	79	98	70
Steel industry	100	112	121	95

Source: François Visine, *L'Economie Française face au Marché Commun* (Paris: Pichon, 1959)

TABLE XX
ESTIMATE OF EVOLUTION OF POPULATION DENSITY
(according to natural causes only)

Country	Surface in sq. km.	No. of inhabitants per sq. km.			
		1951	1961	1965	1971
Luxembourg	2,586	113	121	121	121
Belgium	30,507	283	296	300	300
Netherlands	32,450	314	358	376	400
West Germany	247,946	195	205	216	220
Italy	301,181	155	167	170	178
France	551,208	76	81	82	84
Community	1,165,878	134	143	146	150

Source: *Résumé Statistique* [2023/2/58/1] (Paris: Service des Publications de la Communauté Européenne)

APPENDIX

TABLE XXI
ESTIMATE OF EVOLUTION OF USEFUL AGRICULTURAL
SURFACE (SAU) AVAILABLE PER INHABITANT
(in ha.—Agricultural surface constant)

Country	Sau	1951	1961	1971	1991
Netherlands	2,320,000	0.23	0.20	0.18	0.15
Belgium	1,752,660	0.20	0.19	0.19	0.18
Luxembourg	142,000	0.48	0.48	0.48	0.46
West Germany	14,300,000	0.30	0.28	0.27	0.26
France	33,644,000	0.80	0.75	0.73	0.68
Italy	16,930,000	0.36	0.33	0.31	0.27
Community	69,088,000	0.44	0.41	0.40	0.36

Source: B. Oury, *L'Agriculture au seuil du Marché Commun* (Paris: Presses Universitaires de France, 1959).

TABLE XXII
ITALY: INCOME DIVIDED BY SECTOR
(% of Territorial Distribution)

Region	Agriculture	Industry	Services
North	67	81	84
South	33	19	16
All Italy	100	100	100

(It should be added that per capita income in the South equals 55 per cent of the average national income and 44 per cent of the income of the North. In the North, 17 per cent only of industrial workers are employed in handicraft-type enterprises, while this percentage attains 39 per cent in the South. In the North, 82 per cent of labor is employed in mechanized enterprises, in the South the percentage is only 52 per cent. In the North, 25 per cent of workers are employed in firms with less than ten workers; this percentage increases to 53 per cent in the South.)

Source: EEC: *Rapport 1958*, p. 372.

TABLE XXIII

EMPLOYMENT BY SECTOR IN UNDERDEVELOPED REGIONS OF ITALY

Region	Active Population		Agriculture	%	Industry	%	Services[1]	%
Abruzzo	728,356 plus	22,300[2]	457,092	62.8	139,866	19.2	109,098	15
Campania	1,703,245	,, 104,191	742,412	43.6	432,965	25.4	423,677	24.9
Apulia	1,331,168	,, 60,497	739,980	55.6	279,476	20.9	251,215	18.9
Basilicata	293,669	,, 6,462	209,770	71.4	43,509	14.8	33,928	11.2
Calabria	817,892	,, 34,580	496,476	60.7	156,989	19.2	129,847	15.9
Sicily	1,565,869	,, 82,965	760,080	48.5	338,084	21.6	384,740	24.6
Sardinia	452,207	,, 18,411	221,341	48.9	102,058	22.6	110,397	24.4

[1] Includes commerce, transportation, free professions, arts, etc.
[2] Never employed before, but looking for employment
Source: *Contributo*, I, p. 103.

TABLE XXIV
ITALY: DISTRIBUTION OF TECHNICAL COURSES BY ECONOMIC SECTOR AND GEOGRAPHIC REGION IN 1960

Sector	North Italy	Central Italy	South Italy	Islands	All Italy
Agriculture	793	459	552	124	1,928
Industry	3,287	1,140	1,636	565	6,628
Construction	158	23	83	16	280
Transport and Communication	17	7	20	18	62
Commerce, credit and insurance	669	150	148	167	1,134
Other activities	240	340	436	142	1,158
Total	5,164	2,119	2,875	1,032	11,190

Source: CEE, *Exposé 1960*, p. 13.

TABLE XXV
ITALY: NO. OF PROFESSIONAL TRAINING CENTERS FINANCED BY THE MINISTRY OF LABOR IN 1960

Activity	Workshops	No. of places
Industry	1,552	36,399
Crafts	905	18,465
Agriculture	28	608
Commerce and services	482	9,364
Total	2,967	64,836

Distribution of Centers by Geographic Region:

Region	Number
North Italy............	395
Central Italy.........	278
Southern Italy........	268
Islands..............	116
Total	1,057

Source: CEE, *Exposé 1960*, p. 50.

413

TABLE XXVI
GROSS PRODUCT IN THE SIX COUNTRIES OF
THE COMMUNITY[1] (1954–60)
(1954 = 100)

Country	1954	1955	1956	1957	1958	1959	1960[2]
Belgium	100	103.8	108.0	110.7	108.8	111.4	116.4
Federal Republic of Germany[3]	100	111.5	119.2	125.6	129.7	138.4	149.5
France	100	105.7	111.0	117.3	119.0	121.5	129.1
Italy	100	106.7	111.2	118.3	123.5	131.6	141.5
Luxembourg	100	104.4	109.9	115.4	117.2	—	—
Netherlands	100	107.8	111.9	114.6	116.3	122.7	132.5
Community	100	107.7	113.4	119.5	122.1	127.6	136.5

[1] At market prices
[2] Provisional figures
[3] Including the Saar, not including West Berlin
Source: CEE, *Exposé 1960*, p. 12.

TABLE XXVII
EMPLOYMENT IN THE SIX COUNTRIES OF THE
COMMUNITY (1954–1960)
(1954 = 100)

Country	1954	1955	1956	1957	1958	1959	1960
Belgium	100	101.5	102.6	103.4	102.4	101.5	102.1
Federal Republic of Germany	100	103.7	106.4	108.4	109.2	110.2	111.7
France	100	100.0	100.0	100.6	100.6	100.0	100.2
Italy	100	102.0	103.0	105.0	106.0	107.5	109.7
Luxembourg	100	101.0	103.1	104.4	105.0	105.9	106.4
Netherlands	100	102.2	104.3	105.4	105.0	105.9	108.5
Community	100	101.9	103.5	104.8	105.4	106.2	107.6

Source: *ibid.*, p. 13.

TABLE XXVIII

FRANCE: UNFULFILLED JOB APPLICATIONS				ITALY: ASSISTED UNEMPLOYED AND FIRST JOB SEEKERS			
Month	1958	1959	1960	Month	1958	1959	1960
January	100.1	168.8	174.3	January	1,961.8	1,988.3	1,870.2
February	101.1	179.0	170.0	February	1,940.8	1,932.7	1,804.9
March	96.0	161.3	152.9	March	1,905.7	1,833.2	1,710.5
April	91.8	150.5	140.8	April	1,832.2	1,754.4	1,580.0
May	84.4	136.2	124.9	May	1,700.6	1,656.9	1,481.4
June	77.4	117.0	108.1	June	1,633.4	1,571.3	1,406.3
July	773.6	109.3	103.0	July	1,627.2	1,544.5	1,418.2
August	76.7	110.3	103.2	August	1,610.1	1,517.9	1,388.7
September	85.6	118.0	107.7	September	1,594.8	1,509.7	1,404.4
October	102.0	134.7	116.4	October	1,652.0	1,552.7	1,413.4
November	117.8	146.6	127.7	November	1,740.0	1,632.4	1,472.7
December	133.7	156.1	132.9	December	1,905.7	1,774.2	1,607.8
Annual Mean	93.1	139.7	131.1	*Annual Mean*	1,758.7	1,689.0	1,546.4

Source: *ibid*., p. 15.

415

TABLE XXIX
AVERAGE ANNUAL UNEMPLOYMENT
IN THE COMMUNITY
(in thousands)

Country	1954	1955	1956	1957	1958	1959	1960
Belgium[1]	181	139	101	83	120	142	120
West Germany[2]	1,228	935	767	667	689	480	237
France[3]	184	159	110	80	97	140	131
Italy[4]	1,959	1,913	1,937	1,757	1,759	1,689	1,546
Luxembourg				Negligible			
Netherlands[5]	74	53	40	52	98	77	49
Community	3,626	3,199	2,955	2,639	2,763	2,528	2,083

[1] Includes those employed on public projects
[2] Including the Saar, not including West Berlin
[3] Unplaced job seekers
[4] First two categories on placement bureau lists
[5] Includes those employed on public assistance projects
Source: *ibid.*, p. 24.

TABLE XXX
INDEX OF EVOLUTION OF GROSS NATIONAL
PRODUCT PER CAPITA, 1962–1965
(1953 = 100)

Year	Belgium	France	Germany	Italy	Luxembourg	Netherlands
1962	123.8	138.5	166.0	145.9	130.0	142.7
1963	126.4	142.6	173.3	151.1	133.2	147.4
1964	129.0	146.7	180.6	156.3	136.4	152.1
1965	131.6	150.8	187.9	161.5	139.6	156.8

Source: *Contributo*, iii, p. 52.

TABLE XXXI
FRANCE: FOREIGN WORKERS PLACED BY NATIONAL
IMMIGRATION OFFICE (1958–1960), BY NATIONALITY
(in thousands)

Nationality	1958	1959	1960
	Permanent Workers		
Belgium	0.3	0.3	0.3
Federal Republic of Germany	1.0	1.0	1.0
Italy	51.1	21.3	19.5
Luxembourg	0.01	0.02	0.02
Netherlands	0.2	0.2	0.2
All countries of Community	52.8	22.7	21.0
Spain	22.7	14.7	21.4
Portugal	5.1	3.3	4.0
Various	2.3	3.4	2.4
Total	82.8	44.2	48.9
	Seasonal Workers		
Belgium	8.1	6.7	6.7
Italy	37.0	35.2	33.0
Spain	18.4	21.8	69.2

Source: Exposé 1960, p. 13.

TABLE XXXII
LAND EXPROPRIATED AND REASSIGNED IN ITALY

	North		*Mezzogiorno*		*Italy*	
	Amount	*%*	*Amount*	*%*	*Amount*	*%*
Surface expropriated (hectares)	223,244	30.6	506,886	69.4	730,130	100.0
Surface reassigned (hectares)	183,375	34.6	345,891	65.4	529,266	100.0
% reassigned out of expropriated land	82.1	—	68.2	—	72.5	—
Reassigned small-holdings[1]	13,445	23.0	45,031	77.0	58,476	100.0
" plots[2]	11,118	26.3	31,085	73.7	42,203	100.0
Average size of small-holding (hectares)	11.0	—	6.3	—	7.4	—
Average size of plot (hectares)	3.1	—	2.0	—	2.3	—

[1] "Smallholding" implies a piece of land large enough to support a family

[2] "Plot" implies a piece of land allotted to a family which has another means of livelihood

Source: SVIMEZ, *Notizie*, p. 100.

TABLE XXXIII
NUMBER OF ITALIAN AND FOREIGN CUSTOMERS IN SOUTHERN ITALIAN HOTELS
1962–1963 (SEPT.)

	ITALIANS					FOREIGNERS				
	1962		1963			1962		1963		
Region	Regis-tering	Overnight Stays	Regis-tering	Overnight Stays	% Diff.	Regis-tering	Overnight Stays	Regis-tering	Overnight Stays	% Diff.
Lombardy	1,559,701	5,185,147	1,599,418	5,518,687	6.4	891,420	2,725,543	900,438	2,785,245	2.2
Emilia-Romagna	1,174,063	7,275,768	1,249,313	7,761,741	6.7	601,940	6,012,773	609,557	6,137,785	2.1
Abruzzi e Molise	247,347	701,353	260,473	785,564	12.0	27,942	66,620	26,005	62,396	-6.3
Campania	877,303	2,267,952	897,126	2,346,505	3.5	481,488	1,730,678	468,310	1,827,442	5.6
Apulia	328,012	899,900	355,684	917,971	2.0	53,380	144,658	60,888	172,138	19.0
Basilicata	52,017	151,031	53,452	140,398	-7.1	5,367	10,851	5,347	11,593	6.8
Calabria	337,175	706,524	505,073	941,493	33.3	19,026	29,514	23,722	47,478	60.9
Sicily	838,497	2,281,751	824,705	2,194,456	-3.8	177,128	634,899	167,986	611,446	-3.7
Sardinia	181,363	472,492	182,111	519,058	9.9	23,635	120,623	30,349	165,297	37.0

Source: *Statistica del Turismo*, Bollettino Tecnico Trimestrale dell'Ente Nazionale Italiano per il Turismo, No. 55 (Rome, December 1963).

BIBLIOGRAPHY

DESCRIPTION AND TRAVEL: UNDERDEVELOPED AREAS

FRANCE

Comité d'Expansion Economique Régionale. *Bordeaux et le Sud-Ouest.* (Collection: La France vous invite), Bordeaux, 1948.

Firth, Alfred. *French Life and Landscape.* Vol. ii: *Southern France.* London: Elek, 1955.

Institut Français des Economies Régionales. *Provinces Françaises: La Bretagne.* Paris: Cofosco, 1956.

Muirhead, L. Russel. *North-Western France.* London: Benn, 1958.

———. *Southern France with Corsica.* London: Benn, 1954.

Nagel, Guide. *France.* New York: Praeger, 1957.

Shirley, Hon. A. *South from Toulouse.* New York: Scribner, 1959.

White, Freda. *Three Rivers of France: Lot, Dordogne and Tarn.* New York: Transatlantic, 1955.

ITALY

Levi, Carlo. *Christ Stopped at Eboli.* New York: McLeon, 1956.

Maranelli, Carlo. *Considerazioni Geografiche sulla Questione Meridionale.* Bari: Laterza, 1956.

Muirhead, L. Russel. *Southern Italy with Sicily and Sardinia.* London: Benn, 1959

Munthe, Axel. *The Story of San Michele.* London: Murray and Co., 1929.

Ross, Janet. *The Land of Manfred.* London: Murray and Co., 1889.

Sereni, Emilio. *Il Capitalismo nelle Campagne.* Turin: Einaudi, 1948.

Tomasi, Giuseppe, Principe di Lampedusa. *The Leopard.* New York: Signet Books, 1961.

Vailland, Roger. *La Loi.* Paris: Gallimard, 1957.

WORKS OF HISTORICAL SIGNIFICANCE

FRANCE

Bainville, Jacques. *Histoire de France.* Paris: Fayard, 1924.

Guérard, Albert Léon. *France: A Modern History.* Ann Arbor: University of Michigan, 1959.

Guizot, François Pierre Guillaume. *France.* (With supplementary Chapter by M. W. Hazeltine.) New York: Collier, 1898.

BIBLIOGRAPHY

Lavisse, Ernest. *Histoire de France Illustrée depuis les Origines jusqu'à la Révolution.* Paris: Hachette, 1911.

Maurois, André. *Histoire de la France.* Paris: Michel, 1958. (New ed.)

Michelet, Jules. *Histoire de France.* Paris: Chamerot, 1867.

Sedillot, René. *Survol de l'Histoire de France.* Paris: Fayard, 1955.

Seignobos, Charles. *Histoire Sincère de la Nation Française.* London: Penguin Books, 1944.

Wright, Thomas. *The History of France.* London: The London Printing and Publishing House, 1862.

ITALY

Barbagallo, Corrado. *Cento Anni di Vita Italiana.* Milan: 1948.

Barraco, A. *I Demani Comunali dell'Antico Regno di Napoli.* Naples, 1894.

Cicero, Marcus Tullius. *In Verrem.* Rome: I Classici Bignami, Ed. Bignami, 1941.

Croce, Benedetto. *Storia del Regno di Napoli.* Bari: Laterza, 1925.

Fortunato, Giustino. *Il Mezzogiorno e lo Stato Italiano.* Florence: Vallecchi, 1926.

Moscati, Ruggero. *Il Mezzogiorno d'Italia nel Risorgimento.* Messina: d'Anna, 1953.

Salomone, A. William. *Italian Democracy in the Making: The Political Scene in the Giolittian Era, 1900–1914.* Philadelphia: University of Pennsylvania Press, 1945.

Scarfoglio, Carlo. *Il Mezzogiorno e l'Unità d'Italia.* Florence: Parenti, 1953.

Sturzo, Luigi. *Italy and the Coming World.* New York: Roy and Co., 1945.

Villari, Luigi. *Liberation of Italy.* New York: Devin, 1960.

PROBLEMS OF UNDERDEVELOPMENT

Buchanan, Norman S., and Howard S. Ellis. *Approaches to Economic Development.* New York: Twentieth Century, 1955.

Higgins, Benjamin. *Economic Development.* New York: Norton, 1959.

Lacoste, Yves. *Les Pays Sous-Développés.* Paris: Presses Universitaires de France, 1959.

Mazerik, Avrahan. *Social Factors in Economic Development.* New York: International Review Service, 1959.

Myrdal, Gunnar. *An International Economy.* New York: Harper Bros., 1956.

———. *Economic Theory and Underdeveloped Regions.* London: Duckworth and Co. Ltd., 1957.

421

Staley, Eugene. *The Future of Underdeveloped Countries.* New York: Harper, 1961, rev. ed.

Ward, Barbara. *The Rich Nations and the Poor Nations.* New York: Norton & Co., 1962.

ECONOMIC, SOCIOLOGICAL, AND POLITICAL CONDITIONS

FRANCE

Bauchet, M. *La Planification Française.* Paris: Editions du Seuil, 1963.

Baum, W. C. *French Economy and the State.* Princeton: Princeton University Press, 1958.

Cameron, Rondo E. *France and the Economic Development of Europe, 1800–1941.* Princeton: Princeton University Press, 1961.

De Tocqueville, Alexis. *L'Ancien Régime et la Révolution.* Paris: Lévy, 1856.

Carrère et Dugrand. *La Région Méditerranéenne; La France de Demain.* Paris: Presses Universitaires de France, 1961.

Cazes, Bernard. *La Planification en France et le IVme Plan.* Paris: Editions de l'Epargne, 1962.

Chesné, Guy. *L'Etablissement des Etrangers en France et la Communauté Economique Européenne.* Paris: Librairie Générale de Droit et de Jurisprudence, 1962.

Duverger, Maurice. *French Political System.* Chicago: University of Chicago Press, 1958.

Gravier, Jean-François. *Paris et le Désert Français.* Paris: Flammarion, 1958.

Godchot, J. E. *Les Sociétés d'Economie Mixte et l'Aménagement du Territoire.* Nancy: Berger-Levrault, 1958.

Jeanneney, J. M. *Forces et Faiblesses de l'Economie Française.* Paris: Colin, 1956.

Luchaire, A. *Social France at the time of Philip Augustus.* London: Ungar, 1957.

Luethy, H. *France Against Herself.* New York: Meridian Books, 1957.

Maillet, Pierre. *La Structure Economique de la France.* Paris: Presses Universitaires de France, 1958.

Maurois, André. *Portrait de la France et des Français.* Paris: Hachette, 1955.

Pisani, Edgard, *et al. L'Agriculture en France.* La Nef, Juillard, July–September 1962, Paris.

Rueff, Jacques. *Epitre aux Dirigistes.* Paris: Gallimard, 1949.

Siegfried, André. *Tableau Politique de la France de l'Ouest sous la Troisième République.* Paris: Colin, 1913.

Tannenbaum, Edward R. *New France*. Chicago: University of Chicago Press, 1961.

Thomson, D. *Democracy in France*. Oxford: Oxford University Press, 1958.

Wallace-Hadrill, J. M., and J. McManners. *France: Government and Society*. New York: Methuen, 1951.

ITALY

Barbagallo, Corrado. *La Questione Meridionale*. Milan: Garzanti, 1948.

Caizzi, B. *Antologia della Questione Meridionale*. Milan: Edizioni di Comunità, 1955.

Compagna, Francesco. *Mezzogiorno d'Europa*. Rome: Editoriale Opere Nuove, 1958.

D'Alessandro, Giovanni. *La Questione Meridionale*. Rome: Edizioni della Bussola, 1946.

Dickinson, Robert E. *The Population Problem of Southern Italy*. Syracuse: Syracuse University Press, 1955.

Niceforo, Francesco. *L'Italia Barbara Contemporanea*. Palermo: Sandron, 1898.

———. *Italiani del Nord e del Sud*. Turin: Bocca, 1901.

Nitti, Francesco Saverio. *Nord e Sud*. Turin: Roux, 1900.

Rosenstein, Rodan. *Remarks on Economic Effects of Agrarian Reform— Economic Development in Italy*. Cambridge: MIT Center for International Studies, 1954.

Saraceno, Pasquale. *The Economic Development of the Mezzogiorno*. Milan: Giuffré, 1955. (Published in English.)

EUROPEAN INTEGRATION—ECONOMIC AND GENERAL

Allais, Maurice, *et al. Le Marché Commun et ses Problèmes*. Paris: Sirey, 1958.

———. *L'Europe Unie, Route de la Prosperité*. Paris: Calman-Lévy, 1960.

Byé, M., C. Magaud, *et al. Demain l'Europe sans Frontières?* (Les Documents de Tribune Libre, ed. Racine.) Paris: Plon, 1958. (spec. edn.)

Cartier, Raymond. *Les Dix-Neuf Europes*. Paris: Plon, 1960.

Cassin, R., Waline, M. *Le Marché Commun et le Droit Public*. Paris: Sirey, 1959.

Catalano, Nicola. *La Comunità Economica Europea e l'Euratom*. (Preface by Gaetano Martino.) Milan: Giuffré, 1957.

De Carmoy, Guy. *Fortune de l'Europe*. Paris: Domat, 1954.

De Sainte Lorette, Lucien. *Le Marché Commun.* Paris: Colin, 1958.

Dehousse, Fernand. *L'Europe et le Monde.* Liège: Comité Organisateur de la Manifestation pour le fédéralisme européen, 1962.

Deniau, Jean-François. *Le Marché Commun.* Paris: Presses Universitaires de France, 1959.

Elgozy, George. *La France devant le Marché Commun.* Paris, Flammarion, 1958.

Florinsky, Michael. *Integrated Europe?* New York: Macmillan, 1955.

Giscard d'Estaing, Edmond. *La France et l'Unification Economique de l'Europe.* Paris: Genin, 1953.

Gross, Felix (ed.). *European Ideologies.* New York: Philosophical Library, 1948.

Hallstein, Walter. *United Europe: Challenge and Opportunity.* Cambridge, Mass.: Harvard University Press, 1962.

Langrod, Georges. *Les Institutions Européennes et leur Aspect Administratif.* Turin: Unione Tipografico-Editrice Torinese, 1959. (Published in French).

Lapie, P. O. *Les Trois Communautés.* Paris: Fayard, 1960.

Madariaga, Salvador de. *Portrait de l'Europe.* Paris: Calman-Lévy. 1952.

Massip, Roger. *Voici l'Europe.* Paris: Fayard, 1958.

Maury, René. *L'Intégration Européenne.* Paris: Sirey, 1958.

Monnet, Jean. *Les Etats-Unis d'Europe ont Commencé.* Paris: Laffont, 1955.

Ohlin, Bertil and Byé, Maurice. *Les Aspects Sociaux de la Coopération Européenne.* Geneva: Bureau International du Travail, 1956.

Oury, Bernard. *L'Agriculture au Seuil du Marché Commun.* Paris: Presses Universitaires de France, 1959.

Perroux, François. *L'Europe sans Rivages.* Paris: Presses Universitaires de France, 1954.

Research and Policy Committee of the Committee for Economic Development. *A Statement on National Policy: The European Common Market and Its Meaning to the United States.* New York, 1959.

Sandys, Duncan. *European Unity.* Speech made to the Association of Anglo-Saxon Press, December 1, 1948. Paris: Archives of the Institut d'Etudes Politiques, Université de Paris.

Visine, François. *L'Economic française face au Marché Commun.* Paris: Pichon, 1959.

HISTORY OF THE IDEA OF EUROPEAN INTEGRATION

Alpert, Paul. *Twentieth Century Economic History of Europe.* New York: Schuman, 1951.

BIBLIOGRAPHY

Aron, Raymond. *L'Age des Empires*. Paris: Editions Défense de la France, 1944.

Benda, Julien. *Discours à la Nation Européenne*. Paris, 1933.

Billotte, Pierre. *L'Europe est Née*. Paris: Fayard, 1955.

Bonnefous, Edouard. *L'Idée Européenne et sa Réalisation*. Paris: Editions du Grand Siècle, 1953.

Boyd, Andrew and Frances. *Western Union*. Washington: Public Affairs Press, 1949.

Churchill, Sir Winston. *Europe Unite: Speeches, 1947 and 1948* (ed. Randolph S. Churchill). London: Cassell, 1950.

Coudenhove-Kalergi, Richard. *Pan-Europe*. New York: Knopf, 1926.

———. *L'Europe Unie*. Paris: Glaris, 1938.

———. *Europe Must Unite*. London: Secker and Warburg, 1940.

———. *Crusade for Pan-Europe*. London: Putnam and Sons, 1943.

Hawtray, R. G. *Western European Union*. London: Royal Institute of International Affairs, 1949.

Jennings, W. I. *A Federation for Western Europe*. London: Cambridge University Press, 1940.

Madia, Luigi. *Che Cosa è il Mercato Comune*. Milan: AEIOU, 1960.

Miller, F. and H. Hill. *The Giant of the Western World: America and Europe in a North Atlantic Civilization*. New York: Morrow, 1930.

Sforza, Carlo. *O Federazione Europea o Nuove Guerre*. Florence: La Nuova Italia, Collana Orientamenti, 1948.

Spinelli, Altiero. *Dagli Stati Sovrani agli Stati Uniti d'Europa*. Florence: La Nuova Italia, Collana Orientamenti, 1950.

Tersen, E., *et al*. *L'Europe, Mythes et Réalités*. Paris: Editions Sociales, 1954.

Zampaglione, Gerardo. *Breve Storia dell'Integrazione Europea*. Rome: Cinque Lune, 1958.

Zurcher, Arnold J. *The Struggle to Unite Europe, 1940–1958*. New York: New York University Press, 1958.

PUBLICATIONS OF THE FRENCH GOVERNMENT AND ITS AGENCIES

Ambassade de France, Service de Presse et d'Information. *France and Economic Planning*. New York, 1963.

Bureau de la Statistique Générale. *Mouvement Économique français de 1929 à 1939*. Paris: Imprimerie Nationale, 1941.

Commissariat Général au Plan de Modernisation et d'Equipement. *Rapport sur la Réalisation du Plan de Modernisation et d'Equipement*, 1947, '48, '50, '51, '52, '54 through 1960. Paris: Imprimerie Nationale.

――――. Commission de Modernisation, de l'Enseignement, de la Recherche et de la Vulgarisation en Agriculture. *Rapport.* Paris, 1948.

――――. Commission de Modernisation des Industries du Coke et Gaz. *Rapport.* Paris, 1948.

Conseil Economique. *Communauté Européenne du Charbon et de l'Acier.* Paris, 1951.

Institut National de la Statistique et des Etudes Economiques (INSEE). *Annuaire Statistique.* Paris: Imprimerie Nationale, 1951 through 1960.

――――. *Recensement Général de la Population de Mai 1954.* Paris: Imprimerie Nationale, 1955.

――――. Direction Régionale de Limoges. *Conséquences des Migrations à l'Intérieur de la France.* Limoges, 1955.

――――. *Etudes et Documents Démographiques,* No. 7. Paris, 1956.

――――. *Tableaux de l'Economie Française.* Paris, 1958.

――――. *Etudes et Conjonctures: L'Evolution des Revenues Agricoles.* Paris, December 1959.

――――. *Statistiques Industrielles 1900–1959.* Paris, 1960.

――――. Direction Régionale de Marseille. *Annuaire Statistique de la XIème Région Economique—Basses-Alpes, Hautes-Alpes, Corse, Gard.* Marseille, 1960.

――――. Direction Régionale de Rennes. *Annuaire Statistique Régional.* Rennes, 1961.

――――. *Etude de l'Evolution Démographique.* Paris, 1964.

Journal Officiel. Several issues.

Journal Officiel. Région Midi-Pyrénées. Paris, 1959.

Ministère des Travaux Publics et des Transports: *Le Tourisme en France,* Commissariat Général au Tourisme, Paris, 1962.

Secrétariat Général du Gouvernement Français. *L'Economie Française.* Paris: La Documentation Française, 1959.

Service Economique Français. *La Politique Commerciale et Douanière de la France.* Paris, May 1958.

PUBLICATIONS OF THE ITALIAN GOVERNMENT AND ITS AGENCIES

CASSA PER IL MEZZOGIORNO

Bilancio: 1951 through 1960. Rome: Istituto Poligrafico dello Stato.

Centro Studi. *La Politica di Sviluppo nel Mezzogiorno* (Quaderno 39 by G. Pastore). Rome, December 1960.

――――. *Per lo Sviluppo della Sardegna* (Quaderno 29 by G. Pastore).

BIBLIOGRAPHY

Contributo alla Conoscenza dell'Agricoltura dei Paesi della Comunità Europea. 3 Vol. Rome, 1961.

Comitato dei Ministri per il Mezzogiorno. *Relazione sulla Attività di Coordinamento.* (Rome: Istituto Poligrafico dello Stato, 1962).

Comitato Italiano per la Ricostruzione: *Lo Sviluppo dell'Economia Italiana nel Quadro della Ricostruzione e Cooperazione Europea.* Rome: Istituto Poligrafico dello Stato, 1952.

Commercial Office of the Italian Embassy. *Italy—An Economic Profile, 1962.* Washington, D.C., June 1963.

Documenti di Vita Italiana: Monthly publication of the Presidency of the Council of Ministers of the Italian Republic; Rome: Istituto Poligrafico dello Stato. (Published in English as *Italian Affairs—Documents and Notes*).

Inchiesta Parlamentare sulle Condizioni dei Contadini nelle Provincie Meridionali. Rome: Istituto Poligrafico dello Stato, 1910.

Istituto Nazionale di Economia Agraria (INEA). *Indagine sulla Stagionalità e sul Grado di Impiego dei Lavoratori in Agricoltura.* Appended to *Atti della Commissione Parlamentare d'Inchiesta sulla Disoccupazione.* 2 Vols. Rome: Istituto Poligrafico dello Stato, 1953.

————. *Annuario dell'Agricoltura Italiana, 1952–53.* Rome: Istituto Poligrafico dello Stato, 1954.

————. *Rapporto sulla Situazionne Idrica nell'Italia Meridionale.* Rome, 1959.

Italian Information Office, New York. *Italian Report* (monthly bulletin).

————. *Economic News from Italy.*

————. *Tourist News from Italy.* (Monthly supplement to *Economic News*).

Ministero di Agricoltura e Foreste: Direzione-Generale della Bonifica e della Colonizzazione. *Relazione sullo Stato dell'Irrigazione in Italia.* Rome, 1961.

Ministero del Bilancio (Ministry of the Budget). *Relazione Generale sulla Situazione Economica del Paese in 1962.* Rome, 1963.

Ministero del Turismo. *Statistica del Turismo.*

Pescatore, Gabriele. *Dieci Anni di Esperienze della Cassa per il Mezzogiorno.* Rome, 1961.

SVIMEZ PUBLICATIONS (ASSOCIATION FOR THE DEVELOPMENT OF THE MEZZOGIORNO)

Informazioni SVIMEZ. (Weekly bulletin) Rome.

Notizie sull'Economia del Mezzogiorno. Rome, 1956.

427

BIBLIOGRAPHY

Popolazione e Forze di Lavoro. Rome: Istituto Centrale di Statistica, 1954.

Saraceno, Pasquale. *Elementi per un Piano Economico, 1949–1952.* Rome: Centro di Studi e Piani Tecnico-Economici, 1948.

———. *Economic Effects of an Investment Program in Southern Italy.* Rome, 1951.

———. *Interim Report* (A Study of the Italian Economy in View of a Future Plan). Rome, 1963.

Statistiche sul Mezzogiorno d'Italia, 1861–1950. Rome, 1954.

PUBLICATIONS AND DOCUMENTS OF THE EUROPEAN COMMUNITIES

PUBLICATIONS OF THE INFORMATION OFFICE OF THE EUROPEAN COMMUNITIES COMMON MARKET, COAL AND STEEL COMMUNITY, EURATOM

Communaté Européenne (Monthly Information Bulletin)—various issues.

Les Cahiers de Communauté Européenne:
1. *L'Agriculture dans le Marché Commun* and Supplement, *Premières Propositions sur l'Organisation Commune des Marchés Agricoles Européens.*
2. *Euratom prépare l'Europe à la révolution nucléaire.*
3. *L'Europe a dix ans.*
4. *Europe 235.*
5. *C.E.C.A.*
6. *Où en est le Marché Commun?*
7. *Le Marché Commun Agricole.*

En bref:
  La C.E.C.A. en 1959.
  La Communauté Européenne: les faits.
  Douze mois de Marché Commun.
  Le calendrier du Marché Commun Agricole.
  La Communauté Européenne: Bilan 1960.
  L'aide de la Communauté Européenne aux pays d'outre-mer.
  La liberté d'établissement et des services dans le Marché Commun.

Les Documents de Communauté Européenne:
1. *Bilan et perspectives de l'Euratom.*
2. *Les budgets familiaux des travailleurs de la C.E.C.A.*
3. *Le Marché Commun, réalité économique et politique.*
4. *Les voies de communication de l'Europe de demain.*

5. *L'association des pays d'outre-mer dans le Marché Commun.*

6. *Le rôle des Institutions Communautaires dans la construction européenne.*

7. *Les problèmes du pétrole et du gaz naturel.*

8. *Les salaires des travailleurs de la C.E.C.A. 1954–1959.*

9. *La Réglementation des ententes dans le Marché Commun.*

10. *Le Coût de la Main-d'oeuvre dans le Marché Commun.*

11. *Les objectifs généraux acier de la C.E.C.A.*

12. *Euratom; Deuxième programme de recherches.*

13. *Le Marché Commun de l'Energie.*

14. *Comment fonctionnent les institutions du Marché Commun.*

La Communauté Européenne, Bruxelles, March 1963.

PUBLICATIONS OF INTERNATIONAL ORGANIZATIONS

ORGANIZATION FOR EUROPEAN ECONOMIC COOPERATION

Seventh Annual Report. 1955.

Situation et Problèmes de l'Economie Italienne. 1956.

L'OECE au Service de l'Europe. 1956.

Statistiques de l'Agriculture et de l'Alimentation. 1956.

La Situation Economique en France. 1958.

Statistiques Industrielles 1900–1957. 1958.

Statistiques de Base de l'Energie pour les Pays de l'OECE, 1950–1958. 1959.

L'Europe et l'Economie Mondiale, 1960.

L'Energie en Europe. 1960.

UNITED NATIONS

Economic Commission for Europe: *Economic Survey of Europe, 1960.* Geneva, 1961.

———. *Economic Survey of Europe, 1961.* Geneva, 1962.

———. *Economic Survey of Europe, 1963.* (Summary, published as Document ECE/98, April 7, 1964 by the Press Services of the Office of Public Information, New York.)

Economic and Social Council: ECE: *Report on Manpower Problems in Europe in 1963.* Transmitted by the ILO (Document E/ECE/508, Geneva, February 27, 1964).

International Labour Organisation: *The Parliamentary Enquiry into Destitution in Italy.* (Reprinted from *International Labour Review*, LXXI, No. 1), Geneva, January 1955.

———. *Yearbook of Labour Statistics, 1963.* Geneva, Spring 1964.

BIBLIOGRAPHY

PUBLICATIONS SERVICE OF THE EUROPEAN COMMUNITIES

CEE. Commission. *Rapport sur la Situation Economique dans les Pays de la Communauté.* 1958.

————. *Document de Travail sur la Situation de l'Agriculture dans la Communauté.* (Etabli à l'intention des membres de l'Assemblée Parlementaire Européenne.) 1958.

————. *L'Evolution Recente de la Situation Economique.* 1958.

————. *Exposé sur la Situation Sociale dans la Communauté.* 1958–1961.

————. *Annexe Statistique à l'Exposé sur l'Evolution de la Situation Sociale dans la Communauté en 1960.*

————. *Rapport Général sur l'Activité de la Communauté.* 1958–1961.

————. *Mémorandum de la Commission sur le Programme d'Action de la Communauté pendant la deuxième Etape.* Bruxelles, October 24, 1962.

CEE. Office Statistique. *Mémento de Statistiques.* 1961.

CECA. Haute Autorité. *7ème Rapport Général sur l'Activité de la Communauté.* 1959. Also issues for 1960 (8ème) and 1961 (9ème).

————. *Budget de la Communauté pour le Huitième Exercice (1959–1960).* 1961.

————. *L'Europe en Action.* 1958.

————. Discours de M. Piero Malvestiti, Président de la Haute Autorité. *Les Sources d'Energie et les Révolutions Industrielles.* 1962.

CECA. *Développement Economique et Mobilité des Travailleurs.* 1956. (Study made for the CECA by Institut National d'Etudes Démographiques.)

CEEA (Euratom). Commission: *Discours* de M. Etienne Hirsh, Président de la Commission devant l'Assemblée Parlementaire Européenne à Strasbourg. 1961.

EIB (European Investment Bank). *Budget 1960–1961.* 1961.

Journal Officiel des Communautés Européennes, IV Year, No. 57, August 26, 1961 and No. 80, December 13, 1961.

MISCELLANEOUS

M. E. Danvin and L. Degeer: *Dynamique Economique de la Région Liègeoise,* Liège: Editions de l'A.S.B.L., 1959.

W. O. Henderson, *The Zollverein.* London: Cambridge University Press, 1939.

William Miller, *A History of the United States.* New York: Dell Publishing Co., 1958.

BIBLIOGRAPHY

José Ortega y Gasset. *La Rebelión de las Masas.* Madrid: Revista de Occidente, 1956.

The Columbia Lippincott Gazetteer of the World. New York: Columbia University Press, 1952.

The Statesman's Yearbook. Various issues. New York: St. Martin's Press.

PERIODICALS AND MAGAZINES

AMERICAN

The Atlantic Community. 1963–64.
Foreign Affairs. 1963.
The New Yorker. 1964.
Time. 1962–64.
Holiday. 1961.

FRENCH

Réalités. 1959; 1961.
Entreprise. 1961.
Economie. 1961–64.
Economie et Humanisme. 1954; 1961.
L'Economie Française. 1961.
Le Fédéraliste. 1962.
Revue de l'Economie Méridionale. 1962–63.
Revue Juridique et Economique du Sud-Ouest. 1962–63.
Cahiers de l'Exagone. 1962.
Population (Revue de l'Institut National d'Etudes Démographiques). 1963.
Paris-Match. 1960.

BELGIAN

Communautés Européennes. Special number of *Bulletin Officiel Hebdomadaire de la Chambre de Commerce de Bruxelles.* Brussels, 1961.

ITALIAN

Mondo Economico. 1961; 1963.
Prospettive Meridionali. 1959–63.
Confluenze Economiche. 1962.
Cronache Meridionali. 1958.
Agricoltura. 1961.

BIBLIOGRAPHY

BRITISH

The Economist. 1961; 1964.
New Statesman. 1961.

NEWSPAPERS

AMERICAN

The New York Times. 1959–64.
Wall Street Journal. 1963.

FRENCH

Le Monde (Sélection Hebdomadaire). 1961–64.
Le Monde Diplomatique. 1963–64.
Le Monde. 1959–61.
Le Figaro. 1961.

ITALIAN

Corriere della Sera. 1961.
La Stampa. 1961.
Il Messaggero. 1960.
24 Ore. 1961.
Il Popolo. 1961.

BRITISH

The Observer. 1961–62; 1964.

RUSSIAN

Krasnaya Zvezda. 1963.

INDEX

433